TRUST WITHIN AND BETWEEN ORGANIZATIONS

TRUST WITHIN AND BETWEEN ORGANIZATIONS

Conceptual Issues and Empirical Applications

edited by

CHRISTEL LANE and REINHARD BACHMANN

OXFORD UNIVERSITY PRESS
1998

Oxford University Press, Great Clarendon Street, Oxford OX2 6DP
Oxford New York
Athens Auckland Bangkok Bogota Bombay Buenos Aires
Calcutta Cape Town Dar es Salaam Delhi Florence Hong Kong Istanbul
Karachi Kuala Lumpur Madras Madrid Melbourne Mexico City
Nairobi Paris Singapore Taipei Tokyo Toronto Warsaw
and associated companies in
Berlin Ibadan

Oxford is a registered trade mark of Oxford University Press

Published in the United States
by Oxford University Press Inc., New York

British Library Cataloguing in Publication Data
Data available

Library of Congress Cataloging in Publication Data
Trust within and between organizations: conceptual issues and empirical applications /
edited by Christel Lane and Reinnhard Bachman.
p.   cm.
Includes bibliographical references.
1. Organizational behavior.   2. Trust (Psychology)   3. Corporate culture.
4. Organization.   I. Lane, Christel.   II. Bachmann,
Reinhard.
HD58.7.T745   1998
302.3'5—dc21   97-51508
ISBN   0-19-829318-6

1 3 5 7 9 10 8 6 4 2

Typeset by Best-set Typesetter Ltd., Hong Kong
Printed in Great Britain
on acid-free paper by
Biddles Ltd, Guildford and King's Lynn

CONTENTS

LIST OF FIGURES

LIST OF TABLES

NOTES ON CONTRIBUTORS

REINHARD BACHMANN is a Research Fellow at the Technical University of Hamburg-Harburg, and a Lecturer at the Technical University of Vienna. His research interests include: social theory, the modernization of industrial organizations, interfirm co-operation, and advanced information technologies. Recent publications in *Organization Studies*, *Cambridge Journal of Sociology*, *British Journal of Sociology*.

GEORGE BRENKERT moved to the School of Business Administration, Georgetown University, in August 1997. He was formerly Professor of Philosophy at the University of Tennessee. His most recent book is *Political Freedom* (Routledge). He is currently working on a book on marketing ethics.

JOHN CHILD is the Guinness Professor of Management Studies at the University of Cambridge. His interests include strategic alliances, organizational learning, and management in China. He has written *Management in China During the Age of Reform* (Cambridge University Press 1994) and is co-author of *The New Strategy: The Formation and Management of Strategic Alliances* (Oxford University Press 1998).

SIMON DEAKIN is a Lecturer in the Faculty of Law and Assistant Director of the ERSC Centre for Business Research at the University of Cambridge. He researches in the economic theory and analysis of law, with particular reference to corporate governance, labour-market regulation, and competition policy. His books include *Labour Law* (1995, with G. Morris) and *Enterprise and Community: New Directions in Corporate Governance* (1997, edited, with A. Hughes).

CYNTHIA HARDY is Professor of Strategy and Organization in the Faculty of Management, McGill University, Montreal, Canada. Her research interests include organizational power and politics, and interorganizational collaboration. Her recent publications include (co-) edited volumes on *Power and Politics in Organizations* (1995) and *Handbook of Organization Studies* (Sage 1996).

JOHN HUMPHREY is a Fellow of the Institute of Development Studies at the University of Sussex. He has been researching on the spread of Japanese management techniques in Brazil, India, and Southeast Asia. He has recently completed a book on industrial restructuring in India with Professor Raphael Kaplinsky at IDS. Publications include 'The Triple C approach to Local Industrial Policy', *World Development*, 24/12 (Dec. 1996) (with H.

Schmitz) and 'New Manufacturing Strategies and Labour in Latin America', *Asia–Pacific Business Review*, 2/4 (Summer 1996).

HORST KERN is Professor of International Social Studies, Centre for European and Northamerican Studies, University of Göttingen. His publications include: *Das Ende der Arbeitsteilung?*, 4th edn. (1990), 'New Concepts or Production', in P. Adler (ed.), *Technology and the Future of Work* (1992), and 'Rationalization and Work in German Industry', in B. Kogut (ed.), *Country Competitiveness* (1993).

CHRISTEL LANE is a lecturer in Social and Political Sciences, a Fellow of St. John's College, and a member of the ESRC Centre for Business Research at the University of Cambridge. She is the author of *Industry and Society in Europe* (Edward Elgar 1995) and of numerous journal articles on interfirm co-operation and trust. Her research interests focus on European business systems and the institutional embeddedness of European business organizations.

THOMAS LAWRENCE is an Assistant Professor at the University of Victoria in Canada. For the past four years, his research has examined the relationship between power and interorganizational collaboration in a range of Canadian industries.

JULIA PORTER LIEBESKIND is a faculty member in the Marshall School of Business at the University of Southern California. Her research interests include the scope of the firm, corporate governance, and the governance of transactions of intellectual property. Her work has appeared in the *RAND Journal of Economics*, *Organization Science*, *Industrial and Corporate Change*, *Strategic Management Journal*, and the *Academy of Management Review*.

DAVID MARSDEN is Reader in Industrial Relations at the London School of Economics and Political Science, and a member of the LSE's Centre for Economic Performance. He is currently working on *A Theory of Employment Systems: Micro-foundations and Societal Diversity* (Oxford University Press forthcoming), and on a major study of pay and management reforms in the British and German public services. He is vice-president of a group of advisers to European Commissioner, Edith Cresson, on education and training policy in Europe.

AMALYA LUMERMAN OLIVER, currently an Assistant Professor at the Department of Sociology and Anthropology, the Hebrew University of Jerusalem. She graduated from the department of Sociology at UCLA in 1993. Her research focuses on interorganizational networks, trust, new organizational forms, and intellectual capital exchanges. Recent publications in *Organization Studies*, *Organization Science*, and *Sociological Inquiry*.

NELSON PHILLIPS is an Assistant Professor of Strategy and Organization in the Faculty of Management of McGill University. He has published in the *Academy of Management Journal*, *Organization Science*, *Organization Studies*, and *Organization* as well as having published a number of book chapters. His research interests include interorganizational collaboration, corporate reputation, and the management of cultural industries.

MARI SAKO is Reader in Industrial Relations, London School of Economics and Political Science. Major publications include: *Prices, Quality and Trust: Interfirm Relations in Britain and Japan* (Cambridge University Press 1992), *How the Japanese Learn to Work* (Routledge 1989, co-authored with Ronald Dore), and *Japanese Labour and Management in Transition: Diversity, Flexibility and Participation* (Routledge 1997, co-edited with Hiroki Sato).

JÖRG SYDOW is Professor of Management at the Freie Universität Berlin and co-editor of *Managementforschung* (De Gruyter, Berlin and New York) and *Industrielle Beziehungen—The German Journal of Industrial Relations* (Hampp, Munich and Mering). His research interests are in the area of organization and management theory, strategic alliances, information technology, and industrial relations.

FRANK WILKINSON is a Senior Research Officer in the Department of Applied Economics and the ESRC Centre for Business Research, University of Cambridge. His research interests are in the areas of industrial and labour market economics. His most recent publications have been in the areas of interfirm co-operation and trust.

Introduction: Theories and Issues in the Study of Trust

CHRISTEL LANE

Recent changes in the global business environment have radically increased the demands which businesses have to fulfil to stay in the competitive race. Firms in the advanced countries are facing tremendous challenges from a number of sources: demands for enhanced quality and variability of goods and constant innovation in product development; severe price competition from low-wage countries; and much increased costs of new technology. Some of these demands are also beginning to impinge on newly industrializing societies (NIS). To cope with these new challenges, firms have begun to implement organizational innovations within firms and in their relations with other firms. Among the latter, relational contracting, networks, strategic alliances and horizontal co-operation in industrial districts have become particularly prevalent (Piore and Sabel 1984; Powell 1990; Ring and van de Ven 1992; Alter and Hage 1993; Sydow 1996). Within organizations, networking, semi-autonomous working groups, and reciprocity are also accorded new importance (Rajan, van Eupen, and Jaspers 1997: 36; Turner and Auer 1994), as are forms of organizational decentralization of responsibility.

Both the steep increase in the number and variety of exchange relations and the increased complexity and uncertainty of the business environment cannot be handled without the presence of interpersonal and/or interorganizational trust. Additionally, more knowledge-intensive products and a more information-based mode of production, necessitating more sharing of often sensitive information, have made trust a highly desirable property. Trust has not only become regarded as an important co-ordination mechanism (Bradach and Eccles 1989) but is increasingly being viewed as a precondition for superior performance and competitive success in the new business environment (ibid; Ring and van de Ven 1992; Sako, Chapter 3, this volume). Fukuyama (1995: 7) goes even further when he claims that 'a nation's ability to compete is conditioned by a single, pervasive cultural characteristic: the level of trust inherent in a society'.

At the same time, however, the climate of greatly intensified competition and the development of more global business horizons have made it much more difficult to develop and preserve trust within and between organizations, as well as making it very risky to invest in trust. The establishment of many new ties between firms and constant reorganization within firms have disturbed common background assumptions, thereby weakening existing trust relations. Uncertainty and risk are greatly enhanced in business relations across national borders where common background assumptions cannot be taken for granted.

All these developments have made trust both more necessary and more problematic. They have led to a new preoccupation with trust both among managers and among social and management scientists—with its elusive qualities, its social organization and control, and, above all, with possible ways to maintain it, as well as create it anew. The consequences of trust for organizational performance have not so far received systematic study, and an alleged connection between societal trust and superior performance of whole economies (Fukuyama 1995) has so far received only rudimentary attention.

To gain a better understanding of the theoretically highly complex concept of trust and of the ways it impinges on organizations requires a fresh and sustained investigation of trust relations within and between organizations. Such an investigation has to draw on the established literature on trust in the social sciences, economics, philosophy, and management studies. Contributors to this book are exceptionally well equipped to tackle the challenge and to apply their theoretical notions to the analysis of empirical problems in a range of organizational settings, and industrial and social-institutional contexts. Between them, they cover the subject areas of economics, management, industrial relations, philosophy, socio-legal studies, and sociology, and many have a cross-disciplinary, as well as a comparative perspective. The book considers trust primarily as a social phenomenon, to be studied at interpersonal, interorganizational and systemic levels, rather than as an aspect of individual personality. By applying a variety of theoretical perspectives to a wide range of new organizational challenges, the book will clarify central issues in the study of trust, as well as develop new insights. Several of the contributors have previously written on trust (Arrighetti, Bachmann, and Deakin 1997; Burchell and Wilkinson 1997; Deakin, Lane, and Wilkinson 1994; Lane and Bachmann 1996, 1997; Loose and Sydow 1996; Oliver 1997; and Sako 1992).

Among the substantive problems around which trust relations form and unravel are the following: the new partnership sourcing; networks in a service industry; intellectual property rights of academics in a high-tech industry; supplier relations in a newly industrializing country; trust in joint ventures and international business in general; in relations between employers and employees; trust and power; and the relationship between trust and law. These substantive issues are discussed in such diverse societal contexts as Britain, Germany, France, Canada, the USA, Japan, India, and China, as well as in the supranational sphere of international business.

Although much has been written on trust in various contexts, there is no previous study of trust within and between business organizations which brings such broad expertise to bear on the problem of trust. Existing studies on trust between organizations are mainly scattered over a wide range of journals. The book-length study closest to our subject matter, Kramer and Tyler (1996), is much narrower in scope. It is written by American academics on American organizations, is mainly concerned with intraorganizational relationships and the dominant perspective is from social psychology.

This introductory chapter has the following objectives: first, to offer an extended review and analysis of the main approaches to the study of trust in social, economic, and organization theory. In doing so it will address the following questions: what are the social bases and functions of trust and what is the relationship between trust and risk? Second, and transcending specific theoretical traditions, this chapter will raise a number of important issues surrounding trust within and between organizations: how can trust be conceptualized at different levels of analysis; the relationship between trust and performance; how is trust recognized, generated, and sustained; and, finally, an exploration of the notions of opportunism and distrust, and of the mechanisms to lessen the risk of opportunism and contain the negative effects of distrust. Most of these issues are taken up and further investigated in the following chapters. The third and final section of this introduction will provide a brief overview of the contributions to this book.

1. TRUST IN ECONOMIC, SOCIAL, AND ORGANIZATION THEORY

Trust is a concept with many meanings, but most concepts of personal trust share three common elements. First, theories assume a degree of interdependence between trustor and trustee. Expectations about another's trustworthiness only become relevant when the completion of one's own consequential activities *depend* on the prior action or co-operation of another person (Luhmann 1979; Dasgupta 1988). Individuals would have no need to trust apart from social relationships (Lewis and Weigert 1985: 969). Second is the assumption that trust provides a way to cope with risk or uncertainty in exchange relationships. In economic theory, risk arises because trusting behaviour exposes the agent to the presumed opportunistic behaviour of her business partner. Sociological theorists throw light on the conditions which provide scope for opportunism in exchange relationships. Uncertainty and risk are seen to be inherent in social relationships, due to problems of time and information. Response to action in a social-exchange relationship is usually delayed in time, posing an information problem about how the other person will react. This requires a risky precommitment on the part of one actor (Simmel 1978; Luhmann 1979). The third common assumption in the writing on trust is a belief or an expectation that the vulnerability resulting from the acceptance of risk will not be taken advantage of by the other party in the relationship.

Where theorists begin to diverge from each other, however, is in their identification of the grounds or social bases on which such expectations may be based. Such divergencies depend partially on the model of human nature and/or of social interaction underlying theories, i.e. whether man is primarily seen as a rational egoist, or whether social interaction is viewed as being informed by either moral considerations or by cultural scripts and meaning systems. Divergencies may also arise both from the object of trust and the context in which the trust relationship is situated. A small group mainly of economists, who see trust based on calculation, can be contrasted with a group of mainly sociologists and organization scholars who insist on common values/moral orientations as the foundation of trust. Yet a third social basis identified consists of common cognitions. Last, it should be noted that Luhmann (1979) completely sidesteps the question of the grounds of trust and, instead, concentrates on the complexity-reducing function of trust.

Many theorists, however, hold that the grounds will vary with the social context/object of trust, or that the nature of trust will vary with the stage of a relationship reached. Hence they envisage a multidimensional concept of trust and elaborate a typology of trust which rests on more than one basis. Common combinations are cognitive trust with either value- or emotion-based trust (e.g. Barber 1983; Lewis and Weigert 1985) and a combination, popular among economists, of calculative with either cognitive or morally-based trust (Dasgupta 1988; Chiles and McMackin 1996). Some theorists combine all three of the above dimensions. Sheppard and Tuchinsky (1996), for example, talk of deterrence, knowledge, and identification-based trust which roughly approximate to calculative, value-based, and cognition-based trust.

Another multidimensional concept of trust results from distinguishing between different contents of expectations, i.e trust based on qualities one expects the other person to possess. Thus, Parsons (1969: 128) distinguishes between trust in the integrity of, and trust in the competence of the trustee which, in Barber's account, becomes fiduciary and competence trust. Mishra (1996) introduces as many as four different dimensions: competence, openness, concern, and reliability. The expectation of technically competent role performance, as Barber (1983: 14) points out, is particularly prevalent in task-oriented social systems, and it is thus not surprising that this dimension of trust has become adopted in organization studies. (See Sako 1992, and Chapter 3, this volume; Humphrey, Chapter 8, this volume.)

1.1 Calculative Trust

In this view of trust—common in agency theory in all the social sciences (Axelrod 1984; Coleman 1990; Dasgupta 1988) and in transaction costs economics (e.g. Chiles and McMackin 1996)—trusting involves expectations about another, based on calculations which weigh the cost and benefits of certain courses of action to either the trustor or the trustee. It is based on a view of man as a rational actor, and rationality is understood in utilitarian terms where the individual chooses the course of action likely to gain her the maximum utility.

In game-theoretical approaches to trust, which usually build on the work of Axelrod (1984), co-operation and trust can emerge in two situations: either the players expect repeated games and a lasting relationship (where the future casts a shadow back upon the present); or when both actors interact intensively with a third person in other contexts and wish to preserve their reputation. One of the best-known developments of Axelrod's work for the analysis of trust is Coleman's rational choice or decision-theoretic approach (1990). For Coleman, as for Luhmann (1979), trust is a decision under risk. But departing fundamentally from Luhmann, Coleman views trust as a unilateral transfer of resources to another actor, based on the expectation that the other actor might satisfy the trustor's interests better than she could herself (Preisendörfer 1995). A rational actor bestows trust only if her calculation suggests that the gain from reciprocated trust is higher than the loss threatened by a betrayal of trust and when trust relations are supported by negative sanctions (ibid. 115). Coleman recognizes that trusting behaviour requires the making of a precommitment which he likens to issuing 'social credit slips'. He has coined the notion of social capital to refer to the totality of such social credit slips issued by an individual.

The rational choice or decision-theoretical approach has been welcomed by many social and economic analysts because it is seen to permit a more precise assessment of the conditions and strategies in the presence of which repeated games and dense social networks (underlying the reputation effect) are conducive to generating trust (Preisendörfer 1995: 267). There are, however, also weighty objections. Criticisms hinge on the observation that rational actor theories fail to consider how the social nature of action undermines any effort to predict their outcomes. As Max Weber (1978: 63, 69–70) has made clear, a view of instrumentally rational, egoistical man is far too narrow, and substantive rationality (*Wertrationalität*) can be an equally powerful motivator of social action. Axelrod (1984) and Coleman (1990) simply assume that actors share expectations about the future, whereas more sociological accounts would stress that the emergence of the future is in itself in need of explanation. Neither gains nor losses can ever be calculated with the certainty inferred by rational choice theorists for the following reasons: trust is built up incrementally and the relationship may change in an unpredictable fashion as trust develops. In the words of Bradach and Eccles (1989: 108), 'the future is rarely preordained'; magnitude and timing of the trustee's response is influenced by social norms which complicate calculation; and, most importantly, the first step in 'a game without history', taken in the face of incomplete information about the trustee, requires a one-sided precommitment from the trustor based on mere beliefs/expectations about the trustee. As many authors point out (Luhmann 1979; Barber 1983; Zucker 1986; Gambetta 1988; Preisendörfer 1995), trust begins where rational prediction ends as trust bridges the information uncertainty. As Simmel (1950) has noted, to trust means making a leap beyond that which reason alone would warrant. The degree of preparedness to make such a precommitment in the face of imperfect knowledge is not only situationally variable but also culturally (Preisendörfer 1995; Fukuyama 1995; Sako, Chapter 3, this volume).

In transaction costs economics (Williamson 1975, 1985, 1993), the key behavioural assumptions are bounded rationality (the recognition that actors are limitedly rational) and opportunism. The agent copes with the risk of opportunistic behaviour of a potential business partner by employing control mechanisms and by making opportunism costly. Only if an agent expects calculation of the balance of costs and benefits derived from either opportunistic or co-operative behaviour to favour co-operative behaviour is she willing to trust. Williamson (1993: 458) explicitly allows for bounded rationality and claims that by internalizing into his theory 'the use of organization as a means to economize on bounded rationality' the problem is overcome. His claim that agents are able to do this by acting in a 'far-sighted' manner, i.e. by anticipating changes in the condition of the environment, likely outcomes and even unintended consequences, however, amounts to nothing less than negating the problem of bounded rationality which he previously identified. His advocacy of extensive control and monitoring procedures may reduce the need for trust, but they hardly eliminate it.

Williamson's emphasis on pervasive calculation and his claim that bounded rationality is unproblematic lead him to the logical conclusion, that 'calculative trust is a contradiction in terms' (1993: 463) and has no place in economic transactions. This view is entirely plausible within his 'rational actor' model of *Homo economicus*. (Williamson's earlier work (1975: 108) did not exclude trust, and the 1993 article still presupposes trust in close personal relations.) This model assumes an individual who is simultaneously highly prescient **and** aware of the limits of her rationality, who is able completely to divorce economic relations from social ties, and who manages to blend out the question of the subjective meaning of economic action. This undersocialized view, however, finds limited acceptance among economic sociologists and even among many economists. The objections have already been rehearsed in the previous paragraph.

Other adherents to the transaction costs approach, however, show more consistency in their stress on the element of 'bounded rationality' and hence wish to retain the notion of trust because it bridges the information gap (Arrow 1974; Lorenz 1988; Nooteboom 1993; Chiles and McMackin 1996). Arrow, for example, sees trust either as 'a lubricant' of business transactions or even as the most efficient governance mechanism (Arrow 1974). However, given that much economic theorizing ignores the social embeddedness of economic action, trust cannot become integrated into transactions costs theory but, as Ingham (1996: 250) points out, is simply bolted on to it. Also the assumption that the governance mechanism chosen is always the most efficient for the transaction in question would be difficult to justify in relation to trust (Zucker 1986).

Bradach and Eccles (1989), in contrast, modify the transaction costs approach in important ways. First, they do not assume that the risk of opportunism is always present in economic transactions. Second, they adopt a sociologically informed notion of economic exchange which allows for the development of trust in two distinctive contexts: where there exist between exchange partners common values and norms, grown out of a long process of association (see the discussion of value-based trust below); and, second, where economic relations are embedded in personal relations of friendship. This more sociological understanding of economic relations permits them to designate trust as a third mechanism of social control which is seen as both functionally equivalent to price (market) and authority (hierarchy), and as a complement to them. Sako (this volume, Chapter 3), too, sees trust as an alternative governance mechanism.

Chiles and McMackin (1996) also try to insert a more sociological view of trust into the transaction costs approach. But, in contrast to Bradach and Eccles (1989), they do not modify Williamson's assumption about opportunism to make integration credible. Despite extensive rehearsal of sociological views of trust, their references to socially embedded and norm-based trust remain 'bolted on', rather than integrated into transaction costs theory.

The argument so far suggests that the calculative view of trust does not stand up to sociological scrutiny. However, this does not imply that trust always presupposes altruism. Nor can it be assumed that trusting behaviour, particularly within and between business organizations, is completely free of calculation. As pointed out by Kramer, Brewer, and Hanna (1996: 384) and Zucker (1986), an element of calculation may be present in most trusting behaviour. The importance of this element changes both with the context and object of trust, as well as varying between the stages of a trusting relationship. A collectivity-orientation is present at the beginning of the game when rules are being established, but self-interest and calculation are often present at later stages (Zucker 1986). In economic exchange, people play the game to win, and self-interest is explicitly legitimated. The necessity to consider a mixture of motivations now also informs the work of some economists (Elster 1989: 274, quoted by Misztal 1996: 81;

Dasgupta 1988: 71; Lorenz 1988). We merely need to abandon the assumptions of hyperrationality and of rational calculation as a sufficient basis of trust.

1.2 Value- or Norm-based Trust

The claim that trust cannot develop unless individuals share common values has been most forcefully argued by Talcott Parsons (1951) who rejected the idea that rational self-interest could become the basis of collective order. Instead, the concept of solidarity is placed at the centre of such order. Solidarity, identified with institutionalized shared values, is seen as the main characteristic of a legitimate order of societal community, whose primary function is to define the obligations of loyalty to the societal collectivity (Parsons 1971, quoted in Misztal 1995: 67). Hence for Parsons, trust is 'the attitudinal ground—in affectively motivated loyalty—for the acceptance of solidarity relationships' (Parsons 1969: 142). For Parsons, trust entails the suspension of self-interest in favour of a collectivity-orientation. It is based on the expectation, on the part of the trustor, that the trustee—particularly if she is in a position of power—will meet her social obligation and exercise responsibility. The moral aspect of trust thus is given prime emphasis. Parsons envisages that the solidary community exercises a social control function and assumes common values and norms, based on kinship, familiarity, or common background and interest (ibid. 126–7). This theoretical approach is taken up by Fukuyama (1995) who states that 'trust comes out of shared values', stresses commonly shared norms and sees economic actors support each other where they share 'a community of trust'.

To posit common values and norms as the **sole** basis of trust is as one-sided as the notion of calculative trust. Empirical work tells us that trust can be built even between people from different cultural backgrounds or between individuals who share no values beyond their narrow business goals. To insist on common socialization and a solidary community to generate and police the common values underpinning trust would make trust an extremely scarce commodity in advanced society. Even in a fairly settled, locality-based system of economic interaction, Lorenz (1988) points out, ties of friendship between buyers and suppliers are rare. A solidary community would be an impossibility in many types of cross-border interorganizational relations in an increasingly more internationalized, if not globalized economic system. Parsons' notion of trust excludes the incremental, step-by-step construction of trust between individuals/organizations who start out with very imperfect knowledge/experience of each other (Luhmann 1979; Zucker 1986; Lorenz 1988; Gambetta 1988; Sabel 1992).

Parsons' notion of a generalized morality also implies what Granovetter

(1985) calls an over-socialized conception of social interaction. It neglects the fact that social conflict may be as frequent as social harmony in relationships within and between organizations. The necessity to take into consideration such value conflict and the problems it poses for relying on trust is theoretically elaborated by Hardy, Nelson, and Phillips (Chapter 2, this volume). An analysis of value conflict between academic and commercial scientists and of the problems for trust production this entails is a central subject of Chapter 4 (Porter Liebeskind and Lumerman Oliver).

One should, however, not conclude from this discussion of Parsons' notion of trust that common values and/or moral obligation have no role to play in the development of trust. A notion of value-based trust, although not always labelled as such, is adopted by a large number of writers in the fields of economics, and organizational and management studies. Many do not share, or are quite unaware of, sociologists' well-founded scepticism about the existence, in advanced, highly differentiated societies, of 'solidary communities', based on value consensus (e.g. Barney and Hansen 1994; Chiles and McMackin 1996).

Several writers, however, have moved away from a notion of generalized morality and use a concept of more limited norm-based trust which by-passes some of the sociological objections. Such approaches suggest that values and norms may enter into trust relations in very specific substantive areas or specific cultural contexts, or, following Granovetter (1985), view trust relations as embedded in particular social relations and the obligations inherent in them. Thus, common values and norms of obligation can develop in a long-standing relationship where trust was initially created in an incremental manner but where value-consensus emerges from the relationship.

Barber's notion of 'fiduciary trust', the expectation that trustees will carry out their fiduciary obligations and responsibility (1983: 9), for example, is based on Parsons' approach. But for Barber it is one of three types and applicable only in certain clearly defined circumstances. For Sako (1992 and Chapter 3, this volume), common internally generated norms can be expected even in interorganizational business relations, but, following Dore (1983), she recognizes that her notion of 'obligational trust' may be largely confined to a certain cultural context—that of Japanese society. Bradach and Eccles (1989), too, see norms of obligation as one of the bases of trust within and between organizations. Such norms, for them, imply the existence of 'some sort of community of shared values' in a country, industrial district, or a particular network. Although they concede that it is difficult to determine how such common values arise in the first place their review of a number of cases of obligational trust implicates either societal norms or, alternatively, suggests that process-based trust may, with sufficient time, become transformed into value-based trust.

Barney and Hansen's notion of 'strong-form trust', too, is value-based trust in the Parsonian mould. 'Strong-form trust . . . reflects values, principles, and standards that partners bring to an exchange' (1994: 179). This form of trust, which may be vested in organizations or in individuals, is said to reflect an organization's history and culture, or the personal beliefs and values of critical individuals associated with it (ibid). Although Barney and Hansen recognize both the difficulty and the risk of developing strong-form trust between business partners—it has, in their view, no need of legal and contractual protections—they do not limit it to certain cultural contexts or exceptional situations. Hence it remains ultimately unexplained how such trust, which presupposes common values and principles, comes about in relations between business partners.

1.3 Common Cognitions as the Basis of Trust

Cognitions, defined as the 'rules that constitute the nature of reality and the frames through which meaning is made' (Scott 1995: 40), are embodied in the expectations we hold both about the social order in general and about specific interactions with others. Expectations are held in common structure behaviour in certain predictable ways and thus can form the basis of trust. Cognition- or expectation-based trust is a notion held in slightly different forms by theorists from such diverse backgrounds as social exchange theory (Simmel 1978 and Blau 1967), ethnomethodology (Garfinkel 1967), phenomenology (Zucker 1986), systems theory (Luhmann 1979) and structuration theory (Giddens 1984), as well as Barber's (1983) structural-functionalist theory.

The highly general expectation of the persistence of the natural and social order (Barber 1983) forms the basis of trust in several social theories. Simmel's (1950) notion of trust as a constitutive element of society resurfaces in the work of Blau (1967) and has also inspired the concepts of trust central to the work of Luhmann (1979) and Giddens (1990). For Simmel, society is made up by relations of social exchange, and exchange would not be possible without trust. Simmel was the first to identify the 'problem of time and knowledge' in social exchange and the uncertainty this can generate. He points out that, in social interaction, response is often delayed and the initial move has to be made without full knowledge of how the exchange partner will respond, requiring a degree of trust. Trust, for Simmel, is not the only force motivating exchange but is nevertheless one of the most important synthetic forces within society (Simmel 1950: 318). Blau (1967) amplifies and develops Simmel's insights. He points out that all social exchange, during which individuals discharge their obligations for services received in the past, entails *unspecified* obligations, i.e. the exact nature of the return is not specified in advance and is left to the discretion of the one responding (Blau 1967: 93, 113). As there is no way to assure an appropriate

return, social exchange requires trusting others to discharge their obligations. Such an open-ended conception of reciprocity is quite unlike the
notion of reciprocity held by most economists where exchanges are seen to
have roughly equivalent value (Powell 1991: 272).

In Garfinkel's approach to trust from ethnomethodology, the cognitive
content of expectations moves centre stage. He regards the grounds of
trust as 'expectations of persistence, regularity, order and stability in the
everyday and routine moral world'. Trust resides in actors' expectations of
things 'as usual', with the actor 'being able to take for granted, to take under
trust a vast array of features of the social order' (Garfinkel 1967: 173).
Garfinkel thus underlines the unreflective qualities of trusting. He distinguishes between background expectancies (mental habits which explain the
role of social routines) and constitutive expectancies (ibid. 35 f.). He
thereby introduces a useful device for moving from the notion of general
existential trust to trust in specific social contexts, oriented to specific meaning systems. For Garfinkel the two types of expectations are complementary, with abundant background expectations diminishing the need for
constitutive ones. These three theorists—Simmel, Blau, and Garfinkel—
have thus provided some of the general theoretical groundwork on which
subsequent sociological theorists have been able to base their more extended studies of trust.

Zucker builds on Garfinkel's general sociological treatment of trust and,
blending it with insights from New Institutionalism, develops it in directions
which make it highly relevant to studies of organization. In common with
Garfinkel and phenomenology, she stresses the cognitive content of expectations, placing emphasis on social rules and common understandings.
Background expectations contain common interpretative frames and, by
making use of socially warranted knowledge, provide a general framework
for behaviour. Constitutive rules, in contrast, may define roles and rules and
legitimate media of interaction in a given sectoral or interaction context.
The more common background expectations are present—due to homogeneity in certain vital characteristics—the easier it is for trust to develop
spontaneously. Zucker's three types of trust—characteristic-, process-, and
institutionally-based trust—differ in the way they either assume unity of
expectation to be present and be taken for granted or, alternatively, to have
to be produced.

Process-based trust—which is tied to past or expected exchange—entails
the incremental process of building trust through the gradual accumulation
of either direct or indirect knowledge (e.g. reputation, brands, warranties of
quality) about the other. Process-based trust presupposes a degree of stability where there is a low turnover of firms and other market institutions, and
such trust is deliberately developed by firms. If the cultural congruence
necessary for this form of trust is not present at the societal level it can
sometimes be rebuilt at organization level, in the form of corporate culture.

But Zucker assumes that process-based trust has become more difficult to produce in the twentieth century, due to dramatically increased heterogeneity in background expectations.

Her second notion, characteristic-based trust, rests on social similarity and assumes cultural congruence, because trustor and trustee belong to the same social group or community. They may share a common religion, ethnic status, or family background which guarantee that they possess 'a world in common'. Such trust, being based on ascribed characteristics, cannot be deliberately created and, in most advanced societies, is becoming a scarce commodity.

Institutional-based trust moves away from the widely held assumption that trust can only be generated by interpersonal familiarity. Where organizational actors can no longer rely on commonality of personal characteristics or a past history or guaranteed future of exchange they have to turn to this impersonal form of trust. The latter is tied to formal social structures which 'generalize beyond a given transaction and beyond specific sets of exchange partners', and trust becomes part of 'the external world known in common', i.e. it becomes institutionalized (Zucker 1986: 63). Such trust is thus particularly apposite where relations go beyond group boundaries—an increasingly common occurrence in international business. Structures may be either person- or firm-specific, such as a professional credential or membership of an association, or they may be intermediary mechanisms—such as insurance, legal/statutory rules, or an institution, e.g. a bank, 'which protect the interests of all parties to the exchange' (ibid. 64). Thus, legal mechanisms, for Zucker, reduce the risk of trust and make it easier to trust. (Zucker does not envisage, as inferred by Sitkin and Roth (1993), that legal/ legalistic mechanisms restore *violated* trust.) Institutional-based trust can be deliberately produced by individuals, firms, and entire industries, with the proviso that such mechanisms have to be socially legitimated to be effective and they have to remain related to the underlying property signalled.

The most extended and insightful theoretical analysis of trust has been accomplished by Luhmann (1979). He explains the notion of trust by reference to the social function it performs. Luhmann's functionalist approach bypasses the question of the grounds of trust. However, by emphasizing the role of expectations, he implies the importance of cognitive structures in as far as shared meanings reduce complexity in social interaction and thus are assumed as a precondition for making it possible. In contrast to phenomenologists, however, he approaches meaning from a systems-theoretical angle (Poggi 1979: p. xiv).

For Luhmann, trust is a mechanism by which actors reduce the internal complexity of their system of interaction through the adoption of specific expectations about the future behaviour of the other by selecting amongst a range of possibilities. Trust absorbs complexity in so far as someone who trusts acts as if the trustee's actions are, at least to some degree, predictable. Luhmann is concerned only with those expectations concerning others' conduct, 'which would lead one to commit one's own action and which, if unrealised, would lead to regret' (Luhmann 1979: 24–5). Following Simmel, he views trust as a mechanism which overcomes 'the problem of time' (Luhmann 1979: 10 f.) and bridges uncertainty in the face of imperfect information. In common with Zucker, he distinguishes between personal and impersonal trust.

For Luhmann, as for Simmel and Blau, trust is a vital component of every interaction system. But, given 'the problem of time and knowledge', trust is a risky investment because it requires a precommitment (*Vorleistung*). Hence, argues Luhmann, trust has to be supplemented by mechanisms which contain the risk of misplaced trust. Luhmann regards law as one such mechanism as 'legal arrangements . . . lend special assurance to particular expectations and make them sanctionable'(Luhmann 1979: 34). Legal regulations are seen as deterring cheating, but it is important to realize that they act only as background structures which provide assurance and which are not activated (ibid. 36). The actual use of legal sanctions, for Luhmann as for most other social scientists, is incompatible with a trust relationship. Thus law and other social institutions are viewed as mechanisms to co-ordinate expectations which make the risk of trust more bearable. Although actors who trust take cognizance of the possibility of excessive harm resulting from the breach of trust, in Luhmann's view (ibid. 24), risk and the grounds for trust are not weighed up rationally before doing anything else. In common with phenomenologists and ethnomethodologists, he sees trust as often thoughtless, careless, and routinized (ibid.).

Given that Luhmann defines trust in functional terms, he is not concerned with the actual characteristics of different trust relationships and, in the words of Misztal (1995: 76), empties the concept of any objective reference. Hence his theory makes it difficult to distinguish between different kinds of trust according to the object and context of trust, as well as explore varying implications for the building of trust. Although it is extremely valuable for analytical purposes and has, indeed, inspired many subsequent approaches to trust both in sociology and organization studies, without adaptation Luhmann's theory gives limited purchase for empirical analysis of trust within and between organizations.

The theoretical approaches reviewed above have informed work in more empirically oriented organization studies which have been more or less self-consciously placed in a given theoretical tradition. This overview of understandings of trust in economic, social, and organization theory has concentrated on how different theoretical traditions conceptualize the social grounds and/or functions of trust. A distinction between trust based on/ referring to calculation, value-consensus and shared meanings has brought out the different presuppositions about human nature and society. It has also highlighted the context-dependency of varieties of trust, as well as giving some indication of the different implications for creating and sustaining trust in different social and societal contexts. These latter aspects and various other important issues in the study and experience of trust from an organizational perspective will be elaborated in Section 2.

2. ISSUES IN THE STUDY OF TRUST

2.1 Trust at Different Levels of Analysis

Trust may be viewed at the interpersonal level or as a systemic property, and any useful theory of trust must see it as 'a multidimensional social reality' which can bridge the micro and macro levels (Lewis and Weigert 1985: 967). Although it is difficult to envisage trust without an interpersonal dimension any theory which fails to go beyond this level cannot do justice to understanding and building trust within and between organizations in the current business environment. In this environment social stability at the micro level has become problematic; organizational ties need to be established more and more across social, geographical, and national/cultural boundaries; and personal ties, common histories, and 'worlds held in common' can be less and less assumed.

2.1.1 Trust at the micro-level   At the micro level, trust is envisaged both between individual persons and between organizations. Interpersonal trust between individuals is based on familiarity, developed in previous interaction or derived from membership in the same social group. Trust between organizations refers to trusting behaviour of corporate actors who differ from the sum of individuals constituting the corporate unit. Organization theorists perceive organizations which, despite their dependency on individual agency, are nevertheless seen to possess a corporate identity. They presume interorganizational relationships which transcend those of the agents establishing or breaking them off. Barney and Hansen (1994), for example, see firms as trustworthy in so far as they have developed a culture which, although it originates in critical individuals, may become independent from them. It is institutionalized in decision-making mechanisms and becomes perpetuated through control systems which reward trusting behaviour. Furthermore, an organization with a high-trust culture does not require that each one of its members is trusting, they need merely be self-interested (ibid. 180–1). Interpersonal and interorganizational trust are widely seen as informal, interactive processes which do not necessarily have to be sustained by formal structures or institutional mechanisms. In reality, however, informal and formal structures usually coexist.

2.1.2 Institutional-based Trust   Interpersonal trust is contrasted with either institutional-based trust (Zucker 1986) or system trust (Luhmann 1979 and 1988; Barber 1983; Giddens 1990). Both of the latter concepts refer to impersonal trust and the contexts within which it develops, but the various theorists approach impersonal trust in very different ways. Whereas system trust is trust or confidence in an abstract system, institutional-based trust refers to institutions as **sources** of trust.

For Zucker, institutional-based trust is not so much a matter of trust at a higher level of analysis as a different mechanism to produce trust. It is a type of trust which is not dependent on interpersonal familiarity and common history but where reliance is on formal, socially produced and legitimated structures which guarantee trust. It is likely to emerge when there is: (a) exchange across group boundaries and hence significant social distance between groups; (b) exchange across geographical distance; and (c) exchange involving a large number of interdependent, non-separable transactions (ibid. 82).

Luhmann (1979) also ponders on the conditions which make personal trust easier and develops ideas which overlap with Zucker's institutional-based trust. Although trusting behaviour always comes up against the problem of insufficient information about the object of trust, for Luhmann, acquisition of knowledge about the structural properties which one shares with others overcomes the need for information and hence provides supports for building trust. For both Luhmann and Zucker, structural properties or institutions *form the basis or provide supports for* trust production in more complex societies where common histories can no longer be assumed.

Shapiro also examines trust 'when economic transactions are not embedded in social relations' (1987: 624) and institutional mechanisms provide a source for trusting behaviour. But, in contrast to Zucker's work (1986), her analysis portrays impersonal trust as highly problematic. Shapiro, like Zucker, views impersonal trust as exceedingly common in developed societies. Using the concepts of principal and agent, she investigates the many relationships where 'faceless and readily interchangeable individual or organizational agents' act as trustees for principals and exercise considerable delegated power on their behalf (ibid. 634). Managers acting on behalf of shareholders, banks on behalf of firms, brokers or pension fund managers on behalf of investors, are only a few of such impersonal trust relations she has in mind.

Shapiro's contribution to the debate lies in pinpointing the dilemma posed by the wide-spread reliance in modern society on institutional-based trust, and she identifies the development of a 'spiral of distrust'. Her main concern is with the vulnerability of the principals of impersonal trust and with how their agents, supposedly acting on behalf of principals in a disinterested manner, are controlled through a variety of mechanisms. Among these are social control frameworks of procedural norms (e.g. codes of practice), organizational forms (e.g. professional associations) and social-control specialists (e.g. auditors) 'which institutionalize distrust' (ibid. 635). But to institute such 'guardians of trust' to watch over trustees provides no solution to principals' vulnerability to abuse of trust. Guardians of trust, in turn, need to be controlled, and, given their greater physical and social distance from principals, pose an even greater problem of social control. Shapiro thus exposes 'an inflationary spiral of escalating trust relationships and the paradox that the more we control the institution of trust, the more dissatisfied we will be with its offerings' (ibid. 652). These insights about the difficulty of controlling impersonal trust, it will be shown in the following section, were first developed by Luhmann (1979) and later elaborated by Giddens (1990).

2.1.3 System Trust   The notion of impersonal or system trust first appeared in the work of Simmel (1950: 313), received systematic development by Luhmann (1979) and Giddens (1990) and has also been used in a less abstract manner by Barber (1983). This notion of impersonal trust is very important for an understanding of the distinctive nature of modern societies and thus for the changed social context within which relations of trust within and between organizations occur.

Luhmann distinguishes between personal trust, based on familiarity and taking things for granted, and system trust or trust in the reliable functioning of certain systems, which no longer refers to a personally known reality (Luhmann 1979: 50). As the social order becomes more complex it tends to lose this taken-for-granted familiarity, while, at the same time, the need for co-ordination and for 'determining the future'—and hence for trust—becomes more urgent (Luhmann 1979: 20). He develops his notion of system trust via the notion of generalized media of communication—money, truth, and political power—which enable us to connect much longer chains of selectivity in the process of complexity reduction. Luhmann is concerned, as was Simmel before him, with public trust or confidence (Luhmann 1988) in the authority, reliability and/or legitimacy of political power, money, the legal system, and other cultural systems (Lewis and Weigert 1985: 974).

The cognitive basis of this form of trust lies in that 'each trusts on the assumption that others trust' (Luhmann 1979: 75). System trust is built up by continual affirmative experiences with using the system. Thus trust in generalized media of communication requires a minimum of real foundation for trust to be sustained. On the one hand, such trust does not require specific built-in guarantees, but on the other, it is more difficult to control than trust in persons. To control system trust requires expert knowledge, beyond that possessed by most people putting their trust into the system. They must therefore rely on these experts and have trust in them. Finally, for Luhmann as for Zucker (1986), impersonal trust underwrites interpersonal trust. In other words, for Luhmann a system is both the **object** of trust and its **source**.

Giddens' distinction between personal and system trust, developed in the context of his work on modernity (Giddens 1990), owes a large debt to Luhmann (1979 and 1988) and differs mainly in the terminology used. System trust, for Giddens as for Luhmann, is trust in societal systems or abstract principles, characteristic of the institutions of modernity. As in Luhmann's work, these mechanisms are media of exchange or symbolic tokens—money and political legitimacy, and systems of technical and professional knowledge, and they are seen to guarantee individual expectations. Luhmann's bridging of time and space in Giddens' work becomes time–space distanciation and is explicitly linked to processes of globalization and social disembedding, i.e. the lifting out of social relations from local contexts of interaction and their restructuring across undefined spans of time and space (Giddens 1990: 21). Impersonal trust develops in social contexts where the social disembedding of relationships prevails. Sydow, in Chapter 1 of this volume, further develops Giddens' concepts and makes them applicable to the analysis of trust between organizations.

Whereas Luhmann and Giddens are concerned with trust in highly abstract systems, Barber (1983: 18) equates these systems with societal institutions, such as legal, educational, and political institutions. System trust becomes confidence in major societal institutions, and it is in this sense that it is used in some of the chapters of this book.

2.1.4 Societal Trust The idea of societal trust, although implied in many comparative studies (Fox 1974; Sako 1992; Fukuyama 1995), has received relatively little systematic analysis in the literature on trust. Three alternative approaches suggest themselves. Societal trust can either refer to a generalized notion of value/norm-based trust, seeing a society as a solidary cultural community; or it can refer to institutional arrangements at a meso and macro level; a third variant is linked to the concept of system trust where one is concerned with trust or confidence in certain crucial abstract societal principles or systems.

The first of the above notions of societal trust has been associated particularly with the recent work of Fukuyama (1995) whose concept of trust has already been examined critically above. Fukuyama sees societies as cultural communities, and trust, for him, 'is the expectation that arises within a community of regular, honest, and co-operative behaviour, based on commonly shared norms, on the part of other members of the community' (ibid. 26). The prevalence of trust in a society, for him, results in social capital—a notion borrowed from Coleman (1990). In Fukuyama's view, societies are distinguished from each other by the extent to which trust penetrates the whole of society, rather than remainining confined to family, clan, or close friends. Although, for Fukuyama, a society may increase or diminish its social capital over time, he also points out that societal trust is hard to develop systematically. It is therefore implied that it is difficult, if not impossible, to cultivate trust intentionally at this level and to change from a low-trust to a high-trust society. Given his value/norm-based notion of trust, this conclusion is inescapable. Other theorists reviewed above, however, are sceptical of such a broad-grained, common values-based notion of societal trust, presupposing a solidary community.

The notion of societal trust is arguably more useful for comparative organizational study if the culturalist approach is replaced by an institutional one. Such an institutional analysis would not only focus at the meso level, but would encompass societal institutions at the macro level. Zucker (1986) makes it clear that institutional mechanisms to produce trust are many and varied, and her analysis concludes that they can be intentionally produced. Although such mechanisms will possess a degree of cultural specificity, cross-national borrowing of organizational forms from societies perceived as economically successful is less categorically excluded, and changes in the level of trust depend on instituion building and reconstruction.

System trust (Luhmann 1979; Giddens 1990), trust in abstract systems, such as the political system, differs from the other two in that it refers to abstract societal properties which make a society appear more or less stable and predictable. The strength or weakness of such system trust will influence the degree to which individuals are prepared to extend trust beyond familiar primary groups. The absence of system trust in some newly industrializing countries and the impact of this on interorganizational relations is an important theme in Child's description (Chapter 9 of this volume) of the Chinese business environment, but trust in a specific system may also be low in more advanced societies, as found by Arrighetti, Bachmann, and Deakin (1997) when considering the Italian legal system.

Adopting a notion of societal trust does not imply a structural determinism and denial of managerial strategic choice. It should merely be interpreted as positing societal variability in the presence of structural facilitators of/constraints on the production of trust. The impact of societal institutions must be viewed as mediated by factors at industry level and by managerial action. The diversity of such societal institutionalized rule systems, which stabilize trust relations within and between firms, is well illustrated by Deakin and Wilkinson (Chapter 5, this volume) and Marsden (Chapter 6, this volume). Whereas Marsden highlights the impact of societally diverse interfirm labour market institutions on the maintenance of trust in employment relations, Deakin and Wilkinson examine the impact of differing legal rules on supplier relations. Similar concerns are also more or less central in the chapters in this volume by Sako (3), Humphrey (8), and Child (9).

2.2 Trust and Economic Performance

The issue of whether trust enhances organizational performance receives different answers in the literature. A few writers, e.g. Williamson (1993), claim it has no role to play at all. Others see trust as a very necessary and desirable property of organizational interaction but nevertheless dispute that it is the most efficient governance mechanism (Zucker 1986) or that it is invariantly associated with high performance (Kern, Chapter 7, this volume). But the majority of organization scholars connect trust with highly positive effects on performance. Arrow (1974: 26) and Fukuyama (1995) even connect the absence of trust with economic backwardness or underdevelopment.

Zucker's claim about 'bounded efficiency' is based on the recognition that the production of trust 'has supernormal costs associated with it' (1986: 67). Inefficiency arises from the fact that trust is often unplanned and unacknowledged, and the fragility of trust also poses obvious problems. Kern (Chapter 7, this volume) goes further and contends that, in certain circumstances, trust is connected with suboptimal performance. For Kern, a surfeit of trust in industrial districts may cement interorganizational relations to such a degree that organizations become locked into them and lose the flexibility to forge new ties outside the district. He sees this as being particularly damaging for radical innovation in new high-tech industries where the dependence on the combination of different bodies of knowledge presupposes the easy establishment of transterritorial relations.

For trust to have an impact on performance and competitiveness, it is pointed out by Barney and Hansen (1994), it has to be assumed that both opportunism and trust are not constants of exchange relationships but are unevenly distributed between them. Those who connect trust with enhanced business performance put forward different reasons for why this may be the case. The economic literature points mainly to the impact of trust on the level of transaction costs, resulting from a reduced need for contractual or monitoring devices (Lorenz 1988; Chiles and McMackin 1996). According to Arrow (1974: 23), 'trust . . . is extremely efficient'; it saves people a lot of trouble to have a fair degree of reliance on other people's word and enables them to produce more (ibid). For some scholars (e.g. Granovetter 1985; Sako 1992; and Barney and Hansen 1994) a high level of trust removes the need for any contractual and monitoring devices, because personal obligation and/or value-consensus are seen to ensure against opportunism. However, for these and many other organization scholars, enhanced performance results not only or even mainly from savings in transaction costs.

A high level of trust between exchange partners is said to incline them towards expanding the amount of knowledge they make available to each other (Sako, Chapter 3, this volume; Child, Chapter 9, this volume). In a relationship of trust, information exchanged may be more accurate, comprehensive, and timely (Chiles and McMackin 1996: 89), and under conditions of high trust, developed in a long-standing relationship, both implicit and proprietary knowledge considered confidential is made available to the exchange partner (Ring and van de Ven 1992). Such easy exchange of information, in turn, makes exchange partners more open to each other and thus inclines them to explore new opportunities of collaboration, such as the enhancement of product quality (Sako, Chapter 3, this volume) and the joint exploitation of a new technology. This effect of trust on performance will also be of increasing importance for intrafirm relations where team-working and organizational learning are now given considerable weight (Rajan, van Eupen, and Jaspers 1997: 36).

Ring and van de Ven (1992), in contrast to Barney and Hansen (1994), do not envisage a complete abandonment of safeguards but point towards the adoption of *mutually* negotiated mechanisms which provide greater flexibility in the relationship—another advantage of a trust relationship. Such flexibility is also derived from the greater openness between exchange partners, allowing them to leave production-related issues, such as cost, quality or volume, open-ended (Barney and Hansen 1994: 493). Ring and van de Ven (1992), together with many other authors, see such increased flexibility and hence the trust to facilitate it, as **the** distinguishing characteristic of a new, and increasingly popular organizational form/governance mode, i.e. networks or relational contracting.

For answers to the question of why organizations of some countries are performing at a higher level than those of others on a number of mainly production-related indicators (Womack, Jones, and Roos 1990; Sako 1992) we need to turn to the notion of societal trust. (See discussion above.) Here we have to move beyond Zucker (1986) who claims that institutional mechanisms to develop trust can be bought on the market. We need to explore why one and the same mechanism, e.g. legal contracts or membership of a certain association, is more closely related to trust production in one society than another. A first step towards an answer has been made by a recent comparative study of supplier relations in Britain, Germany, and Italy (Lane 1997; Deakin, Lane, and Wilkinson 1997). This work points to the differing degrees of institutionalization of trust-producing mechanisms, as well as the varying degree of congruence between them. Such differences then endow rules and norms with varying degrees of legitimacy and thus account for their differential impact on managerial expectations, behaviour, and performance. An alternative culturalist approach implies the much more problematic assumption that some societies enjoy more social solidarity than others and have been better able to preserve a common set of values and norms.

2.3 How to Build and Maintain Trust

Given that trust is seen to confer important advantages on exchange partners, it raises a number of questions and concerns which will be addressed both in this subsection and in 2.4. First, it is obviously important to know whether it can be consciously developed and if so, how, particularly in an environment seen to be more conducive to distrust. An equally strong concern, arising from the fragility of trust and hence its riskiness, is how to maintain and expand it. A third problematic issue is how to recognize trust and distinguish it from simulated trust, disguising opportunism (Hardy, Phillips, and Lawrence, Chapter 2, this volume). Opportunism and its social control, as well as the negative consequences of distrust and the ways to contain them, will be examined in subsection 2.4.

There is wide agreement in the literature that opportunism can be detected and that trust needs to replace distrust if positive effects on performance are to be realized. While some theorists claim that trust cannot be intentionally created but that it is emergent, others hold the opposite opinion. These differences can largely be explained by reference to the different grounds for trust identified. Those theorists who recognize only characteristic-based trust and/or socially embedded trust (Granovetter 1985) tend to hold the first view, as do **some** of the theorists adhering to the value/norm-based version of trust. Others hold that trust can be systematically created or produced, but that the way in which it is produced differs between kinds of trust. Different methods are seen as being required, for example, for process-based trust and institutionally-based trust. (See the discussion of Zucker 1986, above.) The notion of process-based trust or studied trust (Sabel 1993) is relevant both to the distinction of genuine from simulated trust (Hardy, Phillips, and Lawrence, Chpater 2, this volume) and to the development of trust where there previously was none (Humphrey, Chapter 8, this volume; Child, Chapter 9, this volume).

The literature is agreed that interpersonal trust in business relations is rarely offered spontaneously but requires an extended period of experience. During this time, knowledge about the exchange partner is accumulated through direct contact or is acquired indirectly through reliable third parties. The search for trustworthy partners is eased by the fact that it is in the interest of such potential partners to make their trustworthiness known by sending out signals of trustworthiness, providing indirect information. Reputation, brands, and adoption of quality standards are among the signals, highlighted in the literature. For such signals to be reliably perceived, there must be established channels of communication, and these cannot be presumed in cross-border co-operations. The potential trustor will often still want to check whether such signals correspond to actual behaviour and initiate direct contact.

In the case of direct contact, the building of trust occurs in a gradual process and the amount of trust conferred is expanded in very small steps. Exchange partners gradually test whether the other party is trustworthy. The incremental expansion of trust entails that the object of trust and the levels of risk entailed are gradually increased, i.e. the stakes are being raised over time (Ring and van de Ven 1992: 489). Such a 'stages' model of trust is well illustrated in Child's account (Chapter 9, this volume) of joint ventures in China. It is even suggested that calculus-based trust may become transformed into affect-based trust (ibid.), or competence trust into good-will trust (Sako, Chapter 3, this volume). Sako's notion of a hierarchy of trust well sums up this transformation process.

It is also being suggested that the process of building trust may be shortened if boundary-spanning persons in exchange relationships have regular personal contact (Bradach and Eccles 1989), if auditing of the exchange by a third party is accepted, or if unilateral transaction-specific investments (Barney and Hansen 1994) or precommitments are being made (Sako, Chapter 3, this volume).

2.4 Opportunism, Distrust and Their Social Control

Trust, it is widely held, is a risky investment, and the risk is due to the fact that the trustee may exploit the vulnerability of the trustor. Such behaviour is referred to as opportunism in the economic and organizational literature. The notion of opportunism is given particular emphasis in Williamson's (1985) transaction costs approach where opportunism is defined as 'self-interest seeking with guile'. This approach assumes that the risk of opportunism is always present in exchange relations and that it is impossible to detect it. As opportunism reduces the efficiency of transactions, it has to be controlled through various contractual and monitoring devices. The adoption of a variety of governance devices is seen to make opportunism costly and thus deter rational exchange partners from adopting it (Barney and Hansen 1994: 178). Marsden (Chapter 6, this volume) addresses the problem of opportunism in the employment relationship and points to the importance of institutionalized rule systems to control it.

In other approaches, opportunism is seen to be less likely in relationships where both sides are committed to a common future (Axelrod 1984), or where exchange partners wish to protect their reputation (Zucker 1986; Coleman 1990). The risk of opportunism is lessened and the need for elaborate formal governance structures reduced where economic transactions are embedded in personal relationships (Bradach and Eccles 1989: 109), or where action is governed by ethical principles (ibid.; Hosmer 1995), i.e. where value-based trust is present. As the adherence to ethical principles cannot be assumed in business partners there is always a danger that trust may be merely simulated (Williamson 1985; Hardy, Phillips, and Lawrence, Chapter 2, this volume).

If a variety of governance mechanisms are adopted to deter opportunism, Barney and Hansen (1994) claim, only 'weak form' trust or, in Sako's (1992) terms, 'contractual trust' may develop. Such a view is widely endorsed by economists (e.g. Arrow 1974). A more sociologically informed approach stresses that first, the entering into contract already presupposes trust (Durkheim 1984: 215) and that a contract may be seen as a token of trust. Another view is that legal and similar devices, provided they are kept as background expectancies, make it easier to trust (Luhmann 1979; Zucker 1986; Deakin and Wilkinson, Chapter 5, this volume). Thus, no incompatibility between the two is envisaged, and most empirical studies of business organizations would attest to the common use of trust, together with other control mechanisms.

In the sociological literature concern is also focused on the betrayal of trust and on the distrust which may develop in the face of opportunism. Distrust is seen both as the opposite of trust and as a functional alternative to it. Following Luhmann (1979: 27 f.), two qualities of trust explain both its fragility and the highly emotional reaction when trust is betrayed: the first is the fact that trusting, learnt from infancy onwards by a process of generalizing from isolated experiences, is closely tied up with the self-developing identity of the learner; second, the persons and social arrangements in which one puts trust become symbolic complexes, which are especially sensitive to disturbance. Hence, one falsehood may be reacted to with great emotional intensity and upset trust for ever. These facts explain not only the fragility of trust and the likelihood of its transformation into distrust, but they also point to the necessity to sustain trust through appropriate actions.

But not all negative feedback information about the trustee threatens or disrupts trust. The trustee enjoys a certain credit which allows even unfavourable experiences to be reinterpreted and absorbed (Luhmann 1979: 29; Zucker 1986). Depending on the circumstances and the object of trust, certain symbolic thresholds are erected to determine when trust is considered broken (ibid. 72). Zucker (1986) connects distrust with the violation of either background or constituent expectations. In her view, the threshold considered to constitute a violation of trust is reached when it is suspected that violation of trust in one exchange will be generalized to other exchanges. Chapter 7 by Kern in this volume illustrates the loss of trust in German employers who have violated the constitutive expectation that employees' identification with their firm will be reciprocated by the guarantee of employment security.

For Luhmann, distrust is not simply the opposite of trust but also a functional equivalent to it. Anyone who chooses not to trust another must adopt another negative strategy to reduce complexity. But complexity reduction through distrust is much more burdensome and difficult to implement as the person who distrusts becomes more dependent on information and, at the same time, feels compelled to narrow down the information on which she is able and willing to rely. 'Strategies of distrust . . . often absorb the strength of the person who distrusts to an extent which leaves him little energy to explore and adapt to an environment in an objective and unprejudiced manner, and hence allow him fewer opportunities for learning' (Luhmann 1979: 72). Luhmann thus points to the negative consequences for organizational learning of distrust and makes clear why there is a strong incentive to start a relationship with trust. Marsden (Chapter 6, this volume), develops the work of Fox (1974) on the 'low trust' syndrome in the context of industrial relations. He points to the negative impact of distrust on the employment relationship, in that it reduces room for manœuvre and flexibility in the shaping of work roles.

Distrust becomes visible to the exchange partner who eventually reacts with distrust on her own part, feeling herself relieved of moral obligation and free to act in her own interest. This reaction further confirms the initial distrust and leads to a downward spiral or a self-fulfilling prophecy which can totally paralyse an organization or an interorganizational co-operation. Hence organizations must develop mechanisms which keep distrust from turning into a destructive force. They can either explain away trust-threatening actions as mistakes or as something caused by an external force, i.e. as actions which explain away distrust as an attitude and instead portray it as a unique or accidental event, or they can use sanction to stop the destructing cycle (Luhmann 1979: 75).

The argument in section 2 has identified important issues and problems in the study of trust and has shown how these are analysed in the different theoretical treatments of trust, opportunism, and distrust. In doing so, it has not only drawn on the general theoretical literature on trust, but reference has also been made to how the authors in this volume have contributed to the various debates around trust. Section 3, in contrast, will provide more focused brief summaries of the argument presented in the chapters of this book.

3. CONTRIBUTIONS TO THE BOOK

Chapter 1 by Jörg Sydow combines Giddens' structuration theory with Zucker's typology of trust to study the evolution of trust in the German financial services industry. It analyses the interplay of Zucker's three different sources of trust in disembedding and reembedding processes. His analysis of both interpersonal and system trust and his focus on structural features of organizational configurations and their institutional supports enable him to explore the possibilities for network management to intentionally create trust, as well as the limitations faced in this endeavour.

Cynthia Hardy, Nelson Phillips, and Tom Lawrence (Chapter 2) start from the premise that any study of trust between organizations needs to take account of asymmetrical power and conflict in interorganizational relations and draw attention to the risk of simulated trust. They have developed a concept of trust, based on expectations and good will, which emphasizes shared meaning and shared power. This conceptualization enables them to distinguish between trust-based and power-based relationships and to develop a model which identifies both forms and façades of trust. Their analysis is illustrated with examples of different types of relations within and between Canadian voluntary and business organizations.

Chapter 3 on the new supplier relations in the auto industry by Mari Sako is devoted to the examination of several very important issues: how trust in business relations may lead to enhanced performance; and how trust can develop where there was previously none. She offers not only theoretical conceptualizations of these matters but also develops a methodology for operationalizing both trust and performance to make them amenable to measurement. Additionally, she explores the issue of trust as a societal property and attempts to explain differential national competitive performance in these terms.

Julia Porter Liebeskind and Amalya Lumerman Oliver (Chapter 4) describe how the increasing commercial value of scientific discoveries in molecular biology has transformed the notion of trust within the academic scientific community, and how this transformation has in turn impacted the social structure of academic scientific research. They develop the concept of credibility or scientific trust and explore how the delicate social system of academic research may become unbalanced by the intrusion of commercial interest. Drawing on a recent study of relations between academic scientists and biotechnology firms in California, they provide some fascinating insights into the problems and opportunities encountered in building research networks which link commercial and non-commercial organizations.

Trust is often viewed as a mechanism of co-ordination and control in interorganizational relations. There is a fundamental disagreement in the literature on trust whether the deployment of legal contracts should be regarded as an alternative mechanism of control which undermines trust (Macaulay 1963; Sako 1992; Fukuyama 1995), or whether legal regulation of business relations is an important precondition for trust as it makes business relations more predictable and less risky (Luhmann 1979; Zucker 1986). Chapter 5 by Simon Deakin and Frank Wilkinson examines the theoretical arguments on both sides of this long-standing academic debate.

Drawing on a comparative study of supplier relations in Britain, Germany, and Italy, they develop the case for the proposition that trust and law are compatible and that the latter may contribute to the development and strengthening of the former. Legal regulation is conceptualized as being part of a societal institutional framework, and varying institutional frameworks are shown to significantly affect firm's strategies with regard to interorganizational co-operation.

David Marsden, in Chapter 6, moves the discussion of trust to the terrain of industrial relations, and his theoretical analysis is concerned with the fragility of trust in this area. He investigates how external institutions can provide the necessary stability to make trust possible in the inherently unstable context in which industrial relations are situated. In doing so he explores the variabilty in societal institutions between European countries and examines their differential impact on trust production and maintenance.

Horst Kern (Chapter 7) tackles one of the main problems confronting managements in advanced industrial societies today: how to preserve and develop the trust necessary for the realization of a production regime based on constant innovation and speedy application of new knowledge in the face of constant organizational rationalization and heightened employment insecurity among employees. He also poses the more challenging thesis that unquestioning trust can create blockages to learning and innovation and thus maintains that both a lack and a surfeit of trust may have harmful consequences. In his analysis of these dilemmas, Kern addresses one of the most pressing problems facing German industry today and, in doing so, draws on his immense knowledge of German production regimes in several industries.

John Humphrey (Chapter 8) studies the transformation of supplier relations towards partnership in the automobile industry of India. Humphrey is preoccupied with the crucial issue of how to develop trust where there was previously none. This issue poses itself particularly starkly in the business environment of a newly industrializing country which often lacks the conditions conducive to the production of trust. Hence Humphrey's theoretical concern is as much with distrust as trust. He postulates that, in the Indian business environment, trust has to be backed up with distrust, at least in the early stages of the process of building trust.

The problem of how to build trust in the business environment of a low-trust society is also a central concern of John Child's study of trust-building in Chinese joint ventures (Chapter 9). Western managers, trying to establish joint ventures, are faced with formidable problems: in Chinese society trust is largely based on social familiarity and confined to relations within families or local communities, and institutional mechanisms to produce trust are lowly developed and unreliable; managers additionally have to contend with problems, posed by the absence of common background assumptions and understandings in intercultural exchange relations characterized by a high degree of physical and cultural distance. Child develops a 'stages model' of trust which allows for the possibility of a gradual transition from 'weak form' trust to 'strong form' trust (Barney and Hansen 1994). This model is utilized to structure a rich body of empirical data about Chinese joint ventures and to generate insights for Western managers on how to approach and handle this increasingly common and important type of interorganizational co-operation.

In the context of a greatly intensified internationalization of business organization George Brenkert (Chapter 10) contributes a very timely and valuable exploration of the relation between trust and morality among commercial agents, operating on the international level. Marrying a theoretical approach from philosophy with one of organization studies, he argues for the establishment of an international business ethics. This would provide guidance on such questions as exploitation of workers in developing nations, child labour, and environmental despoilation. Brenkert emphasizes that such an ethics has to be a morality, i.e. an ethics whose rules, principles, and values are capable of being communicated and taught to others. Trust is viewed as a necessary condition for an international business morality in so far as conditions of trust sustain the contexts in which moral principles achieve their embodiment. Brenkert does not underestimate the difficulties entailed in the development of trust in international business and offers some suggestions on how these may be met. Finally, the Conclusion by Reinhard Bachmann draws out some of the important issues around trust appearing in the various chapters, as well as further developing some of the ideas first rehearsed here.

REFERENCES

Alter, C. and Hage, J. (1993), *Organizations Working Together*. Newbury Park, Calif.: Sage.

Arighetti, S., Bachmann, R., and Deakin, S. (1997), 'Contract law, Social Norms and Inter-firm Cooperation', *Cambridge Journal of Economics*, 21/2: 171–96.

Arrow, K. (1974), *The Limits of Organization*. New York: Norton.

Axelrod, R. (1984), *The Evolution of Cooperation*. New York: Basic Books.

Barber, B. (1983), *The Logic and Limits of Trust*. New Brunswick, NJ: Rutgers University Press.

Barney, J. B. and Hansen, M. H. (1994), 'Trustworthiness as a Source of Competitive Advantage', *Strategic Management Journal*, 15: 175–90.

Blau, P. M. (1967), *Exchange and Power in Social Life*. London: John Wiley.

Bradach, J. L. and Eccles, R. G. (1989), 'Price, Authority and Trust: From Ideal Types to Plural Forms', *Annual Review of Sociology*, 15: 97–118.

Burchell, B. and Wilkinson, F. (1997), 'Trust, Business Relationships and the Contractual Environment', *Cambridge Journal of Economics*, 21/2: 217–39.

Chiles, T. H. and McMackin, J. (1996), 'Integrating Variable Risk Preferences, Trust, and Transaction Costs Economics', *Academy of Management Review*, 21/1: 73–99.

Coleman, J. S. (1990), *The Foundations of Social Theory*. Cambridge, Mass.: Harvard University Press.

Dasgupta, P. (1988), 'Trust as a Commodity', in Gambetta (ed.), *Trust: Making and Breaking Cooperative Relations*, 49–72.

Deakin, S., Lane, C., and Wilkinson, F. (1994), 'Trust or Law? Towards an Integrated Theory of Contractual Relations Between Firms', *Journal of Law and Society*, 21/3: 329–49.

——————(1997), 'Performance Standards in Supplier Relations: Relational Strategies, Organisational Processes and Institutional Structures', paper presented to the EMOT Workshop on Performance Standards, Wissenschaftszentrum, Berlin, Jan. 1997.

Dore, R. (1983), 'Goodwill and the Spirit of Market Capitalism', *British Journal of Sociology*, 34/4: 459–82.

Durkheim, E. (1933), *The Division of Labour in Society*. London: Macmillan.

Fox, A. (1974), *Beyond Contract: Work, Power and Trust Relations*. London: Faber and Faber.

Fukuyama, F. (1995), *Trust: the Social Virtues and the Creation of Prosperity*. London: Hamish Hamilton.

Gambetta, D. (1988), 'Can we Trust Trust?', in D. Gambetta (ed.), *Trust: Making and Breaking of Cooperative Relations*. Oxford: Blackwell.

Garfinkel, H. (1984), *Studies in Ethnomethodology*. Cambridge: Polity Press in association with Oxford: Blackwell.

Giddens, A. (1984), *The Constitution of Society*. Cambridge: Polity Press.

——(1990), *The Consequences of Modernity*. Cambridge: Polity Press.

Granovetter, M. (1985), 'Economic Action and Social Structure: A Theory of Embeddedness', *American Journal of Sociology*, 91: 481–510.

Hosmer, L. T. (1995), 'Trust: The Connecting Link Between Organizational Theory and Philosophical Ethics', *Academy of Management Review*, 20/2: 379–403.

Ingham, G. (1996), 'Some Recent Changes in the Relationship Between Economics and Sociology', *Cambridge Journal of Economics*, 20: 243–75.

Kramer, R. M. and Tyler, T. R. (1996) (eds.), *Trust in Organizations*. London: Sage.

——Brewer, M. B., and Hanna, B. A. (1996), 'Collective Trust and Collective Action', in Kramer and Tyler (eds.), *Trust in Organizations*.

Lane, C. (1997), 'The Social Regulation of Inter-firm Relations in Britain and Germany: Market Rules, Legal Norms and Technical Standards', *Cambridge Journal of Economics*, 21/2: 197–216.

——and Bachmann, R. (1996), 'The Social Constitution of Trust: Supplier Relations in Britain and Germany', *Organization Studies*, 17/3: 365–95.

——————(1997), 'Cooperation in Inter-firm Relations in Britain and Germany: The Role of Social Institutions', *British Journal of Sociology*, 48/2: 226–54.

Lewis, J. D. and Weigert, A. (1985), 'Trust as a Social Reality', *Social Forces*, 63/3: 967–84.

Loose, A. and Sydow, J. (1994), 'Vertrauen und Ökonomie in Netzwerkbeziehungen', in J. Sydow and A. Windeler (eds.), *Management interorganisationaler Beziehungen*. Opladen: Westdeutscher Verlag, 160–93.

Lorenz, E. H. (1988), 'Neither Friends nor Strangers: Informal Networks of Subcontracting in French Industry', in Gambetta (ed.), *Trust: Making and Breaking of Cooperative Relations*, 194–210.

Luhmann, N. (1979), *Trust and Power*. Chichester: John Wiley.

——(1988), 'Familiarity, Confidence, Trust: Problems and Alternatives', in Gambetta (ed.), *Trust: Making and Breaking Cooperative Relations*, 94–107.

Macaulay, S. (1963), 'Non-contractual Relations in Business: A Preliminary Study', *American Sociological Review*, 28/2: 55–67.

Mishra, A. (1996), 'Organizational Responses to Crisis: The Centrality of Trust', in Kramer and Tyler (eds.), *Trust in Organizations*.

Misztal, B. (1995), *Trust in Modern Societies*. Cambridge: Polity Press.

Nooteboom, B. (1993), 'Networks and Transactions: Do They Connect?', in J. Groenewegen (ed.), *Dynamics of the Firm*. Aldershot: Edward Elgar, 9–26.

Oliver, A. L. (forthcoming), 'On the Nexus of Organizations and Professions: Networking Through Trust', *Sociological Inquiry*, 67.

Parsons, T. (1951), *The Social System*. London: Routledge & Kegan Paul.

——(1969), 'Research with Human Subjects and the "Professional Complex"', in P. A. Freund (ed.), *Experimentation with Human Subjects*. New York: George Braziller, 116–51.

——(1971), *The System of Modern Societies*. Englewood Cliffs, NJ: Prentice Hall.

Piore, M. and Sabel, C. (1984), *The Second Industrial Divide. Possibilities for Prosperity*. New York: Basic Books.

Poggi, G. (1979), 'Introduction', in N. Luhmann, *Trust and Power*.

Powell, W. W. (1991), 'Neither Market, nor Hierarchy: Network Forms of Organization', in G. Thompson, J. Frances, R. Levacic, and J. Mitchell (eds.), *Markets, Hierarchies and Networks*. London: Sage, 265–76.

Preisendörfer, P. (1995), 'Vertrauen als soziologische Kategorie: Möglichkeiten und Grenzen einer entscheidungstheoretischen Fundierung des Vertrauenskonzepts', *Zeitschrift für Soziologie*, 24/4: 263–72.

Rajan, A., van Eupen, P., and Jaspers, A. (1997), *Britain's Flexible Labour Market: What Next?*. London: CREATE.

Ring, P. S. and van de Ven, A. H. (1992), 'Structuring Cooperative Relationships Between Organizations', *Strategic Management Journal*, 13: 483–98.

Sabel, C. (1992), 'Studied Trust: Building New Forms of Cooperation in a Volatile Economy', in F. Pyke and W. Sengenberger (eds.), *Industrial Districts and Local Economic Regeneration*. Geneva: IILS, 215–50.

Sako, M. (1992), *Prices, Quality and Trust: Inter-firm Relations in Britain and Japan*. Cambridge: Cambridge University Press.

Scott, W. R. (1995), *Institutions and Organizations*. London: Sage.

Shapiro, S. P. (1987), 'The Social Control of Impersonal Trust', *American Journal of Sociology*, 93/3: 623–58.

Sheppard, B. H. and Tuchinsky, M. (1996), 'Micro-OB and the Network Organization', in Kramer and Tyler (eds.), *Trust in Organizations*, 140–65.

Simmel, G. (1950), *The Sociology of Georg Simmel*, ed. K. H. Wolff. New York: Free Press.

—— (1978), *The Philosophy of Money*. London: Routledge & Kegan Paul.

Sitkin, S. B. and Roth, N. L. (1993), 'Explaining the Limited Effectiveness of Legalistic "Remedies" for Trust/Distrust', *Organization Science*, 4/3: 367–92.

Sydow, J. (1996), 'Inter-organisational Relations', *International Encyclopedia of Business and Management*. London: Routledge.

Turner, L. and Auer, P. (1994), 'A Diversity of New Work Organization', *Industrielle Beziehungen*, 1/1: 39–61.

Weber, M. (1978), *Economy and Society*. Berkeley: University of California Press.

Williamson, O. E. (1975), *Markets and Hierarchies*. New York: Free Press.

—— (1985), *The Economic Institutions of Capitalism*. New York: Free Press.

—— (1993), 'Calculativeness, Trust and Economic Organization', *Journal of Law and Economics*, 36 (April), 453–86.

Womack, J. R., Jones, D. T., and Roos, D. (1990), *The Machine That Changed the World*. New York: Rawson.

Zucker, L. G. (1986), 'Production of Trust: Institutional Sources of Economic Structure, 1840–1920', *Research in Organizational Behavior*, 8: 53–111.

1

*Understanding the Constitution of Interorganizational Trust**

JÖRG SYDOW

1. ORGANIZATIONAL AND INTERORGANIZATIONAL TRUST: AN INTRODUCTION

Trust is a social phenomenon which makes work within organizations easier and collaboration among organizations possible. Specifically in a world of increasing uncertainty and complexity, flat hierarchies, more participative management styles, and increased professionalism, trust is thought to be a more appropriate mechanism for controlling organizational life than hierarchical power or direct surveillance (e.g. Fox 1974 and, for more recent sources, Heisig and Littek 1995; Hosmer 1995; Zaheer and Venkatraman 1995; Lane and Bachmann 1996). Beyond *intra*organizational trust, the increasingly close collaboration among organizations as in cases of joint research and development, just-in-time delivery or relationship marketing requires trust among organizations, that is *inter*organizational trust (Dodgson 1993).

Interorganizational trust is believed to have several economic advantages: above all, trust may serve as an alternative control mechanism in interorganizational relations where it may substitute or at least complement market prices and hierarchical authority (Bradach and Eccles 1989), especially since legalistic remedies are now considered to be only weak institutional substitutes for trust (Sitkin and Roth 1993). Moreover, interorganizational trust is likely to enhance allocative efficiency when it encourages the disclosure of confidential information, and to reduce the costs of interorganizational transactions (Sako 1992). Once established, trust stabilizes exchange relationships which in turn increase chances to enhance trust (Ring and van de Ven 1992, 1994). Not only are trust relations regarded as generally important from a marketing perspective (Håkansson 1987; Young and Wilkinson 1989; Wilson and Möller 1995), strong form trustworthiness, similar to 'reputation capital' (Fombrun 1996), is even

* A previous version of this paper was presented at the 8th International Conference on Socio-Economics organized by the Society for the Advancement of Socio-Economics (SASE), University of Geneva, Switzerland, 12–14 July 1996. The revised version which was written during my 1996/7 sabbatical leave at Bentley College, Mass., USA, has profited much from comments by Anthony Buono, Christel Lane, Udo Staber, and, in particular, Reinhard Bachmann. I thank the Deutsche Forschungsgemeinschaft (DFG) for its financial support of my sabbatical leave to the USA.

assumed to constitute a competitive advantage. This applies to firms (Barney and Hansen 1994), as well to regions (e.g. Ernste and Meier 1992; Scott 1996; Staber 1996).

It is true that *inter*organizational trust is regarded as offering economic advantages within hierarchical organizational forms, in trusts or holding companies for instance, as well as under rather ideal-type market conditions.[1] The organizational form, however, which is said to rely most heavily on trust relations is known as the 'hybrid' (Williamson 1985; Borys and Jemison 1989), the 'relational contracting' (Ring and van de Ven 1992; Borch 1994), the 'constellation' (Lorenzoni and Ornati 1988; Gomes-Casseres 1996), the 'relational governance' (Zaheer and Venkatraman 1995), or the 'interorganizational network' (Miles and Snow 1986; Powell 1990; Sydow 1992; Alter and Hage 1993). This interorganizational trust, which, above all, refers to mutual trust among organizations, is sometimes even regarded as being constitutive for organizations working together in such networks. For interorganizational trust within interorganizational networks, although not a valuable asset in every respect,[2] is mostly assumed to

- support the formation of 'collective strategies' (Astley and Fombrun 1983);
- facilitate the co-ordination of economic activities;
- promote open exchange of information and 'interorganizational learning' (Hamel 1991);
- ease the management of interorganizational conflicts;
- contribute, hence, to a significant reduction of transaction costs; and open up opportunities for strategic action, enhance system stability, and yet support organizational change.

However, while trust in interorganizational networks may be particularly important, especially if these are intended to be stable and efficient, it is particularly difficult to develop and sustain. The reason for this contradiction which managers of organizations and interorganizational relations have to face will become clear later.

The conditions and mechanisms which contribute to the constitution of interorganizational trust—less so the consequences enumerated—are the focus of the following analysis which heavily draws on Anthony Giddens' (1984) theory of structuration and, thus, offers a more informative and realistic view of the constitution of interorganizational trust than most other theoretical approaches. For interorganizational trust, from this theoretical perspective, is conceptualized as an outcome of the subtle and recursive interplay of action and structure (Section 3), thus avoiding an 'undersocialized' conception of this constitution process as is typical of much of economic theory, but also an 'oversozialized' conception which is characteristic of many sociological theories (Granovetter 1985).

Structuration theory, then, is used to investigate the sources of interorganizational trust constituted as system trust in disembedding and reembedding processes, facilitated and moderated by trust enhancing structural properties of interorganizational networks (Section 4). One of the major implications of this theoretical analysis for network management is that while agents should refrain from direct management of trust they should certainly act in a trust-sensitive way when building and sustaining interorganizational relations or networks (Section 5).

Empirical evidence which mainly, but not exclusively, stems from our own research on financial services networks in Germany (Sydow *et al.* 1995; Sydow, van Well, and Windeler 1998) is referred to wherever possible in order to illustrate the theoretical argument.[3] The financial services industry presents itself for an analysis of the constitution of interorganizational trust for at least two reasons: (1) Leading insurers have transferred most of the production and distribution of financial services from their own (employed) sales force to networks of more or less independent agents and brokers with which they usually maintain long-term business relations. (2) Trust is particularly important in this industry, since financial services exhibit neither search nor experience but 'credence qualities' (Nelson 1970), i.e. the real quality of these services cannot even be established reliably after consumption. The quality of the business relations, therefore, supplies an important interpretative scheme for the evaluation of the service quality from the perspective of all actors in this industry: insurers, agents, brokers, and, not least, private and industrial customers.

2. INTERORGANIZATIONAL NETWORKS AND TRUST: DEFINITIONS

Although networks have been defined in different ways (Miles and Snow 1986; Thorelli 1986; Jarillo 1988; Powell 1990), for the purpose of this paper, an *interorganizational network* is conceived of as a long-term institutional arrangement among distinct but related organizations. The relationships among the network organizations, i.e. the network relations, are typically complex and reciprocal, co-operative rather than competitive, and relatively stable (Sydow 1992). Even if interorganizational relations are less stable as in the case of 'dynamic networks' (Miles and Snow 1986) or 'virtual corporations' (Davidow and Malone 1992) project networks of this kind most probably assume the existence of at least latent stable relations which may be activated in the case of a customer's demand for a particular product or service.

Interorganizational networks emerge either due to a quasi-externalization or due to a quasi-internalization of business functions

(Sydow 1992). That is, while specific functions are farmed out or organizations refrain from vertical or horizontal integration respectively, the same organizations try to keep the execution of these functions under their control. In both cases, this assumes a respective social organization of network relations which are only 'loosely coupled' (Weick 1976) with respect to *intra*organizational relations. The social organization of the relations results from different organizing modes such as procedural, personal, technological, and gratificational (Sydow and Windeler 1996, for details).

Interorganizational networks should not only be looked at as an institutional arrangement or as a governance structure but also as processes. While the current emphasis on network processes is considered a necessary countermovement to the prevailing comparative-static analysis of formal structures, a more balanced view of structure and process such as the one put forward by Zaheer and Venkatraman (1995) is certainly desirable, especially if the dynamic relationship between the two dimensions is emphasized. However, the differentiation of structure and process, still very common not only in organization but also in interorganization theory is, at least from a structuration perspective, inapt, because it simply reproduces the common dualistic thinking on the interplay of action and structure (see Section 3).

In the literature on interorganizational networks, trust is mostly considered to be a constitutive feature of network relations (Powell 1990, 1996). In fact, there are many indications of trust relations in interorganizational networks. Two examples should be sufficient for purposes of illustration: (1) In addition to outsourcing production-related functions, car manufacturers are also transferring such basic functions as quality control and purchasing checks to their network counterparts; simultaneously, very early in the development process, they exchange confidential information about new products with their suppliers (Helper 1993). (2) Insurance companies that market their policies via independent intermediaries such as insurance brokers refrain from the usage of their own risk experts although they are the ones who have to carry the risk in the end. On the other hand, independent intermediaries, trusting in the later acceptance of the risk by the insurer, provide immediate interim coverage. And clients reveal confidential data to insurance intermediaries, which allow those intermediaries a deep insight into their personal or business situation (Sydow *et al.* 1995). Nevertheless, trust in all these cases is neither blind nor limitless. Rather, from a structuration perspective which conceives agents to be knowledgeable, it has to be assumed that the constitution of trust is to a significant extent based upon a relatively close monitoring of the foundations of trust.

Since trust relations are considered to be constitutive properties of interorganizational networks, most studies simply assume this kind of relationship exists. At least they point to the fact that trust is a necessary even if not sufficient condition to speak of interorganizational relationships as network relations. It is true that both high rewards and high risks usually associated with this kind of relationship create the necessity of trust. But few studies have investigated the actual development, emergence, or constitution of interorganizational trust (see Lorenz 1988; Ring and van de Ven 1994; Loose and Sydow 1994, as exceptions). From a structuration perspective one would prefer the notion of *trust constitution* because, in contrast to other concepts, it emphasizes both the possibility of intentional creation *and* the emergent development of trust and, in particular, the subtle interplay of these two dimensions of the constitution process.

Trust, the medium and outcome of this process, is usually defined in different ways, but there is some consensus that it is not absorbed by a mere predictability of events, but rather begins where knowledge ends. Trust, for this reason, always implies *confidence in face of risk* (Lewis and Weigert 1985). One of the more convincing definitions of trust is supplied by Giddens (1990) himself:

Trust may be defined as confidence in the reliability of a person or system, regarding a given set of outcomes or events, where that confidence expresses a faith in the probity or love of another, or in the correctness of abstract principles.   (p. 34)

Trust, which may be of a more rational, self-interested, calculative, or a more non-rational, cultural or social nature (see the Introduction to this book), is always associated with a particular risk on the side of the trusting party. This is said to 'be one of the few characteristics common to all trust situations' (Mayer, Davis, and Schoormann 1995: 712).

In face of the willingness to take such risk and to accept vulnerability, *interorganizational trust*, therefore, is the confidence of an organization in the reliability of other organizations, regarding a given set of outcomes or events. This latter proviso takes into account that one does not usually trust a person, an organization or another system in every respect (global trust) but only with respect to certain kinds of behaviour (specific trust).

In actual fact, interorganizational trust which does not necessarily have to be (but most likely will be) of a mutual nature, is a possible attribute of interorganizational *relationships*. As such, interorganizational trust may be spread across a network, or simply be restricted to a dyad of organizations.[4]

The theoretical and empirical analysis of the constitution of interorganizational trust within networks which will follow is based upon Giddens' (1984) theory of structuration, developed originally as a social theory but currently applied not only to the analysis of organizations (e.g. Reed 1992, 1996; Whittington 1992; Kilduff 1993; Boden 1994; Ortmann, Sydow, and Windeler 1997) but also to the analysis of interorganizational networks (Sydow 1996a; Sydow and Windeler 1996; Sydow *et al.* 1995; Sydow, van Well, and Windeler 1998).

3. TRUST AS A SOURCE AND OUTCOME OF ACTION AND STRUCTURE: DUALITY AND RECURSIVENESS

Only apparently trivial, trust, even if attributed to certain personal or organizational characteristics, is mainly produced and reproduced via action, in the case of interorganizational networks via management interaction in particular. (Inter-)action, however, is not possible without structures. This latter statement implies that the relationship of action and structure is not—as common to social sciences thus far—conceptualized as a dualism but as a duality.

3.1 Duality of Structure

The duality of structure, i.e. the conception of structure as a medium and outcome of action, is one of at least two central messages of Giddens' theory of structuration (cf. Sydow and Windeler 1996; Ortmann, Sydow, and Windeler 1997). Structures, in the light of this theory, not only constrain but also enable action. Consequently, structure and action (or process, or practice) are not usefully separated, especially since structures only exist—apart from memory traces—in social practices.

The theorem of the duality of structure requires a two-dimensional investigation of social practices in general and of the constitution of trust via such practices in interorganizational networks in particular: on the dimension of structure and on the dimension of action (see Fig. 1.1).

The *dimension of structure* comprises rules[5] of signification, i.e. modes of signifying and of meaning constitution, rules of legitimation, and resources of domination. The *dimension of (inter-)action* involves communication, sanctioning, and power respectively. Agents act by referring to structural properties of their action context via modalities of structuration. For this purpose, they make use of interpretative schemes, norms, and facilities (see, once again, Fig. 1.1).

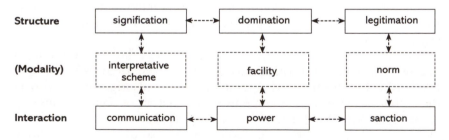

FIG. 1.1. Duality of structure

Source: Giddens 1984: 29.

To give an example, the theorem states: A manager *communicating* with managers of other organizations uses in her concrete 'talk-in-interaction' (Boden 1994) the *interpretative scheme* 'an efficient network organization is based upon interorganizational trust'. In doing so she refers to a rule of *signification*, which makes it possible that her communication is understood. Such a rule could be that managers in general and network managers in particular share the view or the implicit theory that interorganizational networks are a more efficient governance structure than other organizational forms of economic activity only and only if they are based upon trust. In the course of this communication this rule of signification is reproduced by the communicating managers.[6] Thereby, the rule becomes increasingly institutionalized, finally is taken for granted, and is thus likely to produce even more shared assumptions and background expectancies among the interacting managers, which in turn enhance interorganizational trust even further.

While the duality of structure assumes the possibility of agents to refer to rules (of signification and legitimation), it also takes into account that agents need *resources* for exercising power and for influencing social praxis. These resources, which are reproduced in this very action, are either of an allocative or an authoritative nature. While the former refer to capabilities which generate command over objects, the latter refer to transformative capacities generating command over agents. In fact, trust creates, in most situations, additional opportunities for interaction thus adopting the character of an authoritative resource.

3.2 Recursiveness of Social Praxis

Recognizing the recursiveness of social praxis is the second central message of Giddens' theory of structuration. This recursiveness, on the one hand, is exemplified by the continuous reference of agents to structures of signification, legitimation, and domination, and the reproduction of these structures (illustrated by the vertical arrows in Fig. 1.1). On the other hand, the recursiveness of social praxis manifests itself in the interrelationships between the three dimensions of action and the three dimensions of structure (illustrated by the horizontal arrows in Fig. 1.1). And this message too is of outstanding importance for an enhanced understanding of the constitution of interorganizational trust as will be explained later (see Subsection 3.3).

Trust, according to this theorem of recursiveness, is as much an outcome as a medium of co-operative interaction. Thus interorganizational trust— via the opening of additional opportunities for action—contributes to a more powerful position of an actor in a network of relationships. Although power and trust are often regarded as substitutes (e.g. Luhmann 1979), social praxis seems to be more complicated. First of all, we cannot necessarily trust trust. For 'power can be hidden behind the facade of "trust" and the rhetoric of "collaboration", and used to promote vested interests through the manipulation of and capitulation by weaker partners' (Clegg and Hardy 1996: 679). Secondly, powerful organizations have been found to be more inclined to be trusting while the less powerful tend to be less confident of the trustworthiness of their exchange partners, even if the relationships proceeded smoothly (Young and Wilkinson 1989). And if trust is sustained, this gives actors even more power and opportunities to reproduce trust as an important component not only of the structures of signification and legitimation but also of the structures of domination. Hence, power may not necessarily substitute or even destroy trust but, at least if exercised in a certain manner, enhance trust and thus in turn lead to an even more powerful position in a network. The mechanisms of positive recursiveness in a nutshell: trust increases power, and power offers the opportunity (*sic*) for developing even more trusting relations, however only if the powerful action remains within the confines of certain rules of signification and legitimation. This escalating recursiveness of trust is path-depending and was labelled many years ago a 'self-heightening cycle of trust' (Golembiewski and McConkie 1975).

However, a negative recursiveness, a spiral of distrust, is also possible and rather common, as Sitkin and Stickel (1996) demonstrate in the case of the introduction of quality control systems ill-suited to the task and as Ortmann (1994) shows in the case of traditional supplier relations he contrasts with 'Japanized' supplier relations. The outcome of such a cycle of distrust is not only reduced transaction efficiency but also disempowerment. While a cycle of trust is supposed to be incremental and step-by-step in nature, such a cycle of mistrust is likely to have a more catastrophic quality (Burt and Knez 1996, who refer to dyads of persons rather than organizations) and to be extremely difficult to reverse.

Of course, the development of a positive cycle of interorganizational trust is much favoured by the selection of trustworthy organizations, an adequate management of the selection process itself, and the signalling of shared assumptions and understandings at the very beginning. Competence, benevolence, and integrity, which are assumed to be important antecedents of trustworthiness on an interpersonal level (Mayer, Davis, and Schoormann 1995: 717–24), should have a similar effect at the interorganizational level, as long as those characteristics are attributed to the organization (i.e. the system rather than the person) in question. Nevertheless, the task of identifying trustworthy organizations is not easy to accomplish, since on the one hand, the assessment of these antecedents is affected by context and since, and on the other, exchange partners generally have a strong incentive to pretend to be strong form trustworthy. Despite this incentive and the resulting complication of trust detection process, organizations should not stop looking out for respective signals (Nohria 1992; Barney and Hansen 1994: 186–8) and then react by giving their counterparts a trust advance or by acting *as if* trust were in place. Signals often used by insurance brokers are: number of risk experts and membership to a particular broker association, both signalling the level of competence and thus being a potential source of competence-based trust, or promptness of service and shared views on how to do business, both signalling rather the motivational foundations of interorganizational trust.

Kinship and friendship ties as well as other rather reliable sources of interorganizational trust aside, a cycle of trust almost always begins with what might be called a *policy of small steps*, which is characterized, above all, by a sparse use of resources and a careful reference to the prevailing rules of signification and legitimation. This policy may first lead to what has been called 'tentative trust' (Barnes 1981), before this kind of trust changes into more persuasive, resilient, and durable forms. Insurance intermediaries, for instance, report that at the outset of a business relation they signal credibility and reliability *vis-à-vis* clients as well as insurance companies by close adherence to dates, deadlines, formal contracts, and informal agreements. For, at the beginning of a relationship, intermediaries have very little chance to actually demonstrate the full range and real quality of their services. On the other hand, neither clients nor insurers can check their service quality with performance-related criteria because of the credence quality of financial services. In later phases of the development of an interorganizational relation credible commitments may act as signals for trustworthiness and strengthen the trust relationship. Thus social relations may give way to economic exchange as much as the former may emerge from purely contractual relations and economic exchange (cf. Larson 1992, for similar results in a different industrial setting). It is under these conditions that the employees of an insurance broker, for instance, will communicate critical information more openly with the risk experts of an insurance company, although not without care. These experts in turn will then sanction the trust placed with them positively and strengthen it by communicating more openly.

3.3 Trust Constitution in the Light of Duality and Recursiveness

Fig. 1.2 illustrates this process of trust constitution which is characterized by the duality of structure *and* the recursiveness of social praxis with respect to all three aspects: (1) signification, (2) domination, and (3) legitimation (cf. Loose and Sydow 1994: 174–8).

1. Interorganizational trust may be conceived of as a *rule of signification*. Agents are assumed to refer to this rule via a scheme which helps to interpret the social world as a trusting context of action. Thus insurers, brokers, and customers may refer to the rule of signification that 'a trust relationship increases communication efficiency and effectiveness among these parties of the insurance industry'. While this assumption corresponds to the view of psychologists distinguishing individuals with high- and low-

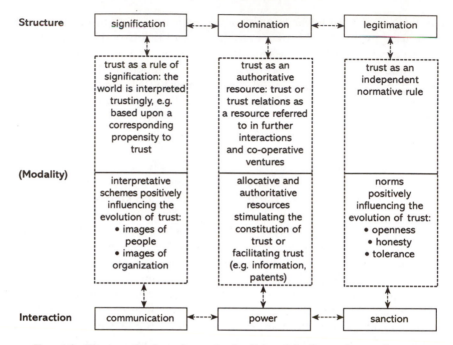

FIG. 1.2. The constitution of trust in the light of duality and recursiveness

trusting personalities (e.g. Rotter 1980), this allegedly transsituationally invariant disposition, from a structurationist point of view, results from concrete social practices which are always tied to social structures. These structures, structures of signification in particular, e.g. established implicit theories or images of organizations (cf. Barnes 1981) and interorganizational relationships, may well enhance the constitution of interorganizational trust if and only if agents refer to them in their interorganizational interactions. By referring to these *in praxi*, agents reproduce these very structures of signification.

2. Trust relations among organizations may be considered as an *authoritative resource* to which agents refer in their interaction via facilities, thus enabling them to intervene intentionally or unintentionally but in any case powerfully into interaction sequences. Trust relations to insurance companies, for instance, make it easier for brokers to develop and maintain trust relations with their clients (and vice versa). In both cases, interorganizational trust expands the agent's control of the resources of other agents and opens up additional opportunities to give and reciprocate trust and, thereby, leads to a recursive strengthening of trust relations. This, once more, demonstrates the suble interplay of power and trust *in praxi*, which should not be assumed to substitute for each other.

A permanent, trust-sensitive way of interacting stabilizes the prevailing order of domination as a trust relation and, simultaneously, trust as a resource. In fact, trust and other elements of the moral order belong to those 'resources whose supply may well increase rather than decrease through use' (Hirschman 1970: 4). In this structured process of interaction, trust that stimulates action should exceed a certain threshold. Where these thresholds lie, derives from the history of the specific interaction sequence (Luhmann 1979). In all these cases, recursively reproduced trust relations serve as a form of 'social capital' (Coleman 1990), which is a specific kind of authoritative resource making possible actions that might otherwise not be feasible. On the other hand, any trustful action itself requires resources beyond trust. For instance, the granting of trust presumes the existence of and the access to respective allocative and other authoritative resources. Moreover, it requires the willingness and capacity of agents adequately to interpret the—trusting or distrusting—actions of others, and to refer competently to the prevailing rules of signification and legitimation.

3. Interorganizational trust may finally be seen as a *rule of legitimation* to which agents refer via social norms in order to sanction a particular behaviour or event within the network as trusting or distrusting. For example, all parties within the insurance industry may believe that brokers should sustain trust relations to insurers as well as clients. The theorem of the duality of structure, however, states that agents, by their very action, must reproduce this rule of legitimation, if its legitimizing or sanctioning effect is to be preserved. Several other related norms, such as openness, honesty, reciprocity, tolerance, and fairness, may make it easier for agents to reproduce trust as a rule of legitimation.

Beyond the theorems of the duality of structure and the recursiveness of social life Giddens (1990) introduces in his discussion of *The Consequences of Modernity* additional concepts which further our understanding of the constitution of interorganizational trust in networks. Among these are: 'practical consciousness', 'reembedding' and 'disembedding', 'facework commitments' and 'faceless commitments', 'access points' and last but not least trust in 'abstract systems'. These concepts will be explained when they are used in the following investigation of the conditions facilitating and/or impeding the development of trust relations in interorganizational networks.

4. TRUST IN INTERORGANIZATIONAL NETWORKS: SYSTEM TRUST

If interorganizational trust is produced and reproduced via actions that refer to structures of signification, legitimation, and domination, its constitution is inevitably tied to persons and, thereby, to personalities. Nevertheless agents can not only trust concrete persons but also abstract systems, technical and social. Since an organization—as much as an interorganizational network—is such an abstract (social) system, the theoretical and empirical analysis of the constitution of interorganizational trust has to acknowledge this system character, without disregarding the personal embeddedness of trust and trust attributions. The latter has been expressed by many brokers questioned in our study:

Sympathy is important in our business, since the product is extensively shaped by the individual. . . . The chemistry among the partners has to fit, otherwise it would not be possible to do business.

The system character of trust, however, often remains opaque but can be understood from a structuration perspective.

4.1 From Personal Trust to System Trust: Disembedding and Reembedding

The constitution of trust in social systems such as organizations and networks can be explained at first by means of two conceptual differentiations which have been much used in organizational and interorganizational research on trust. On the one hand, it concerns the differentiation between personal trust and system trust already mentioned, on the other the differentiation of three quite distinct sources of trust. The combination of these sources of personal and system trust and their interplay in disembedding and reembedding processes is at the heart of a structurationist explanation of the constitution of interorganizational trust which assumes that trust in organizations and interorganizational networks is both tied to, and decoupled from, individual actors and their personalitites.

In her historical analysis of the constitution of trust and its relevance for the development of the US economy Zucker (1986) distinguishes three different *sources of trust*: 'process-based trust', 'characteristic-based trust', and 'institutional-based trust'. Thereby she observes a relative increase in significance of the latter, especially both process-based and characteristic-based trusts 'need to be (at least) backed up by a form of trust which is rooted in the existence of stable societal institutions' (Lane and Bachmann 1996: 371).

Process-based trust develops from concrete experience of social and/or economic exchange and is brought as an expectation to future transactions. This kind of trust seems to emerge particularly when the quality of exchanged goods or services is uncertain (Kollock 1994), as in the case of financial services with their credence qualitites. Process-based trust may be firsthand or transferred through the hands of a 'trust intermediary' (Coleman 1990). The relevance of firsthand experience of trust for the development and maintainance of interorganizational relationships has often been demonstrated (e.g. Gulati 1995; Uzzi 1996). Despite the relevance of firsthand experience (and institutions, see below) this type of earned trust is deeply rooted within stable personal relationships and, hence, the social embeddedness of economic action (Granovetter 1985).

These relationships are important, even if trust is experienced second hand. Uzzi (1996) finds in his study of the New York apparel industry referral networks to be as important a source of social embeddedness as previous personal ties. Intermediaries, such as insurance brokers in financial services networks, often act as 'trust intermediaries'. Given these relationships, even third-party gossip may contribute to the constitution of trust relations (Burt and Knez 1996). For instance, we experienced that insurers' opinion on the trustworthiness of a particular broker plays a major role for the readiness of other brokers to co-operate with him or her.

Process-based trust may finally cumulate into reputation, which is a set of attributes ascribed to a particular person or system, typically inferred from its past practices, and which for both, a person and a system, makes it significantly easier to enter into new relationships. In fact, Dollinger, Golden, and Saxton (1997) find in their experimental study that the better a firm's reputation the more likely it is to be targeted as an alliance partner. Once a reputation has been established it operates as an effective safeguard, especially within dense social networks. Reputation, as much as trust, may be transferred from one organization to another, given the existence of another trust relationship.

Characteristics-based trust is independent of a concrete exchange experience. The sources of this kind of trust are rather personal characteristics such as age, sex, or belonging to a particualar ethnic community or social system (or system characteristics, respectively). In this context, even stereotype reference to such characteristics, often on the level of 'practical consciousness' (Giddens 1984), may be the point of departure for the constitution of characteristics-based trust. In addition, such characteristics may be anchored in the subconsciousness where they relate to an actual disposition to (dis-)trust which may have been learned in early life experiences (Erikson 1950, to whom Giddens usually refers when he discusses trust).

Institutional-based trust finally transcends the concrete exchange experience and does not depend upon the concrete exchange partner either. Consequently it is considered as being generated more diffusely in a wider network of relationships. Sources of institutional-based trust are first of all traditions, professions, certifications, licences, brand names, or memberships in certain associations. A further source of institutional-based trust is the social practices of intermediaries which create trust relations among third persons or systems, whilst they themselves have to

Object of trust \ Source of trust	Experiences	Characteristics	Institutions
Person	positive experience with persons in exchange relations	personal characteristics features relevant for trust	regulations concerning interpersonal exchange relations
System	positive experience with social systems in exchange relations	social system properties relevant for trust	regulations concerning interorganizational exchange relations

(left margin between rows: disembedding ↑↑ reembedding ↓↓)

FIG. 1.3. Conditions of the constitution of personal and system trust

rely on trust relationships with their interaction partners. In the financial services industry, independent intermediaries may profit from the reputation capital of the insurer(s) to which it or they maintain business relations, even if to a lesser extent than dependent agents who are tied to one insurer only. Financial intermediaries, however, are able to act as trust intermediaries and, as such, may better create trust relations among actors than they could do themselves in personal interaction. Moreover, formal rules which contribute to a higher level of reliability of actions may stimulate the emergence of institutional-based trust if agents truly refer to these in their actions (see Fig. 1.3). Institutions in this sense do not necessarily remain exogenous to a relationship but rather develop within it.

Although trust is the property of a relationship, the distinction of personal trust from system trust or from trust in abstract systems places the *object of trust* at the centre of the analysis. *Personal trust*, whether in the technical competence or in the goodwill of a person,[7] generally refers to personal agents and is usually dependent upon 'facework commitments' (Giddens 1990: 80), which are expressed by concrete interactions in which agents necessarily refer to structures of signification, domination, and legitimation. Characteristics-based and process-based trust can develop only in the course of such 'facework commitments'; institutional-based personal trust assumes that agents (not systems!) are linked with institutional sources of trust.

Objects of *system trust* are technical or social systems, or parts of such systems. Social systems, such as organizations or even networks of organizations, are from a structurationist perspective seen as corporate agents with distinct structural properties not reduceable to the individual agents whose social and possibly contradicting practices contribute to the constitution of the system. These systems are taken as the outcome of complex structuration processes in which individual agents from the system—as much as from its 'environment' (including other social systems)—refer to the 'systems' and other social structures. As Whitley (1987) puts it with regard to the firm:

This question need not imply a unitary belief system or the absence of conflict in firms, it simply imputes collective characteristics to an administrative organisation and top management group which are not reducible to features of individual actors and which ensure some continuity of activities and direction when those actors change. (p. 133)

From this follows, that organizations—and even less likely interorganizational networks—do not exhibit a homogeneous or unified 'system rationality' or 'system culture'. Rather, they reflect divergent interests of actors and are more likely to be and to remain heterogeneous and contested in nature. This can be examplified by a regional network of seven medium-sized insurance brokers from our empirical study (Sydow *et al.* 1995: 344–89; Sydow 1996*b*). At the time of investigation, these brokers had intensified co-operation and quasi-internalized many activities ranging from purchasing to marketing for more than two years. Following a step-by-step approach which offers many opportunities for process-based trust, and given many shared assumptions and understandings on which quality of financial services to offer and on how to run the broker business (i.e. the existence of network rules of signification and legitimation, in structurationist terms), they even started to consider creating a joint-venture firm which would take over administrative services and provide information technology services for all network firms. Nevertheless, the regional network, neither at that time nor today, turned into a unified (new) social system in which system members, the individual broker firms, gave up their identity and their particular interests. Although the regional network can be considered as a success story, it continued to exist not only as separate firms with clear identities and interests but, in addition, of at least two sub-networks, the established brokers and the innovative newcomers. And, despite that the network had started to communicate the emergence of a new system to customers by the use of a logo, it also experienced severe reservations on the part of suppliers to accept the network as a unified—and possibly more powerful—business partner.

A social system, a particular organization, or this regional network of insurance brokers for example, is trusted even though not necessarily all or most of the organizational members are trustworthy.[8] One reason for this is that the system, here the regional network, is attributed trusted characteristics through what Giddens (1990) calls 'disembedding': 'the "lifting out" of social relations from local contexts of interaction and their restructuring across indefinite spans of time-space' (p. 21). A related reason is that trust in 'abstract systems' (Giddens 1990) is not only based upon personal inter-action but to a significant extent upon the 'faith in the correctness of principles' (ibid. 33–4). Trust in this case is not only constituted via face-to-face interactions, but is rather disembedded from these and assumes instead 'faceless commitments' (ibid.).

Nevertheless, system trust, the trust in the willingness and capability of a network of brokers or one of its sub-systems, for instance, to handle an insurance contract in an acceptable manner, not only depends upon con-tinual positive experiences with using the system but also upon processes of personal 'reembedding' via 'facework', and for this reason upon the availability of respective resources. Due to the necessity of personal reembedding, independent intermediaries acknowledge their limited capacity to develop and maintain trust relationships with customers and insurers. However, there seems hardly to be any substitute for personal reembedding of relationships when it comes to the building of system trust of a more resilient nature.

This reembedding usually takes place at certain 'access points' (Giddens 1990: 85), which in organizations may typically be found in boundary span-ning-roles. In the case of our regional network of medium-sized brokers these roles were mainly filled by the entrepreneurs themselves, but at a later point in time, also by risk experts and even by administrative personnel. Boundary-spanning personnel of this kind should be considered as repre-senting the correctness of the principles upon which the functioning of the abstract system is based. For this reason alone these personnel have to act according to the prevailing rules of signification and legitimation, especially in a way which meets the expectations of the partner if the trust in the system, here in the regional network, is not to be undermined. For building up trustful relationships among organizations boundary spanners have to do a lot of facework with those persons at the blurred boundaries of the networked organizations. Moreover, their capacity to build such relations relies heavily and recursively on the trustful relationships they maintain within and across their organization.

As much as friendship ties evolve from those activities at the access points of the system, the inter*organizational* network is overlaid by a net-work of inter*personal* relations which contributes to the stabilizing of busi-ness relations (Granovetter 1985; Larson 1992; Ring and van de Ven 1992, 1994; Staber 1996). Both networks interact in subtle ways. The network of personal relationships not only opens up opportunities for enhancing a better mutual understanding of shared or diverse schemes, norms, and actions, but makes it also possible that exchanges between trustworthy individuals in different organizations 'lead to strong form trust, even though the firms, themselves, may not be strong form trustworthy' (Barney and Hansen 1994: 182).

The access points mentioned are of critical importance in the insurance industry. The access of customers to qualified brokers, and their access to insurers, is typically granted by customer and broker advisor, or departments specialized for servicing industrial customers. All these access points are usually positioned in distance accessible to customers (including brokers). If the 'chemistry does not fit' among the acting persons, as we were told again and again in the insurance industry, the constitution of interorganizational trust is very unlikely. Then investigating the constitution of trust within interorganizational networks, it is of outstanding importance to pay attention to these access points where agents meet and do facework. For these are not only the points where agents refer to structures of signification, legitimation, and domination, but where these structures are reproduced in organizational and interorganizational practices via 'reembedding'.

4.2 Trust-Enhancing Structural Properties of Interorganizational Networks

According to all that has been said, the analysis of the constitution of interorganizational trust requires the investigation of the processes in which agents interact and refer, in a way which enhances trust, to the structural properties of their action context. This occurs on different levels, which not only include the personal and the organizational level, but also the network level and even the level of the industries, sectors, or fields, i.e. the network environment.

On the *personal* level features such as the individual propensity to trust, the particular style of leadership and negotiation of key boundary-spanners (Hart 1988), or any other idiosyncratic assumption and expectation may be relevant. On the *organizational* level, to give just one example, the impact of the organizational climate on the internal interaction among organizational members should be considered because the quality of intraorganizational interaction very much affects the reliability of interorganizational interaction. On the level of the *network environment* it would be important to take into account differences of national cultures and particular 'industry recipes' (Spender 1989), which embody the history of an industry, the sharing of particular understandings of strategic concepts and frames, including the trust or distrust cultures of a particular industry, sector or field. In this respect, the German financial services sector may offer a context for the development and maintainance of interorganizational trust which is very different from the Japanese biotechnological industry, due not only to national character, but also with respect to professional values and norms. Along these lines, Lane and Bachmann (1996), for instance, find evidence for the different impact of societal institutions (such as trade associations, chambers of commerce, legal and financial systems, and systems of industrial relations and training) upon the development of trust-based interfirm relations in Britain and Germany.

Being aware of the necessity to conceptualize and empirically research the constitution of interorganizational trust not only within each of these levels of analysis but also among them, I shall only be concerned with structural properties on the *network* level which has hitherto largely been disregarded. However, it should be kept in mind that a more comprehensive analysis of the constitution of interorganizational trust would have to take into account not only these different levels and their interplay,[9] but also the fact that any structural property contributes only to the constitution of interorganizational trust if, and only if, agents refer to it in their interactions, i.e. in communicating, sanctioning, and powerfully intervening in interactions sequences in a way which is trust enhancing because 'appropriate' interpretative schemes, norms and facilities respectively are used.

Disregarding the importance of the type of network (e.g. regional network, strategic alliance) for a moment, six such properties on the network level will be looked at in some detail (see Fig. 1.4). The first four concern, in the main, network relations, the latter two predominantly organizations tied together by a network. All of these structural properties are not unique to a structurationist perspective on interorganizational trust. Rather, being either suggested by other theoretical approaches or found to matter *in praxi*, these properties and their impact upon the constitution of organizational trust are to be reinterpreted from a structurationist perspective.

A *first* structural property which can stipulate the constitution of interorganizational trust is the *frequency and openness of interorganizational communication*. Frequent, repeated and multifaceted contacts among organizations and an open exchange of information increase the possibility of trust building in networks. While game theory explains that the absence of communication makes trust building much more difficult, most authors assume that the quantity and quality of communication stimulates the emergence of trust relationships (e.g. Luhmann 1979; Golembiewski and McConkie 1975; Sako 1992: 126–33; Borch 1994). One major reason is that communication increases the opportunity for better mutual understanding and makes it easier to predict each others' behaviour. The frequency—or, in terms of network analysis, density—of interorganizational communication itself much depends, not only upon task interdependencies and common interests, but also upon spatial proximity.

In all these respects, the regional network of insurance brokers already mentioned provides favourable circumstances for the constitution of interorganizational trust. Following implicitly the model of 'flexible specialization' (Piore and Sabel 1984), the task interdependencies among the brokers inevitably increase. The growing level of system integration produces more common interests and shared views, although separate firm

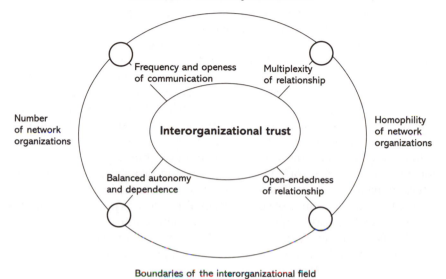

FIG. 1.4. Trust-enhancing structural properties on the network level

interests and perspectives certainly do not entirely disappear. Finally, spatial proximity not only provides the brokers with many opportunities for face-to-face communication, but enhances a common understanding of the business among them.[10]

Openness is an important norm fostering the constitution of inter-organizational trust via which agents may refer to the prevailing rules of legitimation when they sanction particular kinds of network behaviour. Here it is essential that the agents acknowledge the advantage of open, trust-enhancing communication (cf. Ortmann 1994). In the case of the financial services networks investigated, independent intermediaries usually trust those insurers which inform them on time and comprehensively, and the intermediaries try to establish trust relationships with insurers by communicating to them the actual quality of the risks to be insured. Since, in this case, the constitution of system trust is required, it is important that the frequency and openness of communication is not attributed to the boundary-spanners but to the social system.

A *second* structural property which, according to structural network theory is likely to promote the constitution of interorganizational trust is the *multiplexity of network relations*. Multiplexity means that organizational actors, at a given point in time, transact for a variety of reasons and exchange different contents. Products and services are among those contents as are information and emotion. Based upon this argument, relationships are the more likely to exhibit trust properties the more different contents are exchanged (and vice versa). Accordingly, insurance intermediaries are more likely to conceive interorganizational relations as trust relations when they are used for the exchange of services *and* ideas, *and* when they, in addition, contain personal elements of exchange (see also Lorenz 1988, for evidence from a different industry setting).

Products, services, information, and emotion may also be characterized in more general terms of plasticity. High plasticity, typical of research and development rather than production and distribution projects (Alchian and Woodward 1987: 116), means that agents are able to manipulate the process and outcome of co-operation without the partner noticing this manipulation. Thus not only the exchange of multiple but especially of plastic content, as in the case of financial services and products, is a seedbed of interorganizational trust. Trust, under these circumstances, is not only demanded, but the exchange of such content also provides more opportunities to demonstrate trustworthiness. From a structurationist perspective it is decisive as to whether agents actually refer to the multiplexity and plasticity of relations in this manner and, thereby, reproduce them not only as muliplex but also as trusted relations.

A *third* structural condition is the *open-endedness of the relationship*. Again, especially game theory makes clear that an unlimited game tends to promote trust and co-operation, while an a priori limited game is confronted with the problem of backward induction (Selten 1978). The expectancy of a continuation of relations, known as the 'shadow of the future' (Axelrod 1984), is decisive for co-operative behaviour in networks if the prevailing rules of signification and legitimation require such an expectation (Parkhe 1993).[11] However, agents must refer to this structural property in their interaction by means of appropriate schemes and norms. This helps them to develop respective expectations on which interorganizational trust may be built.

A *fourth* structural condition which may contribute to the constitution of trust within interorganizational networks is a *balanced relation between autonomy and dependence*. Thereby it is of outstanding importance that the agents, eventually embedded in intraorganizational structuration processes such as the use of friendship and advice networks and their interplay (cf. Gibbons 1996), come to the conclusion that the network relationships are balanced. In this process of perceiving, categorizing, evaluating, and eventually acting, rules of signification as well as rules of legitimation become important since they influence what agents consider to be balanced or unbalanced. If they come to the conclusion that autonomy and dependence are balanced fairly well this promotes a certain permanence in network relations which, however, could also be achieved through either reciprocal task interdependence (Thompson 1967) or transaction-specific investments (Williamson 1985). Although interorganizational trust may well develop under these latter circumstances too, long-term relationships among insurers, intermediaries, and clients *per se* do not indicate a high level of trust in persons or social systems.

In the case of complete autonomy and in the case of total dependence, trusted network relations are—at least from a functionalist perspective— rather dispensable. The theory of structuration with its third theorem, not yet mentioned, namely the 'dialectic of control' (Giddens 1984), however points to the fact that complete autonomy as well as total dependence are very unlikely to occur, especially within interorganizational networks. For this reason alone, a certain mimimum level of interorganizational trust seems to be essential. In fact, independent insurance brokers emphasize that they consider themselves not dependent upon insurers and clients *per se* but upon the maintainance of trustful relationships with both. Important reasons for this are:

- the credence qualities of insurance and other financial services;
- the importance of trustful relations with insurers for maintaining and stabilizing relations with clients (and vice versa); and
- the potential for a more efficient way of doing business, including a possible reduction of transaction costs.

A *fifth* structural property enhancing the constitution of trust on the network level, and the first concerning the structure of the network actors rather than the structure of the network relationships, is the *number and homophility of network organizations* (Powell 1990: 326). The constitution of interorganizational trust is more likely in networks with a small number of network firms, especially if spared from turnover. In addition, the constitution of network trust is the more likely the more similar the structural properties of the network firms are, at least if network managers refer to these similarities by means of interpretative schemes, norms, and facilities, when reproducing interorganizational relationships. It is mainly for this reason that interorganizational trust will be difficult to build up if the network cuts across national borders and regional cultures. Belonging to the same social sub-system (e.g. economy, industry, profession), on the other hand, should, according to systems and neo-institutional theory alike, increase the probability that interorganizational trust emerges among actors (cf. Luhmann 1979; Zündorf 1994; Oliver 1995; Powell 1996; Staber 1996). A medium-sized insurance broker refers, among others, to organizational size, another important source of homophility, when he explains: 'Our strengths are firms which have a similar structure and size as we have, and where the entrepreneur risks his head. Entrepreneurs love to have entrepreneurs on the other side [of the broker] as well. . . . Moreover, both are likely to have similar social interests. . . . It is different with corporations, which are rather attached to large-sized firms.' In a study of investment banking relationships Podolny (1994) found that, especially in face of great market uncertainty, organizations not only prefer exchange relationships with those organizations with whom they have transacted in the past but also with those of a similar reputation or status.

However, one qualification seems important: it is true that homophility, which may result from a goal-directed selection of network partners based either upon a strategy of differentiation on the part of insurers towards insurance brokers for example (Illner 1994 on the strategy of the German *Allianz*) or upon the selection of insurers (and clients) by the brokers, facilitates the development of interorganizational trust in vertical network relations. In the case of horizontal relations, as in the case of the regional networks of insurance brokers for instance, this homophility may imply a greater likelihood of competition which, in turn, makes trust building more difficult. However, and again as in the case of vertical relationships, much depends upon the agents and how they refer to this structural property in their interactions.

A *sixth* and final structural property relevant for the constitution of interorganizational trust is the *structure of the interorganizational field* from which potential network organizations are recruited.[12] If, for instance, this field is rather *narrow and bounded*, as in the case of well-established industrial insurance brokers, the chance is relatively high that an organization, even if presently not included in a focal network, will become (again) a member in it. The more the reputation of such a (potential network) organization is implicitly threatened, the greater the chance for future interaction. For this reason, a narrow and well-defined interorganizational field may in fact enhance the constitution of interorganizational trust (cf. Meyerson, Weick, and Kramer 1996: 181). Once tied to the network, such an organization has little alternative scope for action which is likely to strengthen the basis for interorganizational trust even further.

Several of these six structural properties which may enhance the constitution of trust within networks are somewhat closely related to the particular *type of interorganizational network* in question. For instance, for a 'strategic network' (Jarillo 1988) the conduct of strategic leadership by the focal organization is decisive, though trust enhancing and destroying processes among the other network organizations are also important. Yet, because the trustworthiness of the focal organization may even serve as a substitute for a concrete experience of exchange, the trust-building process within this type of interorganizational network may be somewhat centralized.

In regional networks of more equal firms interorganizational trust emerges due to the small size of the network, the intensity of communication among the network firms, shared interpretative schemes and norms based upon regional bonds, and the operational closeness of the network (Piore and Sabel 1984; Sabel 1992). The process of trust constitution in this type of network is most likely be be of a more decentralized nature. Sydow *et al.* (1995) found in fact empirical evidence for the different character of these processes in distinct types of broker networks. Powell (1996) also makes the point that the type of network very much affects the process and outcome of trust constitution. He believes that regional networks within industrial districts, R&D networks, and strategic networks within business groups exhibit, although for different reasons, almost a 'natural' level of interorganizational trust. This, however, is hardly the case within more formal strategic alliances and networks which 'lack the "natural" basis of trust that other networks possess' (Powell 1996: 59).

In the context of the six structural properties fostering the development of interorganizational trust, which have been mentioned only as examples, four other points should be acknowledged:

1. Structural properties, neither on the network level nor on any other level, are not simply 'given', nor do they determine a certain level of interorganizational trust. Rather they reveal opportunities and constraints for actors to refer to them in acting, i.e. in communicating, sanctioning, and power executing, namely in ways that enhance the level of interorganizational trust.

2. The obvious question whether these structural properties are causes or rather consequences of interorganizational trust, does not arise from a structurationist perspective, which emphasizes the recursiveness of structure and action. From this perspective, the openness of communication or the multiplexity of network relations, for example, are conditions fostering the constitution of trust as much as they manifest the existing level of trust. Trust relations simply offer actors the potential for a recursive increase of the level of trust within the network.

3. The structural properties discussed may reinforce or weaken each other in their effect upon the level of interorganizational trust, depending upon the agents and how they refer to these properties in their interaction. Especially if the agents refer to the organizational form of a network as a success, a self-heightening cycle of trust is likely to develop which—conversely—will increase the economic success attributed to the network form.

4. Trust in general and interorganizational trust in particular, even in the case of an 'optimal' pattern and combination of these structural properties and of an 'optimal' reference to these properties by the agents, is never certain. For this reason alone, trust in the social reality of networks will always coexist with other means of control, i.e. substitutes for trust (cf. Loose and Sydow 1994, for details).

5. IN PREFERENCE TO A MANAGEMENT OF TRUST: TRUST-SENSITIVE MANAGEMENT IN INTERORGANIZATIONAL NETWORKS

Management is of course interested whether and to what extent interorganizational trust may be created intentionally, or at least how conditions may be created which stimulate the constitution of trust in interorganizational networks. The notion of 'trust management' would certainly have some appeal for managers of organizations and interorganizational networks, especially for those who recognize the need for 'transorganizational development' (Cummings 1984), 'network development' (Chisholm 1996), and related approaches to intervene purposefully in network organizations (Buono 1997).

The structuration perspective, however, makes clear that interorganizational trust is an outcome of social practices which are often routed in the practical consciousness of an actor, and that it is often the unintended by-product of otherwise intended action. In the extreme, interorganizational trust may even be the unintended outcome of action which is not acknowledged by the agent and incorporated into his or her future action.

This, however, does not imply that trust is a state 'that is *essentially* a by-product' (Elster 1979: 85). To the contrary and as shown above, trust may be created intentionally and reflexively if interorganizational networks exhibit trust-enhancing structural properties and if agents refer to these in a competent way. Nevertheless, managers usually tend to overestimate the possibility of intentional trust creation, not least if the exchange partner may discover this intention. For this reason, a *trust-sensitive management* rather than a trust management seems more appropriate—having supposedly the initially mentioned economic effects. Trust-sensitive management, here of interorganizational relationships in particular, requires a close 're-flexive monitoring' (Giddens 1984) of any action with respect to its impact upon trust, whereby the object of monitoring is the necessity of trust as well as the foundation of trust relations. When agents continuously monitor the conditions under which trusted behaviour will be possible in the future they act as a kind of 'intuitive auditor' (Kramer 1996). Thereby they should pay special attention: (1) to the processes, characteristics, and institutions which enhance not only trust in persons, i.e. interpersonal trust, but also in organizations; and (2) to the disembedding and reembedding processes at work in the constitution of interorganizational trust. Not least (3) they should reflect upon the structural properties which enhance the constitution of interorganizational trust on the level of the network as well as on other levels of analysis.

If compared to the effect of spontaneous trust, the disadvantage of this kind of reflexive trusting behaviour is that it reduces the complexity of the action situation to a much lesser extent (cf. Luhmann 1979). Despite the insight that trust may well—even if only to the extent demonstrated—be considered a 'principle of organizing' (Gondek, Heisig, and Littek 1992), it is and always will be above all the outcome of a collective, co-operative, and successful experience, especially in paradoxical situations (Barnes 1981) where, however, this kind of experience is particularly unlikely to be free of conflict. If this is true then it seems to be useless to search for hands-on instruments of trust management which bridge any lack of interorganizational trust. Rather, it seems necessary to reflect on *every* management action within and across organizations with respect to its impact upon interorganizational trust. This is particularly recommendable for those activities which aim at organizing a network, be it in terms of the procedural, the personal, the technological, or the gratificational mode, and most of all for those actions, such as formal procedures or well specified contracts, which are believed to be substitutes for trust.

If compared with the constitution of trust within organization—a process whose relationship with the constitution of interorganizational trust is still far from clear—a trust sensitive management of interorganizational networks has to overcome *additonal barriers*:

1. Interorganizational networks are not only more complex but *ex definitione* more loosely coupled and less institutionalized than formal organizations, i.e. 'hierarchies' (Williamson 1985). Trusted interorganizational relations, however, require a certain degree of social institutionalization, especially if they cannot rely on specific individual actors. Put differently, dynamic and plastic objects of trust require special efforts so that they will be trusted. Consequently, trust among organizations will mostly be tied more strongly to specific individuals, i.e. boundary-spanners, than trust within organizations. Hence, the development and maintainance of interorganizational trust will require more human resources. And, of course, it is all the more important that under these conditions management cares about continuity in the staffing of boundary-spanning roles.

2. Interorganizational networks typically have less clear, more permeable internal and external boundaries (i.e. among the network organizations as well as between the interorganizational network and the network environment). The constitution of trust, however, is facilitated by the differentiation of the system from its environment, i.e. by the constitution of the system's boundaries (Luhmann 1979), although national cultures or professional norms may partly compensate for this. Since management cannot rely on the emergence of systems boundaries, especially if some breaking of boundaries is required to create more 'boundaryless organizations' (Ashkenas *et al.* 1995), boundary-spanners, access points, and relationship managers are extremely important to the constitution of trust within interorganizational networks.

3. Interorganizational networks are characterized by the coexistence of co-operation *and* competiton, and this to a greater extent than organizations, since the 'market test' (MacMillan and Farmer 1979) continues to be effective. This is exemplified by the fact that, *ceteris paribus*, a lower price does not result in an immediate switch to the supplier offering the same

quality at a cheaper price but, as Dore (1983: 463–4) notes for the Japanese textile industry, in rebargaining with the *current* supplier. Market forces working this way and domesticized within networks are believed to contribute much to the strategic flexibility of this organizational form. Co-operation and competition, autonomy and dependence, and not least trust and control are specific tensions which are effective in interorganizational relations and which have been analysed elsewhere (Sydow *et al.* 1995; Sydow 1996a).

4. Interorganizational networks not only evolve as a result of more intensified co-operation among independent organizations, i.e. from quasi-internalization, but also from quasi-externalization. In the case of the latter, where interorganizational relations substitute for former organizational relations, the building and maintaining of trust is a particularly difficult task. For at least some employees are usually directly threatened by this development, many indirectly. So quasi-externalization, very much in contrast to network formation by means of quasi-internalization, is extremely challenging in terms of trust-sensitive management.

In summary, whether trust relations among organizations are considered to be a constitutive property of interorganizational networks or not, interorganizational trust certainly is of outstanding importance for building and maintaining effective network relations. Paradoxically, this organizational form which is believed to require more trust than others does not make it easy for management to develop and maintain trust relationships. More than in other organizational forms, management has to consider all three: process-based, characteristic-based, and institutional-based trust. Moreover, management should reflexively monitor how these relate to persons and systems in disembedding and reembedding processes, how they are influenced by such structural properties as the frequency and openness of interorganizational communication, the multiplexity and open-endedness of relations, the balance of autonomy and dependence achieved within these relations, the number and homophility of network organizations, and the structure of the interorganizational field, and how these structural properties are reproduced by specific trust-enhancing interorganizational practices.

NOTES

1. Consider, for example, Arrow's (1974) statement that trust is an efficient lubricant for any economic exchange.

2. For instance, a high level of trust may preserve the *status quo* and, sometimes, make interorganizational change more difficult. Moreover, such a high level of trust creates opportunities for malfeance and manipulation.

3. Methodologically, the study, commissioned by the ISDN-Forschungs-kommission des Landes Nordrhein-Westfalens, is based upon interviews with diverse experts in insurance companies and industry associations and, above all, upon semi-structured interviews with 47 independent insurance intermediaries. A detailed description of the study may be found in Sydow *et al.* (1995).

4. While trust in the persistence of the moral social order (Barber 1983) or in institutions such as markets or jurisdiction *per se* thus seems to be excluded from the analysis, it in fact constitutes an important facet of the social context in which interorganizational trust does or does not evolve (see Chapter 4 for details).

5. In structuration theory the notion 'rule', as much as the notion of structure, is used very differently than in organization theory. Rules, i.e. structures of signification and/or legitimation, are to be found only embedded in action or in memory traces, nowhere else. This theory, hence, focuses on rules of signification and legitimation as practised (or at least as memorized), rather than on formal rules codified in contracts or handbooks.

6. It should be recognized that the notion of reproduction includes the possibility of change. Structuration theory, at least in this respect, corresponds to the recent claim 'that there is a pressing need for more "naive theories" about trust. . . . It is, after all, the naive [or implicit] theory that provides individuals with the perceived links between *their* cognitions and *their* actions' (Kramer 1996: 238).

7. Barber (1983: 14) differentiates accordingly 'competence trust' and 'goodwill trust', both of which are considered important in network relationships, among a focal firm and its subcontractors, for example (Berger *et al.* 1993: 91–2).

8. The trustworthiness of the social system in the case may stem either from an organizational culture and associated control systems that reward trustworthy behaviour (Barney and Hansen 1994: 180–1) or from a general reputation of the organization in the field.

9. This the more so as, from a structurationist perspective, as much as from any other social constructionist view, such levels are neither distinct nor independent.

10. Concerning supplier and customer relations of brokers, some spatial closeness in the insurance industry is (still) intentionally created, for example, by the establishment of broker advisors or of departments specialized in servicing industrial customers.

11. For this reason alone, a more or less project-based co-operation, which is typically to be found in dynamic networks and virtual corporations, is very likely to require additional sources of trust rather than pure experience, i.e. characteristics-based and institutional-based trust in persons and/or systems. While dynamic networks or temporary systems certainly require additional conditions and effort to create and maintain trust relations, the limited time horizon also makes some things easier (see Meyerson, Weick, and Kramer 1996: 190–1, for details).

12. This structural property demarcates the line to another level of analysis, the network environment.

REFERENCES

Alchian, A. and Woodward, S. (1987), 'Reflections on the Theory of the Firm', *Journal of Institutional and Theoretical Economics*, 143: 110–36.

Alter, C. and Hage, J. (1993), *Organizations Working Together*. Newbury Park, Calif.: Sage.

Arrow, K. (1974), *The Limits of Organizations*. New York: Norton.

Ashkenas, R., Ulrich, D., Jick, T., and Kerr, S. (1995), *Boundaryless Organization*. San Francisco: Jossey-Bass.

Astley, W. G. and Fombrun, C. J. (1983), 'Collective Strategy: Social Ecology of Organizational Environment', *Academy of Management Review*, 8/4: 576–87.

Axelrod, R. (1984), *The Evolution of Cooperation*. New York: Basic Books.

Barber, B. (1983), *The Logic and Limits of Trust*. New Brunswick, NJ: Rutgers University Press.

Barnes, L. B. (1981), 'Managing the Paradox of Organizational Trust', *Harvard Business Review*, 59/2: 107–16.

Barney, J. B. and Hansen, M. H. (1994), 'Trustworthiness as a Source of Competitive Advantage', *Strategic Management Journal*, 15: 175–90.

Berger, H., Noorderhaven, N., Nooteboom, B., and Pennink, B. (1993), 'Understanding the Subcontracting Relationship: The Limitations of Transaction Cost Economics', in J. Child, M. Crozier, and R. Mayntz (eds.), *Societal Change Between Markets and Organizations*. Aldershot: Avebury, 77–98.

Boden, D. (1994), *The Business of Talk: Organizations in Action*. Cambridge: Cambridge University Press.

Borch, O. J. (1994), 'The Process of Relational Contracting: Developing Trust-Based Strategic Alliances Among Small Business Enterprises', *Advances in Strategic Management 10B*. Greenwich, Conn.: JAI Press, 113–35.

Borys, B. and Jemison, D. B. (1989), 'Hybrid Arrangements as Strategic Alliances: Theoretical Issues in Organizational Combinations', *Academy of Management Review*, 14/2: 234–49.

Bradach, J. and Eccles, R. G. (1989), 'Price, Authority and Trust: From Ideal Types to Plural Forms', *Annual Review of Sociology*, 15: 97–118.

Buono, A. F. (1997), 'Enhancing Strategic Partnerships: Intervening in Network Organizations', *Journal of Organizational Change Management*, 10/3: 251–66.

Burt, R. S. and Knez, M. (1996), 'Trust and Third-Party Gossip', in R. M. Kramer and T. R. Tyler (eds.), *Trust in Organizations*. London: Sage, 68–89.

Chisholm, R. F. (1996), 'On the Meaning of Networks', *Group & Organization Management*, 21/2: 216–35.

Clegg, S. R. and Hardy, C. (1996), 'Conclusions: Representations', in S. R. Clegg, C. Hardy, and W. R. Nord (eds.), *Handbook of Organization Studies*. London: Sage, 676–708.

Coleman, J. S. (1990), *Foundations of Social Theory*. Cambridge, Mass.: Harvard University Press.

Cummings, T. G. (1984), 'Transorganizational development', in B. Staw and L. L. Cummings (eds.), *Research in Organizational Behavior, 6*. Greenwich, Conn.: JAI Press, 367–422.

Davidow, W. H. and Malone, M. S. (1992), *The Virtual Corporation*. New York: Harper.

Dodgson, M. (1993), 'Learning, Trust and Technological Collaboration', *Human Relations*, 46: 77–95.

Dollinger, M. J., Golden, P. A., and Saxton, T. (1997), 'The Effect of Reputation on the Decision to Joint Venture', *Strategic Management Journal*, 18/2: 127–40.

Dore, R. (1983), 'Goodwill and the Spirit of Market Capitalism', *British Journal of Sociology*, 34/4: 459–82.

Elster, J. (1979), *Sour Grapes: Studies in the Subversion of Rationality*. Cambridge: Cambridge University Press.

Erikson, E. H. (1950), *Childhood and Society*. New York: Norton.

Ernste, H. and Meier, V. (1992) (eds.), *Regional Development and Contemporary Industrial Response*. London: Pinter.

Fombrun, C. J. (1996), *Reputation: Realizing Value from Corporate Image*. Boston: Harvard Business School Press.

Fox, A. (1974), *Beyond Contract: Work, Power and Trust Relations*. London: Faber and Faber.

Gibbons, D. E. (1996), 'Friendship and Advice Networks in Organizations: Interlacing Change with Stasis', *Best Paper Proceedings of the 1996 Meeting of the Academy of Management*. Cincinatti, Oh.

Giddens, A. (1984), *The Constitution of Society*. Cambridge: Polity Press.

——(1990), *The Consequences of Modernity*. Cambridge: Polity Press.

Golembiewski, R. T. and McConkie, M. (1975), 'The Centrality of Interpersonal Trust in Group Processes', in C. L. Cooper (ed.), *Theories of Group Processes*. London: Wiley, 131–85.

Gomes-Casseres, B. (1996), *The Alliance Revolution: The New Shape of Business Rivalry*. Cambridge, Mass.: Harvard University Press.

Gondek, H.-D., Heisig, U., and Littek, W. (1992), 'Vertrauen als Organisationsprinzip', in W. Littek, U. Heisig, and H.-D. Gondek (eds.), *Organisation von Dienstleistungsarbeit*. Berlin: Sigma, 33–55.

Granovetter, M. (1985), 'Economic Action and Social Structure: The Problem of Embeddedness', *American Journal of Sociology*, 91: 481–510.

Gulati, R. (1995), 'Does Familiarity Breed Trust? The Implications of Repeated Ties for Contractual Choice in Alliances', *Academy of Management Journal*, 38/1: 85–112.

Håkansson, H. (1987), *Industrial Technological Development: A Network Approach*. London: Croom Helm.

Hamel, G. (1991), 'Competition for Competence and Interpartner Learning Within International Strategic Alliances', *Strategic Management Journal*, 12: 83–103.

Hart, K. M. (1988), 'A Requisite for Employee Trust: Leadership', *Psychology*, 25: 1–7.

Heisig, U. and Littek, W. (1995), 'Trust as a Basis of Work Organisation', in W. Littek and T. Charles (eds.), *The New Division of Work*. Berlin and New York: De Gruyter, 17–56.

Helper, S. (1993), 'An Exit-Voice Approach to Supplier Relations: The Case of the US Automobile Industry', in G. Grabher (ed.), *The Embedded Firm: On the Socioeconomics of Industrial Networks*. London: Routledge, 141–60.

Hirschman, A. (1970), *Exit, Voice, and Loyalty*. Cambridge, Mass.: Harvard University Press.

Hosmer, L. T. (1995), 'Trust: The Connecting Link Between Organizational Theory and Philosophical Ethics', *Academy of Management Review*, 20/2: 379–403.

Illner, M. (1994), 'Strategische Orientierung der Allianz gegenüber im Industriegeschäft tätigen Versicherungsmaklern', in J. Sydow (ed.), *Strategien in Versicherungsnetzwerken*. Karlsruhe : Verlag Versicherungswirtschaft, 101–11.

Jarillo, J. C. (1988), 'On Strategic Networks', *Strategic Management Journal*, 9: 31–41.

Kilduff, M. (1993), 'The Reproduction of Inertia in Multinational Corporations', in S. Ghoshal and D. E. Westney (eds.), *Organization Theory and the Multinational Corporation*. New York: St Martin's Press, 259–74.

Kollock, P. (1994), 'The Emergence of Exchange Structures: An Experimental Study of Uncertainty, Commitment, and Trust', *American Journal of Sociology*, 100/2: 313–45.

Kramer, R. M. (1996), 'Divergent Realities and Convergent Disappointments in the Hierachic Relation: Trust and the Intuitive Auditor at Work', in Kramer and Tyler (eds.), *Trust in Organizations*, 216–45.

Lane, C. and Bachmann, R. (1996), 'The Social Constitution of Supplier Relations in Britain and Germany', *Organization Studies*, 17/3: 365–95.

Larson, A. (1992), 'Network Dyads in Entrepreneurial Settings: A Study of the Governance of Exchange Relations', *Administrative Science Quarterly*, 37: 76–104.

Lewis, J. D. and Weigert, A. (1985), 'Trust as a Social Reality', *Social Forces*, 63: 967–85.

Loose, A. and Sydow, J. (1994), 'Vertrauen und Ökonomie in Netzwerkbeziehungen', in J. Sydow and A. Windeler (eds.), *Management interorganisationaler Beziehungen*. Opladen: Westdeutscher Verlag, 160–93.

Lorenz, E. H. (1988), 'Neither Friends Nor Strangers: Informal Networks of Subcontracting in French Industry', in D. Gambetta (ed.), *Trust: Making and Breaking Cooperative Relations*. New York: Blackwell, 3–13.

Lorenzoni, G. and Ornati, O. A. (1988), 'Constellations of Firms and New Ventures', *Journal of Business Venturing*, 3: 41–57.

Luhmann, N. (1979), *Trust and Power*. Chichester: Wiley.

MacMillan, K. and Farmer, D. (1979), 'Redefining the Boundaries of the Firm', *Journal of Industrial Economics*, 27: 277–85.

Mayer, R. C., Davis, J. H., and Schoormann, F. D. (1995), 'An Integrative Model of Organizational Trust', *Academy of Management Review*, 20/3: 709–34.

Meyerson, D., Weick, K. E., and Kramer, R. M. (1996), 'Swift Trust and Temporary Groups', in Kramer and Tyler (eds.), *Trust in Organizations*, 166–95.

Miles, R. E. and Snow, C. C. (1986), 'Organizations: New Concepts for New Forms', *California Management Review*, 28: 62–73.

Nelson, P. (1970), 'Information and Consumer Behavior', *Journal of Political Economy*, 78: 311–29.

Nohria, N. (1992), 'Information and Search in the Creation of New Business Ventures: The Case of the 128 Venture Group', in N. Nohria and R. G. Eccles (eds.), *Networks and Organizations*. Boston: Harvard Business School Press, 240–61.

Oliver, A. L. (1995), *On the Nexus of Organizations and Professions: Networking Through Trust*, unpub. paper, Department of Sociology and Anthropology, Hebrew University of Jerusalem, Israel.

Ortmann, G. (1994), '"Lean"—Zur rekursiven Stabilisierung von Kooperation', in G. Schreyögg and P. Conrad (eds.), *Managementforschung 4*. Berlin and New York: De Gruyter, 143–84.

——Sydow, J., and Windeler, A. (1997), 'Organisation als reflexive Strukturation', in G. Ortmann, J. Sydow, and K. Türk (eds.), *Theorien der Organisation*. Opladen: Westdeutscher Verlag, 315–54.

Parkhe, A. (1993), 'Strategic Alliance Structuring: A Game Theoretic and Transaction Cost Examination of Interfirm Cooperation', *Academy of Management Journal*, 36: 794–829.

Piore, M. J. and Sabel, C. F. (1984), *The Second Industrial Divide*. New York: Basic Books.

Podolny, J. M. (1994), 'Market Uncertainty and the Social Character of Economic Exchange', *Administrative Science Quarterly*, 39: 458–83.

Powell, W. W. (1990), 'Neither Market nor Hierarchy: Network Forms of Organization', in Staw and Cummings (eds.), *Research in Organizational Behavior, 12*, 295–336.

——(1996), 'Trust-Based Forms of Governance', in Kramer and Tyler (eds.), *Trust in Organizations*, 51–67.

Reed, M. I. (1992), *The Sociology of Organizations*. Hemel Hempstead: Harvester.

——(1996), 'Organizational Theorizing: A Historically Contested Terrain', in Clegg, Hardy, and Nord (eds.), *Handbook of Organization Studies*, 31–56.

Ring, P. S. and van de Ven, A. H. (1992), 'Structuring Cooperative Relationships Between Organizations', *Strategic Management Journal*, 13: 483–98.

————(1994), 'Developmental Processes of Cooperative Interorganizational Relationships', *Academy of Management Review*, 19/1: 90–118.

Rotter, J. B. (1980), 'Interpersonal Trust, Trustworthiness and Gullibility', *American Psychologist*, 35: 1–7.

Sabel, C. F. (1992), 'Studied Trust: Building New Forms of Co-operation in a Volatile Economy', in W. Sengenberger and F. Pyke (eds.), *Industrial Districts and Local Economic Regeneration*. Geneva: IILS, 215–50.

Sako, M. (1992), *Prices, Quality and Trust: Inter-firm Relations in Britain and Japan*. Cambridge: Cambridge University Press.

Scott, A. J. (1996), 'Economic Decline and Regeneration in a Regional Manufacturing Complex: Southern California's Household Furniture Industry', *Entrepreneurship and Regional Development*, 8: 75–98.

Selten, R. (1978), 'The Chain Store Paradox', *Theory and Decision*, 9: 127–59.

Sitkin, S. B. and Roth, N. L. (1993), 'Explaining the Limited Effectiveness of Legalistic "Remedies" for Trust/Distrust', *Organization Science*, 4: 367–92.

Sitkin, S. B. and Stickel, D. (1996), 'The Road to Hell: The Dynamics of Distrust in an Era of Quality', in Kramer and Tyler (eds.), *Trust in Organizations*, 196–215.

Spender, J.-C. (1989), *Industry Recipes: An Enquiry into the Nature and Sources of Managerial Judgement*. Oxford: Oxford University Press.

Staber, U. H. (1996), 'The Social Embeddedness of Industrial District Networks', in U. H. Staber, N. V. Schaefer, and B. Sharma (eds.), *Business Networks: Prospects for Regional Development*. Berlin and New York: De Gruyter, 148–74.

Sydow, J. (1992), 'On the Management of Strategic Networks', in H. Ernste and V. Meier (eds.), *Regional Development and Contemporary Industrial Response*. London: Pinter, 113–29.

——(1996a), 'Inter-organizational Relations', in M. Warner (ed.), *International Encyclopedia of Business and Management*. London: Thomson, iii. 2360–73.

——(1996b), 'Flexible Specialization in Regional Networks', in Staber, Schaefer, and Sharma (eds.), *Business Networks*, 24–40.

——and Windeler, A. (1996), 'Managing Inter-firm Networks: A Structurationist Perspective', in C. G. A. Bryant and D. Jary (eds.), *Anthony Giddens: Critical Assessments*. London: Routledge, iv. 455–95.

——van Well, B., and Windeler, A. (1998), 'Networked Networks: Financial Services Networks in the Context of Their Industry', *International Studies of Management and Organization*, 28.

——Windeler, A., Krebs, M., Loose, A., and van Well, B. (1995), *Organisation von Netzwerken*. Opladen: Westdeutscher Verlag.

Thompson, J. D. (1967), *Organizations in Action*. New York: McGraw-Hill.

Thorelli, H. B. (1986), 'Networks: Between Markets and Hierarchies', *Strategic Management Journal*, 7: 37–51.

Tyler, T. R. and Kramer, R. M. (1996), 'Whither Trust?' in Kramer and Tyler (eds.), *Trust in Organizations*, 1–15.

Uzzi, B. (1996), 'The Sources and Consequences of Embeddedness for the Economic Performance of Organizations: The Network Effect', *American Sociological Review*, 61: 674–98.

Weick, K. E. (1976), 'Educational Organizations as Loosely Coupled Systems', *Administrative Science Quarterly*, 21: 1–19.

Whitley, R. (1987), 'Taking Firms Seriously as Economic Actors: Towards a Sociology of Firm Behaviour', *Organization Studies*, 8/2: 125–47.

——Henderson, J., Czaban, L., and Lengyel, G. (1996), 'Trust and Contractual Relations in an Emerging Capitalist Economy: The Changing Trading Relationships of Ten Large Hungarian Enterprises', *Organization Studies*, 17/3: 397–420.

Whittington, R. (1992), 'Putting Giddens into Action: Social Systems and Managerial Agency', *Journal of Management Studies*, 29/6: 693–712.

Williamson, O. E. (1985), *The Economic Institutions of Capitalism*. New York and London: Free Press.

Wilson, D. T. and Möller, V. (1995), 'Dynamics of Relationship Development', in V. Möller and D. T. Wilson (eds.), *Business Marketing: An Interaction and Network Perspective*. Boston: Cleever, 53–69.

Young, L. S. and Wilkinson, I. F. (1989), 'Characteristics of Good and Poor Interfirm Relations', *European Journal of Marketing*, 23/2: 109–22.

Zaheer, A. and Venkatraman, N. (1995), 'Relational Governance as an Interorganizational Strategy: An Empirical Test of the Role of Trust in Economic Exchange', *Strategic Management Journal*, 16/5: 373–92.

Zucker, L. G. (1986), 'Production of Trust: Institutional Sources of Economic Structure', in Staw and Cummings (eds.), *Research in Organizational Behavior 8*, 53–111.

Zündorf, L. (1994), 'Manager- und Expertennetzwerke in innovativen Problem-verarbeitungsprozessen', in J. Sydow and A. Windeler (eds.), *Management interorganisationaler Beziehungen*. Opladen: Westdeutscher Verlag, 244–57.

2

Distinguishing Trust and Power in Interorganizational Relations: Forms and Façades of Trust*

CYNTHIA HARDY, NELSON PHILLIPS, AND TOM LAWRENCE

1. INTRODUCTION

During recent years, the role of trust in interorganizational relationships has become an increasingly popular topic in organizational studies. Furthermore, as Sydow discusses in Chapter 1 of this volume, much of the literature has heralded the virtues of trust. Trust is supposed to make interorganizational relations function more effectively by curtailing opportunistic behaviour, by reducing complexity, and by fostering co-ordination and co-operation in ways that more formal contracts cannot (e.g. Ouchi 1980; Zucker 1986; Lewis and Weigert 1985*a*,*b*; Bowen and Jones 1986; Dasgupta 1988; Gambetta 1988; Donaldson 1990; Hill 1990; Ring and van de Ven 1992; Morgan and Hunt 1994). In this way, trust has been suggested as an alternative or supplement to hierarchies and markets (e.g. Barney and Hansen 1994) and to rational prediction (Lewis and Weigert 1985*a*). Trust has also been considered, implicitly or explicitly, as an important component in interorganizational co-operation (e.g. Alter 1990; Knoke 1990; Alter and Hage 1993), collaboration (e.g. Gray 1989; Nathan and Mitroff 1991), joint ventures (Harrigan 1985) and strategic alliances (Kanter 1990). For such 'collective' strategies (Astley 1984; Bresser and Harl 1986) to be successful, trust is needed to reduce uncertainty, produce co-operation, solve problems, and uncover innovative solutions (Dodgson 1993; Sabel 1993).

In this paper, we examine two definitions of trust commonly found in the organizational and management literature; one that defines trust as predictability, and one that emphasizes the role of goodwill. Both approaches tend to see trust as inherently functional and beneficial, and to ignore issues of asymmetrical power and conflicting interests. As a result, we suggest that

* The authors would like to acknowledge the financial support of McGill University, the Social Sciences and Humanities Council of Canada, and Les Fonds pour la Formation des Chercheurs et l'Aide à la Recherche.

neither definition is completely satisfactory: definitions focusing on predictability are unable to distinguish between relationships based on trust and
those based on power; definitions that emphasize goodwill make assumptions of common goals that are not always realistic and that have little to say
about how trust can be created. We argue that to effectively differentiate
trust from power, we must consider *both* predictability and goodwill; and to
understand how trust is created we must attend to the processes of communication that create shared meanings between partners.

In adopting this approach, we address an important anomaly that characterizes the literature not only on trust, but on interorganizational co-
operation and collaboration in general; the tendency to avoid issues of
power:

[Studies] have tended to be 'heavy' on notions of negotiations and trust between
members of the network and exceptionally 'light' on domination and power relations . . . networks continue to be portrayed as interdependent relationships based
on reciprocity and mutual trust where self interest is sacrificed for the communal
good. (Knights, Murray, and Willmott 1993: 979)

Despite calls to the contrary (e.g. Granovetter 1985), a functionalist emphasis persists in the literature on interorganizational relations (Hazen 1994).
Such a perspective tends to focus on surface dynamics and to ignore the
fact that power can be hidden behind a façade of 'trust' and a rhetoric of
'collaboration' and can be used to promote vested interests through the
manipulation and capitulation of weaker partners. In addition, approaches
that concentrate on the 'rational' aspects of interorganizational co-
operation downplay the very real difficulties in creating co-operative
relations, especially where new partners, from different organizations, industries, and sectors, are thrown together (e.g. Waddock 1989). In these
circumstances, exactly what constitutes 'rational' is problematic. Consequently, trust is unlikely to emerge spontaneously and, so, we need to learn
how to *create* trust between partners with very different goals and values.

Conceptualizations of trust need to accomplish two objectives: first, they
must show how trust is generated; second, they must differentiate between
trust-based relationships and relationships where power is used to create a
façade of trust. The latter may be convenient for more powerful partners,
but we demonstrate that it is unlikely to produce the synergistic creativity
that more reciprocal interorganizational relations promote (e.g. Gray
1989). The conceptualization presented in this chapter addresses both these
objectives. We begin by critiquing two definitions of trust commonly found
in the literature, showing how definitions based on predictability are unable
to distinguish trust from power, while definitions based on goodwill make
unrealistic assumptions that curtail their usefulness. We then discuss how
trust arises as a result of a communicative process through which meaning
is shared. We use empirical examples to explore this process further.

Finally, we present a model that distinguishes a variety of trust and power-based interorganizational relationships.

2. DEFINITIONS OF TRUST

The literature on trust is burgeoning and the topic has been considered by economists, psychologists, and sociologists, as well as management theorists (see Sitkin and Roth 1993; Hosmer 1995; Mayer, Davis, and Schoorman 1995; and Kramer and Tyler 1996 for reviews). While there is agreement on the importance of trust, there is little consensus on how to define it (Mayer, Davis, and Schoorman 1995; McAllister, 1995). Consequently, trust has been equated with individual expectations, interpersonal relations, economic transactions, and social structures (Hosmer 1995; McAllister 1995). In this section, we will develop a communicative approach to examine trust in the context of interactions between organizations. We commence by critiquing two commonly used definitions of trust found in the literature on interorganizational relations: trust as predictability and trust as goodwill (see Zucker 1986; Ring and van de Ven 1992).

2.1 Trust as Predictability

The first definition relates trust to predictability, which is defined as the probability with which an actor assesses that another actor will act in a certain way (e.g. Luhmann 1979; Lewis and Weigert 1985a; Zucker 1986; Gambetta 1988). Luhmann (1979), for example, argues that we make predictions (or have expectations) concerning the behaviour of others. If we are confident that our predictions will come to pass, we trust them:

Trust exists in a social system in so far as the members of that system act according to and are secure in the expected futures constituted by the presence of each other or their symbolic representations.   (Lewis and Weigert 1985a: 968, original emphasis removed)

Trust reduces complexity by ensuring that the social system is based on mutual expectations about actors' future behaviour, encouraging social actors to select specific options of social action and reaction. The basic function of co-ordinating social interaction is thus achieved and co-operation is the result (see Lane and Bachman 1996).

This approach to trust often ignores the fact that power is, in fact, a functional equivalent of trust, serving also to ensure predictability in coordination (Lane and Bachmann 1996). When writers identify interdependency between partners as a factor in trust, they need also to consider *relative* dependency and its power implications. For example, Provan and Skinner (1989) found that high dependency of individual farm-dealers on a single equipment supplier reduced opportunistic behaviour by the dealer, increasing the likelihood of co-operation. This situation conforms to the definition above: the suppliers could be confident that the dealers would act according to expectations. But it is not clear whether the dealers co-operated due to a trusting relationship or because they had no choice (i.e. supplier power forced them to). Hasenfeld and Chesler (1989: 515) draw the former conclusion regarding the dependency relationship between social service providers and their clients:

Functional trust emerges when there is considerable interdependence, and thus some degree of power balance between the service provider and the client, nor does it neutralize power's advantage; rather trust is a derivative of power-dependence relations.

The situation is further complicated when writers turn their attention to the *creation* of trust, usually through the institution of relevant procedures (Zucker 1986), or the display of the appropriate symbolic representation (Lewis and Weigert 1985*a*). Such actions could equally well be interpreted as the management of meaning (Pettigrew 1979; Phillips and Brown 1993), where power is used unobtrusively to ensure the co-operation of others (e.g. Hardy 1985*a*). For example, the idea that the symbols employed by the medical profession create trust in the minds of patients has also been seen as a strategy by doctors to retain power over their clients (e.g. Barber 1980). Similarly, definitions that focus on trust as confidence in the reliability and integrity of another actor (e.g. Rotter 1967; Moorman, Deshpande, and Zaltman 1993) are problematic because reliability and integrity may be a façade if predictability of behaviour is the only condition.

In other words, many of the complexities of interorganizational interactions may be resolved, not by trust, but 'by implicit or explicit power relations *among* firms' (Granovetter 1985: 502):

'We've got to trust them' means in fact: 'We don't trust them but feel constrained to submit to their discretion.' This simply describes, of course, a power relationship.   (Fox 1974: 95)

It is, however, important to differentiate between trust-based interactions and power-based interactions since there is a substantive difference between co-operation achieved through power differentials that render some partners *unable* to engage in opportunistic behaviour, and a willingness to *voluntarily sacrifice* the benefits of opportunistic behaviour in order to co-operate with a trusted partner. While the first kind of co-operation may produce predictable behaviour, it will not produce the kinds of advantages that have been associated with trusting relationships. Therefore, a concept of trust that cannot distinguish co-operation derived from the political realities of powerlessness from co-operation based on reciprocity and goodwill; nor differentiate between the self-serving management of meaning to create a façade of trust and attempts to create shared meanings on which a trusting relationship can be built, is helpful to neither researchers nor practitioners.

2.2 Trust as Goodwill

This definition argues that trust is more than predictability: it also includes goodwill—mutual expectations of reciprocity—between partners (e.g. Ring and van de Ven 1992) which, in turn, lead to co-operation rather than conflict or opportunistic behaviour. According to Zucker (1986), this definition draws (directly or indirectly) on the work of Parsons (1969) whose conditions for the creation of trust included the existence of common values that can be translated into common goals. Trust is generated by realizing these conditions through relevant symbolic representations (Lewis and Weigert 1985*a*; Zucker 1986).

While the introduction of the condition of goodwill avoids conflating efforts to create trust with self-interested attempts to manage meaning; many writers subscribing to this definition assume the *ex ante* existence of convergent goals or a sense of community (e.g. Ouchi 1980; Ring and van de Ven 1992). The question remains, however, whether such assumptions are useful in the context of complex interorganizational relations in which partners may have different values, pursue different goals, be subject to pressures from different constituencies, and are socialized into different cultures (e.g. Rainey 1983; Waddock 1989). In this situation, it is more likely that stereotypic views of the 'other' will inhibit the creation of community (Sebring 1977; Gray 1985), making it unlikely that common goals will pre-exist and making it difficult to develop them. Moreover, in new relationships between different organizations, the norms and values about what constitutes trustworthy behaviour often differ markedly between partners. In such circumstances, how does goodwill arise and, if it does, how can it be signalled to other partners?

Many writers have avoided this issue of building trust altogether, arguing that it arises either spontaneously or not at all (see Sabel 1993). Other writers, drawing on the work of Granovetter (1985), link trust to the social relations within which business transactions are embedded. In other words, trust exists as a result of frequent interactions and previous trusting relationships (e.g. Dasgupta 1988).

Reliance on trust by organizations can be expected to emerge between business partners only when they have successfully completed transactions in the past and they perceive one another as complying with norms of equity.   (Ring and van de Ven 1992: 489)

Butler and Gill (1995) argue that this approach tends towards the tautological, begging the question: how do organizational partners achieve a trusting relationship *in the first place*? Furthermore, even if we accept that trust builds slowly through repeated interactions, we are left with the question of what is it that *changes* through multiple interactions to create trust? In other words, what is the foundation of a trusting relationship?

In summary, these two common definitions of trust—trust as predictability and trust as goodwill—fail to address the complexity of trust in interorganizational relationships. The first definition is problematic because, although it acknowledges the possibility of conflicting interests, its emphasis on predictability makes it difficult to distinguish between attempts to reduce power differentials and attempts to exploit them. The second definition hinges on the existence of common goals or a sense of community that does not always characterize the situations in which interorganizational trust is supposed to develop. Finally, neither definition has much to say about how to create trust. To address these problems, we turn to the conceptualization of trust as a process of communication.

3. TRUST AS COMMUNICATION

We believe that trust is a meaningful concept only when conditions concerning both predictability and goodwill are met, and when attention is paid to the communicative foundation of trust. Trust can be said to exist between partners when relations involve a high degree of predictability, on all sides, that the others will not engage in opportunistic behaviour. This definition is not unlike that of Sabel (1993) who sees trust as the mutual confidence that no party will exploit the vulnerabilities of another (also see Gulati 1995). We, however, place power at centre-stage by arguing that trust rests on reciprocal communication, and does not involve communication undertaken in order to sustain asymmetrical power relations or to exploit a position of power. In this way, predictability arises from shared meaning; while goodwill arises from the participation of all partners in the communication process whereby this shared meaning is created. Thus, we can distinguish between partners who are trustworthy and those who merely claim to be so while manipulating the confidence of the other.

In an interorganizational relationship, trust grows out of a communication process in which shared meanings develop to provide the necessary foundation for non-opportunistic behaviour. Accordingly, trust can be conceptualized as a communicative, sense-making process that bridges disparate groups (e.g. Lewis and Weigert 1985a,b; Zucker 1986; Sabel 1993). This approach emphasizes the *shared* meanings that partners use to signal trust and trustworthiness to each other.

Sociologically, trust is conceptualized as a reciprocal orientation and interpretive assumption that is shared, has the social relationship itself as the object, and is symbolized through intention action. Sociological trust is not derived from, nor reducible to the psychological states of atomistic individuals. (Lewis and Weigert 1985*b*: 456)

Trust is therefore an intersubjective social 'reality' that cannot exist, regardless of the good intentions of partners, *unless* the symbols used to signal trustworthiness have meaning for all parties.

Many writers have shown how social action hinges on interpretive, communicative, sense-making activities (Berger and Luckmann 1967; Geertz 1973; Schutz 1970), as meaning is created through specific communicative events, or conversations (Collins 1981). These conversations invoke a common reality or 'myth' (Collins 1981) which promotes action based on the tacit understandings and meanings that underlie it. In the case of trust, a myth is created which facilitates the sharing of information, subtle reading of signals, and informal interactions that signal trustworthiness and which, in turn, lead to predictable social action; reduce the likelihood of conflict and opportunistic behaviour; and obviate the need for more formal, bureaucratic controls (e.g. Ouchi 1980; Granovetter 1985; Bowen and Jones 1986; Gambetta 1988).

Such a process of myth creation is, however, problematic for two reasons. First, the creation of a common myth is difficult when symbolic meanings are not consistent between individuals with different values and backgrounds, or when intended symbols have no meaning at all. The task of finding the appropriate presentational signals of trust may not be easy, particularly when a relationship is new and involves disparate groups. To *build* trust between partners who share no common meanings, partners must create shared meaning where none existed before.

Second, such processes of communication run the risk of being 'hijacked' by those who would manage meaning for their own vested interests (e.g. Pettigrew 1979; Pfeffer 1981; Phillips and Brown 1993; Hardy 1985*a*). In other words, the claims made in these conversations may be systematically distorted in ways that produce domination.

When organizations or politics are structured so that their members have no protected recourse to checking the truth, legitimacy, sincerity, or clarity claims made on them by established structures of authority and production, we may find conditions of dogmatism rather than of social learning, tyranny rather than authority, manipulation rather than co-operation, and distraction rather than sensitivity. In this way, critical theory points to the importance of understanding practically and normatively *how* access to, and participation in, discourses, both theoretical and practical, is systematically structured. (Forester 1989: 239–40)

In this case, the myth that is created is one of 'spurious' trust (Fox 1974): conversations have been deliberately exploited to convey a façade of trust, without any consideration of reciprocity, but in order to consolidate power. Spurious trust may produce predictable behaviour, reduce opportunism, and result in co-operation since, as we have already argued, trust and power are functional equivalents. But these advantages are one-sided, accruing to the dominant partner only and, as a result, the more creative outcomes associated with trust are unlikely to ensue.

To guard against this situation, Habermas (1984) recommends that those engaged in dialogue strive for a *communicative ethic*. In practical terms (see Keller 1981; Payne, 1991) it means that conversations should ideally include all stakeholders, on an equal basis, with the freedom to represent their interests and participate in a fair and open dialogue, unfettered by coercion, manipulation, secrecy, concealment, or deception. More powerful stakeholders should be responsive to the arguments and interests of less powerful counterparts (Bowen and Power 1993). They should not appeal to a priori principles but foster a truly dialogic process in which *all* participants contribute equally (e.g. Freire 1992).

Such [high trust] relations do not exclude the challenge of plans by those affected; their submission of new information; their querying of the wisdom of means. But the shared purpose converts what would otherwise be power bargaining based on distrust into problem solving based on trust. During the 'working through' process which clarifies the available acts and probable consequences the participants trust each other and decide courses of action to which they commit themselves. Such a pattern of relations represents a high order of achievement in human affairs. (Fox, 1974: 358)

Synergistic outcomes are thus produced through the contribution of all participants in a communicative process that builds the necessary foundation for a trusting relationship.

The discussion so far raises a number of important points. First, trust results from a communicative process in which shared meanings either exist, or are created through a reciprocal relationship that involves all partners. Second, the spontaneous emergence of trust is unlikely in new relationships between disparate groups because such shared meanings will not exist. Third, trust can be built by using symbolic power to create shared meanings. Fourth, such management of meaning need not necessarily be undertaken with reciprocity in mind and may, on the contrary, be intended to maintain or increase power differentials. In such a case, it is not trust, but a façade of trust that results. Finally, the co-operation and predictability associated with trust is not always the product of voluntary self-sacrifice, but can also result from a lack of alternatives that follow from being the weaker partner in a relationship of asymmetrical power. While the use of power (e.g. the control of resource dependencies, the manipulation of participation, and the management of meaning; see Lukes 1974; Clegg 1989; Hardy 1994*a*) may increase predictability and serve the purposes of the dominant partner, it also reduces synergy. Consequently, it is useful, analytically and practically, to distinguish such cases from situations where all partners are willing to co-operate voluntarily and contribute to synergistic outcomes (Fox 1974; Lewis and Weigert 1985*b*; Sabel 1993). In the following section, we explore these issues further by contrasting two empirical examples of interorganizational co-operation.

4. TRUST-BASED AND POWER-BASED INTERORGANIZATIONAL RELATIONSHIPS

The following examples illustrate two interorganizational relationships involving co-operation. As we will show, co-operation can be produced by both trust and power, but each has different implications for the nature and outcome of that co-operation. In this way, we draw attention to the need to distinguish between trust-based and power-based relationships, and we offer some insights into how trusting relationships are built.

4.1 Trust-Based Co-operation

In this example, we describe a trusting relationship between the Ghana Refugee Union, a refugee-based organization formed to protect the interests of Ghanaian refugees and asylum-seekers, the Committee for Aid to Refugees (CAR), a Montreal-based non-government organization that advises and helps refugees, and the Canadian Council for Refugees (CCR), a national umbrella group of over 100 non-government organizations (NGOs) that deals with the protection and settlement of refugees.

In the late 1980s, a number of Ghanaian asylum-seekers claimed refuge in Canada. At the time, the large backlog of cases was taking a considerable time to process, leaving many Ghanaians (and other asylum-seekers) in limbo for months, often years, waiting to know their fate. The early signs were not promising since the acceptance rate for Ghanaian asylum-seekers was low. Consequently, some members of the Ghanaian refugee community in Montreal decided to take action to address this situation. They turned to the Committee for Aid to Refugees for help. While appreciative of the need for support and advice from this agency, the Ghanaians wanted to ensure they did not become too dependent on it.

I realized that what we needed to do is organize because almost all the refugee communities were disorganized. When the government turned the heat on, they got scared and ran to the NGOs for help. But I thought that was not the solution. It was too paternalistic and the NGOs were part of the system. They can help—up to a point.   (member of Ghanaian Refugee Union)

The Committee for Aid to Refugees, at that time, believed strongly in a 'self-help' philosophy, as an employee explained:

We understand that self-help is important. Our goal has always been the political agenda and it's better to have thousands of people screaming rather than one group. So let's get the refugees to build links so they can take their cases, themselves, instead of just us. . . . The self-help aspect is extremely important and the self-help aspect is what we put across to our funders. Our rationale is a self-help model so these people can help each other. . . .

Accordingly, the Ghanaians, with the help of the Committee for Aid to Refugees, embarked on a strategy to organize in order to influence the decision-makers responsible for refugee determination.

Part of this strategy hinged on more direct and influential involvement by the Ghanaians in the national body, the Canadian Council for Refugees (CCR). A group of Ghanaians attended the Council's meeting in 1990 which was run by members of established NGOs at that time, and was notable for the lack of refugee participation.

We were the only [refugee organization] there and we were surprised. All the resolutions that were being passed about helping refugees were from NGOs. We were very confused so we asked them how they went about determining which refugees needed help . . . 'Where are the refugees you claim to be helping? Is it from your office because people just come to you, or do you go out to the communities? We are the only ones here and we are here not because anyone invited us—we invited ourselves'. (member of Ghanaian Refugee Union)

As a result of the Ghanaians' intervention, a resolution to increase refugee participation in CCR passed and, at the following meeting, a Ghanaian was elected to the executive committee.

Over the following five years, the NGO community became more responsive to the needs of refugees. For example, the meetings of the Canadian Council for Refugees broadened in scope to include more participation from refugee organizations and more sessions on specific refugee issues. In addition, the Ghanaians became increasingly active and, for example, helped to found the Montreal Coalition for Refugees in 1991, becoming a role model for other refugee organizations. Over time, the Ghanaians moved from a subordinate position in relation to the established agencies to become an equal partner.

With the NGOs, I think now we have an equal partnership. The initial stages was more of a client–helper relationship. When we first attended CCR, we were there on that basis, but soon we were on the same level as other NGOs. . . . I think now, after this last consultation [May 1992], they are committed to refugee participation. Earlier there had been much debate about whether refugees, by which I mean refugee-based organizations, should participate. Whether it was their function or not. . . . But a resolution was passed by the end of the session to examine refugee participation and with [another Ghanaian] on the [executive] committee, it is an indication that they are serious. (Ghanaian refugee)

We argue that this relationship is based on trust. Originally, very little trust existed between the parties: the Ghanaians were wary of becoming too reliant on the Committee for Aid to Refugees and were suspicious of the Canadian Council for Refugees, at whose meetings refugees were conspicuous by their absence. Over time, however, a trusting relationship was generated as the partners deliberately tried to establish goodwill towards each other and refrain from opportunistic behaviour at each other's expense. As such, the example illuminates a number of important points about the process of building trust.

First, trust produced considerable benefits for all sides. By organizing, the Ghanaians were able to increase the acceptance rates of Ghanaian asylum claims; be accepted as an equal by the NGOs; and become a driving force in the refugee community. The Committee for Aid to Refugees, a small organization with limited funding and resources, acquired a 'champion' to help it with its goal of organizing refugees and to offset the strictures of limited resources. The Canadian Council for Refugees was able to incorporate refugee opinions and skills, thereby helping to carry out its mandate of representing refugees more effectively. We can see, then, that the creation of trust produced a co-operative, synergistic relationship between the partners through the involvement of the Ghanaians in a communicative process that helped them to organize, act, and participate more effectively.

Second, it is important to note that despite the mutual benefits, this process was not without its tensions. It took a fairly lengthy period, from 1987 to 1994, for trust to be built. During this time the various partners had to learn to communicate in a way that produced shared meaning. Such meaning is essential to trust: without it, the partners, regardless of how sincere their intentions, cannot signal their trustworthy intentions. For example, one obstacle confronting the established NGOs working with refugees concerned the latter's mode of communication, and the issues that had particular meaning for them in the light of their particular experiences, anxieties and cultures.

It becomes a more difficult communication problem [when you involve refugees]. You end up with a refugee standing up and spilling his gut about the pain he has suffered for the past years taking ten or fifteen minutes at the mike. Those who are familiar with that method of communication and understand what's happening there allow it to happen. Other people can get very impatient with that and say we shouldn't have refugees participating because they don't know what's appropriate to say where. . . . Many activist refugees that I've met feel that we Canadians don't understand their pain so they take a long time explaining in great detail their pain. That can both be very hard to listen to and sometimes it's not within the familiar pattern of communication. So, that's going to be a dilemma. (member of an established agency)

So, refugees expected certain signals and protocols to ensue in their communication with representatives from the established agencies in order to trust them. Conversely, members of established agencies expected a different, rather more task-oriented approach from refugees.

[One of our members asked of a refugee]: 'Can you give us some ideas of what we should do?' There was no answer to that. So there was some frustration among the white, non-refugees in terms of: 'We want you to participate but how do we do it?' (CCR member)

One can, then, expect 'teething problems' as partners learn how to communicate and create the meaning from which trustworthiness is signalled and trust is forged. The existence of sincerity and mutual goals will not generate trust, unless partners can communicate with each other.

Third, trust does not preclude conflict. For example, by pointing out the lack of refugee participation, the Ghanaians challenged the very essence of how the Canadian Council for Refugees conducted its business and the assumptions that underlined it. It would be surprising if challenges to established ways of thinking did not provoke some degree of conflict, even when partners are responsive to change. So, when criticized by the Ghanaians, members of the Canadian Council for Refugees felt attacked by charges of racism.

People felt attacked and felt they were being charged with racism . . . The original resolution was something like 'Whereas there has been systemic racism at CCR'. The touchy part was reworded to something like 'CCR has suffered from systemic racism'. I can't remember the first version but it was more active. The change showed that we suffered from it rather than actually doing it . . . I haven't heard that anyone wants less participation but there is some tension about the implications and demands that come with that. (CCR member)

As new partners engage in the communication process that builds trust, such tensions continue precisely *because* they develop the ability to challenge their more established counterparts; the fact that partners are reassured that no one will engage in opportunistic behaviour means that the conflict can be resolved in synergistic and innovative ways.

In summary, this example illustrates the building of a trusting relationship, which produced co-operation between the various organizations and, in turn, innovation and mutual benefits. We found no evidence of systematic distortion in the communication process, and all partners contributed to the new meanings that were created. The example also suggests that the generation of trust is a complex, dynamic, and continuous process. It depends upon signalling trustworthiness in ways that create meaning for others. Sincerity and mutually compatible goals are, by themselves, irrelevant if their meaning cannot be demonstrated. Broadening participation to include less powerful partners in co-producing this meaning helps to produce synergy and innovation, but it also increases the likelihood of conflict. Trust, rather than power, allows partners to resolve this conflict creatively and arrive at a mutually advantageous, co-operative relationship.

4.2 Power-Based Co-operation

In this example, we focus on the actions of a stakeholder to manage the meanings surrounding a situation to create the appearance of trust when, in fact, its aim was to consolidate its power. As we will demonstrate in the following example of a factory closure, the symbolic and communicative aspects of trust are open to manipulation.

Andersons (a pseudonym; all names are disguised) was a Canadian-based multinational producing industrial engineering products.[1] In September 1978, following major losses, Andersons started a review of its world-wide operations, and announced a study into a product manufactured at both *Newlands*, in Scotland, and in France. The results, announced three months later, recommended switching production to France, while transferring a second product from France to Newlands, at a cost of $2 million, to save 500 jobs. In November 1979, however, the company announced that worsening market conditions necessitated the complete closure of Newlands, with the loss of all 1,500 jobs. The company guaranteed generous redundancy payments (severance terms). It also announced an attempt to find a buyer for the site, which it was willing to sell for a nominal amount. When this initiative failed, Andersons provided financing and expertise to help employees establish *Merryvale Ltd.*, a small engineering company. In February 1980, Andersons finally withdrew from Newlands, leaving 200 employees at Merryvale.

These actions might be interpreted as an attempt to respond to employees' needs and to create convergent goals around the closure by saving jobs and providing redundancy compensation. But did the actions undertaken by management constitute a real attempt to build trust with national unions to ensure their co-operation around the closure? As we will see, Andersons managers succeeded in increasing the predictability of union behaviour by manipulating trust and consolidating their own power at the latter's expense.

The Newlands workforce was renowned for its militancy: both white and blue collar workers belonged to national unions, and the plant had recently been the target of a long strike and lockout. The unions reacted quickly to the threat of job losses and formed a Joint Union Coordinating Committee (JUCC) of union representatives. They commissioned professors at a local university to study the commercial basis and social implications of Andersons' decision; lobbied politicians and other unions;

and organized a demonstration in London. Managers were worried that the unions had sufficient power to disrupt the closure: recent factory occupations in the area, where workers united to prevent management from closing plants, provided at least one means of doing so while high unemployment rates provided ample motivation. When the JUCC obtained pledges of support from other British factories, it also became clear that any local action could escalate into a national strike, jeopardizing the entire UK operation and disrupting the transfer of production to France. UK managers were, then, anxious to secure the co-operation of the powerful unions. Accordingly, they engaged in a deliberate strategy to increase the chances of co-operation by manipulating key symbols of trust to demonstrate both their goodwill and the legitimacy of the closure decision.

First, the feasibility study was intended to legitimate the closure by 'proving' to unions and employees, on the basis of 'objective' criteria, that it was necessary to safeguard the future of the larger organization. Second, managers released the results of the study in such a way as to convey the impression that it was willing to discuss the recommendations before reaching a final decision. They wanted 'to make sure that in no way could we be criticized for not having given the trade unions every opportunity to be consulted' (UK director). They initiated a dialogue into which the unions were drawn. However, on grounds of confidentiality, the company refused to release certain key figures, making it difficult for unions to construct effective counter-arguments.

We were using a method of argument which in the end we could never win. For every set of statistics we attacked, the company would come back and produce new ones.   (academic involved in the union study)

Third, management initially offered to transfer production to Newlands to save jobs, then to find a buyer for the factory and, finally, to help to set up Merryvale. These actions helped to persuade employees and union officials that there was a possibility of saving jobs—*if* they co-operated.

Our aim was to perpetually convince people that war would have a bad effect and they would lose out; that peace gave them hope and a chance. People perpetually had hope that something would come out of it that would leave them with jobs. (UK director)

In summary, managers signalled they were trustworthy through their attempts to protect jobs, consult unions, compensate employees, and justify the closure. In this way, they achieved the predictability they wanted—co-operation from national unions. The unions 'trusted' management and, consequently, did not use their power to strike or occupy the plant and, thus, management secured union co-operation while production was transferred. However, these actions were not based on a commitment to reciprocity on the part of managers; rather they used the union involvement in the communication process to enhance their power.

The focusing of our work on the accounts may have meant that other avenues were not explored. It is possible that the contribution we made helped to reinforce, quite inadvertently, a strategy which, in the end, has produced the closure of that factory.   (academic in union study, published article, 1981)

So, while management's actions meet the definition of trust based on predictability, and involved managing the symbols of trust, they do not meet the conditions concerning goodwill. Shared meaning was created, but this meaning was distorted. In Forester's terms (1989), truth and clarity, because of the secrecy concerning 'confidential' figures, as well as the legitimacy and sincerity of management's actions, are suspect. Dialogue was *not* free from coercion, manipulation, secrecy, concealment or deception, and symbols were employed in a deliberate, instrumental attempt to create a façade of trust, behind which co-operation was secured through the consolidation of power (see Hardy 1985*b*). Interactions were couched in the trappings of trust, but it was management's *power* that produced predictability and co-operation.

5. FORMS AND FAÇADES OF TRUST

Co-operation between organizations can, then, be produced by both trust and power, but each has different implications for the nature and outcome of that co-operation. The model depicted in Table 2.1 shows four different interorganizational relationships involving co-operation. It describes two forms of trust—spontaneous trust and generated trust, and two power-based relationships—manipulation and capitulation. The latter two look, on the surface, very much like forms of trust but are, in fact, façades where the aim is not to create trust *per se*, but to create an illusion that is instrumental in securing the goals of one or some of the partners at the expense of others. The model describes these relationships and discusses their implications.

5.1 Spontaneous Trust

Spontaneous trust refers to situations where trusting relationships emerge 'naturally' and instinctively in the absence of any deliberate intent or intervention to create them (see Fox 1974 on spontaneous consent; also Sabel 1993). Co-operation between partners and predictable behaviour ensues as partners decide to gamble on a reciprocal relationship which, in turn, creates synergy that offsets any risk in embarking on such a

TABLE 2.1. Forms and façades of trust

	Spontaneous trust	Generated trust	Manipulation	Capitulation
Nature of co-operation	Co-operation is trust-based	Co-operation is trust-based	Co-operation is power-based	Co-operation is power-based
Dynamics of co-operation	Co-operation emerges naturally, through gamble	Co-operation is achieved through management of meaning	Co-operation is achieved through management of meaning	Co-operation is achieved through dependency and socialization
Synergy, innovation, and risk	Trust emerges spontaneously: synergy is high; risk is high	Trust is created through equal participation which increases synergy but also increases risk	Dominant partner uses symbolic power to reduce risk and to increase predictability; synergy is reduced	Subordinate acts as a tool of dominant partner: risk to dominant partner is low; synergy is low
Power	A 'win-win' view of power is implicit although power is largely ignored	A 'win-win' view of power prevails as asymmetrical power is decreased	A zero-sum view of power prevails as asymmetrical power is either maintained or increased	A zero-sum view of power prevails as asymmetrical power is either maintained or increased
Meaning	Shared meaning already exists between partners	Shared meaning is mutually constructed by all partners	Meaning is shared but it has been distorted by one partner	Meaning is shared but is imposed by one partner on another
Implications for research/practice	Shared meaning may not be as 'spontaneous' as it may appear	Process of creating shared meaning is difficult and may involve conflict	Relationship may look like trust when it is based on power	Power imbalance may mean that partners are not as 'independent' as they may appear

relationship. Much of the literature is clearly interested in such a conceptualization of trust; in fact, some writers argue that trust can *only* arise spontaneously (see Sabel 1993). Drawing on our conceptualization of trust as a communicative process, spontaneous trust arises when shared meaning allows a trusting relationship between partners who may be personally unknown to each other.

We identify two likely sources of such shared meaning. First, meaning may already be *institutionalized* within the larger community. For example, police officers and doctors use institutionalized symbols to signal that their position is worthy of trust; at the organizational level, financial institutions do much the same thing (see Zucker 1986). Trust exists in these cases because these symbols are widely recognized by community members and associated with unequivocal meanings. As long as the behaviour of these individuals and organizations corresponds to that expected by community members, trust will not only endure, it will be 'spontaneously' extended to new actors who display the relevant symbols. Second, shared meaning may be a *by-product* of other social interactions in which the particular relationship is embedded and in which trust has already been demonstrated (Granovetter 1985; Dasgupta 1988; Ring and van de Ven 1992; Sydow Chapter 1, this volume). In this case, trust arises as it is transferred from one setting to another. In other words, spontaneous trust produces co-operation because shared meaning exists either through highly institutionalized symbols or through a communal identity established through relationships and interactions in other activities.

The communicative framework presented here suggests, however, that this form of trust may not be as spontaneous, instinctive, or natural as is often suggested: while partners may not personally know each other, institutionalized symbols mean that they can at least recognize and communicate with each other; or, if they do not know them in the context of this particular relationship they know, and know they can trust them, in the context of others. By conceptualizing trust as a 'natural' phenomenon, unsullied by intervention, adherents of this view may be missing the underlying structures of shared meaning which underpins the relationship and makes trust possible. Accordingly, we know very little about whether trust can really arise spontaneously—in the absence of indirect knowledge of each other, and without a foundation of shared meanings. We also question whether the concept of spontaneous trust is particularly helpful in the context of interorganizational relationships that are new and bring together individuals from very different backgrounds, and where there are neither institutionalized symbols nor previous interactions. In this situation, the institutionalized symbols of one community may be unfamiliar to, or looked on with suspicion by, members of the other; the relevance of personal and process sources (Zucker 1986) is limited when people have different values and no history of positive interaction. Moreover interorganizational relations may involve different people handling different interactions at different times, and the basis of trust must extend beyond the personal and the individual if it is to endure.

5.2 Generated Trust

We refer to attempts to create trust as generated trust. Co-operation is achieved through the use of symbolic power to create shared meanings where none existed before, along the lines suggested by Forester (1989) and Bowen and Power (1993). These actions, coupled with reciprocal participation, ensure that this shared meaning is mutually constructed by all partners and, in so doing, leads to synergy and, as trust develops, predictability. The risks of such activities are relatively high, but a 'win-win' view of power assumes that they are worthwhile (Fox 1974). Generating trust thus involves attempts to free the communicative activity on which trust is built from the effects of distortion and to ensure that shared meaning is co-produced by all participants in order to bring about synergistic and innovative outcomes that benefit all members of the trusting relationship, including the weaker partners.

We suggest that the generation of trust is a particularly fruitful area of research in the context of organizational relationships. In Fox's (1974: 358) terms, it promises a 'high order' of achievement. However, such a process is not necessarily a smooth one, as partners must learn how to communicate and create the meaning through which trustworthiness is signalled and trust is forged. As social, business, and global relationships call for more complex co-operation between more different partners, the ability to generate trust in the absence of shared meaning becomes both more important and more problematic. It is important, however, for work in this area not to become overly seduced by a sanitized version of trust: the generation of trust may provide benefits to all parties but it does not, and should not, preclude conflict. Conflict is a sign that all partners are contributing to the creation of shared meaning and, as such, contributing to a reciprocal relationship in which synergistic outcomes are possible.

5.3 Manipulation

Manipulation looks much like generated trust in that symbolic power is used to manage meaning and to bring about co-operation. However, these actions are part of a strategy to increase power: as one party accumulates it, the other loses it. The aim is to secure agreement and reduce the chances of opposition by creating legitimacy for both actor and actions through language and symbols (e.g. Edelman 1964, 1971, 1979; Hardy 1985b). Claims to truth, legitimacy, sincerity, and clarity are deliberately manipulated and packaged for the benefit of particular actors (Forester 1989). The result is increased predictability and reduced risk for the partner who engages in this strategy because its counterparts' alternatives are reduced; however, synergy and creativity are constrained for the same reasons.

If we compare generated trust and manipulation, both involve attempts to create meaning to influence behaviour and increase predictability. Where they differ is in terms of reciprocity, and the latter's deliberate manipulation of symbols to distort meaning and to mask the consolidation, rather than the dispersal, of power. Dominant partners may be predisposed to use power rather than trust to ensure co-operation because predictability offers more immediate and calculable benefit than potential, but uncertain, synergy. If this is the case, research on trust generation must take care not to conflate it with sophisticated attempts to use power to secure co-operation.

5.4 Capitulation

Our communicative framework allows us to identify another façade of trust, which we call capitulation. In this situation, co-operation is not achieved through trust but, rather, through dependency. Socialized into dependency, weaker partners act as the tools of dominant ones:

> Conditioning and power combine, then, to produce acceptance and submission. . . . If inequalities are being imposed upon people by forces which they shrink from challenging, one way by which they can avoid psychological discomfort is to be receptive to all those influences.   (Fox 1974: 285)

Capitulation can be said, then, to refer to a situation in which co-operation between parties with vastly differing power reserves creates a façade of trust. As Granovetter (1985: 502) points out, if the power position of one firm is obviously dominant, the other is apt to capitulate early so as to cut its losses (also see Thorelli 1986). The subordinate organization acts—or fails to act—because of anticipated reactions (Bachrach and Baratz 1962) or because it has been socialized to accept, unquestioningly, the limits of its room for manœuvre (Warren, Rose, and Bergunder 1974). The weaker organization knows what is required of it and acts accordingly (Granovetter 1985): shared meaning exists but it has been imposed by the dominant partner.

Capitulation conforms to the first definition of trust i.e. a high degree of predictability in the form of co-operation and, on the surface, it looks much like a trusting relationship. But it fails to conform to the second definition concerning goodwill: the terms and conditions of the co-operative relationship are not mutually determined, but are enforced by the dominant partner and asymmetrical power relations are sustained. In Forester's (1989) terms, the dialogue is *not* free from coercion. Through these actions, dominant partners can 'trust' their partner to behave in a particular way because the partner lacks the power to do anything else.[2] But, as the power of the weaker partner is reduced so is its independence and, in addition, any prospects for synergy.

In summary, our model allows us to distinguish between trust and power-based co-operation through the examination of the way in which shared meaning is created. Both rest on shared meaning but, in the case of trust, shared meaning either already exists or is actively and mutually constructed by all partners; in power-based relationships, meaning is either distorted or imposed by dominant partners.

6. CONCLUSIONS

Our model shows some of the complexities involved in studying trust. Co-operative relations that appear to reflect trust can hide attempts to consolidate asymmetrical power relations. As Barney and Hansen (1994) note, it is difficult to know whether a partner is truly trustworthy (also see Arrow 1974; Williamson 1985). Since trust is a 'risky investment' (Luhmann 1979: 24), it should not be surprising if partners prefer to use power to achieve the necessary co-ordination instead. In fact, neither economic nor behavioural theories are optimistic about the possibility of trust existing in exchanges when one partner is vulnerable to the power of the other (Barney and Hansen 1994). Through power, dominant actors can ensure co-operation and even dictate its terms. It may not bring about the creative synergy that collaboration is supposed to stimulate, but it certainly reduces risk and increases the likelihood of predictable behaviour. We cannot, then, afford to ignore power when studying trust.

Our conceptualization has two advantages. First, since illusory trust looks much like the real thing, it is important to define trust in a way that takes into account power relations. Otherwise, we risk making recommendations that invite managers to be more sophisticated in their use of power to create a façade of trust. Second, by linking trust to communication and meaning, we can start to identify the means to build trust, even in situations where new and diverse partners are brought together. Clearly, more work needs to be done using this model. If 'sincere' and 'political' actors cloak their actions in terms of the common interest and the common good, there are major problems concerning attributing political motives. It may, as a result, be difficult to distinguish between trust and power-based relationships. To complicate the matter further, real-life situations are likely to involve mixed motives. None the less, this paper has started to lay the groundwork for a conceptualization of trust which has both academic and practical benefits.

NOTES

1. This example is drawn from a study of plant closures. For more details see Hardy (1985*b*, 1990); Hardy and Pettigrew (1985).
2. In fact, even the weaker partner might be said to be able to 'trust' its more powerful counterpart to derive maximum advantage from its power.

REFERENCES

Alter, C. (1990), 'An Exploratory Study of Conflict and Coordination in Interorganizational Service Delivery Systems', *Academy of Management Journal*, 33: 478–502.

——and Hage, J. (1993), *Organizations Working Together*. Newbury Park, Calif.: Sage.

Arrow, K. J. (1974), *The Limits of Organization*. New York: Norton.

Astley, W. G. (1984), 'Toward an Appreciation of Collective Strategy', *Academy of Management Review*, 9/3: 526–35.

Bachrach, P. and Baratz, M. S. (1962), 'The Two Faces of Power', *American Political Science Review*, 56: 947–52.

Barber, B. (1980), *Informed Consent in Medical Therapy and Research*. New Brunswick, NJ: Rutgers University Press.

——(1983), *The Logic and Limits of Trust*. New Brunswick, NJ: Rutgers University Press.

Barney, J. B. and Hansen, M. H. (1994), 'Trustworthiness as a Source of Competitive Advantage', *Strategic Management Journal*, 15: 175–90.

Benson, J. K. (1975), 'The Inter-organizational Network as a Political Economy', *Administrative Science Quarterly*, 20: 229–45.

Berger, P. L. and Luckmann, T. (1967), *The Social Construction of Reality: A Treatise on the Sociology of Knowledge*. Garden City, NY: Anchor Books.

Bowen, D. E. and Jones, G. E. (1986), 'Transaction Cost Analysis of Service Organization–Customer Exchange', *Academy of Management Review*, 31/2: 428–41.

Bowen, M. G. and Power, F. C. (1993), 'The Moral Manager: Communicative Ethics and the *Exxon Valdez* Disaster', *Business Ethics Quarterly*, 3/2: 97–116.

Bresser, R. K. and Harl, J. E. (1986), 'Collective Strategy: Vice or Virtue?', *Academy of Management Review*, 11: 408–27.

Butler, J. and Gill, J. (1995), *Learning and Knowledge in Joint Ventures: The Importance of Trust*, paper presented at the British Academy of Management, Sheffield, 11–13 Sept.

Clegg, S. R. (1989), *Frameworks of Power*. London: Sage.

Collins, R. (1981), 'On the Microfoundations of Macrosociology', *American Journal of Sociology*, 86/5: 984–1013.

Dasgupta, P. (1988), 'Trust as a Commodity', in D. Gambetta (ed.), *Trust: Making and Breaking Cooperative Relations*. New York: Blackwell.

Dodgson, M. (1993), 'Learning, Trust and Technological Collaboration', *Human Relations*, 46/1: 77–95.

Donaldson, L. (1990), 'The Ethereal Hand: Organizational Economics and Management Theory', *Academy of Management Review*, 15/3: 369–81.

Edelman, M. (1964), *The Symbolic Uses of Politics*. Champaign, Il.: University of Illinois Press.

——(1971), *Politics as Symbolic Action*. Chicago: Markham.

——(1979), *Political Language*. London: Academic Press.

Forester, J. (1989), *Planning in the Face of Power*. Berkeley: University of California Press.

Fox, A. (1974), *Beyond Contract: Work, Power and Trust Relations*. London: Faber and Faber.

Freire, Paulo (1992), *Pedagogy of the Oppressed*. New York: Continuum.

Gambetta, D. (1988), *Trust: Making and Breaking Cooperative Relations*. New York: Blackwell.

Geertz, Clifford (1973), *The Interpretation of Cultures*. New York: Harper Collins.

Granovetter, M. (1985), 'Economic Action and Social Structure: The Problem of Embeddedness', *American Journal of Sociology*, 88: 489–515.

Gray, Barbara (1985), 'Conditions Facilitating Interorganizational Collaboration', *Human Relations*, 38/10: 911–36.

——(1989), *Collaborating: Finding Common Ground for Multiparty Problems*. San Francisco: Jossey-Bass.

Gulati, R. (1995), 'Does Familiarity Breed Trust? The Implications of Repeated Ties for Contractual Choice in Alliances', *Academy of Management Journal*, 38/1: 85–112.

Habermas, J. (1984), *The Theory of Communicative Action*, i. Boston: Beacon Press.

Hardy, C. (1985a) 'The Nature of Unobtrusive Power', *Journal of Management Studies*, 22/4: 384–99.

——(1985b), *Managing Organizational Closure*. Aldershot, Gower Press.

——(1990), *Strategies for Retrenchment and Turnaround: The Politics of Survival*. Berlin: De Gruyter.

——(1994a), *Managing Strategic Action: Mobilizing Change*. London: Sage.

——(1994b), 'Understanding Interorganizational Domains: The Case of Refugee Systems', *Journal of Applied Behavioral Science*, 30/3: 278–96.

——and Pettigrew, A. M. (1985), 'The Use of Power in Managerial Strategies for Change', in R. S. Rosenbloom (ed.), *Research on Technological Innovation, Management and Policy*, ii. Greenwich, Conn.: JAI Press.

Harrigan, K. R. (1985), *Strategies for Joint Ventures*. Lexington, Mass.: D. C. Heath/ Lexington Books.

Hasenfeld, Y. and Chesler, M. A. (1989), 'Client Empowerment in the Human Services: Personal and Professional Agenda', *Journal of Applied Behavioral Science*, 25/4: 499–21.

Hazen, M. A. (1994), 'A Radical Humanist Perspective of Interorganizational Relationships', *Human Relations*, 47/4: 393–415.

Hill, C. W. L. (1990), 'Cooperation, Opportunism, and the Invisible Hand: Implications for Transaction Cost Theory', *Academy of Management Review*, 15: 500–13.

Hosmer, L. T. (1995), 'Trust: The Connecting Link Between Organization Theory and Philosophical Ethics', *Academy of Management Review*, 20/2: 379–403.

Kanter, R. M. (1990), 'When Giants Learn Cooperative Strategies', *Planning Review*, 18/1: 15–25.

Keller, P. W. (1981), 'Interpersonal Dissent and the Ethics of Dialogue', *Communication*, 6: 287–303.

Knights, D., Murray, F., and Willmott, H. (1993), 'Networking as Knowledge Work: A Study of Strategic Interorganizational Development in the Financial Services Industry', *Journal of Management Studies*, 30/6: 975–95.

——and Willmott, H. (1985), 'Power and Identity in Theory and Practice', *Sociological Review*, 33/1: 22–46.

Knoke, D. (1990), *Organizing for Collective Action*. Berlin: De Gruyter.

Kramer, R. M. and Tyler, T. T. (1996) (eds.), *Trust in Organizations: Frontiers of Theory and Research*. London: Sage.

Lane, C. and Bachmann, R. (1996), The Social Constitution of Trust: Supplier Relations in Britain and Germany', *Organization Studies*, 17/3: 365–96.

Lewis, J. D. and Weigert, A. (1985*a*), 'Trust as a Social Reality', *Social Forces*, 43/4: 967–85.

——— (1985*b*), 'Social Atomism, Holism, and Trust', *Sociological Quarterly*, 26/4: 455–71.

Lukes, S. (1974), *Power: A Radical View*. London: Macmillan.

Luhmann, N. (1979), *Trust and Power*. Chichester: Wiley.

McAllister, D. J. (1995), 'Affect- and Cognition-Based Trust as Foundations for Interpersonal Cooperation in Organizations', *Academy Management Journal*, 38/1: 24–59.

Mayer, R. C., Davis, J. J., and Schoorman, F. D. (1995), 'An Integrative Model of Organizational Trust', *Academy of Management Review*, 20/3: 709–34.

Moorman, C., Deshpande R., and Zaltman, G. (1993), 'Factors Affecting Trust in Market Research Relationships', *Journal of Marketing*, 57 (Jan.), 81–101.

Morgan, R. M. and Hunt, S. D. (1994), 'The Commitment–Trust Theory of Relationship Marketing', *Journal of Marketing*, 58: 20–38.

Nathan, M. L. and Mitroff, I. I. (1991), 'The Use of Negotiated Order Theory as a Tool for the Analysis and Development of an Interorganizational Field', *Journal of Applied Behavioral Science*, 27: 163–80.

Ouchi, W. G. (1980), 'Markets, Bureaucracies, and Clans', *Administrative Sciences Quarterly*, 25: 129–41.

Parsons, T. (1969), *Politics and Social Structure*. New York: Free Press.

Payne, S. L. (1991), 'A Proposal for Corporate Ethical Reform: The Ethical Dialogue Group', *Business and Professional Ethics Journal*, 10: 67–88.

Pettigrew, A. M. (1979), 'On Studying Organizational Cultures', *Administrative Science Quarterly*, 24: 570–81.

Pfeffer, J. (1981), *Power in Organizations*. Cambridge, Mass.: Ballinger.

Phillips, N. and Brown, J. (1993), 'Analyzing Communication In and Around Organizations: A Critical Hermeneutic Approach', *Academy of Management Journal*, 36/6: 1547–76.

——and Hardy, C. (forthcoming), 'Managing Multiple Identities: Discourse, Legitimacy and Resources in the UK Refugee System', *Organization*.

Provan, K. A. and Skinner, S. J. (1989), 'Interorganizational Dependence and

Control as Predictors of Opportunism in Dealer–Supplier Relations', *Academy of Management Journal*, 32/1: 202–12.

Rainey, H. G. (1983), 'Public Agencies and Private Firms: Incentive Structures, Goals, and Individual Roles', *Administration and Society*, 15/2: 207–42.

Ring, P. S. and van de Ven, A. H. (1992), 'Structuring Cooperative Relationships Between Organizations', 13: 483–98.

Rotter, J. B. (1967), 'A New Scale for the Measurement of Interpersonal Trust', *Journal of Personality*, 35/4: 651–65.

Sabel, C. F. (1993), 'Studies Trust: Building New Forms of Cooperation in a Volatile Economy', *Human Relations*, 46/9: 1133–70.

Schutz, A. (1970), *On Phenomenology and Social Relations*. Chicago: University of Chicago Press.

Sebring, R. H. (1977), 'The Five Million Dollar Misunderstanding: A Perspective on State Government–University Interorganizational Conflicts', *Administrative Science Quarterly*, 22: 505–23.

Sitkin, S. B. and Roth, N. L. (1993), 'Explaining the Limited Effectiveness of Legalistic "Remedies" for Trust/Distrust', *Organization Science*, 26/4: 367–92.

Thorelli, H. B. (1986), 'Networks: Between Markets and Hierarchies', *Strategic Management Journal*, 7: 37–51.

Waddock, S. A. (1989), 'Understanding Social Partnerships: An Evolutionary Model of Partnership Organizations', *Administration and Society*, 21: 78–100.

Warren, R., Rose, S. R., and Bergunder, A. (1974), *The Structure of Urban Reform*. Lexington, Mass.: D. C. Heath.

Weick, K. (1979), 'Cognitive Processes in Organization', in B. M. Staw (ed.), *Research in Organizational Behavior*. Greenwich, Conn.: JAI Press, i. 41–74.

Williamson, O. E. (1981), 'The Economics of Organizations: The Transaction Cost Approach', *American Journal of Sociology*, 3: 548–65.

——(1985), *The Economic Institutions of Capitalism*. New York: Free Press.

Zucker, L. G. (1986), 'Production of Trust: Institutional Sources of Economic Structure, 1984–1920', in Staw (ed.), *Research in Organizational Behavior*, 8, 53–111.

3

*Does Trust Improve Business Performance?**
MARI SAKO

Does trust improve business performance? And if so, how can trust be created in business where there is none? These are the two questions which this chapter addresses. The main aim of the chapter is to evaluate various theories which touch on the causes and outcomes of trust, and to provide empirical tests of those theories using a large-scale survey of automotive parts suppliers in the United States, Europe, and Japan.

A growing interest in building trust between organizations stems from the belief that trust enhances business performance. For instance, trust has been identified as an important component which makes partnerships, strategic alliances, and networks of small firms successful (Brusco 1986; Powell 1996; Smitka 1991). Trust is also of great relevance today because the maintenance of consistently high quality, which is an important source of competitiveness, is easier in a high-trust production system than in a low-trust one (Sako 1992). In a similar vein, Fukuyama (1995) attributes national industrial competitiveness to trust as a societal-level cultural norm and a social capital. According to him, people's capacity to institutionalize trust in the realm of work and business accounts for the industrial success in Japan and Germany. By contrast, the 'missing middle', namely the absence of intermediate social groups in the area between the family and large, centralized organizations like the Church or the State, accounts for the relative economic backwardness of Latin Catholic countries (like Italy, France, and Spain) and Chinese societies (Fukuyama 1995: 55–6).

In Fukuyama's (1995) study, as in others, the link between trust and business performance is plausible but not proven. Nevertheless, the idea is so appealing that at the practitioner level, an increasing number of studies exhort business to create trust as an essential component in making partnerships between firms successful (SMMT and DTI 1994; Ingersoll Engineers 1995). In business strategy, recent work on trust between organizations focuses on the possibility of using it to create and maintain competitive advantage (Barney and Hansen 1994; Jarillo 1988). While theoretical explorations on the link between trust and performance abound, empirical studies in this area are rare (exceptions include Mohr and Spekman 1994). This chapter presents evidence which fills this lacuna.

* The author acknowledges the funding support of the International Motor Vehicle Program (IMVP) at MIT which made this study possible. I also thank Susan Helper for entering into a high-trust loose reciprocity research collaboration, in particular for allowing me to use the US data she collected for this paper.

The second, related, question which this paper addresses—how can trust be created when there is none?—has been the subject of much debate. The extreme positions in this debate are held by those who argue that trust can be cultivated intentionally by farsighted parties who recognize the benefits of long-term co-operation (Axelrod 1984), and those who argue that it is a by-product of the embeddedness of parties who share a common cultural or social norm (Granovetter 1985). Both approaches are not very helpful for thinking about how to create trust when there is none. In the former, if the parties are not farsighted enough, or if they are antagonistic from the start, a process of co-operation may never get started. In the latter, those living in communities which are already endowed with high trust can benefit from it, but those without it are doomed to suffer from the adverse consequences of low trust. This chapter examines whether the two extreme views can be reconciled.

The central concept explored in this chapter is mutual trust between a customer and a supplier organization. Trust is an expectation held by an agent that its trading partner will behave in a mutually acceptable manner (including an expectation that neither party will exploit the other's vulnerabilities). This expectation narrows the set of possible actions, thus reducing the uncertainty surrounding the partner's actions. The notion of trust implies that the partner has freedom of choice to take alternative courses of action. Thus, predictability in behaviour arises not because of constraints which force the other side to stick to a single possible course of action. Sako (1991, 1992) categorized other reasons for predictability in behaviour to distinguish between three types of trust: 'contractual trust' (will the other party carry out its contractual agreements?), 'competence trust' (is the other party capable of doing what it says it will do?), and 'goodwill trust' (will the other party make an open-ended commitment to take initiatives for mutual benefit while refraining from unfair advantage taking?). This three-way distinction will be employed throughout this chapter.

Contractual trust rests on a shared moral norm of honesty and promise-keeping. Competence trust requires a shared understanding of professional conduct and technical and managerial standards. Goodwill trust can exist only when there is consensus on the principle of fairness. Viewed in this way, there seems to be a hierarchy of trust, with fulfilling a minimum set of obligations constituting 'contractual trust', and honouring a broader set constituting 'goodwill trust'. A move from contractual trust to goodwill trust involves a gradual expansion in the congruence in beliefs about what is acceptable behaviour. Because of the three-way distinction made in the concept of trust, opportunism, defined as self-interest seeking with guile by Williamson (1985), is not a mere opposite of trust. A precondition for trust of the contractual and goodwill types is the absence of opportunistic behaviour. However, lack of opportunism is not a sufficient condition for goodwill trust. For example, a supplier that withholds a vital piece of technical information may not be acting opportunistically according to the strict contractual sense. This amounts to fulfilling the letter, but not the spirit, of the contract. Fulfilling the spirit of the contract, by demonstrating commitment and fair behaviour, is close to the notion of goodwill trust.

The chapter is structured as follows. Section 1 reviews various theories which address the issue of whether trust enhances business performance or not. The evidence from a large-scale survey on the impact of trust on supplier performance is reported. Section 2 discusses how trust can be created between organizations particularly when they are in low trust relationships. This section also reports the results of the survey concerning the determinants of trust and opportunism. Section 3 concludes by drawing theoretical and empirical implications of this study.

1. DOES INTERORGANIZATIONAL TRUST ENHANCE BUSINESS PERFORMANCE?

Interorganizational trust may enhance business performance in a number of ways. This section reviews some of the major works by categorizing them broadly into those which focus on (a) reducing transaction costs, (b) investment with future returns, and (c) continuous improvement and learning. The last subsection presents empirical evidence.

Before doing so, however, a brief word on the link between the notion of interorganizational trust and governance. In organizational studies, it has been common to treat trust either as a determinant of 'governance structure' or as a governance structure in itself. 'Governance mechanisms' include such formal arrangements as markets, hierarchies, and intermediate modes including long-term contracts, joint ventures and other forms of alliances (Heide and John 1990; Joskow 1988; Walker and Weber 1984; Williamson 1985). Trust or opportunism enter into some of these analyses as one of the determinants of governance structures. For example, trust is a social norm which lessens the need to use hierarchy to attenuate opportunism. Thus, the higher the general level of trust, the less need there is for vertical integration (Williamson 1985). Similarly, the higher the dyadic trust which develops over time, the less need there is to rely on equity-holding (Gulati 1995). Here, trust tends to be conceptualized as a substitute for various governance mechanisms. The notion of governance structure is closely linked to the idea of 'safeguards' against opportunistic behaviour. Such safeguards, i.e. externally imposed constraints, become unnecessary if actors have an internalized moral norm of behaving in a trustworthy manner. This view of trust as a determinant of governance structures is dominant in the functionalist perspective represented by transaction cost economics, which argues for an effective alignment of governance structures with transactional characteristics (see below).

An alternative conception is to regard trust as a governance structure, albeit an informal one. 'Governance by trust' is an informal control mechanism which enhances the effectiveness of transactions whether they take place in markets or within a hierarchy (Smitka 1991). This conceptualization introduces the possibility that trust may complement, rather than substitute for, hierarchy or market (Bradach and Eccles 1989; Smitka 1992). This paper adopts this 'governance by trust' perspective. It posits that trust exists to a varying degree in different types of formal governance structures, be they markets, long-term contracts, or hierarchies. Whatever the formal governance structures, the higher the level of mutual trust, the better the performance is likely to be. While formal governance structures may act as 'safeguards' against opportunistic behaviour, they are, in themselves, not sufficient to ensure the sort of performance—innovation and learning—which trust induces.

1.1 Reducing Transaction Costs

The performance criterion used by transaction-cost economics (TCE) is the minimization of transaction costs. This is achieved by aligning governance structures to the characteristics of the transaction. In particular, whenever the environment is uncertain and specific assets are required in a transaction, both parties have an incentive to behave opportunistically. Depending on the frequency of trading which determines the costs of recontracting, Williamson (1979) prescribes either vertical integration or relational contracting. In this framework, as long as optimal decisions are made, every governance structure is just as efficient as another at the margin.

The TCE paradigm has been so influential that the minimization of transaction costs is taken as a performance objective even in other areas, such as strategic management. Strategic management is about how firms can create and sustain competitive advantage. For instance, it is said that trust enables a network of firms to adapt to unforeseen circumstances, thus reducing transaction costs; in this sense firms can make use of the network strategically (Jarillo 1988). More recently, Barney and Hansen (1994) examine trustworthiness as a source of competitive advantage. They make a distinction among three types of trust: weak form, semi-strong form, and strong form trust. Weak form trust emerges because there are limited opportunities for opportunism. Semi-strong form trust depends on governance devices such as a market for reputation and contracts to safeguard against the threat of opportunism. Strong form trust emerges in response to a set of internalized norms and principles that guide the behaviour of exchange partners, and is independent of whether or not specific governance mechanisms exist. (In the three-way categorization of trust employed in this chapter, goodwill trust corresponds roughly to strong form trust, and contractual trust to semi-strong trust.) They argue that only strong form trust leads to competitive advantage. The basis for arguing so is that first, strong form trust is more difficult to imitate than weak form or semi-strong form trust. Second, with strong form trust, less safeguards are needed in the form of governance structures, and therefore it is less costly for the firm.

1.2 Investment to Increase Future Returns

This last assertion depends on the time period which is taken into account. Once strong form trust is built and established, firms may enjoy lower costs than those without. But it is quite possible that the process of building trust might have involved a very high initial set-up cost with uncertain or risky returns. A British purchasing manager in a recent interview said that trusting a new supplier requires a leap of faith, even if there are some objective quality standards such as ISO 9000. This is because the formal documentation sought in an initial supplier audit is not revealing about how the quality standard is actually implemented, but the latter is difficult to capture fully in a short visit. Building trust in itself is an investment, and trust between a buyer and a supplier is a 'relation-specific skill' (Asanuma 1989). The returns to investment may be in terms of low monitoring and co-ordination costs—the agency costs in principal–agent theory—and it is this aspect which enables such practices as just-in-time delivery and no quality inspection on delivery. However, at any time, a buyer and a supplier which have just begun trading and are in the process of building a high-trust relationship may be incurring a greater set-up cost than other companies in low-trust relationships. This in turn leads to a hypothesis that the older the trading relationship, the greater the gap in performance between high-trust and low-trust supplier relations, assuming that the parties have been following a strategy of developing mutual trust during the whole period of the trading relationship.

Suppliers in a high-trust trading relationship are also willing to invest in customer-specific and general assets because of the assumed long-term commitment in such a relationship. Greater investment in itself may be considered a performance measure. At the same time, asset specialization is likely to increase productivity (Dyer, forthcoming). Following Williamson (1985), specific assets consist not only of physical capital, but also of human capital and location.

1.3 Continuous Improvement and Learning

The third and the last perspective argues that trust, especially of the goodwill sort, gives rise not only to lower transaction costs or to higher net benefits from investment, but also to more rapid innovation and learning (Sabel 1994). In other words, suppliers in high-trust relations are likely to exploit opportunities to the mutual benefit of both the customer and the supplier, which would otherwise not have been exploited had transactions depended solely on contracts or 'incentives'. As trust is linked to the notion of 'freewill' choice and is seen to obviate the use of 'safeguards' or constraints, trust gives that something extra, a positive motivational force which enhances X-efficiency and dynamic efficiency. These outcomes are achieved through an orientation towards joint problem solving to improve quality, to reduce costs, and to innovate production and management methods. Such collaboration between a customer and a supplier leads to learning-by-transacting. This implies that even after trust is built and established, trading partners which are performing well are likely to interact intensively. Thus, unlike in the previous investment perspective, the cost of interaction, if imputed by time spent by all the multifunctional personnel involved in interfacing between suppliers and customers, may be quite high. Trust is therefore like a renewable resource which atrophies with disuse and multiplies with use.

1.4 Survey Evidence

The main reason for the relative absence of empirical work to date lies in the characteristics of the relevant theories. In particular, the functionalist approach of TCE asserts that whatever governance structure exists is best for the organization given its environment and circumstances. This has led many researchers to test the determinants of governance structures but not the performance outcomes of these structures. Moreover, all the aforementioned three approaches to linking trust to performance put forward measures which are difficult to quantify, such as transaction costs, net benefit of investment in trust, learning, and innovation. Ideally, also, longitudinal, rather than cross-sectional, studies are necessary in order to unravel the direction of causation between trust building and performance. The survey evidence presented in this chapter does not fully overcome the measurement nor the causation problems, but constitutes an attempt at addressing the question of whether trust enhances performance.

The data used to explore the links between trust and performance were collected by the author and Susan Helper during 1993 and 1994. For details on questionnaire design, the sampling framework, and response rates, see Appendix A. The data consist of 1,415 valid responses from first-tier component suppliers in the automotive industry in Japan, the USA, and Europe.

The survey asked respondents to evaluate how much trust they could place on their customer. The items used to measure trust and opportunism in the questionnaire are shown in Table 3.1. Specifically, the concept of

TABLE 3.1. Trust and opportunism in Japan, the USA, and Europe

	Japan (N = 472)	USA (N = 671)	Britain (N = 123)	Germany (N = 51)	Latin Catholic Europe (N = 52)
Contractual trust (We prefer to have everything spelt out in detail in our contract)	24.03	16.62	15.25	27.45	14.00
Competence trust (The advice our customer gives us is not always helpful)	48.37	31.25	35.51	28.57	39.58
Goodwill trust (We can rely on our customer to help us in ways not required by our agreement with them)	38.81	37.24	42.50	50.00	64.00
Fairness (We can depend on our customer always to treat us fairly)	67.88	42.41	40.00	54.00	54.90
Customer oppportunism (Given the chance, our customer might try to take unfair advantage of our business unit)	23.94	55.85	32.50	26.00	26.00

Note: The figures show the percentages responding 4 or 5 on a five-point scale (5 = strongly agree; 4 = agree; 3 = neither agree nor disagree; 2 = disagree; 1 = strongly disagree). The statements for Contractual trust and Competence trust are reversed, so the figures are the percentages responding 1 or 2.

'contractual trust' is operationalized by the reversed statement 'We prefer to have everything spelt out in detail in our contract'; this preference for detailed formal contracts is presumed to arise from the supplier's distrust that the customer would not stick to promises unless formally spelt out in a contract. The concept of 'competence trust' is captured by a reversed statement 'The advice our customer gives us is not always helpful'. 'Goodwill trust' is operationalized by the statement 'We can rely on our customer to help us in ways not required by our agreement with them'. The survey also asked about suppliers' perception of fairness which is a basis for the sustenance of goodwill trust. Lastly, customer opportunism was captured by the statement 'Given the chance, our customer might try to take unfair advantage of our business unit'.

In order to examine intercountry differences in trust, the data were divided into the following locations of the responding supplier companies: Japan, the USA, Britain, Germany, and the Latin Catholic countries in Europe (namely Italy, France, and Spain). The sample size for the European countries is quite small and the results must be interpreted with caution. But Britain was separated out to examine the supposed similarities with the USA. Germany and the Latin Catholic countries were distinguished in order to examine whether there is any evidence of a contrast between the 'spontaneously sociable' and the 'missing middle' countries identified by Fukuyama (1995). The survey asked about interorganizational trust (suppliers' trust of customers). Therefore, we would expect organizational trust in Germany to be higher than in Latin Catholic countries where high interpersonal trust does not extend to trust between organizations.

As shown in Table 3.1, 'contractual trust' is the highest in Germany and Japan, while the suppliers in the Anglo-American and Latin Catholic countries prefer less contractual flexibility. Japanese suppliers exhibit the highest level of 'competence trust' towards their customer companies, while results for the other countries are mixed, with Latin Catholic suppliers exhibiting a rather high level of 'competence trust' in contrast to German suppliers. 'Goodwill trust' as measured in the survey is the highest among the Latin Catholic and German suppliers. The expectations about fair customer behaviour are most evident among the Japanese suppliers, followed by the German and Latin Catholic suppliers, while the majority of Anglo-American suppliers do not expect fair treatment from their customers. Lastly, customer opportunism is more prevalent in the USA and Britain than in Japan, Germany, or the Latin European countries. Although the results are broadly as expected, the anticipated distinction between Germany and the Latin Catholic countries is not evident in the survey.

Next, the impact of suppliers' trust of customers on supplier performance can be examined by looking at the following measures of performance used in the survey: suppliers' costs, profit margins, just-in-time (JIT) delivery, and joint problem solving. The cost measure is in terms of the average annual percentage change in the supplier's total costs for the product it supplied to the customer during the year preceding the survey. The profit measure was in terms of the average annual percentage point change in the supplier's gross margins for the product in the year preceding the survey. The degree of success in implementing JIT was measured by agreement to the statement 'Use of JIT has allowed our business unit to increase delivery frequency without increasing costs'. Joint problem solving, as an indicator of learning and innovation, was measured by the percentage of contact hours the supplier had with the customer which was for the purpose of 'joint efforts to improve the product or process' (other options included 'assigning blame rather than solving problems').

Different types of trust may be presumed to have different impacts on supplier performance. Therefore each type of trust listed in Table 3.1 was correlated with each of the performance measures. The suppliers were divided into high-trust and low-trust groups, with the former

consisting of those who agreed or strongly agreed with each of the statements. The t-test and Kruskal–Wallis test were applied to examine whether
suppliers' performance was significantly different between the high-trust
and low-trust groups. The five-way locational classification (into Japan,
USA, Britain, Germany, and Latin Catholic countries) is applied in this
analysis also.

The only type of trust with which the first measure of supplier performance, cost reduction, is associated significantly is goodwill trust. Moreover,
when each region is examined separately, it is only in Japan that the high-
trust group of suppliers performs significantly better in this respect than the
low-trust group (see Figure 3.1). Although not statistically significant, high
goodwill trust is associated with *less* cost reduction in Germany and the
Latin Catholic countries. The scope for reducing costs may be considered to
depend in part on the starting-cost level; that is, the higher the initial cost,
the greater the scope for cost reduction, and the lower the initial cost, the
more difficult it is to effect further cost reduction at the margin. This
argument makes it doubly surprising that Japanese suppliers in the high-
trust group, which have been engaging in cost reduction activities for much
longer than their counterparts in the USA or Europe, are the ones which
have distinguished themselves in reducing costs further.

With respect to changes in suppliers' profit margins, interestingly it is
only in the USA that all the five measures of trust (including the reverse of
opportunism) listed in Table 3.1 are significantly associated with better
profit margins (in the form of less profit squeeze). In none of the other
countries is the profit performance between high-trust and low-trust groups
significantly different (see Figure 3.2 which shows the result for goodwill
trust only).

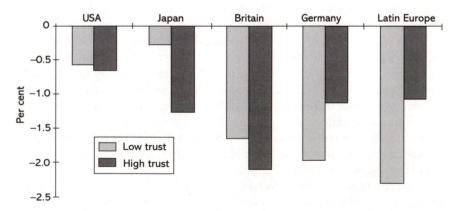

FIG. 3.1. High-trust suppliers controlled costs better in Japan: average annual cost
changes 1991/2–1992/3

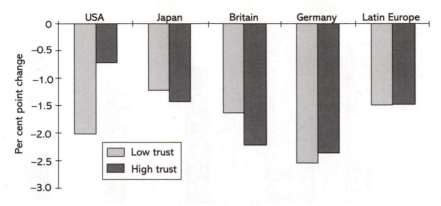

FIG. 3.2. High-trust suppliers defended their profit margins better in the USA: average annual percentage point change 1993/4

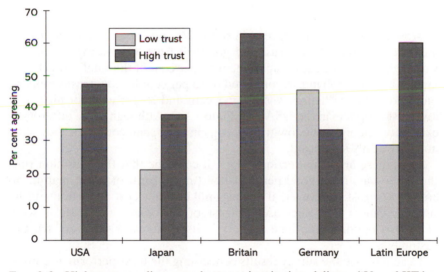

FIG. 3.3. High-trust suppliers were better at just-in-time delivery ('Use of JIT has allowed our business unit to increase delivery frequency without increasing costs')

Next, high trust of all types was associated with suppliers being able to increase the frequency of delivery without increasing costs in the US and Japan. However, in Europe only high goodwill trust significantly enhances JIT delivery in Britain and the Latin European countries (see Figure 3.3 for results on goodwill trust).

Lastly, high-trust suppliers were significantly more likely to spend a greater proportion of their contact time with customers in 'joint efforts to

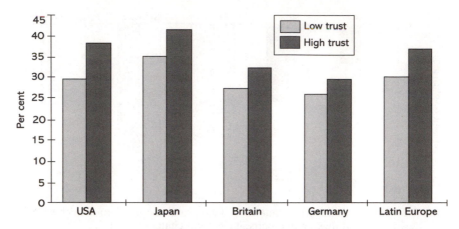

FIG. 3.4. High-trust suppliers are better at joint continuous improvement: average percentage of time spent on 'joint efforts to improve the product or process'

improve the product or process' in the USA and Japan, according to the measures of competence trust and goodwill trust. On average, suppliers with high goodwill trust in Japan spent 43 per cent of the total contact time in joint problem solving, as compared to 35 per cent for low-trust suppliers; the corresponding figures were 38 per cent and 30 per cent for high- and low-trust suppliers in the USA (see Figure 3.4). Although some differences exist between high- and low-trust groups in European countries, they were not statistically significant.

Since these are cross-sectional data, it could be that the causation runs the other way, from good performance (in the form of profit margin increase) to trust. However, it seems unlikely that cost reduction by the supplier causes it to increase its trust of customers, nor does it seem likely that better just-in-time delivery in itself increases suppliers' trust of customers.

To summarize the survey results concerning the trust-performance links, there is some support for the hypothesis that trust is conducive to good supplier performance and that this positive link is stronger for goodwill than for other types of trust. As predicted, suppliers spend more of their time in joint problem solving with their customers, the higher the level of goodwill and competence trust placed upon them. However, differences in the nature of the links between specific types of trust and specific performance measures are not fully explainable. In particular, the impact of goodwill trust on cost reduction is seen only among Japanese suppliers, while profit conditions are better for the high-trust group than for the low-trust group in the USA only.

2. HOW CAN TRUST BE CREATED?

Having obtained some evidence that trust in supplier relations is associated with good supplier performance, we will now turn to the question of how trust may be created. More often than not, this question in practice is asked by managers who face low-trust adversarial customer–supplier relationships. They are in a vicious circle of 'low-trust dynamics' (Fox 1973), in which low trust generates less open communication (leading to misunderstandings) and tighter control to eliminate any scope for discretion, which in turn reinforces the low-trust attitude. The mutually reinforcing nature of low trust between a customer and a supplier makes both parties reluctant to take the first courageous step to break the vicious circle. Breaking the vicious circle is all the more difficult because a trusting first step—e.g. in the form of disclosing confidential information—increases one's vulnerability to the other's opportunistic behaviour.

A number of prescriptions have been offered to break out of the low-trust dynamics in bilateral relationships. The following three sets of approaches are suggested in the existing literature: legalistic remedies including the use of formal contracts, a rational calculative approach, and gift exchange. This section discusses the three approaches, then reviews the relevant institutional environment of bilateral business relationships which is considered to affect the creation and maintenance of trust. The validity of these factors is tested using the survey data.

2.1 Favourable and Adversarial Effects of Legalistic Remedies

Some organizations use legalistic measures to attempt to restore trust. But it has been suggested that such legalistic 'remedies', including formalizing contracts and rules, work for a certain dimension of trust only, namely task reliability (Sitkin and Roth 1993) or competence trust. According to Sitkin and Roth, legal procedures may be used to substitute for interpersonal trust which may not be available in organizations due to the absence of a history of face-to-face contact. Then, legal remedies can be used to guard against bad contingencies which would undermine trust relationships. A greater formalization of rules and procedures can restore competence trust effectively by fostering co-ordination when past violations, in the form of underperformance, are specific to a particular context or task.

At the same time, Sitkin and Roth (1993) argue that legalistic remedies cannot cure another category of distrust which stems from the absence of a shared set of values between the parties, due for instance to a violation of goodwill trust. In their view, legalistic remedies cannot promote value congruence because the formulation of rules and regulations would only exacerbate the problem of distrust, by maintaining the distance between the parties involved, and by increasing the suspicion that rules are imposed in order to reduce the degree of discretion available to each party. So we may hypothesize that:

> H1: Written contracts attenuate customer opportunism and enhance competence trust, but undermine the creation of goodwill trust.

2.2 History of Long-term Trading and Rational Calculation

To the extent that trust is built by demonstrating trustworthiness over time, the historical duration and experience of a relationship is said to matter greatly (Sabel 1992). For instance, Zucker (1986) argues that 'process-based trust' arises from long-term relationships which have proven to be stable over time. On this basis, some studies (e.g. Gulati 1995) use the duration of trading as a proxy for the level of trust in business relationships. Thus:

> H2A: The longer the duration of past trading, the higher is the supplier's trust of its customer.

Expectations of continued trading into the future may be induced by past association. But past association is one of the several ways in which long-term commitment may be made credible (see the next subsection). For those who place importance on the rational calculative basis for creating co-operation, what matters more than the record of long-term trading is the expectation of long-term commitment into the future, what Axelrod calls 'enlarging the shadow of the future' (Axelrod 1984; Heide and John 1990).

> H2B: The longer the informal commitment made by the customer to continue trading with the supplier, the higher is the supplier's trust for its customer.

2.3 Gift Exchange and Credible Commitments

But how can the customer firm create an expectation of informal long-term commitment among its suppliers? One mechanism for creating informal commitment is for the customer to provide technical assistance to a supplier. The customer would receive no return on its investment in training if it fires the supplier. To the extent that the customer demonstrates knowledge and skills by providing technical assistance, it enhances suppliers' competence trust of the customer. Over time, particularly if technical assistance is not fully paid for, suppliers would interpret it as an initiation of 'gift exchange' (Akerlof 1982; Mauss 1966), and it may become a basis for goodwill trust (Sako 1992). In a gift exchange, a long drawn out imbalance of 'favours' done and returned sustains the relationship of interdependence. Thus, we may hypothesize that:

H3A: Technical assistance by customers enhances suppliers' goodwill and competence trust in customers.

Can technical assistance be also a form of credible commitment which attenuates oppportunism (Williamson 1985)? In order to test for the difference between credible commitment and gift exchange, the following procedure is adopted in this paper. 'Gift exchange' is based on loose reciprocity over time. The purpose of this loose reciprocity is to indebt the other party into doing favours in the future. By contrast, in making credible commitments, both parties give out hostages simultaneously so as to signal to the other party that they are committed because defection is too costly. We interpret the simultaneous provision of suppliers' technical assistance to customers and customers' technical assistance to suppliers as more akin to credible commitment than unilateral assistance. Therefore:

H3B: Bilateral technical assistance between customers and suppliers reduces customer opportunism.

Another area in which reciprocity may matter is information exchange. Sharing of information facilitates co-ordination between organizations. But disclosing proprietary or confidential information to the other party exposes one's vulnerability. In this situation, a two-way flow of information reduces information asymmetry, and thus reduces any scope for opportunistic behaviour (Williamson 1975). However, in order for a customer to develop suppliers' trust in the customer, it must engage in gift exchange, namely the disclosure of its information regardless of whether suppliers also disclose their information at the same time. This mechanism is essential to creating and sustaining trust, which feeds on a loose form of reciprocity over time.

H4A: The more suppliers' disclosure of information to their customer is matched by the customer's provision of information to suppliers, the lower the supplier's perception of customer opportunism.

H4B: The more customers provide information to their suppliers, the higher the level of suppliers' trust in customers.

2.4 Embeddedness

Trust between trading partners may vary not only with the attributes of bilateral transactions but also with the trading environment in which they are a part. Here, societal culture, politics, regulation, professionalization, and national institutions are said to be a relevant set of attributes in which a bilateral relationship may be embedded (Granovetter 1985). This embeddedness approach has led some authors to examine a very broadly defined institutional environment of business relationships, including the industrial environment, the financial system, the national legal tradition and system, and the systems of industrial relations and skill formation (e.g. Lane and Bachmann 1996). It is beyond the scope of this chapter to review all these factors for all the countries which are covered in the surveys. This subsection focuses, instead, on two aspects of what is meant by embeddedness, namely the importance of path-dependent evolution of societal norms, and the role of intermediate associational networks in moderating competition with co-operation.

In the first sense of embeddedness, Dore (1983) and Sako (1992) provide evidence that Japanese companies are more predisposed to trusting their trading partners than British companies. This is interpreted to be in part due to prevailing business norms, which are determined by societal-level cultural values. Societal norms may be self-reinforcing. Over time, a history of good experience with trusting behaviour in Japan may have promoted the diffusion of trust. In fact, cultural norms such as trust can be 'the precipitate of history' (Dore 1987: 91). For instance, Japanese suppliers in the automotive industry may trust their customers more today because they have had more customer commitment, more technical assistance, etc. over a much longer period of time than most US suppliers, and their trusting behaviour has been honoured by being given growing orders. In contrast, a typical (though more eloquent) US supplier executive asserted that their customer 'would steal a dime from a starving grandmother' (Helper 1991). Attempts by US or European companies to imitate the Japanese business norm are costly and difficult because the way in which a network of customer–supplier relations developed in Japan is path-dependent.

In the second sense of embeddedness, Fukuyama (1995) argues convincingly that the density of associational networks at intermediate levels between the State and individual firms accounts for the prevalence of institutionalized trust in certain societies such as Japan and Germany. For example, Smitka (1991) argues that 'governance by trust' is more prevalent in the Japanese than in the US automobile industry due to, among other things, the existence of suppliers' associations (*kyoryokukai*) in Japan and their absence in the USA. These are voluntary associations which enhance lateral communication among suppliers, and therefore act as an extra bulwark against customer opportunism (Sako 1996). In Germany, national and regionally based industry associations offer a forum for the exchange of information and the development of common norms and standards, thus creating a favourable environment for the creation and maintenance of trust between firms (Lane and Bachmann 1996). In contrast, trade associations in the US and Britain are relatively weak in their associability and governability (Traxler 1995). While networks of small firms exist in certain parts of the Latin Catholic countries in Europe, they must rely on trust based on common family background, religion, or ethnicity, rather than on institutionally based trust. This, it is argued by Fukuyama (1995), is due to the relative absence of intermediate associations at the level between the family and the State.

It is expected that there are factors common to all countries which contribute towards creating and maintaining trust between firms. However, because of the above reasons, country-specific institutions, and national history gives rise to a unique level of trust in each country.

3. SURVEY EVIDENCE AND DISCUSSION

Using the aforementioned datasets, the four sets of hypotheses elaborated above were tested using the ordered probit regression technique. Four measures were chosen as the dependent variables. Customer Opportunism is measured by the statement 'Given the chance, our customer might try to take unfair advantage of our business unit'. Competence Distrust is measured by 'The advice our customer gives us is not always helpful'. Goodwill Trust is measured by 'We can rely on our customer to help us in ways not required by our agreement with them'. Lastly, Fairness, reflecting a shared principle of fairness between the customer and the supplier which is a basis for goodwill trust, is measured by 'We can depend on our customer always to treat us fairly'. Since all the four scales are ordinal, a response of 4 implies greater agreement than a response of 2, but does not imply twice as much agreement. Thus, the ordered probit regression technique is used. The independent variables are explained in detail in Appendix B. As the

TABLE 3.2. Ordered probit estimation of determinants of trust and opportunism

Independent variables	Contractual Distrust	Competence Distrust	Goodwill Trust	Fairness	Customer Opportunism
CONTRACT	0.088[c]	−0.000	−0.002	−0.001	−0.001
TRADING	0.000	−0.002	−0.002	−0.004	0.004
COMMIT	−0.001	−0.003[c]	0.004[a]	0.004[b]	−0.005[a]
TECHG	−0.003	−0.087[a]	0.064[a]	0.011	−0.003
TECHDIF	0.001	0.001	−0.003[d]	−0.007[a]	0.004[b]
CUSTINFO	0.020	−0.121[b]	0.222[a]	0.188[a]	−0.182[a]
INFODIF	0.029	0.028	0.001	−0.041[c]	0.047[b]
USA	0.563[a]	0.640[a]	−0.210[b]	−0.866[a]	0.758[a]
UK	0.297[d]	0.330[b]	0.034	−0.485[a]	0.671[a]
GERMANY	0.102	0.562[b]	0.089	−0.345[c]	0.619[a]
LATIN	0.475[b]	0.346[c]	0.417[b]	−0.157	0.552[a]
Log Likelihood	−1627.5815	−1660.8079	−1593.8821	−1600.5942	−1836.0586
Pseudo R^2	0.025	0.037	0.025	0.066	0.059
N	1137	1118	1144	1144	1143

[a] $p < 0.001$.
[b] $p < 0.01$.
[c] $p < 0.05$.
[d] $p < 0.10$.

correlation matrices in the appendix show, there is no problem with multicollinearity.

First, the datasets are combined to test the hypotheses, while controlling for country differences by dummy variables. In doing so, we focus our analysis on the question of whether determinants are different for different types of trust and opportunism. Next, dummies for the USA, Britain, Germany, and the Latin Catholic countries in Europe are analysed separately to test the embeddedness hypothesis. Lastly, as is evident in the term 'low-trust dynamics' or 'high-trust dynamics', the analysis will focus on the possibility of mutual and reverse causation between trust and the main independent variables.

3.1 Determinants of Trust and Opportunism

As shown in Table 3.2, each set of hypotheses is supported to a varying degree.

The first hypothesis, H1, that written contracts (CONTRACT) attenuate customer oppportunism and enhance competence trust but reduce goodwill trust, is not supported. It appears that when other mechanisms are present, contract duration in itself fails to be a sufficient enhancer of competence trust or a safeguard to attenuate opportunism.

As hypothesized in H2B, informal commitment (COMMIT) made by the customer enhances all types of trust and reduces customer opportunism. However, contrary to H2A, the length of trading does not have a significant impact on trust. Thus, long-term trading in itself is not sufficient to bring about trust in relationships.

As expected, in accordance with H3A, technical assistance by customers (TECHG) enhances goodwill trust and competence trust but does not have a significant impact on opportunism. H3B is also supported. It was hypothesized that due to credible commitments, a smaller gap between suppliers' technical assistance and customers' technical assistance (TECHDIF) would attenuate customer opportunism, and this is the case. At the same time, a greater gap in bilateral technical assistance reduces goodwill trust significantly and also undermines the notion of fair treatment which is a prerequisite for goodwill trust.

The hypotheses H4A and H4B on information sharing are both supported. In particular, the gap between suppliers' provision of information to customers and customers' disclosure of information to suppliers (INFODIF) increases customer opportunism. Moreover, the customer's provision of information (CUSTINFO) in itself has an independent significant effect of enhancing trust and reducing opportunism.

To summarize, the main determinants of goodwill trust are informal customer commitment, customers' technical assistance and customers' provision of information. The same three factors are significant determinants of competence trust. By contrast, the main determinants of customer opportunism include the information asymmetry between the customer and the supplier, and informal customer commitment. Earlier, it was hypothesized that 'gift exchange' enhances trust but does not attenuate opportunism, while 'credible commitments' attenuate opportunism but do not enhance trust. The survey data provide some suppport for this. In particular, customers' technical assistance enhances trust but does not attenuate opportunism. It is the customers' provision of information, regardless of whether suppliers provide information to customers or not, which matters for enhancing trust, while two-way information sharing (which can be interpreted to be credible commitment) is what matters for attenuating opportunism.

3.2 Country Differences: a Test of Embeddedness

In order to examine differences in the levels of trust and opportunism among countries, dummy variables were created for suppliers located in the USA, Britain, Germany, and the Latin Catholic countries respectively, using those in Japan as the baseline reference group. These dummies capture the embedded national-specific cultural norms and institutions, after taking account of the factors affecting trust and opportunism, which are common to all suppliers regardless of their country location.

As one might expect, the level of customer opportunism anticipated by suppliers was higher in the USA, the UK, and the continental European countries than in Japan (see Table 3.2). The level of competence trust was also lower in these three regions than in Japan. For goodwill trust, the level was significantly lower in the USA than in Japan as expected, but surprisingly, significantly higher in the Latin Catholic countries than in Japan. The German suppliers' goodwill trust was not significantly different from that of Japanese suppliers. Lastly, suppliers' perception of fair treatment by customers was lower in the USA, Britain, and Germany as compared to in Japan, but not significantly different between the Latin countries and Japan. These results largely confirm the impressionistic picture given in Table 3.1, but give a much better indication of the country-specific contribution to raising or undermining different types of trust after controlling for universal factors.

3.3 Trust Dynamics and Written Contracts

In order to test for causality, one would ideally require a longitudinal study. As a second best, the survey asked suppliers about the situation now and four years ago in some of the questions, which enables us to conduct cross-lagged tests. The rest of this paper examines the causation between trust and contract duration. The only measure of trust for 'now' and '4 years ago' was the one concerning fair treatment ('We can depend on our customer to treat us fairly'). Therefore, this subsection uses this measure of trust only.

In the analysis above, written contracts were found not to have any significant impact on opportunism or trust. One of the reasons for this may be that when other mechanisms are present, contracts in themselves fail to be a sufficient enhancer of trust or a safeguard to attenuate opportunism. Another possibility is that besides the formal contract duration, other dimensions (such as the actual content of the contract) may matter in affecting opportunism and trust.

Another added complication is that the implicit contract duration may be different from the explicitly agreed contract duration. For example, according to the survey, in Europe, contracts have lengthened from a median of 1 year in 1990 to 3 years in 1994. In the USA also, the median contract duration has increased, though less dramatically, from 1 year in 1989 to 1.5 years in 1993. However, these figures conceal a sharp decrease in contract duration reported by suppliers to one vehicle manufacturer in the USA. In Japan, contracts between companies typically do not contain specific information about the type of products to be supplied. The practice of general framework contracts (without product-specific contracts) prevailed for two-thirds of the respondents in both 1989 and 1993. Where there were contracts, the implicit contract in Japan tended to be longer than the basic contract which was renewed annually. Therefore, contract duration alone does not truly reflect differences in customer commitment particularly in Japan.

In spite of the above caveat, the survey data make it possible to examine what were the causes and effects of longer-duration contracts at least in the USA and Europe. In order to test whether changes in the level of trust is causing changes in contract duration or vice versa, cross-lagged tests were applied to each regional dataset. As can be seen in Table 3.3, the coefficients in both regressions are negative and significant in the USA, implying that a low level of trust has led customers to offer longer-term contracts, which in turn have led to lower levels of trust. In general, lengthening the duration of the contract has not had the intended effect of restoring trust in the USA. Thus, some US automotive supplier relations appear to be suffering from a low-trust dynamics, and the reason may be the inability of legal 'remedies' to bring about goal congruence when the existing relationships are adversarial (Sitkin and Roth 1993).

In Europe overall, the impact of contract duration on trust is positive and significant in countries other than the UK. Thus in the main countries of Germany, France, Italy, and Spain, it appears that automotive customers have been able to enhance suppliers' trust by offering longer-term contracts. When the Latin Catholic countries are separated out from Germany, the positive impact of contract duration on trust is found to be significant

TABLE 3.3. Cross-lagged tests of the link between contract lengths and trust

	Japan	USA	Britain	Germany	Latin Catholic Europe
Dependent variable: TRUST NOW					
Independent variable: CONTRACT 4 YEARS AGO	−0.035	−0.087[d]	0.028	−0.142	0.273[c]
Adjusted R^2	−0.001	0.005	−0.008	−0.0001	0.056
N	441	457	121	51	51
Dependent variable: CONTRACT NOW					
Independent variable: TRUST 4 YEARS AGO	0.0395	−0.084[d]	−0.027	−0.016	0.094
Adjusted R^2	−0.0007	0.005	−0.008	−0.022	−0.013
N	441	473	123	47	47

[a] $p < 0.001$.
[b] $p < 0.01$.
[c] $p < 0.05$.
[d] $p < 0.10$.

among suppliers in the former only. The German result is not what we expected, but the Latin Catholic countries are seen to share the same civil law tradition with Germany (Arrighetti, Bachmann, and Deakin 1996). In the UK, as in Japan, there has been little change in contract duration, and what little changes there were have had no significant impact on the level of trust among suppliers. This finding, if we contrast the UK with continental Europe, is not inconsistent with Lane and Bachmann's conclusion that (a) adhering to contractual conditions was invariably rated more highly as a trust-creating behaviour in Germany than in Britain, and (b) contracts were used in a more varied and adversarial manner in Britain than in Germany (Lane and Bachmann 1996: 385).

To summarize, the empirical evidence presented in this section shows that the determinants of trust are different from the opposite of the determinants of opportunism. The former are such things as technical assistance and customer provision of information to suppliers regardless of whether the suppliers reciprocate or not; these mechanisms were called 'gift exchange'. The latter include 'safeguards' in terms of credible commitments. After taking account of these universal factors, the levels of suppliers' trust and expectations of customer opportunism were found to be significantly different according to their country location. These differences were interpreted to be due to the embeddedness of business relationships in country-specific institutions and history. The impact of one specific institution, the legal framework, was also examined. There is some evidence that the vicious circle of low-trust dynamics (with longer contracts leading to higher distrust which in turn has led to even longer contracts) developed in the US auto industry in the recent past. But for the Latin Catholic countries, the lengthening of the formal contract appears to have contributed towards enhancing trust. Thus, contract lengths have had different effects on trust creation in different countries.

4. CONCLUSIONS

This chapter conceptualized interorganizational trust into 'contractual trust', 'competence trust', or 'goodwill trust', according to the sources of predictability in mutually acceptable behaviour. The distinction among the three types of trust has proven to be useful particularly in thinking about the outcomes of trust.

In linking trust to business performance, it was argued that there should be a move away from the framework of minimizing transaction costs towards one with a focus on learning and innovation (see also Goshal and Moran 1996). The main hypothesis was that among the three types of trust, 'goodwill trust' would have the strongest impact on performance. This is because the extra edge which 'goodwill trust' offers over and above the formal governance structures of contracts or hierarchies is learning and continuous improvement, not merely in making savings in transaction costs. The survey of first-tier automotive suppliers provides evidence that trust is associated with supplier performance particularly in just-in-time delivery and continuous improvement.

In relation to the creation of trust, this paper recommends a move away from a framework which focuses on safeguards against the abuse of trust towards thinking about enhancers of trust. The latter are like 'gift exchange' based on loose reciprocity over time. According to the survey evidence, the trust enhancers may take the form of customers' technical assistance to suppliers, which does not function as a safeguard against opportunism. One effective safeguard is information sharing (i.e. two-way flow of information), while the unilateral provision of information by customers, regardless of whether suppliers reciprocated simultaneously or not, was found to enhance trust. Other safeguards, such as legal contracts, were found to have differential effects in different countries, with the USA experiencing a low-trust dynamics and the Latin European countries experiencing a positive impact of longer contracts on enhancing trust.

The distinction between 'safeguards' and 'enhancers' of trust roughly corresponds to the difficulty in reconciling the two views on trust alluded to at the beginning of this chapter, namely one regarding trust as an outcome derived from rational calculation and the other equating it with a value traced to culture or social norms. However, 'safeguards' are rarely fool-proof in business, precisely because trust is more than promise keeping, and contracts are always necessarily open-ended. Thus, while law in certain countries may help jump-start trust relations in business, in the end 'good-will trust' has to be found not by resort to law but through learning-by-interacting to fill in the gap left by incomplete contracts. At the same time, gift exchange as an enhancer of trust, in the form of technical assistance for example, may depend on a social norm of loose reciprocity, but in business, there is no such thing as blind faith. The process of gift exchange may be started, and can only be sustained, by intense communication and monitoring of each other's behaviour to find opportunities for continuous improvement, but these are quite different from 'safeguards'.

Appendix A: Questionnaire Development and Data Collection

Data were collected by the author and Professor Susan Helper during 1993 and 1994 from 675 first-tier automotive component suppliers in the USA, 472 first-tier suppliers in Japan, and 268 suppliers in Europe, according to the following procedure.

QUESTIONNAIRE DESIGN

A questionnaire was developed in English and Japanese, in order to enquire into a broad range of questions concerning the nature of suppliers' relationship with their customers, the vehicle manufacturers. Because many companies supply their customers with several different types of products, and their relationships with their customers differ by product, we made a decision to ask respondents to answer the questionnaire for their most important customer regarding one product which was typical of their company's output and with which they were familiar.

Many of the questions were taken from an earlier survey undertaken by Helper in North America in 1989 (Helper 1991) and a short questionnaire on trust and opportunism administered by Sako in the electronics industry in Japan and Britain in 1988–9 (Sako 1992). In particular, the measures of trust and opportunism were developed by surveying the academic literature in economics and psychology (e.g. Anderson 1988; Cook *et al.* 1981). We took the view more common in psychology than in economics that creating composite measures of trust and opportunism would reduce measurement error, as compared to using a single measure. Thus, the questionnaire adopted a number of scales, each reflecting different types of trust and opportunism.

PILOTING THE QUESTIONNAIRE

Next, the draft questionnaire was sequentially piloted at a handful of supplier companies in both the USA and Japan during 1992. As a result, improvements were made to the clarity of questions and the ease of answering them. Much attention was paid to the phrasing of questions in a vocabulary familiar to managers, and to the consistency of meaning in the English and Japanese languages. For instance we asked several people to translate some questions from English to Japanese and others to translate them back from Japanese into English. The process of piloting and revision took around nine months. In 1993, the English language survey was used as a basis for piloting the survey in Europe. As a result, modifications were made to adapt some industry terminology to the European convention. A decision was made to administer the European survey in English.

SAMPLING FRAMEWORK

The sample chosen for the North American questionnaire was every automotive supplier and automaker component division named in the *Elm Guide to Automotive Sourcing* (available from Elm, Inc. in East Lansing, Michigan). This guide lists the major first-tier suppliers (both domestic and foreign-owned) to manufacturers of cars and light trucks in the United States and Canada.

In Japan, the sample consisted of all members of the Japan Auto Parts Industries Association (JAPIA), all automotive suppliers named in *Nihon no Jidosha Buhin Kogyo 1992/1993* (Japanese Automotive Parts Industry) (published by Auto Trade Journal Co. Inc. and JAPIA, Tokyo, 1992), and the component divisions of vehicle manufacturers. This publication lists all the first-tier suppliers (both domestic and foreign-owned) to the eleven manufacturers of cars and trucks in Japan.

The target respondent in the USA was the divisional director of sales and marketing, and the divisional business manager or director of strategic planning in the case of components divisions of vehicle manufacturers. Since they commonly take a lead in interfacing with customers, they were deemed the most knowledgeable informants about customers' procurement practices. Similarly in Japan, the questionnaire was sent to the Director of Sales and Marketing at independent firms. For member companies of JAPIA, the survey was sent to the main contacts named by JAPIA, many of whom were either chief executives or marketing directors. JAMA (Japan Auto Manufacturers Association) took responsibility to identify the respondents for auto-maker components divisions.

In spring 1994, the European survey was sent out to around 1,600 major automotive suppliers located in Western Europe. This sample was compiled from several sources including trade associations and the major vehicle manufacturers in Europe. The target respondent was the director of sales and marketing at each firm. These individuals were selected on the grounds that they would have the broadest knowledge about both customer relationships and about their firms' products and processes.

RESPONSE RATES

The questionnaires were sent out in spring 1993 in the USA, summer 1993 in Japan, and spring 1994 in Europe. The responses were far above the norm for business surveys. They were 55 per cent in North America, 30 per cent in Japan (45 per cent among JAPIA members), and 17 per cent in Europe (26 per cent among UK-based suppliers) after taking into account those firms which were unreachable (mail sent to them was returned undelivered), and those which were not eligible to answer the survey (they were not first-tier automotive suppliers, or they specialized in supplying for heavy truck and buses). In Europe, 45 per cent of responses were from UK-based suppliers, thus making the sample more biased towards UK-based suppliers than the population of European suppliers.

The respondents had a wealth of experience, and were thus the single individual able to answer all of our questions for the customer/product pair they chose. US respondents averaged more than eighteen years in the automobile industry and more than eleven years with their company. Japanese respondents had worked for twenty-two years on average at their company. The European respondents averaged sixteen years in the automotive industry, and 8 years with their company.

Appendix B: Explanations of Independent Variables

This appendix provides the survey questions and explains any manipulation made subsequently to create each independent variable.

VARIABLES

CONTRACT — What is the length of your written contract or purchase order with this customer for this product? (in years)

TRADING — Approximately how long has your firm sold products in this product line to this customer?
1 year 2 years 3 years 4 years 5–10 years 11–19 years 20–40 years 41–60 years over 60 years
The mid-point of each interval was used; thus the variable takes the value of 1, 2, 3, 4, 7.5, 15, 30, 50.5, or 75.

COMMIT — For how long do you think there is a high probability that your business unit will be supplying this or similar item to your customer? (in years)

SUPINFO — What types of information does your business unit provide to your customer about the process you use to make the product you listed above? (Please check all that apply.)

- Detailed breakdown of process steps
- Cost of each process step
- Financial information not publicly available
- Production scheduling information
- Type of equipment used
- Your sources of supply
- Detailed information regarding materials you use.

The seven information items were given one point each if checked, and were added.

CUSTINFO — Does your customer provide you with any of the following types of information? (Please check all that apply.)

- Warranty or other data from final consumers
- Financial information not publicly available
- Information on how your product is used in their process.

The information items were given one point each if checked, and added.

INFODIF | SUPINFO *minus* CUSTINFO

TECHG | Over the last four years, what sorts of technical assistance have you received from your customer? (Please check all that apply, and indicate whether 'provided for zero or nominal charge' or 'provided for a fee'.)

- Provided personnel who visited supplier site to aid in implementing improved procedures
- Arranged for training of your personnel at their site
- Provided personnel who worked two weeks or more on your shopfloor to improve your process.

Given a weight of 2 if 'provided for zero or nominal charge' and a weight of 1 if 'provided for a fee', and summed over the three items.

TECHDIF | Approximately what percentage of the contacts with your customer regarding this product were for the following purposes?

Percentage for 'your business unit providing technical assistance to customer' minus percentage for 'customer providing technical assistance to your business unit'.

USA | *A dummy with 1 for US responses, 0 otherwise.*

UK | *A dummy with 1 for UK responses, 0 otherwise.*

GERMANY | *A dummy with 1 for German responses, 0 otherwise.*

LATIN | *A dummy with 1 for responses from France, Italy, or Spain, 0 otherwise.*

REFERENCES

Akerlof, G. A. (1982), 'Labour Contracts as Partial Gift Exchange', *Quarterly Journal of Economics*, 97: 542–6.

Anderson, E. (1988), 'Transaction Costs as Determinants of Opportunism in Integrated and Independent Sales Forces', *Journal of Economic Behavior and Organization*, 9: 247–64.

——and Weitz, B. (1989), 'Determinants of Continuity in Conventional Industrial Channel Dyads', *Marketing Science*, 8: 310–23.

Arrighetti, A., Bachmann, R., and Deakin, S. (1996), 'Contact Law, Social Norms and Inter-firm Cooperation', Working Paper no. 36, ESRC Centre for Business Research, University of Cambridge.

Arrow, K. J. (1975), 'Gifts and Exchanges', in E. S. Phelps (ed.), *Altruism, Morality and Economic Theory*. New York: Russell Sage Foundation.

Asanuma, B. (1989), 'Manufacturer–Supplier Relationships in Japan and the Concept of Relation-Specific Skills', *Journal of the Japanese and International Economies*, 3: 1–30.

Axelrod, R. (1984), *Evolution of Cooperation*. New York: Basic Books.

Barney, J. B. and Hansen, M. H. (1994), 'Trustworthiness as a Source of Competitive Advantage', *Strategic Management Journal*, 7: 175–90.

Bradach, J. L. and Eccles, R. G. (1989), 'Price, Authority and Trust: From Ideal Types to Plural Forms', *Annual Review of Sociology*, 15: 96–118.

Brusco, S. (1986), 'Small Firms and Industrial Districts: The Experience of Italy', in D. Keeble and F. Weever (eds.), *New Firms and Regional Development in Europe*. London: Croom Helm.

Cook, J. and Wall, T. (1980), 'New Work Attitude Measures of Trust, Organizational Commitment and Personal Need Non-fulfilment', *Journal of Occupational Psychology*, 53: 39–52.

Cook, J. D. *et al.* (1981), *The Experience of Work: A Compendium and Review of 249 Measures and Their Use*. Orlando: Academic Press.

Cummings, L. L. and Bromiley, P. (1996), 'The Organizational Trust Inventory (OTI): Development and Validation', in R. M. Kramer and T. R. Tyler (eds.), *Trust in Organizations: Frontiers of Theory and Research*. London: Sage.

Deutsch, M. (1958), 'Trust and Suspicion', *Journal of Conflict Resolution*, 2/4: 265–79.

Dore, R. (1983), 'Goodwill and the Spirit of Market Capitalism', *British Journal of Sociology*, 34: 459–82.

——(1987), *Taking Japan Seriously*. Stanford: Staniversity Press.

Dyer, J. (forthcoming), 'Does governance matter? Keiretsu alliances and asset specificity as source of Japanese competitive advantage', *Organization Science*.

Fox, A. (1973), *Beyond Contract: Work, Power and Trust Relations*. London: Faber and Faber.

Fukuyama, F. (1995), *Trust: The Social Virtues and the Creation of Prosperity*. London: Hamish Hamilton.

Gambetta, D. (1988) (ed.), *Trust: Making and Breaking Cooperative Relations*. Oxford: Blackwell.

Goshal, S. and Moran, P. (1996), 'Bad for Practice: A Critique of the Transaction Cost Theory', *Academy of Management Review*, 21/1: 13–47.

Granovetter, M. (1985), 'Economic Action and Social Structure: The Problem of Embeddedness', *American Journal of Sociology*, 91: 481–510.

Gulati, R. (1995), 'Does Familiarity Breed Trust? The Implications of Repeated Ties for Contractual Choice in Alliances', *Academy of Management Journal*, 38: 85–112.

Heide, J. B. and John, G. (1990), 'Alliances in Industrial Purchasing: The Determinants of Joint Action in Buyer–Supplier Relationships', *Journal of Marketing Research*, 27: 24–36.

Helper, S. (1991), 'Strategy and Irreversibility in Supplier Relations: The Case of the US Automobile Industry', *Business History Review*, 65: 781–824.

——and Sako, M. (1995), 'Supplier Relations in the Auto Industry in Japan and the USA: Are they Converging?' *Sloan Management Review* (Spring), 77–84.

Ingersoll Engineers (1995), *Partnership or Conflict? The Automotive-Component Supply Industry: A Survey of Issues of Alignment*. Ruby: Ingersoll Engineers.

Jarillo, J. C. (1988), 'On Strategic Networks', *Strategic Management Journal*, 9: 31–41.

Joskow, P. L. (1988), 'Asset Specificity and the Structure of Vertical Relationships: Empirical Evidence', *Journal of Law, Economics and Organization*, 4/1: 95–118.

Lane, C. and Bachmann, R. (1996), 'Risk, Trust and Power: The Social Construction of Supplier Relations in Britain and Germany', paper presented at the Work, Employment and Society Conference, University of Kent, 12–14 Sept.

Macaulay, S. (1963), 'Non-contractual Relations in Business: A Preliminary Study', *American Sociological Review*, 28/2: 55–67.

Macneil, I. R. (1974), 'Contracts: Adjustment of Long-term Economic Relationship under Classical, Neo-classical, and Relational Contract Law', *Northwestern University Law Review*, 72: 584–906.

Mauss, M. (1966), *The Gift*. London and Henley: Routledge & Kegan Paul.

Mohr, J. and Spekman, R. (1994), 'Characteristics of Partnership Success: Partnership Attributes, Communication Behavior, and Conflict Resolution Techniques', *Strategic Management Journal*, 15: 135–52.

Powell, W. W. (1996), 'Trust-based Forms of Governance', in Kramer and Tyler (eds.), *Trust in Organizations*.

Ring, P. S. and van de Ven, A. H. (1994), 'Developmental Processes of Cooperative Interorganizational Relationships', *Academy of Management Review*, 19: 90–118.

Sabel, C. F. (1992), 'Studied Trust: Building New Forms of Co-operation in a Volatile Economy', in F. Pyke and W. Sengenberger (eds.), *Industrial Districts and Local Economic Regeneration*. Geneva: International Institute for Labour Studies.

——(1994), 'Learning by Monitoring: The Institutions of Economic Development', in N. J. Smelser and R. Swedberg (eds.), *The Handbook of Economic Sociology*. Princeton: Princeton University Press.

Sako, M. (1991), 'The Role of "Trust" in Japanese Buyer–Supplier Relationships', *Ricerche Economiche*, 45: 449–74.

——(1992), *Prices, Quality and Trust: Inter-firm Relations in Britain and Japan*. Cambridge: Cambridge University Press.

——(1996), 'Suppliers' Associations in the Japanese Automobile Industry: Collective Action for Technology Diffusion', *Cambridge Journal of Economics*, 20/6: 651–71.

Sitkin, S. B. and Roth, N. L. (1993), 'Explaining the Limited Effectiveness of Legalistic "Remedies" for Trust/Distrust', *Organization Science*, 4/3: 356–92.

Smitka, M. (1991), *Competitive Ties: Subcontracting in the Japanese Automotive Industry*. New York: Columbia University Press.

——(1992), 'Contracting Without Contracts', in S. B. Sitkin and R. J. Bies (eds.), *The Legalistic Organisation*. London: Sage.

Society of Motor Manufacturers and Traders and UK Department of Trade and Industry (1994), *A Review of the Relationships Between Vehicle Manufacturers and Suppliers*. London: SMMT and DTI.

Traxler, F. (1995), 'Two Logics of Collective Action in Industrial Relations?', in C. Crouch and F. Traxler (eds.), *Organized Industrial Relations in Europe: What Future?* Aldershot: Avebury.

Walker, G. and Weber, D. (1984), 'A Transaction Cost Approach to Make-or-Buy Decisions', *Administrative Science Quarterly*, 29: 373–91.

Williamson, O. E. (1975), *Markets and Hierarchies*. New York: Free Press.

——(1979), 'Transaction-cost Economics: The Governance of Contractual Relations', *Journal of Law and Economics*, 22: 3–61.

——(1983), 'Credible Commitments: Using Hostages to Support Exchange', *American Economic Review*, 73: 519–40.

——(1985), *The Economic Institutions of Capitalism*. New York: Free Press.

——(1993), 'Calculativeness, Trust, and Economic Organization', *Journal of Law and Economics*, 36: 453–86.

Zucker, L. (1986), Production of Trust: Institutional Sources of Economic Structure', *Research in Organizational Behavior*, 8: 53–111.

4

From Handshake to Contract: Intellectual Property, Trust, and the Social Structure of Academic Research*

JULIA PORTER LIEBESKIND AND AMALYA LUMERMAN OLIVER

1. INTRODUCTION

Academic science is one area of human activity where trust—in the form of scientific credibility—plays an essential role. Indeed, the entire social structure of academic science comprises a network of trust relationships that are built up through personal experiences, through reputation, and through institutional supports. Without these trust relationships, science itself cannot advance. However, this social structure may be altered when the values and interests of its members change. In this chapter, we describe how the increasing commercial value of scientific discoveries in molecular biology has transformed the notion of trust within the academic scientific community, leading to changes in the social structure of this academic field.

   The observations and arguments we make here are based on over forty interviews at twelve universities and eleven biotechnology firms in the United States, Britain, and Israel that we have undertaken since 1989. We have interviewed not only research scientists in universities and firms, but also university technology transfer staff, academic administrators, and corporate managers. Among the university scientists we interviewed, the majority were currently involved, or had been involved, with commercial research in one form or another, including carrying out commercially sponsored research; patenting and licensing discoveries; founding new firms; consulting to firms; working at an 'NBF' (New Biochtechnology Firm) during a sabbatical or during the summer; and exchanging research materials, equipment, and data with an NBF. However, we also talked to a

   * We thank Sally Hughes, Paul Rabinow, Sharon Traweek, and the editors of this volume for helpful comments and suggestions. We also thank the many university scientists, administrators and staff, and corporate personnel, who gave so generously of their valuable time to be interviewed for this study. Any errors are ours alone. This study was supported by a grant from the Israel–US Binational Science Foundation, Amalya Lumerman Oliver and Julia Porter Liebeskind, principal investigators; and by a grant to the first author from the Center for International Business Education and Research at the University of Southern California.

number of scientists who had none of these involvements. For reasons of brevity, we make relatively few direct quotations from these interviews; however, our entire argument is informed by our interview findings. We also drew on numerous archival sources; these are listed in the references section.

2. TRUST AND CREDIBILITY IN ACADEMIC SCIENTIFIC RESEARCH

We understand 'trust' to be a condition that may or may not exist among two or more social actors. Trust, or distrust, are outcomes of the act of trusting others (Gambetta 1988; Luhman 1988; Coleman 1990). Trusting may also engender trustworthy behaviour in a trustee (Dasgupta 1988; Kramer, Brewer, and Hanna 1996).

Trust may result from social processes, from calculation, or from shared values. Process-based trust is built up over time; as actors interact, the more they will tend to trust or distrust one another, as they update their information about each other's capabilities and character (Zucker 1986; Good 1988; Luhman 1988; Kramer, Brewer, and Hanna 1996). Calculative trust is based on estimates of another's motives and interests (Dasgupta 1988; Williams 1988; Coleman 1990); these will comprise both the gains from behaving in a trustworthy manner (or not), and the costs that may result from untrustworthy behaviour. The benefits and costs of trustworthy or untrustworthy behaviour are both tangible—such as obtaining a faculty position, a promotion, or a grant, and intangible—such as obtaining satisfaction from 'doing good' or from being well regarded within a particular community (Blau 1964; Granovetter 1985; Kramer, Pomerantz, and Newton 1993). Finally, value-based trust is predicated on the understanding that actors share norms of trustworthy behaviour in relation to particular types of exchange (Landa 1994; Fukuyama 1995). Because trust is based upon familiarity, interests, and values, it is significantly influenced by informal social structures and by formal institutions (Zucker 1986; Coleman 1990; Landa 1994; Fukuyama 1995).

Trust is most important in situations where the actions of one social actor impact the welfare of other social actors, and where these impacts cannot be entirely controlled through formal mechanisms such as bureaucratic organization or contracting (Blau 1964; Coleman 1990; Landa 1994; Oliver 1997). Trust is particularly important when the incentives of actors are not well aligned; in these situations, trust can support exchanges between actors that otherwise might not occur (Blau 1964; Axelrod 1984; Brewer and Kramer 1986; Williams 1988; Kreps 1990; Landa 1994).

One area of human activity where trust is particularly important is academic scientific research. Scientific research is a process in which phenomena and relationships between phenomena are examined systematically in a process of prediction and testing through observation or experimentation (Hempel 1966). The goal of scientific research is to produce new 'facts'— new knowledge in the form of scientific discoveries—that can increase society's stock of knowledge (Latour and Woolgar 1979). Typically, scientific research is conducted in small teams of researchers, each investigating a narrow set of phenomena and research questions (Latour and Woolgar 1979; Rabinow 1996). At a macro level, this team specialization can be understood to be efficient, allowing a greater number of new facts to be produced than would be the case were scientists' skills and knowledge more generalized, which would result in more duplication of effort among teams and less incremental learning (Tullock 1966). However, the fact that scientific research teams are highly specialized also means that each team relies on other teams for information that is vital to its own research task: scientists are highly interdependent in terms of knowledge inputs. It is this interdependence that makes credibility such a critical factor in scientific research. Without credibility—trust in the validity of others' scientific research findings—each scientist would be forced to reproduce the work of her predecessors before advancing to the next research question, and the rate of new discoveries and gains to specialization would be drastically reduced (Harding 1991). Thus, the entire progress of science can be understood to depend on whether or not each individual scientist involved in the collective enterprise is credible or not. As Latour and Woolgar (1979) observe:

For a working scientist, the most vital question is 'Is he reliable enough to be believed? Can I trust him/his claim? Is he going to provide me with hard facts?' Scientists are thus interested in one another . . . because each needs the other in order to increase his own production of credible information. (Latour and Woolgar 1979: 202–3)

Because the information produced by one scientist will only constitute a 'fact' if it proves valid to other members of the scientific community (David 1992; Latour and Woolgar 1979), great emphasis is placed on publication in academic science: only published ideas can be subjected to the scrutiny of others (Dasgupta and David 1987). Publication can take many forms, including informal conversations between research collaborators and colleagues; formal presentations at colloquia and professional meetings; working papers; and journal publications. Thus, within academic science, credibility is a social commodity that is produced through social exchange. In turn, scientific credibility determines the patterns of exchange: one scientist will be willing to exchange ideas only with others who are considered credible. As a result, within the academic scientific community, publication and credibility are inextricably interwoven.

The credibility of an academic scientist is also influenced by her reputation for competence and fairness, and her character. A scientist's new research results are more likely to be considered to be credible if she has already established her competence in terms of doing 'good science'. Her 'ownership' of new ideas is also more likely to be acknowledged, if she has a reputation for allocating credit fairly. Because science is conducted in teams, and because any one member of a team may have more or less scientific knowledge, skill, imagination, or judgement than other members of the team, the contribution of individuals cannot be assessed accurately unless allocations of credit are fairly made (Merton 1973; Latour and Woolgar 1979). Furthermore, a scientist can only obtain research funds if she can claim credit for discoveries. Thus, the allocation of credit is a very important issue in scientific research.[1] Credibility also depends on a scientist's character: lax ethics or high personal ambition might induce a scientist to make careless claims, or tempt her not to reveal information in a timely fashion in order to further her own research agenda. Withholding information may delay others' research, or lead them to prematurely abandon promising lines of inquiry.[2] Thus, competence, character and assessments of credibility are interwoven. Again, Latour and Woolgar observe:

Evaluative comments made by scientists *make no distinction between scientists as people and their scientific claims*. . . . Both reward and credibility originate essentially from peers' comments about other scientists. . . . The credibility of the proposer and the proposal are identical.   (Latour and Woolgar 1979: 202, emphasis added)

3. STRUCTURE OF TRUST RELATIONSHIPS IN ACADEMIC SCIENCE

Following Coleman's (1990) classification, we understand trust relationships in academic science to take three different forms, as follows: interpersonal trust; intermediated trust; and institutional trust. Each of these relationships supports scientific credibility in different ways.

3.1 Interpersonal Trust

We define 'interpersonal trust' as trust that is directly engendered when two actors are involved in an exchange relationship over time (Rotter 1980; Good 1988; Luhman 1988).

Interpersonal trust is the most prevalent and the most fundamental type of trust in academic scientific research. Because scientific research is conducted in teams, researchers learn about one another's competence and characters—as well as their interests—as they work together. Thus, within any given research team, a 'sorting' process takes place over time, establishing relationships of trust between credible individuals, and relationships of distrust elsewhere; interpersonal trust in science is process-based trust

(Zucker 1986). Interpersonal trust is absolutely critical to science: without trust, teamwork cannot advance, because collaborators would be unwilling to rely upon one another.

Because the structure of academic careers obligates students, and induces faculty, to move from university to university during the course of their careers, the structure of trust and distrust relations that is observed at any single point in time among a given set of academic scientists will be a reflection of their cumulative interpersonal experiences, as illustrated in Figure 4.1. Here, Scientist A currently works with Scientist B and Scientist C in Lab 1-1, both of whom she trusts. Previously, Scientist A worked with Scientists D and E in Lab 0-1; she trusts D (who now works in Lab 1-3) and distrusts E (who works in Lab 1-4). Scientist B trusts Scientist F (now in Lab 1-2) with whom he previously worked in Lab 0-2.

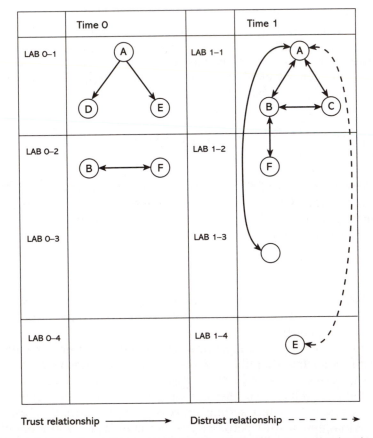

Trust relationship ⟶   Distrust relationship − − − − − ➤

Fɪɢ. 4.1. The dynamic structure of trust relationships in academic science

3.2 Intermediated Trust

Trust among scientists may also be intermediated by trusted others. For example, in Figure 4.1, Scientist A knows and trusts Scientist B in her own team, and Scientist B knows and trusts Scientist F in Lab 0-2. In a situation of intermediated trust, A would trust F's scientific credibility based on B's recommendation. Of course, A will only trust F if she trusts B's assessment of F's trustworthiness. Also, because A does not know F personally, she will most probably consider the interests of both B and F in deciding whether or not to trust F: an intermediated trust relationship will probably involve a more detailed calculation of interest than a directly engendered trust relationship.

Like interpersonal trust, intermediated trust is also critical to scientific research because each research team relies on information produced by others (Latour and Woolgar 1979; Harding 1991). Indeed, 'gossip'—which provides intermediated information about others' credibility—is a notable feature of conversations among scientists (Latour and Woolgar 1979). Gossip is thus an important mechanism through which the personal experiences of individual scientists are transformed into the social capital of scientific credibility. Intermediated trust also plays a central role in shaping the network of interpersonal trust relationships in science. This is because a scientist will usually take others' opinions into account before she enters into a new exchange relationship, such as joining a new research team.

3.3 Institutional Trust

Finally, directly engendered and intermediated trust in academic science is supported and fostered by a variety of formal and informal institutional arrangements that govern its conduct.

First, the credibility of individual scientists is supported by the public granting organizations that support academic research, and by universities. The public funding of academic scientific research is understood to promote unbiased and open research, in contrast to private funding, which is argued to induce partiality and secrecy (Bok 1981; Rosensweig and Turlington 1982; Wade 1984; McCain 1991). Public research funding is typically given only to scientists who produce and publish credible research findings (i.e. facts).[3] Also, promotion and tenure in a university is granted primarily on the basis of peer-reviewed (i.e. credible) publications, also promulgating the practice of 'open science' and thereby, the production of credible scientific information (Nelkin 1984; Dasgupta and David 1987; David 1992). Moreover, because universities and public granting organizations are the sole suppliers of support for traditional academic science, scientists' actions are directed towards meeting the requirements of these institutions (Latour and Woolgar 1979).

Second, informal processes of socialization and social control also support credibility. Entry into the community of academic research scientists requires a lengthy process of education and socialization which engenders cohesion of beliefs and behaviour, and binds scientists together into one 'invisible college' of shared knowledge and understanding (Hagstrom 1965; Crane 1972). Also, because the scientific research community is a bounded community, in which the identity of each individual is known to others, and within which information is freely exchanged, gossip can serve to condition scientists' behaviour towards accepted norms of professional conduct (Merry 1984).

In sum, trust relationships in scientific research—which are essential to scientific progress—are engendered by individual relationships; by intermediaries; and by institutions, both formal and informal. What then happens to this social structure of trust relationships—and the scientific exchanges that both foster it and depend upon it—when academic science has commercial potential, such as it now has in the field of molecular biology?

4. MOLECULAR BIOLOGY, BIOTECHNOLOGY AND INTELLECTUAL PROPERTY

Molecular biology is, broadly stated, the study of the molecular structure of life forms, including the study of genes, proteins, enzymes, and the biochemical functions of cells. Since the 1950s, molecular biology has been understood to be a field with significant humanitarian and commercial potential. Since the early 1970s, new scientific advances have resulted in a plethora of new products including new treatments for many diseases and conditions, and the development of new types of plants, animals, and energy sources. Such commercial application of molecular biology is commonly referred to as 'biotechnology'. Interestingly, to date, the development and commercialization of biotechnology products has been undertaken preponderantly by new, small firms ('NBFs'), rather than by large established firms. By 1995, over 1,200 NBFs had been founded worldwide (Lee and Burrill 1995). In the United States, NBFs have typically been founded by university scientists, and these scientists continue to maintain close ties with the academic research community by funding university research; by collaborating with academic scientists; by employing university researchers as corporate research consultants; and by offering research internships to university faculties and students (Kenney 1986; Eisenberg 1987; Beardsley 1994; Cohen and Noll 1994; Liebeskind, Oliver, Zucker, and Brewer 1996; Rabinow 1996; Werth 1995; Zucker and Darby 1996; Zucker, Darby, Brewer, and Peng 1996).[4] In Britain and Israel, the ties between NBFs and universities are often even closer, because university faculties may be permitted to own and operate NBFs while maintaining their university positions, whereas in the United States, this level of commercial involvement by faculty is generally prohibited (Argyres and Liebeskind 1998).[5]

Despite the commercial potential of biotechnology, its actual commercialization could not have taken place unless firms were able to define and own property rights to commercially valuable discoveries in the form of patents. Without a patent, a firm has no incentive to invest in development and commercialization of a new product, because other firms would be able to imitate it without cost to themselves (Arrow 1962). A patent disallows such imitation.

In the United States, the patentability of biotechnology products was established in a series of landmark court cases during the late 1970s and the early 1980s (Eisenberg 1987). Meanwhile, in 1980 the US Congress passed a law (commonly known as the 'Bayh-Dole Act') that allowed universities to patent biotechnology and other discoveries made by their faculties, and to license these patents to commercial firms.[6] The intention of this legislation was to promote the commercialization of scientific research for the benefit of society. However, it was also recognized that allowing the privatization of knowledge generated in universities might undermine the objectivity of university research, divert faculty attention away from fundamental research, and interfere with the open exchange of research findings (Bok 1981; Nelkin 1984; Wade 1984). Despite these concerns, the patenting of university research in the United States has proceeded rapidly (Henderson, Jaffe, and Trajtenberg 1994). Most large US research universities currently claim ownership of patentable inventions made by their faculties, and license these patents to firms (Argyres and Liebeskind 1998). In Britain and Israel the situation is somewhat different: patentable discoveries by faculties may be owned by either the university or the inventor, depending on the individual university's policies and those of the various granting institutions funding the research. None the less, many universities in these countries also actively promote the commercialization of scientific discoveries made by their faculties.

Commercial considerations have also led to the use of other forms of intellectual property contracts in molecular biology, especially Research Material Transfer Agreements (RMTAs), and confidentiality agreements. RMTAs are used to govern the exchange of cell lines, reagents, and other research materials from one scientist to another; typically, they disallow any patent rights to discoveries made by non-owners' use. Confidentiality Agreements are used to prevent collaborators on commercially valuable research projects from discussing their research with outsiders, in order to protect the patentability of discoveries that have yet to be made.[7]

As the commercial promise of biotechnology has grown, university research in molecular biology is becoming increasingly influenced by intellectual property concerns. First of all, the value of intellectual property rights in biotechnological discoveries is now well established.[8] Because secure intellectual property rights are so critical, biotechnology firms today conduct only those research programmes that offer the prospect of patentable products, and they enter into research collaborations only if they are governed by agreements assuring that the firm will receive patent rights to any discoveries that are made. Second, and equally important, there has been an increasing involvement of university researchers with biotechnology firms. As early as 1986, Kenney reported widespread involvement of university professors in commercially funded research, and even, in the ownership and management of NBFs. Ten years later, this involvement is even more widespread, as the number of NBFs relative to the number of molecular biology faculties has increased dramatically, and as the commercial value of research is increasingly being recognized (Beardsley 1994; Cohen and Noll 1994). As a result:

Scientists working in biotechnology-related fields are increasingly likely to be concerned simultaneously with the norms and rewards of research science and the rules and incentives created by intellectual property law.   (Eisenberg 1987: 195)

5. THE TRANSFORMATION OF TRUST RELATIONSHIPS AMONG ACADEMIC SCIENTISTS

From Handshake to Contract

The combination of commercial emphasis on securing intellectual property rights in biotechnology, and the widespread involvement of individual faculty members with biotechnology firms, has significantly impacted the nature of relationships between academic scientists in molecular biology, because their interests have changed. In 'normal' academic research, scientists

. . . are merely employees of the federal government. No matter how extensive, their scientific capital can neither be sold nor bequeathed and only rarely can it be exchanged for monetary capital. As craftsmen working to produce their own data, they are concerned more or less exclusively with their own accounts.   (Latour and Woolgar 1979: 229)[9]

In commercial research, however, university scientists are no longer exclusively employees of the Federal government, and it becomes possible for them to exchange their knowledge for monetary capital, be it in the direct form of patent royalties and research grants, or in the indirect form of obtaining access to otherwise proprietary research materials, methods, and data that can be used to increase future research funding or personal income.

The potential for monetary exchange can change scientists' interests in a number of ways. One important potential change in interests concerns publicity. In 'normal' academic research, scientists build credibility through publication and garner resources from claiming priority (Latour and Woolgar 1979; Merton 1973; David 1992). Therefore, any valid research findings will be rapidly publicized. In commercial research, however, publication can result in a loss of valuable intellectual property, because once information has been released into the commons (i.e. published), it cannot then be patented (Eisenberg 1987). Thus, if a firm wants to obtain patent rights to discoveries made by a university scientist, that scientist must withhold information for a period of time. The question is to what degree commercial interests increase the period of secrecy relative to normal science, which is also characterized by a certain level of secrecy. University technology transfer staff told us that firms would typically prefer that university scientists never discuss their commercially funded research. The principal reason given for this is that patentable discoveries in molecular biology are typically not discrete entities; many different patents must be filed to obtain complete property rights to discoveries. Because patents are public information, firms have incentives to keep early discoveries secret until more discoveries are made.

To protect the principle of publicity, universities typically disallow firms from binding their faculties to secrecy agreements for long periods of time. However, not all contractual agreements between faculties and firms are governed by universities, and academic scientists are not immune to inducements to secrecy (McCain 1991; Hilgartner and Brandt-Rauf 1994). In addition, if an academic scientist's research is funded by a firm, she can afford not to publish for a longer period than would be the case were she obtaining her funds from public funding institutions: commercial credibility can be substituted for academic credibility, so long as it ensures research funding. For instance, two scientists we interviewed at one university had kept one of their research projects entirely secret for a period of two years, in order to preserve the commercial value of their findings. Scientists have also been increasingly unwilling to submit articles to peer review, and to share research materials, for fear of losing proprietary rights.[10]

Commercial interests may also alter scientists' interest in credit. In normal academic research, individual credit can be exchanged for research grants and other resources necessary to produce more discoveries (Merton 1973; Latour and Woolgar 1979). However, researchers who do not share credit fairly with their collaborators will be identified through personal experience and gossiping, and may be boycotted in the future. When commercial interests intrude, the costs of hoarding credit may be reduced, because academic collaborators may be replaced by commercial collaborators. At the same time, the benefits to hoarding credit are increased, because patent laws typically allow only one or two persons to claim credit for an invention.[11]

Finally, intellectual property considerations cast long shadows: once a scientist has worked on a proprietary project, she may not be free to discuss it for many years. Thus, research relationships entered into at one point in time can effectively prevent a scientist from conducting a specific line of research with 'outsiders' for a long period of time.[12]

As a result of this transformation of interests, there has been an increasing emphasis on using contracts to define the scope and conduct of academic scientific collaborations of all types, including team projects, transfers of research materials, and the preliminary evaluation of research results. As one scientist interviewed for this study remarked:

I never enter into a research relationship without signing a contract governing research materials and confidentiality. These days, everyone signs these agreements before they collaborate. It's just the way that research is done.

It is important to note that this emphasis on contracting is not confined to 'applied' research, but also applies to basic research; this is because even the most basic discoveries in molecular biology can have commercial potential. It is also important to note that these contracts are not merely a 'putting into words' of the traditional handshake agreements that have long existed between academic scientists defining the terms and conditions of their research collaborations. Formal, legally enforceable contracts are both precise and restrictive, and infringement is penalized.[13]

6. THE EFFECTS OF COMMERCIAL INTERESTS ON THE NATURE OF TRUST IN ACADEMIC SCIENCE

These changes in the interests of academic scientists in molecular biology have affected the extent and depth of trust that is necessary to support their research relationships. One such change is that it is no longer sufficient for one scientist to trust another's credibility alone—other aspects of behaviour also become important. For instance, maintaining strict confidentiality is essential if property rights to inventions are to be secured; even informal conversation increases the risk that others will appropriate valuable ideas and findings. Yet, this may be a difficult criterion to satisfy. As Werth (1995: 23) observes:

Academic researchers thrive on publication, attention and credit being the oxygen of their careers. Yet to industrial scientists, whose own success most often depends on keeping their best work secret . . . most academics are . . . loose cannons.

Another aspect of behaviour which becomes important in a commercial research context is commitment: firms are concerned that scientists pursue research programmes in a timely manner, because delays may result in loss of patent rights, or may lead to excessive investment in unpromising avenues of inquiry.[14] Yet in academic research, scientists are socialized and motivated to pursue 'interesting' problems, regardless of their relevance to a particular knowledge goal. Thus, it may be difficult for one academic scientist to trust another to complete a given programme of research, and to complete it on time.

In sum, the success of commercially oriented collaborative research calls for a number of different trustworthy behaviours on the part of the collaborators. *A broader form of trust is required to support a commercially oriented research relationship, than is required to support a normal academic research relationship.*

Collaborative relationships formed with parties who have commercial interests also calls for deeper forms of trust, because incentives for unethical behaviour are increased. As we discuss above, commercial motives sharpen scientists' incentives to hoard credit and to keep research findings secret. One well-known example of credit hoarding in molecular biology concerned Dr Robert Gallo of the National Cancer Institute. Gallo claimed that he discovered the AIDs virus, and so should obtain exclusive royalty rights to a diagnostic test for the disease, although the virus had already been isolated by a group of scientists at the Institute Pasteur, in France.[15] Commercial considerations may also provide incentives not to adhere to norms of impartiality, if this would undermine a given firm's commercial interests. For instance, Boots Corporation forced a team of scientists at the University of California, San Francisco to withdraw a journal article that questioned the efficacy of one of Boots' therapeutic products.[16] Finally, proprietary ownership of research materials, techniques, and data may allow one scientist to hoard credit to another's cost, even if no direct commercial interests are involved. Graduate students and other junior researchers may be at particular risk for being exploited in this way by senior faculties, upon whom they depend for resources and career advancement.

Because involvement in commercial research changes academic scientists' interests, the potential costs of trusting others are increased. As a result, *deeper trust is required to support a research relationship where collaborators have commercial interests, than is required to support a normal academic research relationship.*

These increased demands on the breadth and depth of trust required in commercial research collaborations impact all three types of trust relationships that we have identified and thereby, impact the social structure of academic scientific research.

7. THE EFFECTS OF COMMERCIAL INTERESTS ON
TRUST RELATIONSHIPS IN ACADEMIC SCIENCE

7.1 Changes in the Nature and Structure of Interpersonal
Trust Relationships

When scientists have both academic and commercial interests, it may be
more difficult to establish relationships of complete trust. As broader trust
is called for, scientists may demarcate more carefully what other colleagues
are 'good for' in terms of both credibility and other behaviours, such as
maintaining confidentiality. Similarly, trust that was sufficiently deep to
support an academic collaboration may be insufficient to support a commercial collaboration. Thus, returning to Figure 4.1, we might find that A
now trusts B only in relation to collaborating in academic research, but
trusts C and D in terms of both scientific credibility and confidentiality.

One outcome of the need for increased breadth and depth of trust in the
presence of commercial interests can be a narrowing of the set of trusted
others for any given scientist. For instance, two scientists whom we interviewed had chosen to work on a valuable commercial product almost entirely alone; other colleagues had been deliberately excluded, in part
for fear that they would not be able to maintain confidentiality, and in part
due to their unwillingness to share their intellectual property rights with
others. At some point the two had used the services of a laboratory technician, but as they explained to us, this technician 'knew nothing about the
details of the research' and therefore, was not in a position to leak their
findings to third parties. These two scientists instead had been working
together for many years, and trusted one another to keep their joint research a secret. In addition, they had both signed a formal legal agreement
with the research sponsor; thus, their trust in one another was contractually
supported, consistent with the arguments presented by Deakin and
Wilkinson (Chapter 5, this volume) and Arrighetti, Bachmann, and Deakin
(1997). However, frequently, contractual commitments and the interests
that they engender serve to undermine existing trust relationships among
academic scientists. For instance, another scientist whom we interviewed
had been sharing information and collaborating in research projects for a
number of years with two of his departmental colleagues. However, recently, this scientist and both of his colleagues entered into research
agreements with three different NBFs. As a result, the three scientists
realized that they could no longer collaborate; the contracts they had each
signed prohibited their sharing information, even though their collaborative research was not directly germane to their commercially funded
research.

Consideration of others' commercial interests may also make it more difficult to establish relations of interpersonal trust in the first place, because initial expectations of others' trustworthiness will tend to be lower. Thus, a larger number of confirmatory events will be required within the context of the relationship to assure one collaborator that a colleague is trustworthy, than would be the case were her initial expectations of trustworthiness higher (Williams 1988). Similarly, low initial expectations of trustworthiness may lead potential trustors to interpret some events that occur within the interpersonal relationship in a less favourable light, further undermining the construction of trust (Kramer 1994). Thus, another effect of the intrusion of commercial interests is a certain level of ossification of relationships, as new relationships become more difficult to establish.

A more subtle effect of the intrusion of commercial interests may be a change in the nature of social and collegial relationships between scientists who are not involved in collaborative research with each other (Kenney 1986). These social relationships form the matrix within which scientific collaborations may later be formed; they are also useful for gossiping and therefore for engendering intermediated and institutional trust. Yet commercial interests may lead to an unwillingness of individuals to exchange information freely within the context of social conversations, as well as a reluctance to form new social relationships, for fear that secrets might be let slip. In an extreme example, one university we visited housed an academic research team that was completely isolated, both professionally and socially. This team—which worked on a valuable proprietary technology that it had developed—was located in a locked laboratory within a locked building. No one (not even other faculty members in the same department) was allowed to enter without the advance permission of the head of the team, and each member of the team—faculty, students, and technicians alike—was bound by confidentiality agreements. The content of all publications produced by lab members was reviewed by the lab principals before being publicized, from journal submissions to informal meetings with outsiders. Before any visit by outsiders, all papers were locked away and the computer screens were cleared. Lab members all wore coded identification tags. This research team represented the most complete intrusion of commercial norms of secrecy into an academic department that we have observed anywhere.

Commercial interests have also transformed the nature of hierarchical interpersonal trust relationships, especially between faculties and students. Because it would be unethical for a faculty member to ask a student to become involved in work that she would not be able to publish freely, supervising faculties which are involved in commercial research tend to maintain parallel research programmes, one of which is a normal academic research programme, and the other which is 'closed' to students. In one laboratory we visited, these parallel programmes were crystallized in the architecture: the 'open' research programme was located in an unlocked laboratory where students came and went freely, while the second 'closed' programme was housed in an adjacent locked laboratory, to which only a handful of people were allowed access. The effect of such a separation is to reduce the level of interpersonal contact between students and supervisors, undermining the creation of interpersonal trust. The differing interests of students and faculty may also undermine trust: students may question whether they are obtaining the best research materials and being offered the most interesting research questions, given the commercial interests of their faculty supervisors (Kenney 1986).

In conclusion, commercial interests can lead to the weakening or breaking of both collaborative and social interpersonal trust relationships between academic scientists. Indeed, there is currently somewhat of a social divide within molecular biology between those who do 'pure' research and those who do commercial research; the two groups tend to distrust one another. In particular, purely academic scientists tend to question the impartiality of commercially involved scientists; they also claim that much commercially relevant research is academically uninteresting (Kenney 1986). Conversely, commercially involved scientists complain that purely academic scientists are envious, and that they seek to disrupt relationships with industry.

While commercial interests may weaken and ossify the structure of interpersonal trust relationships among academic scientists, many university faculties have forged new ties with scientists working in NBFs (Liebeskind *et al.* 1996; Zucker *et al.* 1996). In some instances, these relationships result from a university scientist moving to an NBF. New interpersonal trust relationships may also be forged between university and firm scientists during the course of commercially sponsored research programmes or other types of university–firm exchanges. Frequently, these relationships are initiated by NBFs; for these firms, building new interpersonal trust relationships is often a key element in their research strategy (Deutschman 1994; Werth 1995). Managers at one firm we interviewed explained to us that they took great care in designing the process through which they would approach a university scientist in whose work they were interested. For instance, this firm took considerable pains to ensure that the university scientist was approached by a scientific peer—either an academic who was already working with the firm, or a well-known scientist from the firm's own staff. Thus, certain employees or associates of the firm 'broker' trust on the firm's behalf with academic scientists, consistent with Sydow's argument (Chapter 1, this volume) that individuals in boundary-spanning roles are often critical to engendering interorganizational trust. NBFs also frequently appoint well-known university scientists to their Scientific Advisory Boards, in order to engender trust with the academic community. The NBF managers we interviewed also took pains to identify a particular inducement they could offer a given scientist to work on their firm's behalf, be it research materials (e.g. cell lines); equipment or personnel (e.g. protein chemistry services); or money. At the same time, NBFs support such interpersonal relationships by allowing their own scientists to work on purely academic research projects; by relaxing their rules against publication for certain projects; and even, by allowing their own scientists to apply for external grants (Deutschman 1994; Hicks 1995; Oliver and Montgomery 1996; Oliver 1997). However, these relaxations of commercial norms by NBFs are limited and subject to review; firm scientists emphatically do not have the same freedom of either inquiry or publication as academic scientists. None the less, in a study of research collaborations in two successful NBFs, Liebeskind *et al.* (1996) find a very extensive network of collaborative research relationships between NBF and university scientists, suggesting that many scientists in NBFs are able to support interpersonal trust relationships with university scientists.

7.2 Changes in the Nature and Structure of Intermediated Trust Relationships

As in the case of interpersonal trust, the intrusion of commercial interests also makes it more difficult to establish relationships of intermediated trust in academic science, because both the intermediary and the person she vouches for must be trusted more broadly and deeply. Again, this can be expected to have the effect of narrowing the set of trusted others with whom a scientist might be willing to work as she moves from one team to another. On the other hand, commercial interests may sharpen the need for collaborating with others who have needed expertise: the costs to excluding others from collaborations may be much higher in commercial research than in normal academic research. In our experience, these conflicting pressures have been partially resolved within the community of molecular biologists by an increase in the scope of topics covered by gossip: many of the scientists we interviewed were very knowledgeable about the commercial activities and interests of other scientists, and the ways in which these activities and interests influenced their behaviour.

As in the case of interpersonal trust relationships, intermediated trust relationships may also be formed between university scientists and scientists in firms. Indeed, as we discuss above, NBFs are highly aware of the importance of intermediaries in inducing academic scientists to work with them. Consequently, when NBFs hire university scientists onto their own research staff, one of the factors they consider is whether that scientist is sufficiently trusted within the academic community to allow the firm to extend its network of trust relationships with academic scientists.

7.3 Changes in the Nature and Structure of Institutionally Supported Trust Relationships

Finally, the intrusion of commercial interests into academic research in molecular biology has to some degree undermined the ability of the institutions of open science to guarantee the credibility of academic scientists.

One problem in this regard is that neither public funding agencies nor universities are designed, as institutions, to support the extended scope of trust required in commercial research, nor are they well organized to prevent the seepage of commercial values into academic life. Thus, universities in particular at present stand in the invidious position of being criticized both by firms—who often complain that universities do very little to protect their commercial interests when they fund university research—and by the public at large, who complain that universities are not protecting public science from taint by those same interests (Nelkin 1984; Wade 1984). Universities do typically oversee university–industry contracts that pertain to patents and licensing, and to the commercial funding of university research programmes. In particular, universities seek to prevent conflicts of interest between public and privately funded research, and to protect faculties from becoming parties to contracts that restrict their rights to publish, or that might impair their impartiality (David, Mowery, and Steinmueller 1994; Argyres and Liebeskind 1998). However, because faculties are not strictly the employees of the university, the university cannot restrict their private consulting activities, which may create incentives for faculties to be secretive and partial (Williams 1994). In addition, few universities control the terms and conditions of RMTAs to which faculties are signatories, unless these agreements constitute part of a broader agreement governing research funding and/or patent registration and licensing. Thus, there is a large body of university–industry exchanges, many of them governed by contracts, for which universities take no legal or administrative responsibility. Ironically, the university tenure system also makes 'opting out' of public science easier for tenured faculties, because it protects faculties from censure except in the most egregious circumstances. Another problem is that administrators in universities are frequently not as experienced at legal contracting as are the firms with whom they negotiate; consequently, they are occasionally unable to protect their faculties from overly binding contracts. Three scientists we interviewed at one university complained that administrators had signed a contract on their behalf which essentially gave a firm ownership of all their research findings in perpetuity. Finally, universities offer their faculties very attractive incentives to create private intellectual property from their research: typically, faculty inventors can expect to receive between one-third and one-half of all royalties from a university patent (Argyres and Liebeskind 1998). In contrast, a scientist working for a firm might well receive nothing directly from her inventions. This generosity on the part of universities is intended to foster disclosure, and to avoid covert privatization. However, it may also serve to engender secrecy, partiality, and greed. As one university scientist said to us: 'I prefer working for a university to working for a firm: I can make more money in a university.'

For all these reasons, the university—an institution designed for the production of credibility in academic science—is a relatively ineffectual institution for engendering trust in the presence of commercial interests. The involvement of university faculties in commercial research has also placed some strains on the ability of the granting and publishing institutions to support academic credibility. As pointed out in the beginning of this section, many academic scientists no longer work exclusively for the Federal government; many of them obtain funding from commercial sources in one way or another, and so are less sensitive to pressures to maintain academic credibility through the continuous production of published research findings.

It should be remembered that firms are also interested in academic credibility, since university research economizes on research and development costs. None the less, confidentiality concerns are paramount in commercial science; moreover, firms can conduct tests of credibility by replicating research themselves (Rosenberg 1989). Thus it rests on universities to maintain the credibility of their faculty through consciously maintaining and protecting the processes, attitudes, and incentives that ensure credibility, such as publication, academic collaboration, and impartial inquiry. To this end, universities have implemented a number of institutional reforms in recent years that are intended to protect their ability to assure the production of credibility in the presence of commercial interests. For example, it is now common practice in US universities to prohibit faculties from owning equity interests in firms that fund their research, in order to preserve impartiality (Argyres and Liebeskind 1998). Similarly, university faculties must now disclose all their commercial interests to public granting institutions such as the National Institutes of Health and the National Science Foundation.

8. THE NETWORK EFFECTS OF CHANGES IN TRUST RELATIONSHIPS IN ACADEMIC SCIENCE

Changes in the nature of trust relationships in academic science have inevitably affected the network structure of these relationships. Three network dynamics are at work here: erosion of existing ties; exclusion from the formation of new ties; and the extension of network boundaries.

8.1 Erosion of Existing Ties

We have argued that many existing interpersonal trust relationships between academic scientists have been undermined by commercial interests. This is true not only of interpersonal trust relationships, but also of intermediated trust relationships and of institutionally supported trust relationships. As a result, both professional ties and social ties in academic science have been weakened by the intrusion of commercial interests. This is true not only for ties between researchers with commercial interests and those without such interests, but also for ties between researchers with differing commercial interests. None the less, it should be noted that we have observed many instances where existing trust relationships survived changes in the interests of the parties to the relationship. This is especially true where trust relationships were deep in the first place, or where changes in interests have been accompanied by other factors, such as improved access to research funding or materials. For example, increased access to resources may serve to explain why many collaborative research relationships are perpetuated, despite a change in interests, when one collaborator moves from a university to a firm. Thus, the thinning of network ties that has taken place, has taken place primarily among the ties where (a) levels of trust were relatively low in the first place, and/or (b) there have been few benefits to offset the changes in interests of the parties involved.

8.2 Exclusion from the Formation of New Ties

Because commercially oriented research requires broader and deeper levels of trust; because it provides incentives to exclude; because contractual obligations are often long-lived; and because it would be inappropriate for faculties to involve students in research where their ability to publish might be infringed, commercial research projects often have fewer participants than purely academic research projects. Therefore, because collaborative research is the seedbed within which new trust relationships are formed in the academic scientific community, commercial interests serve to reduce the number of new trust relationships that are formed, leading to a condition of 'network ossification'. Hence, the effect of exclusion is also to reduce the total number of trust-based ties within the academic research community. Moreover, exclusion is hierarchical as well as collegial: students are frequently excluded from commercially oriented research, and tenured faculties have the most to gain, and the least to lose, by pursuing it. As a result, the traditional and important role of personal networks in fostering the career development of junior scientists is also weakened.

8.3 Extension of Network Boundaries

While commercial interests have reduced the number of trust-based ties within academic science, new trust relationships have been formed between university scientists and researchers in biotechnology firms. Existing trust relationships have also been transformed by the movement of university faculties and students to these firms. However, these extended boundaries are increasingly being impacted by changes in university rules governing university–industry collaborations. It is possible that in the future, these rules may reduce the rate at which these new boundary-spanning trust relationships are formed.

In the aggregate, these three dynamics have resulted in both a thinning and an extension of the network of trust relationships in academic research. These changes are shown in Figure 4.2. Figure 4.2(a) depicts the situation before commercial interests intruded on academic science in molecular biology. Here, scientists at the four universities depicted, U_1, U_2, U_3, and U_4, have a dense network of research collaborations, and the boundary of this network lies at the boundary of the four universities. The two firms, F_1 and F_2, are not included in this network, and may not even exist at this time. Note that we depict a historical record of collaborations here; thus, there is a high degree of overlap of trust relations between the different scientists, even though at any one point in time we would expect some exclusion between the academic research groups, as different research teams within the overall network compete for priority in discoveries. Because so many scientists collaborate directly, there are also many intermediated trust relationships. In turn, this dense structure of intermediated trust relationships encourages trustworthy behaviour (Granovetter 1985; Burt and Knez 1996) and the formation of new, interpersonal trust relationships.

Figure 4.2(b) depicts the situation after the intrusion of commercial interests. Here, there are fewer ties among the scientists at the four universities. In addition, there is a much lower degree of overlap of interpersonal trust relationships between the university scientists, due to exclusion and ossification. As a result, the network of intermediated trust relationships is very considerably reduced, decreasing the likelihood that these relationships will be able to condition behaviour or foster new academic research relationships. However, the boundaries of the network now extend to the two biotechnology firms.

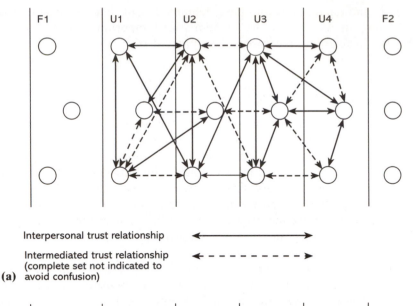

Interpersonal trust relationship

Intermediated trust relationship
(complete set not indicated to
(a) avoid confusion)

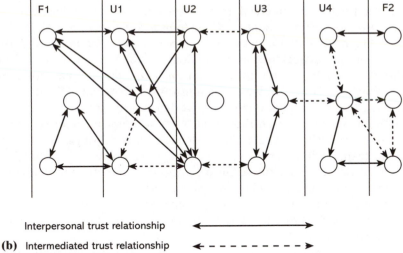

Interpersonal trust relationship

(b) Intermediated trust relationship

FIG. 4.2. Changing networks of trust relationships in academic science in response to the introduction of commercial interests. (a) Networks of interpersonal and intermediated trust in 'normal' science; (b) Networks of interpersonal and intermediated trust after the intrusion of commercial interests

Note: In this scenario, intermediated trust relationships are not likely to be the result of overlapping research collaborations, because this would result in loss of intellectual property interests; they are more likely to be the result of information gathering or gossiping.

9. DISCUSSION

In this study, we have reported how commercial interests have transformed the nature of trust relationships between academic researchers in molecular biology. In turn, this transformation has resulted in a transformation of the social structure of trust relationships in this area of scientific research.

From an academic point of view, this study provides an insight into the interdependence of the nature of trust, the formation and perpetuation of trust-based relationships, and individual interests. We find that trust as a social commodity is not neutral to the interests of individuals or institutions: in many instances, we found evidence that relationships between university scientists were fundamentally changed by changes in the interests of the individuals involved. Many trust-based relationships have been eroded or even severed altogether as a result of the intrusion of commercial interests. At the same time, a different calculus of interests is being used in the formation of new trust relationships. In both cases, formal contractual research agreements are being substituted for the traditional handshake agreements that characterize academic science. In some cases, these contracts support trust relationships, as they do in interorganizational settings (Deakin and Wilkinson, Chapter 5 this volume; Arrighetti, Bachmann and Deakin 1997). In many instances, however, competing contracted interests undermine trust between academic researchers. This is because, while intellectual property contracts serve to engender trust between certain parties involved in exchanges, they also exclude other parties from these exchanges. Because this exclusion particularly concerns the domain in which trust would otherwise be constructed—the exchange of information—the overall effect of contracts on trust is negative. Thus, intellectual property contracts serve in the main to 'disembed' exchange relationships in academic scientific research (Granovetter 1985; Sydow, Chapter 1 this volume).

Our finding that trust relationships and individual interests are closely intertwined in academic science recalls the findings of Parkin (1972), who studied the effects of the introduction of commercial coconut farming on the social structure and culture of the Giriama, a tribe in coastal Kenya. Parkin found that the emergence of new economic opportunities at the individual level led some Giriama to convert to Islam, which provided convertees with a convenient and credibly-binding excuse for not participating in most of the communal activities that formed the social matrix within which redistribution of tribal wealth took place. Similarly, we find that some academic scientists have 'opted out', at least in part, from the communal activities of academic science, in order to pursue their private interests in the domain of commercially oriented research. Their trust relationships with other members of the academic community have been weakened as a result. Furthermore, these scientists are no longer fully contributing parties to the social construction of credibility within the academic scientific community.

Our findings also point to the fact that commercial interests can foster trust-based relationships. Alongside the thinning out of trust relationships among academic scientists, we also found many instances where relationships between academic scientists and NBF scientists that were initially self-seeking in nature evolved into relationships of trust, despite differences in the parties' interests. Thus, trust is not best viewed as a fixed or given commodity that exists within a specific social community or network of relationships (Granovetter 1985), but rather should be understood to be the output of dynamic exchange relationships that are fuelled by individual interests, as well as being the lubricant for the formation of new exchange relationships. Thus, exchange is both embedded in trust, and engenders its formation, consistent with the framework of structuration theory (Sydow, Chapter 1 this volume).

From a policy point of view, the transformation in trust relationships that we have observed must be considered somewhat problematical. In our knowledge-based society, universities are the only institutions that are exclusively devoted to the production of impartial information (Bok 1981; Nelkin 1984; Wade 1984). Thus, any influence that threatens to undermine the institutional regime of open science, especially the norms of publicity and impartiality that are so critical to the production of credible information, must be viewed with concern. In this sense, the argument that the commercialization of research in molecular biology is an unambiguous benefit to society is too narrowly drawn: the costs as well as the benefits of such commercialization must be carefully considered. Moreover, the burden of these costs may be more serious in the long term, than in the short term. At present, the influence of commercial interests on the behaviour of academic scientists in molecular biology is to some degree moderated by their instilled values, as most scientists were socialized into the norms of academic science before the intrusion of commercial interests took place. In the future, however, this may no longer be the case: the next cohort of faculty members is now being socialized into a science that is largely pervaded—either directly or indirectly—by commercial interests and values. At a very minimum, most researchers in molecular biology are now fully aware of the interests that attach to intellectual property rights, contracting, and commercialization; many take property rights into consideration in designing research programmes and choosing collaborators. It is an open question as to whether the ideals of academic scientific conduct—such as publicity, inclusion, and impartiality—can be maintained within this new context. If they cannot, then society's trust in the university as an institution of impartiality will inevitably be undermined.

NOTES

1. Individual scientists frequently demonstrate 'zeal' in ensuring that credit for discoveries is allocated fairly. For instance, Sir John Vane of Cambridge University recently criticized the Laskar Prize Committee for failing to award the prize to Salvador Moncada for his work on the functions of nitric oxide (*Science*, 11 Oct. 1996, 173–4).
2. For instance, early DNA research was characterized by secrecy and intense competition between research teams (Watson 1968; Taubes 1986).
3. Not all granting institutions use peer review. Peer review can also lead to excess production of 'normal' science (Kuhn 1962; Latour and Woolgar 1979).
4. It is commonly argued that this is due to large established firms lacking both the absorptive capacity and the social connections necessary to stay on the forefront of scientific advances in molecular biology.
5. This was not always the case; many US universities have only recently moved to restrict faculty equity ownership or managerial involvement in NBFs in order to avoid conflicts of interest (Argyres and Liebeskind 1998).
6. Similar legislation was subsequently passed in Britain, France, Israel, and Japan.
7. Consider this statement made recently in the corporate report of one NBF: 'It is the Company's current practice to require its employees, consultants [who are usually faculty members], members of its Medical and Research Advisory Board [also usually faculty members], (and) sponsored researchers [also usually faculty members] . . . to execute confidentiality agreements . . . these agreements provide that all confidential information developed or made known to the individual during the course of the individual's relationship with the Company is to be kept confidential and not disclosed to third parties.'
8. Firms' need for secure intellectual property rights to biotechnology products was emphasized in 1982, when the University of California sued Genentech, claiming the firm had illegally obtained and used a cell line for producing insulin that in fact belonged to the university (*Biotechnology Law Report*, 1 Jan. 1982). This lawsuit threatened to bankrupt Genentech, and was rapidly followed by a number of suits over patent rights and patent infringements by other universities and by some NBFs, again signalling the importance of patents to profitability.
9. The same observation would also apply to Britain, France, Israel, and Japan where biomedical research in universities is also funded in large part by government.
10. Eisenberg (1987) recounts that the *Journal of Biological Chemistry* found itself unable to enforce a rule requiring authors to provide cell lines and other research materials to scientists wanting to replicate their findings.
11. For example, the US Patent Office took almost four years to approve the 'Cohen-Boyer' gene-splicing patent, due in part to a dispute as to whether a third scientist should also be cited as an inventor (*Biotechnology Law Report*, 1. May–July and Oct.–Nov. 1982).
12. A university contracting for intellectual property rights may not always protect

faculties from restrictive clauses that apply to future uses of proprietary materials and data. In particular, universities frequently do not regulate RMTAs,
and cannot legally regulate the terms and conditions of faculty consulting agreements, except insofar as they relate to conflicts of interest in academic research.
This is because faculties are not strictly employees of the university (Williams
1994).

13. For instance, consider the case of one scientist we interviewed who was asked to
participate in a research project examining the properties of a given cell line that
was already patented by an NBF. Before joining the project, the scientist had to
sign: (a) an agreement that precisely described the scope of work that he would
carry out, and also restricted him from carrying out any other work on the cell
line; (b) an RMTA that prohibited him from claiming ownership of any patentable discoveries he might make while working with the cell line; and (c) a
confidentiality agreement that required him not to publish his research findings
or discuss them with non-approved third parties without first allowing the NBF
concerned to examine them for the purposes of protecting its own intellectual
property interests.

14. For instance, Rabinow (1996) discusses the challenges faced by Cetus Corporation in trying to induce Kary Mullis, the inventor of PCR, to develop the
technique to the point where the firm could claim patent rights. Cetus
was concerned that a number of other firms were close to developing PCR
on their own account. Moreover, Mullis had talked freely with some
outsiders about his ideas. However, at this critical point in time, Mullis
apparently became distracted by other research questions, and much of the
work required for the patent was ultimately completed by other scientists at
the firm.

15. See the *Biotechnology Law Report*, 5 (1986) and 6 (1987).

16. See 'A Cautionary Tale', *Science*, 293 (26 July 1996), 411.

REFERENCES

Argyres, N. and Liebeskind, J. (1996), 'Privatizing the Intellectual Commons: Universities and the Commercialization of Biotechnology Research', *Journal of
Economic Behaviour and Organization*, 1988 in press.

Arrighetti, A., Bachmann, R., and Deakin, S. (1997), 'Contract Law, Social
Norms and Inter-Firm Cooperation', *Cambridge Journal of Economics*, 21/2: 171–
96.

Arrow, K. (1962), 'Economic Welfare and the Allocation of Resources of Inven-
tion', in *National Bureau of Economic Research, The Rate and Direction of
Inventive Activity: Economic and Social Factors*. Princeton: Princeton University
Press, 609–25.

Axelrod, R. (1984), *The Evolution of Cooperation*. New York: Basic Books.

Beardsley, T. (1994), 'Big Time Biology', *Scientific American* (Nov.), 90–5.

Blau, P. (1964), *Exchange and Power in Social Life*. New York: Wiley.

Bok, D. (1981), 'President's Report: Business and the Academy', *Harvard Magazine* (May/June), 23–35.

Brewer, M. and Kramer, R. (1986), 'Choice Behaviors in Social Dilemmas', *Journal of Personality and Social Psychology*, 50: 543–9.

Burt, R. and Knez, M. (1996), 'Trust and Third-party Gossip', in R. Kramer and T. Tyler (eds.), *Trust in Organizations*. Thousand Oaks, Calif.: Sage, 68–89.

Cohen, L. and Noll, R. (1994), 'Privatizing Public Research', *Scientific American* (Sept.), 72–7.

Coleman, R. (1990), *Foundations of Social Theory*. Cambridge, Mass.: Belknap Press.

Crane, D. (1972), *Invisible Colleges: Diffusion of Knowledge in Scientific Communities*. Chicago: University of Chicago Press.

Dasgupta, P. (1988), 'Trust as a Commodity', in D. Gambetta (ed.), *Trust: Making and Breaking Cooperative Relations*. Oxford: Blackwell, 49–72.

——and David, P. (1987), 'Information Disclosure and the Economics of Science and Technology', in G. Feiwel (ed.), *Arrow and the Ascent of Modern Economic Theory*. New York: Macmillan, 519–42.

David, P. (1992), 'Reputation and Agency in the Historical Emergence of the Institutions of "Open Science"', MS, Stanford University.

——Mowery, D., and Steinmueller, W. (1994), 'University–Industry Research Collaborations: Managing Missions in Conflict', MS, Stanford University.

Deutschman, A. (1994), 'The Managing Wisdom of High-Tech Superstars', *Fortune*, 17 Oct., 197–206.

Eisenberg, R. (1987), 'Proprietary Rights and the Norms of Science in Biotechnology Research', *Yale Law Journal*, 97: 177–231.

Fukuyama, F. (1995), *Trust*. New York: Free Press.

Gambetta, D. (1988), 'Can We Trust Trust?', in Gambetta (ed.), *Trust: Making and Breaking Cooperative Relations*, 213–38.

Good, D. (1988), 'Individuals, Interpersonal Relationships, and Trust', in Gambetta (ed.), *Trust: Making and Breaking Cooperative Relations*, 31–48.

Granovetter, M. (1985), 'Economic Action and Social Structure: A Theory of Embeddedness', *American Journal of Sociology*, 91: 481–510.

Hagstrom, W. (1965), *The Scientific Community*, New York: Basic Books.

Harding, J. (1991), 'The Role of Trust in Knowledge', *Journal of Philosophy*, 88: 693–708.

Hempel, C. (1966), *Philosophy of Natural Science*, Englewood Cliffs, NJ: Prentice-Hall.

Henderson, R., Jaffee, A., and Trajtenberg, M. (1994), 'The Bayh-Dole Act and Trends in University Patenting', MS, Stanford Centre for Economic Policy Research.

Hicks, D. (1995), 'Published Papers, Tacit Competencies and Corporate Management of the Public/Private Character of Knowledge', *Industrial and Corporate Change*, 4: 401–24.

Hilgartner, S. and Brandt-Rauf, S. (1994), 'Controlling Data and Resources: Access Strategies in Molecular Genetics', MS, Columbia University.

Kenney, Martin (1986), *Biotechnology: The University–Industry Complex*. New Haven: Yale University Press.

Kramer, R. (1994), 'The Sinister Attribution Error: Paranoid Cognition and Collective Distrust in Organizations', *Motivation and Emotion*, 18: 199–230.

——Brewer, M., and Hanna, B. (1996), 'Collective Trust and Collective Action: The Decision to Trust as a Social Decision', in Kramer and Tyler (eds.), *Trust in Organizations*, 357–89.

Kreps, D. (1990), 'Corporate Culture and Economic Theory', in J. Alt and K. Shepsle (eds.), *Perspectives on Positive Political Economy*. Cambridge: Cambridge University Press.

Kuhn, T. (1962), *The Structure of Scientific Revolutions*. Chicago: University of Chicago Press.

Landa, J. (1994), *Trust, Ethnicity and Identity*. Ann Arbor, Mich.: University of Michigan Press.

Latour, B. and Woolgar, S. (1979), *Laboratory Life: The Construction of Scientific Facts*. Princeton: Princeton University Press.

Lee, K. and Burrill, G. (1995), *Biotech 95: Reform, Restructure, Renewal*. Palo Alto, Tex.: Ernst and Young.

Liebeskind, J., Oliver, A., Zucker, L., and Brewer, M. (1996), 'Social Networks, Learning and Flexibility: Sourcing Knowledge in New Biotechnology Firms', *Organization Science*, 17/1: 428–43.

Luhmann, N. (1988), 'Familiarity, Confidence, and Trust', in Gambetta (ed.), *Trust: Making and Breaking Cooperative Relations*, 94–108.

McCain, K. (1991), 'Communication, Competition and Secrecy: The Protection and Dissemination of Research-related Information in Genetics', *Science, Technology and Human Values*, 16: 491–516.

Merry, S. (1984), 'Rethinking Gossip and Scandal', in D. Black (ed.), *Toward a General Theory of Social Control*. New York: Academic Press.

Merton, R. (1973), 'The Normative Structure of Science', in R. Merton (ed.), *The Sociology of Science*. Chicago: University of Chicago Press, 223–80.

Nelkin, D. (1984), *Science as Intellectual Property: Who Controls Research?*. American Association for the Advancement of Science, New York: Macmillan.

Oliver, A. L. (forthcoming), 'On the Nexus of Organizations and Professions: Networking Through Trust', *Sociological Inquiry*, 67.

——and Montgomery, K. (1996), 'Creating a Hybrid Organizational Form from Parental Blueprints: The Emergence and Evolution of Knowledge Firms', Working Paper, Hebrew University.

Orsengio, L. (1989), *The Emergence of Biotechnology*. New York: St Martin's Press.

Parkin, D. (1972), *Palms, Wine and Witnesses: Public Spirit and Private Gain in an African Farming Community*. San Francisco: Chandler.

Rabinow, P. (1996), *Making PCR*. Chicago: University of Chicago Press.

Rosenberg, N. (1990), 'Why Do Firms Do Basic Research With Their Own Money?' *Research Policy*, 19: 165–74.

Rosensweig, R. and Turlington B. (1982), *The Research Universities and Their Patrons*. Berkeley: University of California Press.

Rotter, J. (1980), 'Inter-Personal Trust, Trustworthiness and Gullibility', *American Psychologist*, 35: 1–7.

Taubes, G. (1986), *Nobel Dreams: Power, Deceit, and the Ultimate Experiment*. New York: Random House.

Teitelman, R. (1989), *Gene Dreams*. New York: Basic Books.

Tullock, G. (1966), *The Organization of Inquiry*. Durham, NC: Duke University Press.

Twentieth Century Fund (1984), *The Science Business: Report of the Twentieth Century Fund Task Force on the Commercialization of Scientific Research*. New York: Priority Press.

Wade, N. (1984), 'Background Paper', in *The Science Business: Report of the Twentieth Century Fund Task Force on the Commercialization of Scientific Research*.

Watson, J. (1968), *The Double Helix: A Personal Account of the Discovery of the Structure of DNA*. New York: Norton.

Werth, B. (1995), *The Billion Dollar Molecule*. New York: Touchstone/Simon & Schuster.

Williams, B. (1988), 'Formal Structures and Social Reality', in Gambetta (ed.), *Trust: Making and Breaking Cooperative Relations*.

Williams, C. (1994), 'Ownership and Management of Faculty Generated Inventions', MS, University of Washington School of Law.

Zucker, L. (1986), 'Production of Trust: Institutional Sources of Economic Structure, 1840 to 1920', *Research in Organizational Behavior*, 8: 53–111.

——and Darby, M. (1996), 'Star Scientists and Institutional Transformation: Patterns of Invention and Innovation in the Formation of the Biotechnology Industry', *Proceedings of the National Academy of Science*, 93/12: 709–16.

————Brewer, M., and Peng, Y. (1996), 'Organizational Boundaries as Trust Production', in Kramer and Tyler (eds.), *Trust in Organizations*.

5

Contract Law and the Economics of Interorganizational Trust

SIMON DEAKIN AND FRANK WILKINSON

1. INTRODUCTION

Following the seminal study of Macaulay (1963), writers in the socio-legal tradition have generally assumed that the system of contract law is marginal to the process of business contracting. The juridification of commercial relations through contract and regulatory law is seen as inimical to the emergence and preservation of trust. Organization theorists also view legalistic procedures and sanctions both as a threat to trust and as ineffective in restoring trust when contractual relations break down (Sitkin and Roth 1993).

In economic theory, by contrast, it is trust, rather than law, which is regarded as peripheral to contracting. Legal sanctions, operating as a set of implicit prices or incentives, help to ensure an efficient level of performance of contractual obligations (Posner 1993). Trust, on the other hand, is simply an outcome or expression of agents' calculations concerning future contingencies (including the possibility of legal liability). As such, it is a largely redundant or misleading notion (Williamson 1993, 1996: ch. 10).

This chapter seeks to reassess the relationship between organizational trust and the legal-institutional framework governing economic relations. It will be suggested that the assumed opposition between trust and law springs from an unnecessarily rigid and narrow view of legal norms as predominantly coercive in nature. This view assumes that legal norms, along with other formal rules, impose external constraints to which agents respond in a rational, calculative manner. If, however, the assumption of omniscient calculation by agents is replaced by one of decision-making under conditions of pervasive uncertainty, then normative rules no longer *simply* constrain agents' behaviour; rather, they may play an enabling role which opens up certain strategic possibilities for co-operation. Under these circumstances, normative rules, including the rules of the legal system, may provide an important mechanism for the reproduction of trust.

Our empirical research, referred to below, confirms this suggestion by showing that firms operating under similar *sectoral* conditions (in terms of intensity of demand, market structure, and degree of stability) tend to adopt different strategic approaches to supplier relations according to the nature of the different *institutional* frameworks within which their exchange relations are conducted. There is no evidence that either co-operation or trust is necessarily reduced in national systems where the levels of institutional regulation and contract formality are high. On the contrary, there are indications that relations based on conflict and distrust are more likely in systems with minimal normative regulation.

Our discussion proceeds as follows. In Section 2 we look at economic approaches to the definition of trust, including those of the economic analysis of law, game theory, and transaction cost economics. We will argue that rational choice analyses provide us with only a thin and partial account of trust and that, conversely, more institutionally orientated approaches within economics need to incorporate a viable theory of *system trust* if they are to progress. Section 3 illustrates this argument by reference to our empirical work. Section 4 concludes by considering the implications of our analysis for the question of whether the legal system, or other policy mechanisms, can be used actively to foster trust.

2. CONTRACT LAW, TRUST, AND ECONOMIC THEORY

In common with other recent contributions, we take 'trust' to refer to a belief or understanding on the part of one agent in the reliability or capability of another. Although from one point of view trust is 'an element of all social exchange relations . . . and collective action' (Sitkin and Roth 1993: 367), it is also plausible to suggest that the degree of importance attached to trust varies according to the nature of the relationship in question. In this sense, trust becomes particularly important where relationships contain one of a number of elements, including uncertainty arising from unforeseeable future contingencies, a degree of interdependence between agents, and the threat of opportunism (cf. Lane, 'Introduction'). There is also general agreement that trust can be an important means of enhancing the effectiveness of relationships which depend upon extensive co-operation at either an inter- or intra-organizational level. Here, trust may contribute to operational efficiency by reducing transaction costs which are associated with relational contracting. By providing a basis for the sharing of information and risk, it may also promote dynamic efficiency based on innovation and adaptation (Deakin and Wilkinson 1996; Sako, Chapter 3, this volume). At this level, the question of trust is bound up with that of economic development and competitiveness (Humphrey and Schmitz 1996; Deakin, Goodwin, and Hughes (forthcoming)).

But is trust, as just described, a phenemenon which is ultimately reducible to interactions between self-interested, utility-maximizing individuals?

A form of *calculative* or *self-interested trust* could be based on the belief of parties to an economic relationship that it is in their individual self-interest to continue trading (Dasgupta 1988; Lyons and Mehta (forthcoming)). Where the relationship rests upon an agreement to co-operate, this can be maintained by the possibility that any defection will be sanctioned by retaliation of some kind. Expectations may be formed over time on the basis of a 'Bayesian' updating of beliefs, as each agent recalculates the probability of future defection by others in the light of their past behaviour (Axelrod 1984). The same process can be understood as operating at a broader societal level: social practices which are regarded as underpinning contractual relations—such as reputational effects, norms of ethical behaviour, and conventions of standard business practice (cf. Macaulay 1963; Beale and Dugdale 1975)—may be established through the repeated, recursive interactions of individual agents (Coleman 1990; Kreps 1990; Casson 1993*a*, *b*).

Here, the basic insight of game theory is that the success of strategies for future co-operation between contracting parties depends on how far each agent calculates that it is in his or her self-interest to continue observing the norm of co-operation, *given the likely behaviour and response of the other*. A situation in which each party adopts and maintains a strategy which will maximize its own interest, given the choice or strategy of the other(s), is known as a 'Nash equilibrium'. A Nash equilibrium does not necessarily represent a state in which the allocative efficiency of society's resources is maximized. Thus in many of the situations analysed by the 'prisoners' dilemma' game, self-interested behaviour by both of the parties results in a sub-optimal solution.

It can be shown, nevertheless, that under circumstances of repeated exchange, there is a greater likelihood that strategies of co-operation will prevail, as each party now calculates that the costs of defection include the prospect of retaliation by the other party in future rounds of bargaining (Axelrod 1984). In other words, co-operation may be enforced as long as there is a credible threat of retaliatory behaviour, and this, in turn, depends upon the extent of future trading opportunities and of the parties' knowledge or perception of them. Where both parties anticipate the continuation of trading relations between them, their agreement to co-operate may be self-enforcing. However, for complete self-enforcement, it is necessary that the parties are *not* equally well informed about the terminal date of the relationship, since once that is known, the parties enter a bargaining 'endgame' in which, through backward induction, it becomes rational for each party to defect in response to the impending defection of the other. This insight can be thought of as explaining the apparently stable nature of many contracts for an indeterminate duration, such as 'permanent' employment contracts, but, in general, few contracts conform to this model.

Possible 'external' solutions to the problem of non-co-operation in long-term relationships include legal enforcement, on the one hand, and the presence of a shared commercial morality or set of ethical values, on the other. However, it has also been suggested that agents can devise their own governance structures through *private ordering* in such a way as to obviate the need for external intervention. Incentive structures may play a role in supporting long-term exchange relations in contracts of varying degrees of complexity and duration. A substantial body of work in the modern economic theory of contract has been devoted to understanding the operation of exchange relations under conditions of risk, opportunism and asymmetric information, in other words, the very same conditions which are also the focus of study in the debate over trust. From an economic point of view, the effects of relaxing the assumption that all agents are equally well informed about the quality or characteristics of goods, or of the prices of alternative commodities, are far-reaching. If, for example, buyers cannot observe the quality of goods purchased at the time of contracting—the problem of 'adverse selection' or hidden information—individual sellers may have an incentive to lower the quality of the goods offered to the *average* level of quality which buyers expect to receive; higher-quality sellers may then withdraw from the market. The result is a sub-optimal allocation of resources (Akerlof 1970). Similarly, economic relationships involving a divergence of interests between 'principal' and 'agent' may be vitiated by 'moral hazard' or hidden action, that is, by the likelihood that the agent will act to further his or her own interests at the expense of the principal, under circumstances where the latter cannot effectively monitor the former's performance.

One response to adverse selection is 'signalling', whereby a seller takes steps to indicate to potential buyers that the goods which he or she offers for sale are of above average quality. The seller can do this by taking steps which are less costly for him or her than they would be for sellers of lower-quality goods (Spence 1973). Buyers may then draw the necessary inference. In the case of moral hazard, it is argued that the principal can devise a payment schedule which induces the agent to behave in such a way as to maximize the principal's utility. Certain common contractual arrangements, such as piece-work employment contracts, and share-cropping tenancy agreements, have been analysed in this way (cf. Stiglitz 1990).

More generally, where there are transaction-specific rents, contract terms can be used to set up an incentive structure aimed at giving credibility to the parties' commitments. The essential idea is that one or both of the parties undertakes to cede something of value in the event of committing a breach of contract. Bonds, collateral, penalties, and other forms of contractual 'hostages', which might appear to be the result of inequality of bargaining power, may be designed instead to stabilize the exchange in the interests of both parties (cf. Williamson 1983; Kronman 1985). Contracts may also contain incentive structures which embody a positive reward system of some kind in order to elicit co-operation over the long term, such as the informal job security guarantees and more formal pension entitlements which are found in contracts of employment.

Even though these approaches predict considerable scope for self-enforcing agreements, or agreements which do not depend for their effectiveness upon the threat of external legal enforcement, limits to self-enforcement must also be recognized (cf. You and Wilkinson 1994). Even in the case of incentive structures which represent an *ex ante* efficient allocation of risk, there remains the problem that renegotiation of the contract terms may become necessary at some point in the life of the relationship, or that one party may acquire a temporary market advantage which it can use to dictate new terms of trade. The formal conditions under which long-term contracts can be written so as to be 'renegotiation-proof' are so extreme as to have only a tenuous connection with agreements of the kind which are observed in practice, if, indeed, they can be stated formally at all (cf. Harsanyi and Selten 1988). As a result, most analysts see a significant role being maintained for mechanisms of institutional enforcement of various kinds, even if they work in conjunction with, rather than against, those based on private ordering. Hence, 'government policies which enhance complete contracts and improve their enforcement, can be welfare enhancing. Examples are contract law, liability rules, and trade regulations' (Kotowitz 1990: 212).

In the law and economics literature, contract law is generally seen as providing a set of 'default rules' which serve to reduce transaction costs and overcome informational and related barriers to optimal exchange. Legal enforcement of promises is not absolute, but is set by a comparison of the marginal costs and benefits of court-led intervention (Posner 1993). The costs include the time and expense involved in administering and enforcing the remedies concerned. Information and measurement problems make it difficult for the courts effectively to gauge the value of the parties' *ex ante* contractual expectations; nor can they enforce or supervise specific performance of a contract without encountering serious problems of moral hazard (Kronman 1978, 1985). Strict legal enforcement may, indeed, be actively harmful in the context of long-term, relational contracts which rest upon shared assumptions and understandings and on the possibility of extra-legal sanctions which may not be expressed in formal terms. Such arrangements may easily be misinterpreted by the courts, which do not have access to the specialized knowledge or assumptions shared by the parties (Charny 1990; Bernstein 1992).

As a consequence, 'the legal right to enforce a promise can reduce but not eliminate the insecurity associated with all temporally asymmetrical exchanges' (Kronman 1985: 25). *Specific performance*, or the literal enforcement of a promise of contractual performance, is normally only avail-

able where the victim of breach could not have been adequately compensated by other means (such as finding a substitute contract). Moroever, the
extent of damages awarded will be reduced by (amongst other things) the
requirement that the innocent party take steps to minimize his or her losses
through *mitigation*. Damages seek to protect the expectation interest or
opportunity cost of the plaintiff, but the courts will not award punitive or
restitutionary damages in excess of this amount. As a result, the common
law of contract permits an 'efficient' breach of contract which, by redirect-
ing the resources in question to a more efficient use than originally envisaged, would leave all the parties better off (on the assumption that the
victim of breach can be fully compensated out of the resulting surplus).
There are other ways in which the law of contract is seen as providing
incentive structures which promote allocative efficiency. For example, common law rules concerning mistake and misrepresentation can be seen as
providing the parties with incentives to minimize joint search costs in situations of limited information (Kronman 1978). These common law liability
rules can be seen as supplementing private ordering based on specialized
incentive structures and 'signalling'.

The phenomenon of trust in contractual relations may be explained,
therefore, in terms of the rational responses of agents to incentive structures supplied by mechanisms of private ordering, on the one hand, and
by the legal system and other instruments of state intervention, on the
other. But another interpretation would be that these analyses deny any
role at all for trust as an explanatory factor. Williamson, for example, has
argued that:

transaction cost economics refers to contractual safeguards, or their absence, rather
than trust, or its absence. I argue that it is redundant at best and can be misleading
to use the term 'trust' to describe commercial exchange for which cost-effective
safeguards have been devised in support of more efficient exchange. Calculative
trust is a contradiction in terms.   (Williamson 1996: 256)

In other words: from an economic perspective, there may be value in
studying the incentive structures and other processes by which barriers to
efficient contracting are overcome; but the notion of trust does not help us
to understand *these* processes.

Williamson then goes on to suggest that other possible formulations of
trust—personal or process trust, on the one hand, and institutional or
systems trust, on the other—are of limited value as explanations of economic form. The use of the term 'personal trust' is, he suggests, 'warranted
only for very special personal relations that would be seriously degraded if
a calculative orientation were "permitted". Commercial relations do not
qualify' (1996: 275). Institutional trust, which 'refers to the social and
organisational context within which contracts are embedded', also 'has
the appearance of being non-calculative'; but this is deceptive, because

transactions are governed 'with reference to the institutional context (environment) of which they are a part. Calculativeness thus always reappears' (ibid.). In other words, the institutional framework is simply a part, for this purpose, of the incentive structure from which the pattern of transactions emerges. Institutions are important, but to describe their effect in terms of 'trust' is misleading except to the extent that some kind of partial or 'hyphenated' trust can be derived from institutional sources. This 'hyphenated' trust may be worthy of study, but it cannot be properly compared to the kind of trust which is generated at the level of interpersonal relations.

At one level, a calculative, or 'economic-rational' dimension to business contracting cannot be denied. Still less would it be appropriate to talk of co-operative relations involving the denial or submergence of the parties' *separate* interests. If there is no separation of interests, and hence no possibility of a divergence or conflict of interests, then there is no problem of trust worth discussing. In the world of perfect unity of interests, the issue of trust would be as trivial as in the 'zero transaction cost world' of perfect rationality, foresight, and candour on the part of contracting agents. However, if we wish to retain a role for 'calculative' behaviour, this need not be regarded as synonymous with the peculiar 'hyperrationality' which much of economic theory imputes to agents. As Williamson (among others) has noted, this makes 'patently unrealistic assumptions about the cognitive ability of human actors to receive, store, retrieve, and process information' (Williamson 1996: 8). His version of transaction cost economics 'concedes that comprehensive contracting is not a feasible option (by reason of bounded rationality), yet it maintains that many economic agents have the capacities both to learn and to look ahead, perceive hazards, and factor these back into the contractual relation' (ibid. 9).

But if 'hyperrationality' is rejected, the implications for analysis are much more far-reaching than adherents of transaction cost economics seem prepared to accept. Why should it be assumed that choices about the forms of contractual governance—such as the choice between integrating production in a single firm and pursuing extended forms of co-operative relations between firms—represent an efficient, 'economizing' response by agents to their environment? We might expect one result of 'bounded rationality' to be 'bounded effiency' (Zucker 1986: 67). If that were so, there would be limits to the capacity of agents to contract for the safeguards needed to sustain complex exchange relations. Institutions might then have a role to play in the production and reproduction of trust, on the basis of which long-term exchange relations could be sustained notwithstanding the 'incompleteness' of the contracts on which they were based.

This suggestion is admittedly difficult to reconcile with a transaction cost analysis which sees the institutional framework as a coercive and constraining force, to which agents respond by modifying their behaviour: 'taking the institutional environment as given, economic agents purportedly align transactions with governance structures to effect economising outcomes' (Williamson 1996: 5; cf. also North 1993, 1994). It naturally enough follows from this point of view that the legal system, as an external *given* constraint on agents' behaviour, can have little or no part to play in generating inter-personal trust.

This is a theme which is echoed in parts of the organization theory literature, where it has been analysed in detail by Sitkin and Roth (1993). They suggest that while legalistic sanctions and procedures can promote trust in the (arguably limited) sense of enhanced reliability, they can, at the same time, engender *distrust* in the sense of disrupting a sense of shared values. This occurs for three reasons: first, 'legalistic remedies can erode the interpersonal foundations of a relationship they are intended to bolster because they replace reliance on a person's "good will" with objective, formal requirements'. Secondly, legal intervention, by placing distance be-tween the parties, is hostile to the tacit or implicit elements which underlie close interpersonal relations. Thirdly, legal procedures can only address a particular aspect of a dispute or conflict, and so fail to address the wider effects of 'value incongruence' (Sitkin and Roth 1993: 376). In some-what similar vein, Sako (Chapter 3, this volume) advances the hypothesis that formal legal contracts can enhance 'competence' trust, or the expecta-tion of reliability in performance, but are likely to undermine 'goodwill trust'.

What is lacking from these analyses is an appreciation that the social impact of legal and other norms may be more than just coercive. There is no recognition, for example, of the 'normative' and 'cognitive' dimensions of institutional forms which are recognized by writers in the neo-institutional strand within sociology. We may refer briefly here to Scott's formulation, in which the regulative or 'constraining' aspects of institutional rules are offset by normative rules which 'introduce a prescriptive, evaluative, and obliga-tory dimension into social life' (Scott 1995: 32) and by cognitive aspects which 'constitute the nature of reality and the frames through which mean-ing is made' (ibid. 40). The effect is to posit a richer theory of individual agency than the rigidly deterministic one offered by rational choice theory within economics. From a *normative* viewpoint, choice is no longer prede-termined by instrumental considerations, but is influenced by conceptions of appropriate behaviour in particular settings; from a *cognitive* viewpoint, choices are not simply constrained but are also informed by rule-based systems.

If this view is taken, then the relationship between the institutional framework and economic agency must be seen as a multilayered and com-plex one. It cannot be reduced to the (more or less straightforward) adap-tation of individual behaviour to the signals sent out by 'incentive structures' which are derived, in turn, from some 'given' set of institutional forms. Legal and social norms operate on individual agency at a number of levels, so that agency itself can be said to presuppose the prior existence of a system of institutionalized norms and rules. Hence, 'rational' economic agency presupposes the existence of norms concerning acceptable, legitimate, or conventional behaviour by business parties. The operation of business organizations presupposes the existence of constitutive norms relating to the status of the organizational form (as a public limited or joint-stock company, or as a public-sector body) and of its members (employees, managers, and so on). These norms may take a tacit or implicit form, but their relationship to more formal norms at the level, for example, of the legal system, must also be taken into account.

Here, the idea of institutional-based trust, as developed by Zucker (1986), or system trust, as developed by Luhmann (1979), Giddens (1990), and Lane and Bachmann (1996), offers important insights. This point of view holds that trust, by its very nature, cannot be *merely* calculative. This is because the complexity of the environment is such that complete contracting over future contingencies is impossible. But, equally, it is inappropriate to think of institutional rules or social norms as simply filling in the gaps in 'incomplete' contracts, or as providing the necessary 'missing' incentive structures, as in the mainstream 'law and economics' literature. Much of the importance of the legal and regulatory system lies in the 'taken for granted' quality of the norms which it produces. As Lane and Bachmann (1997) put it, if trust is 'a mechanism by which actors reduce the internal complexity of their interaction system and which enables the actors to mutually establish specific expectations about their future behaviour', then the principal function of the legal system is not to 'be activated and imposed on actors who have cheated. Rather it serves as a background structure which provides for the possibility of sanctions and thus deters from cheating'. In other words: norms operate as a set of framework conditions, setting standards which, to a greater or lesser degree, are internalized by agents, and which may serve to reinforce expectations of future behaviour. But it is not being suggested that agents respond in a mechanically instrumental fashion to the presence of norms. Their choice of action is not predetermined. Rather, legal and other normative influences have a potentially 'facilitative' or 'channelling' role. Agents faced with the need to co-operate with one another in a contractual setting have a number of 'strategic' options at their disposal as a consequence of the institutional framework within which they operate, and given the resources or capabilities which they have at their disposal.

To sum up our argument to this point, the notion of 'calculative trust' is, as Williamson suggests, a contradiction in terms. However, it does not follow, as Williamson implies, that the concept of trust more generally is of no interest to economics. On the contrary, economic analysis should be informed by an understanding of how institutional mechanisms can operate to generate trust. In this respect, the role of the institutional framework cannot be confined to that of 'constraining' agents' behaviour, as implied not just by transaction cost economics but also by many accounts in the socio-legal and organizational literature. Instead, attention should also be focused on the role of the institutional framework in 'channelling' economic activity, in particular by creating an environment in which firms view co-operative behaviour as feasible.

It is essential, therefore, to maintain a distinction between, on the one hand, the process by which individual firms form trusting relationships with each other (which we may refer to as personal or *processual trust*) and, on the other, the *system trust* which derives from the operation of collective institutions (Dei Ottati 1994). The more effective this wider framework is in promoting information flows and spreading the costs of conflict, monitoring, and uncertainty, the greater will be the potential for trust-building within individual relationships. Hence the building of processual trust through individual relationships and interorganizational links cannot be seen in isolation from the institutional framework within which contracts are made and performed.

3. SYSTEM TRUST AND CO-OPERATIVE STRATEGIES

In this part, we illustrate the arguments set out above by reference to our empirical work on interfirm relations. As has been suggested elsewhere (cf. Sako, and Kern, both this volume), the idea that high-trust relations might improve economic performance has been widely theorized, but relatively little empirical evidence has been produced in its favour. Problems arise in conceptualizing trust, in measuring it, and in obtaining reliable comparative evidence of the performance of different productive systems. The Cambridge study of vertical interfirm contracting (cf. Arrighetti, Bachmann, and Deakin 1997; Lane and Bachmann 1997; Burchell and Wilkinson 1997), on which we will draw here, involved a cross-sectoral and cross-country comparison which throws into relief the impact of the legal-regulatory system on contractual practice. It also provides evidence of perceptions of trust on the part of business managers operating under different sectoral and institutional conditions. The study is therefore of particular relevance to our hypothesis that the institutional framework may be an important factor in the generation of trust.

The Cambridge study was based on a randomly selected sample of around sixty firms in two engineering sectors (mining machinery and kitchen furniture) in three countries (Germany, Britain, and Italy). Lengthy interviews, using a semi-structured questionnaire, were carried out through visits to the firms which took place during 1993 and 1994. Information was also collected on both the sectoral and institutional conditions under which the firms were operating.

The two industries had strongly contrasting features in terms of market structure, entry and exit costs, the extent of capital investments, and the nature and intensity of competitive pressures. Mining machinery is a highly developed and technically advanced industry, with a relatively small and stable population of firms. Until recently, most manufacturers had close relationships with coal production companies which were all or part-owned by the state (in particular, British Coal and Ruhrkohle in Britain and Germany respectively). Relationships in the supply chain had been subject to a high degree of regulation, much of it either encouraged or simply imposed by the large coal producers in each country. The collapse of demand for coal in the early 1990s, together with the related effects of privatization in the energy sectors, placed manufacturers under severe competitive pressures, and, at the time our interviews were carried out, had led them to diversify into rapidly growing export markets including those in China, the former Soviet Union, and Iran. Kitchen furniture, by contrast, is a developing industry which has enjoyed steady growth for several decades as part of the rise in demand for fitted kitchens. On the whole, start-up costs are low (at least for certain segments of the trade), alternative suppliers are readily available, and neither state bodies nor large private-sector firms play much of a role in the organization of the supply chain.

Significant differences in the institutional frameworks of the countries studied were also identified. These included the prominent role of notions of good faith in German contract law; the strength of trade associations and quality standards in Germany; the prevalence of softer, cultural assumptions about quality in Italy; the perceived expense and rigidity of the Italian legal system; and a strong tendency towards 'voluntarism' in commercial law and relations in Britain. The single most important difference *at the level of legal doctrine* between the three systems concerns the absence from English law of a generalized principle of good faith in contractual dealings. The English courts have had difficulty in formulating an acceptable version of the good faith doctrine, and have insisted instead on the need to preserve the notion that commercial parties deal, for the most part, at arm's length. As a consequence, certain doctrines which are well known in civilian systems, such as requirements of pre-contractual duties of disclosure and the possibility of relief for commercial impracticability, have remained underdeveloped; this is also the case, although to a lesser extent, by way of comparison to the commercial laws of the United States (cf. generally McKendrick 1995; Brownsword 1997).

In Germany, the principle of good faith in Article 242 of the Civil Code has come to have an extensive influence throughout the body of commercial contract law. The immediate aim of Article 242 is 'to spell out what performance entails, for example, to show that one need not accept delivery at an inconvenient time . . .' (Leser 1982: 135) but through the interpretations of the courts its function has become one of 'giving legal force to broad ethical values' (ibid. 138). One of the most important areas in which Article 242 has been applied is to require parties to renegotiate long-term contracts which have been subject to an unanticipated event, such as an unexpected rise in prices or fall in demand, in such a way as to go far beyond what would normally be permitted by the common law doctrine of frustration, which relieves the parties from future performance but only in a much more restricted range of circumstances (Dawson 1983; 1984). In Italian contract law, similarly, it has been said that the application of the notion of good faith means that performance of contractual obligations 'must take place with the loyal and honest co-operation of the parties to achieve the recipro-cal benefits agreed in the contract. Only in that way can the contract play its part as a useful private mechanism in the context of the "social solidarity" which is the inescapable duty of all citizens under Article 2 of the [1949] Constitution' (Criscuoli and Pugsley 1991: 142).

The role of good faith in the civilian systems is not confined to this high level of legal abstraction. In Germany, it operates at the micro-level of interfirm relations by virtue of the close relationship between the Civil Code, legislation governing terms in standard-form contracts, and the contents of the standard-form contracts themselves which are agreed at industry level. The general effect is to confer a very high level of stability upon the normative framework within which interfirm relations are con-ducted. Firms rarely seek to vary either the standard term agreements which derive from the trade association or those implied terms which oper-ate as a matter of law; indeed, there is considerable doubt as to whether they may, legally, contract out of those norms which the courts would read into the contract (Casper 1997). Under English law, on the other hand, the parties to commercial agreements enjoy, from this point of view, almost compete freedom of contract: judicially implied terms and the clauses of standard-term agreements operate only at the level of default rules which can be varied or omitted as the parties wish. The principal difference between the systems, then, resides not so much in the 'quantity' or 'weight' of legal intervention (assuming that this can be measured in any relevant way), but in the way in which the different elements of the institutional framework—legal doctrine, industry-level standards, individual contractual agreements—relate to one another. In Germany the relationship between the levels is one of a high degree of functional interdependence, with normative influences flowing in both directions so that the legal system is affected by the content of agreements as well as vice versa. In Britain, neither legal doctrine nor the terms of industry-level assocations are par-ticularly important by comparison to the scope given to individual parties to 'make their own agreements'.

Italy represents a further variation on the nature of the relationship between contract law and norms set outside the formal parameters of the legal system. Here, legal notions of good faith have limited relevance in commercial life, by virtue of the perceived ridigity and inefficiency of the court system. However, the principle of ethical dealing is reflected in trading standards which operate in particular regions or industries and which are linked to the roles played by local government and by trade associations. On the whole Italian associations play a less important role in setting and enforcing standards than their German counterparts (cf. Lane and Bachmann 1997), but they are not the negligible force which many associations in Britain have become. The artisanal associations, in particular, operate as a 'blend of trade association and government agency' (Best 1990: 210) in providing a framework for interfirm co-operation. Economies of scale and risk-sharing are achieved through such means as collectively owned industrial parks, financial and marketing consortia of firms, and service centres which collect business information and provide technical training (Best 1990; Brusco 1992). Local associations of firms and artisans also operate to set 'benchmark prices' which serve to reduce negotiation costs, limit the opportunistic renegotiation of contracts and, by outlawing cutthroat competition, encourage firms to raise and maintain product quality (Dei Ottati 1994: 473).

How would we expect these sectoral and institutional differences to be reflected in attitudes towards contracting and trust? The 'voluntaristic' framework in Britain would seem to favour adaptation through 'processual trust', since it provides organizations with a high degree of contractual autonomy: formally, at least, firms have the capacity to shape their own agreements to meet changing circumstances. By contrast, firms in Germany and, to a lesser extent, Italy, operate within a framework of legal and extralegal norms which are largely taken for granted, cannot be contracted out of except at high cost, and which can be changed only through collective action at the level of trade associations or through the intervention of the courts. A central question is how firms respond to economic fluctuations, even shocks, in environments which are orientated towards the generation of institutionalized trust: do such systems allow sufficient flexibility for firms to develop strategies to cope with competitive pressures?

The evidence we have relates to the form and duration of contracts entered into by buyer and supplier firms; respondents' perceptions of trust; the use of legal sanctions and procedures; and company performance in terms of profitability and employment growth.

The Form and Duration of Contracts

Sectoral factors had a certain influence on the types of contract agreed by firms, but the country-specific, institutional conditions under which firms operated were found to be far more important. Across the two sectors, a greater degree of contractual formality was observed in the mining machinery industry than in kitchen furniture. Mining machinery firms almost all made use of exclusion or limitation clauses to cover themselves against the risk of extensive liability for the costs of lost production if one of their machines broke down. Few furniture firms were faced with potential costs of this kind, and use of exclusion clauses and other complex risk allocation devices was rare. But apart from this, there were no statistically significant differences by sector in the use by firms of written documentation, in their use of legally binding agreements, in the use of particular contractual clauses, in their understanding of the likely costs of legal action, and in the likelihood of legal action against another firm for breach of contract.

However, statistically significant differences in all of the above factors were found at the level of the cross-country comparisons. In relation to the level of contractual formality, German firms in both sectors were much more likely to make use of clauses indicating a high level of interdependence and of formal planning for contingencies. Contracts in Germany tended to be longer term, in the sense of spanning a number of discrete exchanges. In both Britain and Italy, most agreements tended to be order-specific or, at best, were loose 'framework' or 'requirement' contracts under which the buyer could place orders as required. British firms were the least likely to have formal performance standards based on audits and rating systems incorporated into contracts.

German and British agreements were found to be significantly more likely than Italian ones to contain clauses providing for a degree of exclusive dealing, protection of intellectual property rights, and retention of title over property after sale. In relation to planning, German firms were most likely to have hardship clauses requiring the parties to renegotiate the contract in the event of an unforeseen contingency (see Table 5.1). By contrast, British firms reported finding such terms 'confusing'. German firms were also more likely to have clauses governing the duration of the contract and allowing for termination for breach of condition or by way of notice; as all these are terms which are only necessary in contracts of a certain duration and covering more than one exchange, their presence is an indicator of the greater length and complexity of German contractual arrangements. Numerous German companies also reported making use of gentlemen's agreements; but their function was one of supplementing the more formal agreements. No German respondents used non-binding agreements or understandings to the exclusion of a formal agreement. Italian firms reported the lowest level of formality of contract terms, with little provision for contingencies and very little use of terms indicating a high degree of interdependence. The UK firms occupied a middle position; this is largely accounted for by an important difference between the two sectors,

TABLE 5.1. Types of clauses in contracts

	Germany		Britain		Italy	
	No. of firms	% of firms	No. of firms	% of firms	No. of firms	% of firms
Firms with clauses in contracts for:						
Retention of title[a]	19	86	15	93	1	5
Protection of intellectual property rights[a]	17	77	10	63	2	11
Exclusive dealing[b]	12	57	5	31	3	16
Hardship[a]	15	68	0	0	0	0
Exclusion or limitation of liability[b]	13	59	12	75	4	21

[a] Intercountry distribution significant at the 1% level using the Chi-square test.
[b] Intercountry distribution significant at the 5% level using the Chi-square test.

TABLE 5.2. Performance standards and interfirm linkages

	Germany	Britain	Italy
Percentage of firms with:			
Just-in-time	65	58	42
Quantity guarantees[a]	61	25	53
Formal quality audits[b]	76	37	74
Rating systems[b]	87	35	72
Computerized links[b]	45	42	5
No. of firms	21	19	19

[a] Intercountry distribution significant at the 5% level using the Chi-square test.
[b] Intercountry distribution significant at the 1% level using the Chi-square test.

with the kitchen furniture firms relying on contract formality far less than firms in mining machinery.

Other mechanisms cited by firms as means to promote long-term relationships included use of just-in-time delivery, guarantees of quantities to be supplied, formal quality audits, rating systems and computerized links. The British firms in the sample had a significantly lower incidence of formal performance standards based on audits and rating systems than in the two other countries, and they were also significantly less likely to make use of guarantees of future supply (Table 5.2). British firms valued personal contacts more highly than financial or technical assistance in building long-term relationships (Table 5.3), while in Germany, personal

TABLE 5.3. Types of links for establishing long-term relationships

	Germany	Britain	Italy
Percentage of firms:			
Financing arrangements[b]	47	25	5
Technical assistance[a]	56	65	32
Personal contacts[a]	86	95	68
No. of firms	23	20	19

[a] Intercountry distribution significant at the 10% level using the Chi-square test.
[b] Intercountry distribution significant at the 5% level using the Chi-square test.

contacts were important but not to the exclusion of financial or technical ones.

Taken together, these findings indicate that the most highly formalized linkages were to be found in Germany, while in both Germany and Italy there was a strong emphasis on formal mechanisms for raising quality. British firms placed the greatest emphasis on personal contacts, but such contacts were also important in the other two countries and in particular in Germany. In Britain the tendency was to see personal relations as independent of more formal mechanisms for collaboration, whereas in Germany the perception of managers was that 'gentlemen's agreements' and other personal understandings only operated in the context of an otherwise stable institutional framework.

Perceptions of Trust

When asked what was their understanding of trust in business relations, respondents gave answers which describe trust largely in interpersonal or processual terms. Thus, trust was seen as the ability to depend on other firms being honest, reliable, open, fair and co-operative, and on being able to keep their word, whether given contractually or otherwise. Firms saw the process of building and maintaining trust in terms of both projecting themselves as trustworthy and deciding whether to trust others; in both cases they identified the importance of establishing or investigating a firm's reputation, experiencing its performance, and building personal contacts and long-term relationships.

Nevertheless, even at this general level, intercountry differences in responses were observed. A relatively high proportion of the Italian firms surveyed associated favourable past experience with trust and saw themselves as having no particular strategy for establishing themselves as trustworthy. They saw satisfaction with performance as a means of deciding whether other firms could be trusted and chose to terminate relationships when other firms proved untrustworthy. A relatively large proportion of

British firms said that personal contacts were important in establishing themselves as trustworthy and in deciding whether other firms could be trusted, and a relatively large proportion said they tried to sort out the differences through personal contact when another firm proved untrustworthy rather than end the relationship. This suggests that in establishing and maintaining business relations, informal personal links are relatively important. In Germany, a higher proportion of firms emphasized the importance of reputation of competence, reliability, and straight dealing for establishing themselves as trustworthy; German firms were more likely formally to investigate the reputation of others before they decided whether they could be trusted, and to resort to contractual protection against untrustworthiness. This is indicative of a system in which firms are careful about entering into business relationships, but where, when they do, they expect such relationships to endure.

Respondents were shown a list of actions and were asked to score on a scale 1 to 10 (where 1 was of no importance and 10 was most important) the degree to which they associated each action with trust in business relationships (cf. Burchell and Wilkinson 1997, for a more detailed account of these findings). The actions can be broadly divided into three groups. There was first a set of actions associated with the idea of *contract adherence* (these were: paying and delivering on time; maintaining high product quality at all time; preserving confidentiality; ensuring the relevant standards are complied with; and honouring strictly the terms of contracts). There was secondly a set of actions associated with flexibility. Certain of these can be thought of in terms of gap-filling and discretionary behaviour, or *flexibility beyond contract* (being ready to exchange business information; honouring informal understandings; and being ready to renegotiate the terms of contracts at any time). Other actions could be classified as more social in orientation, and as representing a form of *flexibility regardless of or outside contract* (being ready to help in an emergency, being prepared to give and take and being willing to overlook occasional faults).

There were important intercountry differences in the ranking of the mean scores for responses under these headings. Statistically significant differences in intercountry scores were found for the categories of preserving confidentiality (German 9.1, British 8.0, Italian 7.7); strictly honouring the terms of contracts (Italian 8.3, German 8.0, British 6.0); being prepared to give and take (German 7.8, Britain 7.7, Italian 5.9); and being willing to overlook faults (British 7.3, German 5.6, Italian 4.8). In sum, the Italian respondents put relatively more weight on the association between *contract adherence* and trust than those in the other two countries, especially in Britain, while, on average, the British respondents associated trust more highly with *flexibility outside contract* than with contract adherence. This is indicated in particular by the relatively high mean score given by the British respondents to the category of 'being willing to overlook occasional faults' and the relatively low mean scores to the headings of 'strictly honouring the terms of contracts' and 'ensuring that the relevant standards are complied with'. The German and Italian firms gave high average scores to contract adherence, but the German respondents saw a greater association between flexibility and trust, and in particular *flexibility beyond contract*.

In short, despite the general association of trust with factors operating at an interpersonal or processual level, firms in different systems tended to adopt different strategies for achieving goodwill trust based on flexibility. The role of the contractual environment in fostering certain types of co-operative strategies can be seen more clearly in the context of our findings on the use by firms of legal remedies and sanctions for breach of contract.

Trust and the Legal System

The survey found evidence of important differences in respondents' attitudes in general towards the legal system, trading standards and the role of trade associations in the sectors and countries studied. In Germany, respondents commented that their contracts were shaped by the general law as well as by the 'general conditions of business' applying in their industry. Both the Civil Code and the general conditions were seen to apply 'as a matter of course', as did quality standards laid down by the DIN and by trade associations. These findings, when taken together with the results of the questions on contract form and duration, indicate a high level of awareness on the part of the German firms of the legal and regulatory framework for exchange, as well as a high level of stability within the framework of norms operating at both sectoral and national level. There is a strong contrast here with Italy, where firms were unable to estimate the costs and outcomes of legal action and did not rely extensively on contractual form to shape their relationship. This appears to reflect a system in which the court system is seen as slow, expensive, and uncertain in terms of outcome. In addition, the impact of formal standard setting and regulation by the state and by sectoral bodies alike was seen as limited. In Britain, there was a sectoral divide. Most mining machinery contracts were detailed and sophisticated, but a large proportion of firms in the kitchen furniture sector reported that informal understandings were common, with some firms conducting business over a long period without either legally binding or written agreements.

A clear intercountry difference also arose with regard to methods of dealing with untrustworthy behaviour (Table 5.4). When asked how they dealt with untrustworthiness in business relationships, more than 50 per cent of all firms surveyed said they ended relationships immediately, 21 per cent made contractual arrangements to cover the risk, and 14

TABLE 5.4. How do you deal with untrustworthy behaviour?[a]

	Germany	Britain	Italy
Percentage of firms who:			
Terminate immediately	32	50	88
Terminate eventually	5	5	0
Limit exposure	9	0	6
Contractual protection	41	15	0
Personal contact	14	25	0
Other	0	5	6
No. of firms	22	20	16

[a] Intercountry distribution significant at the 1% level using the Chi-square test. The German column sums to more than 100 because some firms gave more than one response.

per cent made more informal efforts to sort things out. All but two (88 per cent) of Italian respondents to this question claimed that they would terminate relations immediately. Such immediate action would also be taken by 50 per cent of British respondents while 25 per cent tried to sort out differences, and 25 per cent made contractual provisions to cover risk. An even smaller proportion of German firms said that they would respond to untrustworthiness by ending relationships (32 per cent), and a much higher proportion (41 per cent) responded by making contractual provisions to cover risk.

We have described the predominant British strategy in terms of *flexibility outside contract*, because the informal contacts and understandings on which the parties relied to do business most often arose independently of, and sometimes even in contradiction of, the terms of a formal agreement. In Germany, on the other hand, *flexibility beyond contract* meant that flexibility took account of the contract in the sense of filling in gaps or providing for additional elements of performance. In Italy, the absence of 'hard' standards and the cost of using the legal system to enforce contracts was made up for, in part, by the presence of widely accepted social norms governing quality and reliability and by collective provision of public goods, as well as by an implicit threat to cease trading with any firm which failed to match up to these expectations.

Did the voluntaristic approach of the British firms lead to reduced reliance on costly legal procedures for enforcing agreements? There was no evidence that this was the case, indeed, there was evidence to the contrary. German respondents made frequent references to the role of normative influences, in particular the standard form contracts of industry-level trade associations, in shaping contractual practice; but they expressed the greatest confidence in their ability to predict the level of legal costs; and they

TABLE 5.5. Degree of clarity concerning the outcome
of legal action[a]

	Germany	Britain	Italy
Percentage of firms who are:			
Very Clear	77	37	0
Clear	0	26	5
Unclear	23	37	95
No. of firms	13	19	19

[a] Intercountry distribution significant at the 1% level using
the Chi-square test.

TABLE 5.6. Likelihood of legal action against a customer or supplier committing
a breach of contract[a]

	Germany		Britain		Italy	
	No. of firms	% of firms	No. of firms	% of firms	No. of firms	% of firms
Very likely	0	0	9	45	1	5
Fairly likely	0	0	1	5	3	16
Likely	1	5	2	10	0	0
Unlikely	9	41	1	5	6	32
Very unlikely	12	54	7	35	9	47

[a] Intercountry distribution significant at the 1% level using the Chi-square test.

were the most likely to carry insurance against legal liability (Table 5.5).
They were also the least likely to take legal action for breach of contract,
even to recover debts (Table 5.6). By contrast, legal action for non-payment
of the price was regarded as highly likely in Britain in both the sectors
studied, but in particular in the kitchen furniture sector which exhibited the
lowest level of contract formality of any of the industries studied, in the
sense that several firms in this sample reported that they dispensed with
contractual documentation altogether in favour of informal understandings. A number of British firms in both sectors complained about the
practice of late payment of debts and many looked on legal action to claim
the price as a matter of first, rather than last, resort.

On this basis, there is some evidence to suggest that the presence of a
formal legal contract may be part of a strategy of building a 'trusting'
relationship in which the parties are able to avoid the use of the courts
(Germany); alternatively, in the absence of effective court-based ordering,
firms rely on intermediate institutions and on a widely shared commercial

morality, as well as the availability of alternative sources of supply, to achieve co-operation (Italy). By contrast, a strategy of basing the exchange on loose understandings and 'give and take', while it has certain advantages from the point of view of encouraging close personal dealings, may also lead both to distrust and to frequent recourse to the courts (Britain).[1] In Britain, then, the relatively limited role for system trust did not necessarily entail a greater role for interpersonal or processual trust. Rather, the weakness of collective institutions resulted in an environment in which the formation of trustworthy relations was inhibited by the tendency of the more powerful firms to pursue their market advantage for all it was worth. Consider, for example, the following statement, made by a British respondent in the mining machinery industry:

There has been a fundamental change. In the old days of standard form conditions it was easy to place subcontracting work. Now that customers are varying their terms and conditions so quickly, there are enormous costs monitoring this and of customising terms with our own subcontractors. The whole process is much more difficult and twice the cost of before.

British respondents reported that it was becoming common for larger customers to seek to customize the normal industry-level terms, often insisting on the insertion of terms which exposed their subcontractors and suppliers to a high level of risk. Suppliers reported that they were obliged to accept this practice as a condition of continuing to do business with these customers. Instability in this aspect of the institutional framework was put down to the effects of the sharp recession of the early 1990s and also to privatization in the electricity and mining industries, which had led to a reassessment of previously established standard form agreements.

Trust and Economic Performance

We turn finally to the question of how far different modes of contractual organization are reflected in economic outcomes.[2] The data do not reveal a significant link between the adoption of practices which would indicate a high degree of close co-operation, and superior firm-level performance. No significant correlations were found between the adoption by *individual* firms of one of the features of close co-operation listed above (such as financial assistance, or quality audits), and their performance as measured by increases in turnover and/or employment in the five years before the date of the interview. Both within the sample as a whole and within individual countries, the incidence of 'relational' contracting was randomly distributed among more successful and less successful firms.

Evidence was collected from firms concerning changes in turnover and employment between 1988 and 1994. As would be expected, mining machinery firms sustained a greater level of job loss and greater falls in turn-over during this period than firms in the kitchen furniture sector. Differ-ences by country are less marked; nevertheless, only 33 per cent of the British firms reported any growth of turnover in real terms in the period of question as opposed to 61 per cent of German and 50 per cent of Italian firms. 39 per cent of the British firms reported rapid decline in turnover, compared to 14 per cent in Germany and 11 per cent in Italy. In relation to employment, only 27 per cent of British firms reported a rise, compared to 53 per cent of German firms and 67 per cent of Italian firms. At the other extreme, 39 per cent of British firms reported rapid decline in employment, compared to 19 per cent in Germany and 6 per cent in Italy. There is evidence to indicate, then, that the location of a firm may make a difference to its performance in terms of employment and turnover.

If we take the performance of industries as a whole as opposed to that of individual firms, the British pattern stands out: a small group of successful firms at one extreme is set against a long tail of underperformers at the other. This is also indicated by information on the export orientation of firms. A larger percentage of British firms than in either of the other two countries had no overseas customers at all (45 per cent, as opposed to 14 per cent in Germany and 11 per cent in Italy), but at the opposite end of the scale, a sizeable group of British firms had more than half of its customers overseas (15 per cent, as opposed to 9 per cent in Germany and 5 per cent in Italy).

If it is only at the level of particular industries that German and Italian firms on average performed better than their British counterparts, this raises the possibility that the relational linkages which, in different forms, exist in Germany and Italy, have improved the *general* level of performance of firms in those systems, by requiring firms, as an effective precondition of entry, to come up to a certain threshold. Evidence for this view is supported by the findings of Jarvis and Prais (1995), to the effect that the level of quality embodied in German consumer goods in a range of indus-tries was substantially higher than that for equivalent British products. This suggests, in turn, that the export performance of firms is linked both to the nature of consumer demand in their domestic markets, and also to the domestic institutional conditions under which production takes place. The variations in performance within each system which our data reveal reflect the managerial and other capabilities of individual firms to meet the re-quired standards; the institutional influences which serve to promote qual-ity in a given system are necessary but not sufficient conditions for its achievement at the level of the firm. But even if individual firms vary in their capacity to compete, it may still be the case that such institutional support is a prerequisite for the enhanced competitiveness of the system as a whole.

4. CONCLUSION: LEGISLATING FOR TRUST?

This chapter has aimed to reassert the importance of the law–trust relation for the understanding of contractual relations. The long-accepted view that the legal system is 'marginal' to contractual processes needs to be reexamined. This view can only be maintained if law is regarded in a narrowly instrumentalist sense. Closer attention should be paid to the standard-setting functions of law and to the close interdependencies between highly formal, legal norms, and less formal social norms. In particular, intermediate institutions (in particular, trade associations and standard-setting organizations) should be seen as playing an important role in the process by which the meta-values of the legal system come to be translated into the more concrete terms of standard form agreements, and into looser notions of business ethics.

This suggested reassessment of the role of the institutional framework, and of legal-regulatory mechanisms in particular, may help to cast light on the contemporary debate over trust. Economic analysis is right to be sceptical of 'the idea of a disembodied notion of trust floating around somewhere in the social ether' (Kay 1996: 256). On the other hand, little is gained if trust is seen as simply the end product of contractual strategies based on rational choice (Williamson 1993). We have sought to show here that a way forward may be found by adopting a conceptual division between system trust and interpersonal or processual trust. While it is often through experience, reputation and other processual mechanisms that trust is built up and maintained between trading partners, a crucial influence is also provided by the environment in which they operate. The issue at stake here is to explain the ways in which transactions are made possible or facilitated by the presence of systemic rules of a certain kind.

One way in which transactions of a certain kind may be encouraged is through legal sanctions against opportunistic or uncooperative behaviour. According to Williamson, the institutional framework (or environment) may be conceived of as 'a set of parameters, changes in which elicit shifts in the comparative costs of governance' (1996: 112). It follows that 'the need for transaction-specific safeguards (governance) varies systematically with the institutional environment within which transactions are located . . . Accordingly, transactions that are viable in an institutional environment that provides strong safeguards may be nonviable in institutional environments that are weak' (ibid. 267). We may agree that the institutional framework is an important determinant, in this sense, of risk, and hence of the strategies which trading partners may pursue. The empirical research which we have drawn on in this paper provides some support for that view. However, it is necessary also to recognize that penalizing opportunism is just one of a number of techniques through which the institutional framework may influence economic outcomes. In particular, it may be that norms such as the norm of 'good faith', which seek to promote co-operation in a more affirmative way and to set basic standards with regard to contractual behaviour, play a broader role in encouraging the sharing of risk and information between contracting parties.

We should not conclude that it is possible to change the institutional framework at will, or to legislate for trust in any straightforward fashion. The issue, rather, is how regulatory reform might contribute to the establishment of environments which are supportive of economic co-operation. Here, there may be a role for 'reflexive law' which operates on the basis of an understanding of the operation of the economic and social relations which are being made the subject of regulation (Teubner 1993). Even then, as we have seen, the relationship between legal norms and economic outcomes is a highly complex one. A wide range of factors influence organizational strategies. Hence, strategies cannot be expected to respond in a straightforward way to reforms initiated from the centre. Moreover, insofar as there is a link between co-operative strategies and economic performance, then on the data presented here it is one which may be tenuously observed at the level of the relevant system as a whole, that is to say the relevant industry (or region), but not at the level of performance of individual firms. Nevertheless, this is quite different from accepting that the role of the state is confined to one of putting in place the bare minimum of conditions for the functioning of a market, in terms of guarantees of contract and property rights. Just as an excess of regulation may, conceivably, stifle innovation (Kern, Chapter 7 this volume), so its opposite, extreme voluntarism, may result in a form of *anomie*, in which contractual co-operation breaks down under the pressure of short-term self-interest seeking. The precise nature of the relationship between institutional influences and economic outcomes is, as yet, far from being well understood. What is increasingly clear, though, is that the institutional framework plays an important role in determining the success or failure of productive systems.

NOTES

1. Generalizations just given do not describe *all* the firms in the countries in question. The strategies of particular organizations are not pre-ordained by the regulatory framework. Nevertheless, we have persuasive evidence of tendencies which characterize the approach which a majority of organizations have adopted, or which may be thought of as representing a default position to which organizations tend to conform (if only by way of imitation of others) unless they take steps

to do otherwise. Moreover, as we have seen, there is very clear evidence of divergence not simply at the level of the formal rules and norms which govern business relations in the countries in question, but also at the level of contractual practice.
2. This part draws on Deakin, Lane, and Wilkinson (1997).

REFERENCES

Akerlof, G. (1970), 'The Market for "Lemons": Qualitative Uncertainty and the Market Mechanism', *Quarterly Journal of Economics*, 84: 488–500.

Alt, J. and Schepsle, K. (1990) (eds.), *Perspectives on Positive Political Economy*. Cambridge: Cambridge University Press.

Arrighetti, A., Bachmann, R., and Deakin, S. (1997), 'Contract Law, Social Norms and Inter-Firm Cooperation', *Cambridge Journal of Economics*, 21: 171–96.

Axelrod, R. (1984), *The Evolution of Cooperation*. New York: Basic Books.

Beale, H. and Dugdale, T. (1975), 'Contracts Between Businessmen: Planning and the Use of Contractual Remedies', *British Journal of Law and Society*, 2: 45–60.

Bernstein, L. (1992), 'Opting Out of the Legal System: Extralegal Contractual Relations in the Diamond Industry', *Journal of Legal Studies*, 21: 115–57.

Best, M. (1990), *The New Competition*. Cambridge, Mass.: Harvard University Press.

Brownsword, R. (1997), 'Contract Law, Cooperation, and Good Faith: the Movement from Static to Dynamic Market-Individualism', in S. Deakin and J. Michie (eds.), *Contracts, Co-operation, and Competition*. Oxford: Clarendon Press.

Brusco, S. (1992), 'Small Firms and the Provision of Real Services', in Pyke and Sengenberger (eds.), *Industrial Districts and Local Economic Regeneration*.

Burchell, B. and Wilkinson, F. (1997), 'Trust, Business Relationships and the Contractual Environment', *Cambridge Journal of Economics*, 21: 217–38.

Casper, S. (1997), 'National Institutional Frameworks and Innovative Industrial Organization: Supplier Relations in the United States and Germany', mimeo, Wissenschaftszentrum, Berlin.

Casson, M. (1993*a*), *Studies in the Economics of Trust*, i. *Entrepreneurship and Business Culture*. Aldershot: Elgar.

——(1993*b*), *Studies in the Economics of Trust*, ii. *The Organisation of International Business*. Aldershot: Elgar.

Charny, D. (1989), 'Nonlegal Sanctions in Commercial Relationships', *Harvard Law Review*, 104: 375–467.

Coleman, J. (1990), *Foundations of Social Theory*. Cambridge, Mass: Harvard University Press.

Criscuoli, G. and Pugsley, D. (1991), *The Italian Law of Contract*. Naples: Jovene.

Dasgupta, P. (1988), 'Trust as a Commodity', in D. Gambetta (ed.), *Trust: Making and Breaking Cooperative Relations*. Oxford: Blackwell.

Dawson, J. (1983), 'Judicial Revision of Frustrated Contracts: Germany', *Boston University Law Review*, 63: 1039–98.

——(1984), 'Judicial Revision of Frustrated Contracts: USA', *Boston University Law Review*, 64: 1–38.

Deakin, S. and Wilkinson, F. (1996), 'Contracts, Cooperation and Trust: The Role of the Institutional Framework', in D. Campbell and P. Vincent-Jones (eds.), *Contract and Economic Organisation*. Aldershot: Dartmonth.

——Goodwin, T., and Hughes, A. (1997), 'Cooperation and Trust in Inter-Firm Relations: Beyond Competition Policy?', in Deakin and Michie (eds.), *Contracts, Co-operation, and Competition*.

——Lane, C., and Wilkinson, F. (1997), 'Contract Law, Trust Relations and Incentives for Cooperation', in Deakin and Michie (eds.), *Contracts, Co-operation, and Competition*.

Dei Ottati, G. (1994), 'Cooperation and Competition in the Industrial District as an Organisational Model', *European Planning Studies*, 2: 463–83.

Giddens, A. (1990), *The Consequences of Modernity*. Cambridge: Polity Press.

Harsanyi, M. and Selten, R. (1988), *Towards a Theory Equilibrium Selection in Games*. Cambridge, Mass.: MIT Press.

Humphrey, J. and Schmitz, H. (1996), 'Trust and Economic Development', DP 355. Brighton: Institute of Development Studies.

Jarvis, V. and Prais, S. (1995), 'The Quality of Manufactured Products in Britain and Germany', Discussion Paper no. 88. London: National Institute of Economic and Social Research.

Kay, N. (1996), 'The Economics of Trust', *International Journal of the Economics of Business*, 3: 249–60.

Kotowitz, Y. (1990), 'Moral Hazard', in J. Eatwell, M. Milgate, and P. Newman (eds.), *Information, Allocation and Markets*. London: Macmillan.

Kreps, D. (1990), 'Corporate Culture and Economic Theory', in Alt and Schepsle (eds.), *Perspectives on Positive Political Economy*.

Kronman, A. (1978), 'Mistake, Disclosure, Information and the Law of Contracts', *Journal of Legal Studies*, 7: 1–34.

——(1985), 'Contract Law and the State of Nature', *Journal of Law, Economics and Organization*, 1: 3–25.

Lane, C. (1997), 'The Social Regulation of Inter-firm Relations in Britain and Germany: Market Rules, Legal Norms and Technical Standards', *Cambridge Journal of Economics*, 21: 197–215.

——and Bachmann, R. (1996), 'The Social Construction of Trust: Supplier Relations in Britain and Germany', *Organisation Studies*, 17: 365–95.

————(1997), 'Cooperation in Inter-firm Relations in Britain and Germany: The Role of Social Institutions', *British Journal of Sociology*, 48: 226–55.

Leser, H. (1982), 'The Principle of Good Faith: Article 242 BGB', in N. Horn, H. Kötz, and H. Leser (eds.) (trans. T. Weir), *German Private and Commercial Law: An Introduction*. Oxford: Clarendon Press.

Luhmann, N. (1979), *Trust and Power*, Chichester: Wiley.

Lyons, B. and Mehta, J. (1997), 'Contracts, Opportunism and Trust: Self-interest and Social Orientation', *Cambridge Journal of Economics*, 21: 239–57.

Macaulay, S. (1963), 'Non-contractual Relations in Business: A Preliminary Study', *American Sociological Review*, 45: 55–69.

McKendrick, E. (1995), 'The Regulation of Long-term Contracts in English Law', in J. Beatson and D. Friedmann (eds.), *Good Faith and Fault in Contract Law*. Oxford: Clarendon Press.

North, D. (1990), *Institutions, Institutional Change, and Economic Performance*. Cambridge: Cambridge University Press.

——(1993), 'Institutions and Credible Commitment', *Journal of Institutional and Theoretical Economics*, 149: 11–23.

——(1994), 'Economic Performance through Time', *American Economic Review*, 84: 359–68.

Posner, R. (1993), *Economic Analysis of Law* (4th edn.). Boston: Little, Brown.

Pyke, F. and Sengenberger, W. (1992) (eds.), *Industrial Districts and Local Economic Regeneration*. Geneva: IILS.

Scott, W. R. (1995), *Institutions and Organizations*. London: Sage.

Sitkin, S. and Roth, N. (1993), 'Explaining the Limited Effectiveness of Legalistic "Remedies" for Trust/Distrust', *Organization Science*, 4: 367–92.

Spence, M. (1973), *Market Signalling: Information Transfer in Hiring and Related Processes*. Cambridge, Mass.: Harvard University Press.

Stiglitz, J. (1990), 'Principal and Agent', in Eatwell, Milgate, and Newman (eds.), *Information, Allocation and Markets*.

Teubner, G. (1993), *Law as an Autopoietic System*. Oxford: Blackwell.

Williamson, O. (1983), 'Credible Commitments: Using Hostages to Support Exchange', *American Economic Review*, 73: 519–40.

——(1993), 'Calculativeness, Trust, and Economic Organization', *Journal of Law and Economics*, 36: 456–83.

——(1996), *The Mechanisms of Governance*. Oxford: Oxford University Press.

You, J.-I. and Wilkinson, F. (1994), 'Competition and Cooperation: Toward Understanding Industrial Districts', *Review of Political Economy*, 6: 259–78.

Zucker, L. (1986), 'Production of Trust: Institutional Sources of Economic Structure, 1840–1920', *Research in Organisational Behaviour*, 6: 53–111.

6

Understanding the Role of Interfirm Institutions in Sustaining Trust Within the Employment Relationship*

DAVID MARSDEN

1. A PARADOX

There is a paradox in our understanding of the employment relationship. On the one hand, its principal advantage to employers lies in its flexibility and economy compared with other types of transaction, and such flexibility could be deemed dependent upon a good degree of trust between the parties concerned. On the other, the prisoner's dilemma teaches us that co-operation based on trust is very fragile, a point which seems to be borne out by Fox's observation that the great majority of work roles in modern industrial society are of the 'low-discretion–low-trust' kind. If that it is so, why should the employment relation remain far and away the most common way of regulating the exchange of labour services?

Exploring this paradox, which is the goal of this paper, leads to two main conclusions concerning the position of trust in the employment relation. The first is that certain transaction rules, which are shown to be a logically necessary component of the employment relation, play a critical part in preventing the slide into the kind of low-trust relations that would destroy its viability. The second is the degree of support provided to workplace co-operation by institutions and conventions that span several firms, such as employer organizations and labour-market customs.

The central focus of this paper is that of employee work roles and how the parties concerned set boundaries on the demands that can legitimately be made. In his classic study, Fox (1974) stressed the power of management to set the amount of discretion workers can exercise in their jobs unless confronted by well-organized groups. However, a number of recent developments now reveal the limitations of this presumption. The rise of 'new concepts of production' and much recent comparative research on jobs and skills shows that the 'job-based' model of work organization is but one of several economically viable models (e.g. Kern and Schumann 1984). The growth of 'non-standard' forms of employment also highlights the element

* I should like to thank Ron Dore, François Eyraud, Christel Lane, Ned Lorenz, and François Sellier for their helpful comments. The ideas in this chapter are more fully developed in my book: *A Theory of Employment Systems: Micro-Foundations of Societal Diversity* (Oxford University Press), for publication in 1998/9.

of choice that firms and workers face in deciding how to organize the provision and pricing of labour services (e.g. Rubery and Wilkinson 1994). The effect of Fox's presumption was to direct his attention to countervailing work-group power, as with certain craft trades, and to ideology, as instilled by certain types of paternalistic management, as forces avoiding the worst problems of the low-discretion–low-trust syndrome. In contrast, if one recognizes the element of choice, for both workers and firms, between different ways of organizing their economic transactions, then the regulation of work roles and the problem of workplace trust emerges in a different, and complementary, perspective. Taking account of this element of choice between means of contracting leads one to ask why firms and workers should choose the employment relation, and if they do, how can they enforce their different understandings concerning work roles and their adaptation over time.

This leads to a second important question concerning the role of interfirm institutions and conventions in shaping work roles and setting the framework for trust relations. Problems of inflation over the last thirty years have directed most of our attention to the part played by such institutions in wage bargaining and the transmission of wage increases from one group to another. This has obscured their second critical function, which is logically prior, namely the definition of the categories of labour services exchanged. One cannot have a price without first defining the good or service to which that price is attached. In countries with industry bargaining, classification agreements at industry and company level regulate the categories of exchange, and so provide a valuable support to the workplace regulation of work roles. Their contribution has been underestimated again because of the focus on the 'price' of labour services rather than the regulation of their content. As will be shown, despite the existence of a sizeable 'wage gap' between industry- and company-level pay rates, in fact, their influence on the regulation of job categories is considerable. The prime reason for this, it will be argued, is because the interfirm agreements and conventions play an essential part in consolidating the workplace rules that check the slide towards low-trust relations.

In the conclusion, the paper comes back to Fox's problem of high- and low-discretion work roles and trust with a discussion of selected countries' workplace relations as belonging to predominantly 'high-' or 'low-trust' types, and the relationship with functional flexibility, and the quality of co-operation. It is argued that the best way to make sense of the contribution of trust to flexibility in these systems is to do so in the context of the different types of transaction rule that predominate in these countries.

The analysis in this paper makes three key behavioural assumptions about the nature of the work environment. They play an important part in the work of Coase, Simon, and Williamson, and also of Fox. First, the need to adapt continuously to shifting economic conditions gives rise to two kinds of information asymmetry. Job contents are frequently only partially transparent to outsiders. The need to adapt continuously breaks down any attempts to impose uniformity, and related to this, tacit knowledge and skills play an important role. The other asymmetry is that employers are usually better informed about market conditions. Secondly, the actors are subject to bounded rationality: although intentionally rational, they are restricted in their ability to process and use information. Thirdly, they are aware that they have areas of divergent as well as convergent interests. As a result, the conditions are ripe for opportunism to develop, which is not to say that it necessarily will, but that its potential is ever present. In fact, Fox was greatly interested in how certain ideologies could restrain opportunism on the part of workers by convincing them that management had their interests at heart, although he saw these, at the time he wrote, as losing their hold in the face of a more radical ideology which stressed divergent interests.

The type of trust involved in this chapter closely reflects Simmel's 'problem of time and knowledge' referred to in the introductory chapter. In the employment relation, both parties typically agree overall terms and conditions before work demands and worker ability and motivation are known with any precision. It is close to what Zucker (1986) characterized as 'institutional-based' (cf. Lane's introductory chapter). The transaction rules, which will be shown to define the boundaries of management authority in the employment relation, are impersonal, and extend beyond a given transaction and beyond specific sets of exchanger partners. Indeed, it will be argued that the articulation between the job-level transaction rules and those of interfirm conventions and institutions analysed in this chapter is the basis of co-operation within the employment relation. These rules provide protection against opportunistic behaviour by either party, and offer a vital element of predictability in the demands placed on different work roles thus establishing a basis on which trust relations may develop. The rules facilitate non-contractual co-operative action, but as will be apparent by the end of the chapter, the different types of rules allow different degrees of flexibility in work roles.

Finally, some writers, such as Streeck (1992), have argued that the law can provide a powerful framework within which workplace trust relations may develop. The argument of the present chapter does not dispute this possibility. However, its aim is not to give an exhaustive analysis of all the factors contributing to workplace trust relations, but rather to provide a theory of how the actors might develop their own rules in a spontaneous, decentralized, fashion, and to examine the role of the interfirm conventions they develop.

2. THE EMPLOYMENT RELATION AND THE PROBLEM OF LOW TRUST

The analysis of the employment relation developed in this paper takes the work of Coase, Simon, and Williamson as its starting point. Essentially, they ask why certain kinds of transaction should take place within organizations, or firms, rather than on the open market. The increased use of self-employment, and of subcontracting in recent years highlights just how far there is a real economic choice between these different methods of regulating the supply of labour services. The fact that recent surveys, such as those reported by Gallie and White (1994), show that the overwhelming majority of workers are still engaged in open-ended employment relations, tells us something important about that kind of transaction.[1] In similar vein, despite some decline in the importance of long-term jobs in advanced industrial economies, the latest evidence shows that they still represent by far the most common way of organizing work.[2] That there is some growth of alternatives demonstrates the logical and practical possibility of alternatives, and that the parties are indeed able to choose between different types of transaction, and the continued prevalence of the open-ended employment relation, shows how that choice is being exercised.

Why should firms choose to hire workers on employment contracts rather than purchase the specific good or service they require on the open market? First, the employment relation is often much more flexible, enabling the parties to agree a contract, and only later, to determine its precise content in terms of the exact tasks to be undertaken, how hard or how long the person should work, and so on. Given the extreme difficulty for many firms to forecast exactly when they will need certain tasks to be carried out so that their sales plans may be realized, such flexibility is of great benefit. They do not know exactly when certain services will be needed, but they must be sure that they will be available at the right time and they must know at what price. The employment contract enables the entrepreneur to take an 'option' on future labour services at a pre-agreed price. This flexibility, as Coase (1937) argued, can also be a source of economy in that a single, flexible, transaction is substituted for a multitude of individual transactions for each service required by a firm. It greatly reduces the cost of specifying contracts and negotiating prices.

In one of the very few formal presentations of such analysis, Simon (1951) demonstrates that the greater the degree of uncertainty over which tasks a firm will need, the greater the advantage of the employment contract over the 'sales' contract. Although critical of the narrowness of Simon's view of the main co-ordinating mechanism within the employment relation, managerial authority, Williamson (1975) reaches a similar conclusion,[3] and in the process highlights many of the weaknesses of the less open-ended types of employment relation, notably the 'sequential spot' and the 'contingent claims' employment contracts. Where jobs involve 'idiosyncratic' skills and tacit knowledge such that formal codification is either impossible or very costly, neither form of contracting proves viable. The resulting information asymmetries expose the first to chronic opportunism, which Willman (1986) illustrates very aptly in his study of job regulation in the British printing and automobile industries, and the combination of complexity and uncertainty makes the specification of future contingencies too costly under most circumstances. In these industries, shop-floor bargaining had evolved to an extent that approached 'sequential spot' contracting with management having to bargain each new work assignment and agree a price before work could commence. As a result, production and introduction of new equipment were very frequently disrupted by intensive negotiation and wildcat strikes.

If the advantage of the employment relation resides in its flexibility, how then was it possible for Fox to observe that the great majority of work environments were characterized by low-discretion work roles and low trust? His account of the 'low-trust syndrome' heralds later work on the problems of co-operative action as shown in the 'prisoner's dilemma'.

Fox (1974) characterizes work roles in the 'low-trust–low-discretion syndrome' as consisting of five related elements, of which the first is the key:

(a) role occupants perceive management as behaving as if they believe workers cannot be trusted, of their own volition, to deliver desired work performance, and hence:

(b) there is specific definition of job activities and close supervision;

(c) co-ordination of the occupant's with other activities is constrained by standardized rules and routines;

(d) failures draw punishment because they are presumed to stem from careless indifference to job rules and organizational goals; and

(e) conflict with superiors handled by bargaining of an adversarial nature.

The downward spiral into low-trust relations can begin with some shock to an established workplace equilibrium, for example, with management seeking to restrict workers' discretion in some area important to them, which the latter then interpret as showing institutionalized distrust in them, and so strengthening both sides' belief that their goals diverge, which stimulates management to tighten up on supervision and workers to reciprocate by narrowing the scope of co-operation.

Each twist to the low-trust dynamic leads to tighter specification of work roles and tighter controls. In one respect, this may reduce workers' discretion and increase management control over them, but at the same time it reduces the flexibility that management obtains from the employment relation. Slichter and his colleagues (1960) warned of the dangers for management of over-detailed job descriptions: that people begin to work by 'the words in the manual'. This means, of course, that management must foresee exactly which tasks it is going to require in the future, which is just what it sought to avoid in opting for the open-ended employment relation instead of the sales or the contingent claims contracts.

The employment contract imposes a number of additional costs on management as compared with the sales contract. Most notable among these are a wage premium and the expectation of longer-term employment. A wage premium arises because the tasks the employer may need vary in difficulty, and would under a sales contract command different prices to induce workers to undertake them. As the employer does not know in advance exactly which ones will be required, it has to offer enough money to induce the worker to accept assignment to any of the likely tasks, including the most difficult ones should they be needed. Hence the wage premium. A second important cost stems from the expected duration of the relationship. Therefore, if the advantages of the employment contract are lost because of the need to offer very precise job descriptions, it loses its attractiveness compared with the sales contract. So why should firms offer employment contracts at all?

A similar paradox emerges at the 'high-trust–high-discretion' end. In an economic relationship, job descriptions cannot be wholly diffuse. The reason is that both parties have only partially converging goals, and there are substantial areas where they diverge. For Fox, both high and low trust rest upon the parties' perceptions of each other's intentions. These are based largely on continued reciprocity by the other party, but the vagaries of economic life mean that reciprocity often cannot be guaranteed, and then continued reciprocity by the other party depends upon its belief in the good faith of the first. This may withstand a few shocks, but as their number and frequency increase, the likelihood of continued belief in the other's good faith will decline. This would then precipitate moves to reduce discretion, and so set in motion the beginnings of the low-trust syndrome.

It might be objected that Fox also recognized that some jobs fall in between the low- and high-discretion types and by implication that an intermediate level of trust might prevail. Such cases were, however, exceptional, and in those he cited, well-organized work groups had successfully resisted management attempts to reduce worker discretion. Otherwise, there is little in the logic of the low- and high-trust syndromes to suggest that the intermediate position is at all stable. Indeed, Fox recognizes this. He saw two main checks on the tendency towards low-trust behaviour: ideology and power. Workers might refrain from opportunism if they were led to believe that they shared interests with management. Equally, management might be able to hold opportunism at bay by use of power, for example, the threat of discipline or dismissal during periods of high unemployment. Otherwise, the tendency towards reciprocity in human exchange, which plays a central part in his model of trust dynamics, has 'the consequence that unless some compensating mechanism such as power or legitimizing sentiment is present to support a situation of imbalance, institutionalized distrust will evoke its like in return ... the likelihood is that the parties will draw each other into a spiral of distrust' (Fox 1974: 145).

If we take the view that task discretion in jobs is mainly a management decision, then it is hard to see a way out of this paradox, and it is hard to understand why the employment relation has proved so robust as a means of organizing the productive contribution of citizens of the advanced industrial societies. In what follows, I wish to argue that a critical influence on the scope of jobs stems from the transaction rules that underpin the employment relation. These, it will be argued, provide a framework for workplace trust and co-operation, and enable employers to obtain a sufficient degree of task flexibility to make the employment relation worthwhile, although it will also be seen that different rules give different degrees of work role flexibility. These rules set the parameters for workplace trust relations.

3. TRANSACTION RULES AND THE EMPLOYMENT RELATION

Under the employment relation, workers agree to follow management instructions assigning work tasks, and thus enable management to organize and co-ordinate work. But they do so only within certain limits. Without such limits, employment would be akin to slavery. The law recognizes this arrangement and supports it, but of itself does not explain the widespread adoption in many countries of this open-ended form of contracting. Equally, the law sets only very broad limits. In some countries, it may even prescribe maximum weekly working hours, and regulate work at nights and by minors, but only in the case of occupational licensing does it actually set limits on the range of tasks that are undertaken. For the rest, these limits are agreed, but how?

One possible solution might be to agree an inventory of likely tasks that could be assigned to a worker, a variant of the contingent claims contract described by Williamson (1975). However, this is not practical for most jobs because the contingencies rapidly become too complex to define and enforce. A more viable alternative is to establish some rule for defining the scope of jobs and the limits within which management may assign work tasks. The big advantage of a rule, or set of rules over some kind of inventory or very detailed job description lies in simplicity.

Such rules have to fulfil two fundamental conditions to enable an effective employment relation to develop: they must align worker skills with job demands; and they must be sufficiently transparent to be enforceable. Without the first, efficient production will not be achieved. Without the

TABLE 6.1. A typology of employment transaction rules

Type of transparency of definition	Job demands identified by:	
	Production approach	Training approach
Task-centred	Work post (task complementarity)	'Tools of trade' handled
Function-/production-centred	Range of activities/ worker rank	Training procedure or qualification

second, it is unlikely that both workers and employers will agree to an employment relation as each would fear its open-ended nature would be exploited to its disadvantage. A corollary of transparency is that any such rules should be sufficiently robust to be easily applicable in a wide variety of work environments by workers and their supervisors. If the personnel department has to be called in to adjudicate every new work assignment then costs will quickly spiral. This has one very important implication for our argument: the number of different types of transaction rules will tend to be fairly small because the greater their number, the less likely that individual workers and supervisors will be familiar with their application in practice.

The two conditions will be referred to as the competency and the transparency constraints, and are summarized in Table 6.1. Under the first constraint, job demands may be identified by either the 'production' or the 'training' approach. The first focuses on the technology of production or service provision, and in the words of one American production engineer, seeks to 'mould men to jobs not jobs to men' (Piore 1968). Thus the production approach seeks to organize work according to task complementarities arising out of the way production has been set up, seeking to minimize costs, for example, by cutting down worker displacements or concentrating on certain kinds of customer. The second, the training approach, focuses on the economics of skill development, organizing work according to kinds of skills available. It is common under the production approach to rely upon on-the-job training as worker competencies develop around the tasks to which they have been assigned: learning by doing. Alternatively, skills may be developed off the job according to the logic of certain intellectual disciplines and according to the general level of demand across all firms for certain types of skill or knowledge. Thus many skilled occupations have developed following complementarities among intellectual skills and the need for a large enough market to ensure workers an adequate return on their investment in training. As such skills have, by definition, to be transferable, trainees have to bear all, or at least a significant part, of the cost (Becker 1975).[4] The cost structures of the two kinds of skill acquisition are such as to push firms to give priority to one or other mode so that one may consider there exist two distinct and discrete approaches rather than thinking of them as the two poles of a continuum.[5] Sengenberger (1987), and Maurice, Sellier, and Silvestre (1986) provide some good illustrations of the influence of the training approach on job classifications.[6]

Turning to the transparency constraint, one may think of rules that identify the tasks that may be assigned to certain employees as falling into a limited number of categories. The most direct approach is to adopt a rule that identifies or defines some attribute of tasks concerned and uses that in order to decide which tasks go to which individuals. Alternatively, instead of thinking of work as being made up of a large number of discrete tasks, one might focus instead on the function to be carried out. The function itself might be defined in terms of the production or the training approaches: a function within the production process, or a function as identified by the exercise of a particular skill or qualification. A good example would be the treatment of maintenance work either as a separate function because of the way skills are organized, or as an integral part of production work. Although the division into two discrete types may be less strict than between the production and training approaches, it is likely that the number of types of rule along the transparency constraint is limited. First, the need for robustness entails both simplicity and familiarity. The actors need to know what kind of rule is being applied, and they need to be familiar with its application, otherwise the scope for opportunism is too great. The more widely used the rule, the more likely it is to be effective. Secondly, as will be shown later, the functional rules require a higher degree of trust for their operation, in the absence of which, they are likely to degenerate into task-focused rules. Thus, as with the contrast between the production and training approaches, the middle ground in between proves to be unstable. Some very good illustrations of such instability can be found in the difficulty encountered by firms using task-focused rules as they tried to shift to a more functional approach to job definition, and so were suspicious and sought to maintain the *status quo* (see Dugué 1994, and Clarke 1994). In particular, employees feared that the loss of clear lines of responsibility for particular tasks would expose them to arbitrary criticism and sanctions by management.

3.1 Common Examples of Rules Fitting Each Category

Although the theoretical model predicts the existence of four types of transaction rules arising from the transparency and competence constraints, there may well exist a number of different rules that fit into these categories. To prevent the discussion becoming too abstract, in what follows, we shall focus one widely used rule to exemplify each one. Those selected are:

- work post rule
- tools of the trade rule
- competence rank rule
- qualification rule

The *work post rule* establishes a job description covering the range of tasks to be accomplished. All the work to be undertaken in the firm is divided into a set of discrete work posts for each of which individual workers are held responsible: it is their job to do x, y, and z. Of the four rules cited, this comes closest to the idea of defining work roles by an inventory of tasks, it does however stop some way short of this. In practice, the job description often serves not as a list of prescribed tasks but rather as a means of allocating responsibility and a guide to management in periodic 'crack-downs'. The *tools of the trade* rule avoids listing tasks but identifies and allocates them according to the tools needed for, or the materials handled in, their execution. The *competence rank rule* enables a flexible allocation of tasks within a work group which has overall responsibility for fulfilling a particular function in production or service provision. It works primarily by assigning members of the group to ranks according to the range of tasks they are competent to undertake so that the more senior ones in the highest ranks are those usually able to undertake the widest range, and most difficult tasks. Finally, the *qualification rule* allocates tasks according to the possession of some recognized qualification. It is economically viable for the firm to do so because it will have designed jobs taking account of such qualifications.

4. LOW TRUST AND THE CONTROL OF OPPORTUNISM

The principal function of these rules is to control opportunism by either party in the employment relation and so make it an attractive way of co-ordinating economic activity. An exhaustive treatment of the different kinds of opportunism is beyond the scope of this paper, but it is possible to deal with the most important one for the present argument, namely the control of work assignments, and the unilateral addition or subtraction of tasks, the pressures for which may come from either party. Unilateral addition of tasks by employers increases employee workloads,[7] and under certain circumstances, unilateral subtraction can threaten one of the important benefits for employees, namely continuous economic activity. By the same token, unilateral subtraction of tasks by workers can deprive employers of the availability of labour when it is most needed. On the other hand, unilateral increases by workers in the tasks they undertake may impose an inefficient pattern of work organization or generate conflict between different groups of workers.

Where work is organized on the basis of work posts, the clear and unambiguous assignment of each task to a different post controls such tendencies to opportunism. The work post establishes clear individual responsibilities for the execution of certain tasks, and so checks potential moves by employees to cut tasks from their jobs, but it also limits tendencies in the other direction, to take on additional tasks. The clarity of task assignments to work posts identifies who is and who is not responsible for doing certain tasks, so that taking over additional tasks brings the risk of additional responsibilities and of opposition from other groups of employees. The clarity of work assignments also protects employees from unilateral job enlargement by the employer because the demarcation lines have been clearly set out.

The tools of the trade rule, which regulates task allocation by reference to the tools used or materials handled also gives clear answers. Management knows that if a particular task requires the use of certain tools, then it can be assigned without further negotiation to a particular category of employees, and it knows who is responsible if certain tasks are not performed. As with the work post rule, unilateral reassignment of tasks by either party would upset the equilibrium with other groups. For the employee, the same clarity of the rule makes it difficult for management to reassign and to add tasks unilaterally, thus both parties gain protection against opportunism.

For the two functional rules, the indirect link with work tasks makes monitoring more difficult, and increases the scope for opportunism, but there are compensating mechanisms to hold it in check. Taking first the production approach, assignment of tasks by work function depends upon the internal equilibrium of the work group. The indirect reference to individual work tasks creates scope for jobs with diffuse and overlapping boundaries. This enables great flexibility in allocating tasks to different workers, but at the same time, it deprives them of any clear reference point limiting their contractual obligations to their employer. There is no longer any unique relationship between individual tasks and individual jobs as under the work post system. How then can the scope of management authority be limited? It is important to remember that the production approach leads to a heavy emphasis on on-the-job training so that the progression of work group members between work assignments within the group enriches their skills. Such a process is facilitated if senior workers teach their junior colleagues the tricks they need to know to undertake their work effectively. Thus an exchange can develop between the two groups of workers whereby the former pass their skills and know-how to the latter, provided they respect the established rules of progression through work assignments and thus avoid threatening the position of the 'seniors'. The employer gains greatly from more flexible working practices and a greater quality of skills so long as it respects the internal norms of the work group over task allocation. In this case, opportunism is controlled by monitoring certain key indicators. For example, the employer's continued commitment to the rule can be signalled by maintaining long-term employment, essential for OJT and job rotation, and by respecting the pay and other norms which sustain the competence rank model. If these are violated, the work group can retaliate by withdrawing cooperation, and flexible work assignments, which are such a benefit for management, are turned against it as diffuse job boundaries make it much harder for management to pin down non-performance than under the work post system.

The last of the four rules, combining the training and the functional approaches, also involves an indirect link between tasks and jobs, and so also supports a more flexible system of work allocation than the tools of the trade rule. In contrast to the function in production rule, this one centres most commonly on general skills both in terms of their theoretical content and their transferability between firms. Although theoretically possible for such a rule to exist within a single firm, in practice it is unlikely because of the economies of scale in forming this kind of skill. Because employers stand to lose out by providing training for transferable skills, and workers, as a consequence, have to bear a significant part of the cost, the larger the market, the more attractive investment in such skills. A recognized qualification is an essential part of this process, sanctioning the worker's investment, and a common procedure for obtaining it, such as apprenticeships, or traineeships in the professions, helps to instil a professional identity among those holding it. The competencies involved enable the performance of certain kinds of work tasks (both physical and intellectual) without creating a direct link between the tasks and the job.

The price mechanism helps to ensure the system's solidity by discouraging employers from regularly assigning unskilled tasks to skilled workers. The clear labelling of skills by qualifications and their associated training procedures, which is absent under the production approach, enables skilled workers to identify easily who should receive the skilled rate of pay whatever the tasks on which they may be currently engaged. Thus, they are able to control task assignments effectively by making it expensive for the employer to assign them to a whole range of lower-valued tasks.

On the other hand, training and skill development are the vulnerable point of the system. The logic of transferable skills dictates trainees should bear an important part, if not the whole, of the cost. Because of the difficulty of obtaining loans for training, the most common solution has been for the trainee to receive a lower rate of pay during the training period. The gap between the trainee's pay and the value of their output helps contribute to the training costs. However, the low pay of trainees opens up the danger of three kinds of opportunism by the employer. It may economize on the quality of the training given; it may assign trainees to unskilled tasks using them as cheap labour; and especially towards the end of the training period, it may use them to substitute for more expensive skilled workers. Such tendencies may be restricted in several ways. One of the most important is to use the group's professional identity to control the work assignments of trainees. Others include the application of quotas on the number of trainees, or enable the negotiation of higher rates of pay for trainees to eliminate their use as cheap labour (Ryan 1987).

Thus, each of the four types of task allocation rules is able to set limits on managerial authority, and to provide a stable basis for the employment relationship. With the ability to limit possible employer demands, the relationship becomes attractive to workers. On the other side, with suitable guarantees as to the availability of labour for certain tasks, employers also find it a useful form of economic co-ordination.

These rules give potentially stable solutions to the problem of how to build a viable employment relation, avoiding the dangers of the extreme low-trust syndrome which would eliminate the gains of using an employment relationship. They hold a number of important pressures for opportunism at bay and so enable co-operative relations to develop around the employment relation.

In practice, we observe that each of the four rules tends to predominate in certain sectors and in certain economies. The work post rule was very widely used in US manufacturing, as illustrated by Doeringer and Piore's (1971) account of the job structures of North American internal labour markets. In France too it is widely diffused in both manufacturing and services, and stands out in the workplace comparisons between France and Germany (Maurice, Sellier, and Silvestre 1986) and between France and Japan (Maurice *et al.* 1988). The competence rank model is most widely developed in large Japanese industrial firms. Koike and Inoki (1990, ch. 6) contrast the work post model found in their Thai machine tool firm in which each worker is 'in charge of only a small task unit in production of a given part and operates only one machine in fulfilling that task' with the equivalent Japanese plant in which workers are responsible for the production of an entire part using many machines, and also rotate between different production areas. Skill and worker rank are measured by the range of activities a worker can undertake, and her or his ability to deal with unusual operations and to teach other workers, and is not tied to individual work posts. And the tacit nature of these skills means management has to give workers a good deal of autonomy, which Koike compares to semi-autonomous work groups.

The tools of the trade rule has been most commonly found in craft labour markets, for industrial and construction skills in the UK, but also in some other countries using the same methods for regulating skill acquisition and utilization. Finally, a very good example of the qualification rule today can be found in German industry for both skilled blue- and intermediate white-collar workers. The studies of Maurice, Sellier, and Silvestre (1986), and of

Sengenberger (1987) show how the qualification rule both shapes work organization and governs who should undertake it.

The reason why certain transaction rules tend to predominate in whole sectors of activity within individual economies lies in the need for robust rules with which workers and line managers are familiar, and the resulting advantages to whole sectors using the same ones. Elsewhere, I argue that they have some characteristics of 'evolutionary stable strategies' that is, patterns of behaviour which can evolve and diffuse in a decentralized environment, and once they begin to get established they can drive out certain kinds of 'mutant' behaviour patterns (Marsden 1998). The main reasons for this are that, once established, they help control opportunism, and they also then make it difficult to establish one of the other rules in the same environment. Finally, and this is the subject of the next section, because their 'evolutionary stable' qualities are incomplete, they also depend on the support they derive from interfirm institutions and conventions fashioned in their image which also discourage alternative transaction rules.

5. THE ROLE OF INTERFIRM INSTITUTIONS IN SUPPORTING WORKPLACE CO-OPERATION

One of the problems highlighted by the 'prisoner's dilemma' model is the difficulty of achieving trustful and co-operative outcomes in isolation. The 'tit-for-tat' rule proves unreliable because of the 'reverse induction argument' because, in finite games, each party has an incentive to behave opportunistically in the final round, and as a result, it has also in each preceding round, so that the process of co-operation unravels (Dasgupta 1988). 'Reputation' is also insufficient because one can always co-operate with the aim of inducing a false sense of security.

An external support can provide a valuable supplement to co-operation within the firm in a number of ways. First, it may help validate the information exchanged between the parties as this itself is prone to opportunistic manipulation. Secondly, it may help to enforce agreements reached within the workplace. Thirdly, it may enable a more flexible application of the transaction rules in individual instances. The first two arguments have been developed elsewhere (Marsden 1997), but in essence they can be summarized as follows. If we assume the parties wish to co-operate, and are following the 'tit-for-tat' rule, but are uncertain as to the intentions of the other, they will also be leery of any information the other may provide. Because external shocks often make full reciprocity hard to provide, one party may find it is unable to meet the other's expectations. It wishes to assure the other of its continued good faith, but how can it do this, and prevent the other from starting to play 'tit-for-tat' in the reverse direction?

In Fox's analysis this was typically how a low-trust cycle could begin, and as argued earlier, the transaction rules provide partial but not complete protection.

One solution is that both parties should seek to join a wider alliance of their own kind in other firms, in other words, make use of unions and employer organizations. These may play two very important functions. Because they enable each side to escalate retaliatory action, but at an increased cost, they have an in-built interest in weeding out ill-informed and opportunistic disputes raised by their own members as distinct from genuine and serious grievances. Thus, unions and employer organizations have often played an important part in resolving disputes that arise between their members, and by virtue of their ability to support or denounce actions by their own members, have considerable 'policing' powers. They also are often better informed of wider issues than the parties to a local dispute. The union may be better able to assess an employer's claims about the state of the market because it can hire its own expert services, and the employers' organization can advise its members on labour practices across a large number of different firms. It is therefore easier for the parties in a local dispute to judge whether the other party is behaving opportunistically or facing a genuine problem of *force majeure*. The more easily opportunistic action can be detected 'in the bud', the less the incentive to follow this path.

It might be argued that the same problems of co-operative action would recur at the higher level. However, there are a number of limiting factors. The greater cost of conflict at this level increases the incentive to seek other ways of resolving difficulties. Also, there is a greater number of channels of communication and of sources of information so opportunities for communication are considerably greater than presupposed by the prisoner's dilemma.

The third argument concerns the difficulty of allowing more flexible application of a given transaction rule without causing its dilution. If undertaken locally in an environment in which tacit knowledge and skills are important, it is hard to distinguish exceptions made in goodwill for greater flexibility from a gradual transformation of the rule itself. An external standard or point of reference enables the parties to apply the rule more flexibly in the confidence that the other party will not use this as a precedent to argue that the rule has now changed its scope or content. A good example can be found in the observation of Jürgens, Malsch, and Dohse (1993) that although job grades were highly differentiated and clearly defined in the German car plants they studied, there were none of the demarcation restrictions on task allocation they found in British and US plants. In the former plants, the widespread recognition of skills in fact enables the parties to be flexible over job demarcations because there are external criteria to identify goodwill and to distinguish it from minimum required performance. This limits the degree to which either party can manipulate and dilute job rules.

Thus, institutions external to the enterprise may have an important part to play in supporting workplace co-operation, however, the argument so far does not give them much to bite on. It is hard to judge whether one party's claim about work assignments and attached rates of pay or new technology is legitimate or not if there is no general language in terms of which they may be expressed. Workplaces are very varied, and it can be hard for an outsider to judge whether the parties are behaving opportunistically or not. It is much easier if one has to judge whether certain kinds of rules are being followed or not, and it is easier still if one is familiar with the general type of rules being applied. Herein lies one of the bridges between the transaction rules as applied at the job level and those of sector-level classification agreements, but also with certain other kinds of widely observed labour-market conventions and customs.

Multi-Employer Job Classification Agreements

A very important channel through which task allocation rules can be strengthened is by means of job classification agreements. They establish a framework for categorizing jobs within firms, and set up principles for relating them to each other. In many instances, they are a critical supplement to industry bargaining over pay, and play a major role in countries with industry bargaining systems such as France and Germany, but in other countries, equivalent functions can be filled by other processes. In Britain, for example, customary boundaries of skilled work were often backed up by the apprenticeship system, and this was widely recognized in company agreements, and so provided a backbone around which company-level job classifications were constructed for blue-collar workers. In the USA, Jacoby (1985) shows the role played by the Dictionary of Occupational Titles in establishing standard job definitions. As recently as 1994, Lawler (1994) cited it as reinforcing the prevailing 'job-based' pattern of work organization in American firms.

It has long been known that markets need ways of categorizing goods and services in order to function properly. Indeed, it is hard to imagine how the process of competition can function without employers being able to compare the asking wages of different workers offering the same skill, and vice versa. Yet, job classification systems existed in the twilight zone of research until the recent work on France of Eyraud *et al.* (1989), and an international ILO study reported by Eyraud and Rozenblatt (1994). What we learn from these is how the transaction rules regulating the employment relation are supported by the interfirm rules embodied in the classification agreements.

The French case provides a particularly interesting illustration, showing both why such agreements have been neglected in the past, and why their role needs to be re-evaluated in the light of the theory of the employment relation. It is also an important example for our argument because it is generally assumed that employers have considerable discretion over the organization of their internal labour markets. As French firms rely heavily upon this type of labour market, and have generally been reluctant to recognize state vocational qualifications as either a prerequisite for holding jobs of certain levels or as entitling the holders to a certain minimum job grade, one's immediate presumption is that firm-level autonomy would be the rule.

The industry classification agreements in France set up a means of classifying jobs and linking basic rates of pay to them. Although they have evolved considerably over the last five decades, a number of basic principles have remained fairly constant. Job types are assigned to a number of job grades and ranked on a hierarchical scale to which pay indices are attached. In the firm, individual work posts are then assigned to particular job grades such as highly skilled manual, or technician, or supervisor, and so on. Within the grades, there may be a number of levels between which incumbents may progress, or into which certain work posts may be slotted. Individual firms may also have their own classification systems on condition that the workers concerned can be shown to be at least no worse off than under the provisions of their industry agreement.

At first sight, the evidence of a large wage gap between the pay scales set in industry agreements and the gross earnings of workers on the equivalent grades appears to suggest the agreements have only a marginal role. For example, in the chemical industry in the early 1980s, Jobert and Rozenblatt (1985) estimated the wage gap to be about 20 per cent, up slightly on the 1970s. The later work of Eyraud *et al.* (1989) also showed that company-level agreements could also either raise or reduce the wage differentials set in industry agreements. On this evidence, therefore, it would seem that firms have a good deal of freedom and that the industry classification agreements do not impose much in the way of constraints. In that case, how could they reinforce job-level transaction rules and restrain opportunism?

Closer analysis, however, reveals a much greater degree of influence. First, when the earnings gap is analysed at the level of individual workers, it proves to be largely explained by length of service, age, and diploma, all criteria that are fundamental to the industry classification agreements. Secondly, the compression and expansion of intraplant wage differentials as compared with the pay scales of the industry agreements proves to be explicable largely in terms of the same variables: explaining about 50 per cent of the variance overall, and considerably more among blue-collar workers, supervisors and technicians (Eyraud *et al.* 1989: 206 ff.). Thus, the agreements prove to reinforce a number of key rules that are related to the work post system, notably the hierarchical ordering of jobs, the role of length of service in progression, and the recognition of external qualifications as entry points, thus segregating internal and external training.

An impression of the qualitative influence of the industry classification rules is given by methods adopted by French sectoral-level employers and unions to deal with new technology, and the growing demand for skills in between those of skilled blue-collar and technician. The old metal industry classification agreement offered no easy solution to integrating this emerging category. The solution adopted was to establish a new job category of workshop technician ('technicien d'atelier'), inserted in between the blue-collar and technician categories (Carrière-Ramanoelina and Zarifian 1985). Other solutions might have been possible, for example, a complete reorganization of blue-collar and technician skills, bringing more technicians into the workshop, or by aiming at a more flexible pattern of work organization based on the increased competencies of individual workers. Both strategies would have blurred existing work post boundaries, and called into question the principle of determinate categories of jobs and individual responsibility for a set of tasks. Instead, the logic of the classification system was maintained by the insertion of the new grade of work post. The authors also showed how the interests of the incumbent parties were reflected in the solution adopted. Employers insisted that only those competencies required by the post should be rewarded whereas flexible jobs require workers to hold a degree of 'excess' qualifications that can be called on when needed. The white-collar unions, and notably the middle management CGC, wanted the new grade confined to blue-collar work to prevent an erosion of their own work posts, and the blue-collar unions were happy to have an extra grade to which their most skilled members could accede. At the company level, in their study of new technology implementation in French establishments, Maurice *et al.* (1988) also found that the new jobs associated with the new technology were by and large assimilated into the existing job classification categories.

Thus, if one thinks of the sectoral classification agreements as dictating a precise pattern of remuneration or dictating detailed task assignments to particular jobs, then their influence on day-to-day work relations is bound to be small, and the latter would almost certainly be intended so. However, their true importance lies in the principles they enshrine. They have been shown to exert a powerful influence on the principles of work organization and the related pay incentives despite the 'wage gap' in earnings.

Another example within the production approach is given by the function-in-production system as widely practised in Japan. There too the importance of enterprise internal labour markets would suggest a great deal of autonomy, and the pattern of diffuse jobs militates against any parallel to the French and German classification agreements. Is there then a functional equivalent to these, that underpins employee confidence in the principles regulating work organization?

Although there is no formal equivalent of Western European sectoral bargaining, the annual spring offensive is the occasion of intensive information exchange, discussion, and negotiation among firms and enterprise unions and their federations. In these, certain signals play an extremely important part, and bear strongly on the norms governing the employment transaction. The concept of the 'standard worker' (who is also 'regular') serves as the interfirm standard for gauging demands for improvements in pay and conditions, and serves as the 'orbit of comparison' between firms and for changes over time. Focus on the regular worker highlights the second principle, that of long-term or life-time employment, the second orbit of comparison.[8] The power of these rules is well illustrated by the reactions of large Japanese firms to the very deep recession of the early 1990s. Lincoln and Nakata (1997) show that despite wide media coverage of albeit small lay-offs by West European and US standards, firms have gone to great, and expensive, lengths to avoid eroding the principle of long-term employment for their regular workers.

There are two reasons for this. First, as argued earlier, it is the key signal employers can give to their employees of their intention to maintain the competence rank system and any serious departure from it would endanger its associated patterns of co-operation. But, secondly, its very clarity is greatly enhanced because it is a rule followed collectively by large Japanese firms for their domestic regular workforces. Any serious dilution of this commitment by one firm would erode the collective reputation of all large Japanese firms. Whereas cartels are notoriously prone to break down because of the rewards to the first partner to move independently, the intensive contacts among Japanese employers and between them and their unions create powerful informal channels through which moral pressures can be exercised to restrain potential defaulters. Strong links among enterprise unions, especially those grouped in the same federation, likewise help to reinforce pressure to maintain certain key standards and especially valued among these is long-term employment. Indeed, Shirai and Shimada (1978) argued that union pressure was one of the prime causes behind the emergence of the lifetime employment system as union members were dependent largely upon firm-specific skills. Thus, even among firms widely using internal labour-markets, and in the absence of formal sectoral classification agreements, it is possible for an interfirm functional equivalent to develop and which helps to underpin confidence in job-level transaction rules.

Familiarity and Convention

Customs and widely accepted labour-market conventions may play a similar role to that of formal classification systems. Much has been made of their
importance within workplaces, and in most countries where there is a
tradition of empirical workplace research, one can find references to
workplace custom. Brown (1973) highlighted the importance of workplace
custom in shop steward bargaining in the UK, and Doeringer and Piore
(1971), its importance in job regulation in North American internal labour-
markets. But in Germany too, Bosch and Lichte (1982) provide examples of
customary seniority rules in some workplaces, and Morel (1979) provides
examples of such practices in France. When work rules are customary, the
workers and managers concerned know how they will be applied, and know
what outcomes to expect. It is relatively easy then to detect a change of
behaviour by one or other side. Seniority in task allocations is a good
example, as is allocation of work according to the tools required or materials used. There is usually a simple and unambiguous answer, and so rapid
acceptance of a management decision that conforms to them. Morel provides a different kind of example from colder rural areas of France: the
practice of employees being allowed to arrive late on the first day of heavy
snow without prior agreement of management. The employees know this
will not be penalized as absenteeism, but by the end of the first day they
should have made their own arrangements, or come to some agreement
with management.

   What is often less appreciated is the importance of particular practices
being widespread in a particular sector or region. Although one can imagine
repeated games in which such rules might emerge in a firm taken in isolation, they take time to become established. Typically, they would require
the actors to go through several rounds, which in practical terms means
encountering the same kinds of problem many times over. In some cases,
such problems may recur frequently, but in Morel's example of the first
heavy snowfall, this would happen perhaps only once a year or even less
frequently. In the meantime, supervisors and their staff would be in considerable uncertainty as to how such events should be treated with all
the attendant dangers of suspected opportunism. For example, supervisors
might be suspected of using lateness as a way of penalizing union activists,
or they might fear that employees would use the heavy snow as the thin
end of the wedge to gain acceptance for lateness under all kinds of
weather conditions. In another example, that of wet weather compensation,
Dunlop (1958) showed that special treatment of such conditions was common in the construction industries of all the countries his study surveyed. In
some cases it was formalized into collective agreements, in others it was of
a more customary nature. The point is that once the rule is widely recognized within a sector, it is easy to apply because everyone understands

its meaning, and the scope for opportunistic manipulation by either side is limited.

The 'tools of the trade' rule provides another example. Although commonly seen as a restrictive practice, the Webbs' (1920) study shows how useful familiarity with it could be across a host of independent workplaces which all used a large variety of different skills engaged on quite complex work. When management was faced with the complex task of assigning work to people of many different skills on sites in which the stability of factory work was absent, the tools of the trade generally gave clear and unambiguous answers. Plumbers had their work, and other trades, theirs. As work on shipyards was unstable, and people were often hired for the construction of a particular ship, familiarity with such a rule in the local communities enabled orderly work organization to develop.

Similar conventions can also assist operation of formal classification agreements in the workplace. Although the 'work post' rule has been more commonly identified with Taylorist management, there too one can find evidence of such wider understandings. In theory, work posts could follow a number of different contours of tasks complementarity, as Lazear's discussion of why cherry picking and cherry spotting tend to be combined into a single role illustrates[9] (Lazear 1995). However, Touraine (1955) observed that it was common, under this system, for each skilled worker to have 'his machine' a common custom inherited from the craft tradition of people being responsible for their own tools.

So far, it has been argued that interfirm rules and conventions can support workplace transaction rules by making it easier to detect opportunistic action, by dispute-settling procedures and policing the actions of one's own side, and in the last resort, enabling the workplace actors to escalate their action. The argument would however be incomplete unless one could show a strong degree of congruence between the type of rules shaping work roles at the job level, and those of industry-level classifications and conventions. The next section seeks to show that there is indeed a high degree of congruence.

6. CLASSIFICATION RULES AND TRANSACTION RULES

In a recent international comparative study of job classification systems at industry and company level, Eyraud and Rozenblatt (1994) proposed a typology that is quite close to that derived in this paper from the constraints on the employment relation. They argue that job classifications they observed could be situated between two poles: classification according to the attributes of either the work post, or of the individual worker. They identified also a third pole, namely, that of qualification which they sometimes present in an intermediate position in between the other two, and sometimes as a separate pole. Classification of jobs by work post attributes, they argue, is common in France and the United States, and that by worker attributes, in Japan. The use of qualification or trade, which they present as a form of individual attribute, is widespread in Germany, and has been common in many other countries, such as Britain and Australia, but there it is in decline in the face of increased use of work post attributes, notably in job evaluation.

Eyraud and Rozenblatt start from wage determination rather than work role definition, and so concentrate on the link between classification systems and wage rules. Here they identify two types of wage relation under the work post system depending on whether job evaluation alone is used, or whether it is supplemented by the recognition of certain status groups, such as, in France, those of 'blue-collar', 'white-collar and supervisory', and 'managerial employees' (cadres). These systems establish pay classifications according to the demands of categories of work posts, and workers are graded according to the work post they occupy. Under such systems, skill is treated as an attribute of the work post and not of the individual job-holder.

The second broad category, which they identify primarily in Japan, is associated with the individual characteristics pole, namely a classification and remuneration system that is internal to the firm, in which employees are graded according to educational qualifications that are recognized at entry, and service and performance that are recognized thereafter. As the authors point out, there is no direct link between the work post and pay, nor does the personnel department have any information enabling them to establish one.

Two other types of classification system they identify belong to the qualification pole: the British and Australian models in which craft or trade communities receive special recognition and gain the dominant position in company classification systems; and the German model, in which vocational qualifications play the key role. In the British classification systems they studied, the craft skills tended to occupy a prestigious but discrete position, as if the craft-skilled category was of a different nature to lower-level skills; in the German ones, there was more of an idea of skill as a continuous gradation. For example, in many German agreements, length of service may be recognized as a partial equivalent, although not being allowed to displace formally acquired vocational skills.

At first sight, their typology seems to provide partial support for the argument of this paper, but only partial because of their emphasis on the qualification pole as an intermediate case in between the other two. However, I hope to show that if one resolves some of the tensions within their typology, then their model coincides very closely with the typology of transaction rules derived from the constraints on the employment relation.

The basic difficulty of their typology lies in the problematic position of the 'qualification' pole. If one takes the contrast between classification by job or by individual characteristics, then publicly recognized vocational qualifications do not fit. Hence the fluctuation in the authors' treatment of that pole. There are two basic problems: first, skill based on vocational qualifications clearly is not an attribute of individual jobs. If the two coincide, it is because, as argued earlier, the training approach to job design has been adopted. Nor is such qualification really an individual attribute. Its effectiveness depends upon its widespread use by many firms, otherwise, for reasons explained earlier, the size of the market for the skill concerned is too small to warrant workers investing in it. Nor can it be seen as an intermediate case as it clearly is not a mix of two different logics, but follows a distinct one of its own.

The second problem in their classification is that length of service and performance are not strictly individual attributes as practised in the large Japanese firms on which we have most evidence (cf. for example Koike and Inoki 1990). Length of service signals the duration of a person's membership of a particular enterprise community, and performance is carefully assessed by management using such criteria as contribution to the work group's effort. In this respect, length of service and performance have a rather different meaning compared with that they often have under work post systems where the same criteria often apply.

In fact, one can resolve these problems by locating Eyraud and Rozenblatt's examples within the typology of transaction rules. The German and British qualification and craft rules clearly belong to a different logic from that of the US, French, and Japanese systems which are based on variants of the 'production approach'. The French and US classification systems clearly belong together because they classify work posts, even though there may be differences of emphasis in the precise way in which they are divided up. In the Japanese case, the classification systems are not assessing individual characteristics in relation to specific jobs, but in relation to contribution to team output, and the teams are primarily engaged in fulfilling certain functions in production. It is true that, as in the USA and France where employee performance appraisal is also used increasingly, appraisal in the large Japanese firms is by supervisors, but more often these are 'player managers' rather than specialist supervisors, hence the large number of supervisors noted by Jürgens and Strömel (1987) in their comparison of two Japanese and German car plants. The work team, including the supervisors, has been likened by Koike and Inoki (1990) to a semi-autonomous work group. Thus, what is being evaluated is the contribution to a team, and as the job boundaries are diffuse and flexible, that contribution is not identified with certain tasks, but rather with the quality of co-operation or interaction with other team members.

If this argument is correct, then the results of the Eyraud and Rozenblatt study show there is a marked convergence between the micro-level transaction rules needed to establish job-level co-operation and the company- and industry-wide classification systems. This conclusion is especially important for the third of the three ways in which interfirm conventions can sustain workplace transaction rules (cf. Section 5 above). The convergence between the substance of workplace rules and classification principles illustrates how the latter provide the external point of reference for workplace rules that enables the parties to show goodwill and apply them flexibly without fearing to create the kind of precedent that dilutes the rule.

There is a reciprocal relationship between job-level transaction rules and classification rules. As shown in the last two sections, interfirm classification rules and conventions provide valuable support to the transaction rules, a support they need because they share only some of the characteristics of evolutionary stable strategies. But the latter also support the working of the former. The reason is that the employment relation's dependence upon transaction rules for its stability and flexibility mean that employers in fact face a fixed menu of principles for organizing their employment relations. If they wish, say, to opt out of an industry-wide classification agreement or some established labour-market convention, they have to choose something else in its place. There is no long-term option of an employment relation without transaction rules because that would deprive one of protection against the cycle of low trust which, as argued earlier, would destroy the viability of an employment relation. An employer may choose to develop its own system, but the cost would be much higher because of the greater investment required in its credibility in the eyes of current and potential employees. This indeed is one of the problems facing employers that wish to move away from work post systems towards the more functional ones but find employee fear of employer opportunism an obstacle as shown in the examples by Dugué (1994) and Clark (1994) cited earlier.

7. CONCLUSION

This paper has sought to inject a new element into the discussion of work roles and trust relations by considering the problems of designing an effective employment relation. Unlike 'buyer–supplier' relations discussed in Sako's chapter in this book, there is no choice between arm's length and relational contracting within the employment relation: once employment has been chosen as the form of transaction one has embarked upon a relational contract. There may be other forms of contracting, such as variants on the sales and self-employment contracts, but employment is necessarily relational. If one goes too far down the path to fully explicit contracts, then the advantages of employment are lost, and one slides out into some variant of the sales contract. Hence, the degree of flexibility, discretion and with that, trust, are essential problems of the employment relation.

Most of this paper, for reasons of space, has concentrated on the problem of avoiding low trust, and hence on how to control opportunism over work allocation within the employment relation. It has been argued that rules enabling the parties to define their respective obligations and to define the scope of managerial authority in allocating work play a logically necessary part in ensuring a viable employment relation. From a close examination of the nature of the constraints, it has been possible to derive four broad categories of transaction rule and to show that these solve many of the problems of opportunism. They do so to a sufficient degree to make them attractive to the parties in a decentralized economy without legal or collective bargaining constraints, but their power to control opportunism is greatly enhanced if they are supported by institutions or norms outside the individual firm. The paper has given illustrations of the rules backed up by some evidence from workplace studies, and then has shown how interfirm classification norms back up those at the workplace.

Finally, it is worth returning to Fox's argument about discretion and trust, and to look at it in the light of the various national cases discussed in this paper. It has been common in recent discussions of functional flexibility and workplace co-operation, to regard the 'typical' medium- to large-size firm in Germany and Japan as illustrating high flexibility and high levels of workplace co-operation, and work relations in other countries such as the USA, France, and Britain as illustrating predominantly the opposite albeit to varying degrees. The MIT 'Made in America' report for the USA (Dertouzos, Lester, and Solow 1989); Crozier (1963), and Maurice, Sellier, and Silvestre (1986) on France; and Batstone (1988), and Willman (1986), and many others on the UK, have highlighted the kind of low-trust syndrome analysed by Fox.

The analysis of this paper suggests that the position of trust and its contribution to co-operation in the industrial relations literature has been misconstrued, and that it is only part of the story. Fox, and many others since him, have tended to concentrate on the cycle of low-trust behaviour and to focus first of all on the impetus from management who have been widely regarded as determining work roles. There have been some notable exceptions, such as Willman (1986) and Marginson (1993), but they have been few in number. Perhaps this tendency has been accentuated by the popularity of the 'prisoner's dilemma' model which looks at the problem of trust behaviour in abstraction from many features of the employment relation. Hopefully, the argument of this paper sheds some light on the preconditions for trust behaviour within the employment relation. The resulting transaction rules also shed light on the relationship between trust, co-operation, and the degree of work role flexibility. Reading Fox's classic account, one could be forgiven for concluding that low trust reinforces and feeds upon low-discretion work roles, and high trust, on high-discretion roles. Ideology and power may generate exceptions, but they do not alter the underlying dynamic of trust relations.

The different kinds of transaction rule transform the link between the degree of trust and that of work role discretion. It is clear that the two 'task-centred' rules will define the boundaries of jobs in a much more specific way than the two function-oriented rules, and so give rise to much sharper divisions of tasks between workers and more tightly prescribed work roles. In contrast, the two function-oriented rules, by avoiding any direct reference to the tasks workers carry out give rise to a more flexible pattern of work allocation. In Fox's terms, work roles may be more diffuse. Trust may develop around all four types of rule, but the amount of expansion of work roles it enables is more restricted under the task-centred rules than the other two. On the other hand, the two function-centred rules provide less protection against opportunism because responsibilities for non- or sub-standard performance cannot be so clearly attributed, so although they may enable greater task flexibility if work relations are co-operative, if they are not then the danger of drifting into large-scale opportunism is also much greater than under the task-centred rules. In the discussion of functional flexibility and workplace relations of co-operation and trust, the role of interfirm rules and conventions has been largely neglected. The argument of this paper shows how these underpin workplace transaction rules both by restraining the slide into low-trust relations, and by fostering an environment in which higher-trust relations may develop.

NOTES

1. Using the employer survey results from SCELI for the latter part of the 1980s, Gallie and White (1994) showed that 91 per cent of employees were in permanent employment (of which, 74 per cent were in permanent full-time, and 17 per cent in permanent part-time employment), and only 3 per cent in fixed-term contracts of under one year, and 3 per cent in those of between one and three years, and 3 per cent temporary part-time.
2. Another indicator of the continued importance of permanent open-ended employment is given by Burgess and Rees' (1996) findings that job tenures in Britain had proved remarkably stable between 1975 and 1995. Men's job tenures dropped from an average of 10.5 years to 9.4 years, but the authors could not rule

out the possibility of cyclical factors. For women, average job tenures remained stable at about 6–7 years throughout. The one big area of decline was for men on lowest quartile earnings. In the USA, Swinnerton and Wial (1995) have shown evidence for some decline in job tenures during the latter part of the 1980s, but their analysis has been contested by Diebold, Neumark, and Polsky (1996), using the same data set, who argue the amount of change has been very small. Swinnerton and Wial (1996) rebutted Diebold *et al.*'s critique, but the differences in estimates are clearly small enough to be swallowed up by differences in estimation methods on the same data set. The OECD (1993) provides international evidence of only modest change in age-controlled job-tenure profiles during the 1980s. The most dramatic reductions were in the UK and the USA.

3. He takes Simon to task for identifying the employment relation with management authority, and offers his own alternative in the form of a jointly regulated internal labour-market, similar to that described by Doeringer and Piore (1971). However, Simon took care to stress that authority was only one of a number of possible ways of organizing an employment relation, himself taking this one for simplicity of exposition.

4. Becker's argument assumes perfect competition, but in this case, skill transferability ensures competition among employers. In theory, the state could assume the costs of such training, although there are good reasons why this is not likely to be wholly effective (Marsden 1986, ch. 8). Employers may be induced to share the cost if there are sufficient frictions to enable them to retain those they have trained, or if there are means of ensuring that all employers concerned contribute to training costs so that none assumes a competitive disadvantage by providing transferable training.

5. The argument is fully developed in Marsden (1986, ch. 8), and hinges on the distinction between internal and occupational labour-markets. Since intermediate forms are likely to prove unstable, in the long run, firms are faced with a choice between two discrete models.

6. In their study of pay and productivity bargaining in the early 1970s, McKersie and Hunter (1973) described the contrast as follows: 'If, from a theoretical point of view, work can be organised either according to management principles of engineering economy or according to established occupational lines, then the craft system represents the most notable example of the latter approach. The essential feature of a craft-type occupational system is that each single craft maintains a considerable degree of autonomy in regulating the standards and conditions for the performance of particular tasks. The base of this autonomy is the skill and specific knowledge required to perform the tasks. Since it usually takes considerable time and effort to become proficient in performing such tasks, it is more economical to grant monopoly over the service to a certain group which, in return, guarantees certain standards of· performance by apprenticeship, certification and self-supervision . . . (Under) the administrative system . . . rather than allowing job design to be determined by occupational definitions existing in the local labour market, management packages job duties based on technology, scale of operations, and other economic considerations internal to the firm.' (345–6).

7. Recent work on functional flexibility in banking in Britain and France has

illustrated how increased functional flexibility may often be a form of work intensification rather than enrichment, especially if the additional tasks workers are expected to undertake are of limited skill content (O'Reilly 1992).

8. I am grateful to Mitsuharu Miyamoto for explaining how this functions.

9. Lazear suggests that it might be more efficient on incentive grounds to separate the spotting of cherries to be picked and the actual picking. The picker has an incentive to gather the most accessible fruit and to leave the rest, whereas the grower may wish to maximize the return on each tree. By hiring a specialist fruit spotter the grower could ensure that more cherries were picked. However, the gains from the technical complementarity of the two roles means that it may still prove more economical to combine the roles in a single worker.

REFERENCES

Batstone, E. (1988), *The Reform of Workplace Industrial Relations: Theory, Myth and Evidence.* Oxford: Oxford University Press.

Becker, G. S. (1975), *Human Capital: A Theoretical and Empirical Analysis, with Special Reference to Education.* Chicago: University of Chicago Press.

Bosch, G. and Lichte, R. (1982), *Die Funktionsweise informeller Senioritätsrechte: am Beispiel einer betrieblichen Fallstudie*, in K. Dohse, U. Jürgens, and H. Russig (eds.), 205–36. Statussicherung im Industriebetrieb. Frankfurt: Campus Verlag.

Brown, W. E. (1973), *Piecework Bargaining.* London: Heinemann.

Burgess, S. and Rees, H. (1996) , 'Job Tenure in Britain, 1975–1995', *Economic Journal*, 106/435 (Mar.), 334–44.

Carrière-Ramanoelina, M. and Zarifian P. (1985), 'Le Technicien d'atelier dans la classification de la métallurgie: de la référence au métier à l'analyse de l'emploi; vers un ouvrier-technicien?', *Formation Emploi*, 9/1 (Jan.–Mar.), 11–24.

Clark, J. (1994), 'Greenfield sites and the "New Industrial Relations"', in ISVET-IRRU (ed.), *Participation, Involvement and Company Performance in Great Britain.* Milan: Franco Angeli.

Coase, R. H. (1937), 'The Nature of the Firm', *Economica* (Nov.), 386–405.

Crozier, M. (1963), *Le Phénomène bureaucratique.* Paris: Seuil.

Dasgupta, P. (1988), 'Trust as a Commodity', in D. Gambetta (ed.), *Trust: Making and Breaking Cooperative Relations.* Oxford: Blackwell.

Dertouzos, M., Lester, R., and Solow, R. (1989), *Made in America: Regaining the Productive Edge.* Cambridge, Mass.: MIT Commission on Industrial Productivity/MIT Press.

Diebold, F., Neumark, D., and Polsky, D. (1996), 'Comment on Kenneth A. Swinnerton and Howard Wial, "Is job stability declining in the US economy?"', *Industrial and Labour Relations Review*, 49/2 (Jan.), 348–52.

Doeringer, P. B. and Piore, M. J. (1971), *Internal Labor Markets and Manpower Analysis.* Lexington, Mass.: Heath.

Dugué, E. (1994), 'La Gestion des compétences: les savoirs dévalués, le pouvoir occulté', *Sociologie du Travail*, 3/94: 273–92.

Dunlop, J. T. (1958), *Industrial Relations Systems*. New York: Holt.

Eyraud, F. and Rozenblatt, P. (1994), *Les Formes hiérarchiques: travail et salaires dans neuf pays industrialisées*. Paris: La Documentation Française.

——Jobert, A., Rozenblatt, P., and Tallard, M. (1989), 'Les Classifications dans l'entreprise: production des hiérarchies professionnelles et salariales', *Document Travail Emploi*, Paris: Ministère du Travail, de l'Emploi et de la Formation Professionnelle.

Fox, A. (1974), *Beyond Contract: Work, Power and Trust Relations*. London: Faber and Faber.

Gallie, D. and White, M. (1994), 'Employer Policies, Employee Contracts, and Labour-Market Structure', in Rubery and Wilkinson (eds.), *Employer Strategy and the Labour-Market*, ch. 2.

Jacoby, S. M. (1985), *Employing Bureaucracy: Managers, Unions, and the Transformation of Work in American Industry, 1900–1945*. New York: Columbia University Press.

Jobert, A. and Rozenblatt P. (1985), 'Portée et limite d'un accord de branche sur les classifications', *Formation Emploi*, 9 (Jan.–Mar.), 3–10.

Junankar, P. N. (1987) (ed.), *From School to Unemployment? The Labour Market for Young People*. London: Macmillan.

Jürgens, U. and Strömel, H.-P. (1987), 'The Communication Structure Between Management and Shop Floor: A Comparison of a Japanese and a German Plant', in M. Trevor (ed.), *The Internationalisation of Japanese Business: European and Japanese Perspectives*. Frankfurt: Campus.

——Malsch, T., and Dohse, K. (1993), *Breaking from Taylorism: Changing Forms of Work in the Automobile Industry*. Cambridge: Cambridge University Press.

Kern, H. and Schumann, M. (1984), *Das Ende der Arbeitsteilung: Rationalisierung in der industriellen Produktion*. Munich: C. H. Beck.

Koike, K. and Inoki, T. (1990) (eds.), *Skill Formation in Japan and Southeast Asia*. Tokyo: University of Tokyo Press.

Lawler, E. J. (1994), 'From Job-Based to Competency-Based Organization', *Journal of Organizational Behavior*, 15/3: 3–15.

Lazear, E. (1995), *Personnel Economics*. Cambridge, Mass.: MIT Press.

Lincoln, J. R. and Nakata, Y. (1997), 'The Transformation of the Japanese Employment System: Nature, Depth, and Origins', *Work and Occupations*, 24/1 (Feb.), 33–55.

McKersie, R. B. and Hunter, L. C. (1973), *Pay, Productivity and Collective Bargaining*. London: Macmillan.

Marginson, P. (1993), 'Power and Efficiency in the Firm: Understanding the Employment Relationship', in C. Pitelis (ed.), *Surveys in Transaction Costs, Markets and Hierarchies*. Cambridge: Cambridge University Press.

Marsden, D. (1986), *The End of Economic Man? Custom and Competition in Labour Markets*. Brighton: Wheatsheaf.

——(1997), 'The "Social Dimension" as a Basis for the Single Market', in J. Addison and S. Siebert (eds.), *Labor Market Harmonization in Europe: An Investigation of the Issues*. Dryden Press.

Marsden, D. (1998), *A Theory of Employment Systems: Micro-foundations of Societal Diversity*. Oxford: Oxford University Press.

Maurice, M., Sellier, F., and Silvestre, J. J. (1986), *The Social Foundations of Industrial Power: A Comparison of France and Germany*. Cambridge, Mass.: MIT Press.

——Mannari, H., Takeoka, Y., and Inoki, T. (1988), *Des entreprises françaises et japonaises face à la mécatronique: acteurs et organisation de la dynamique industrielle.* Aix-en-Provence: Laboratoire d'Economie et de Sociologie du Travail (CNRS).

Morel, C. (1979), 'Le Droit coutumier social dans l'entreprise', *Droit Social*, 7–8 (July–Aug.), 279–86.

OECD (1993), *Employment Outlook 1993*. Paris: OECD.

O'Reilly, J. (1992), 'Where Do You Draw the Line? Functional Flexibility, Training and Skill in Britain and France', *Work, Employment and Society*, 6/3: 369–96.

Piore, M. J. (1968), 'The Impact of the Labor Market on the Design and Selection of Productive Techniques Within the Manufacturing Plant', *Quarterly Journal of Economics*, 82/4: 602–20.

Rubery, J. and Wilkinson, F. (1994) (eds.), *Employer Strategy and the Labour-Market*. Oxford: Oxford University Press.

Ryan, P. (1987), 'Trade Unionism and the Pay of Young Workers', in P. N. Junankar (ed.), *From School to Unemployment?*, 119–42.

Sengenberger, W. (1987), *Struktur und Funktionsweise von Arbeitsmärkten: die Bundesrepublik Deutschland im internationalen Vergleich*. Frankfurt: Campus.

Shirai, T. and Shimada, H. (1978), 'Japan', in J. Dunlop and W. Galenson (eds.), *Labor in the Twentieth Century*. New York: Academic Press, 241–322.

Simon, H. A. (1951), 'A Formal Theory of the Employment Relationship', *Econometrica*, 19/3: 293–305.

Slichter, S., Healy, J., and Livernash, E. (1960), *The Impact of Collective Bargaining on Management*. Washington, DC: Brookings Institution.

Streeck, W. (1992), *Social Institutions and Economic Performance: Studies of Industrial Relations in Advanced Capitalist Countries*. London: Sage.

Swinnerton, K. and Wial, H. (1995), 'Is Job Stability Declining in the United States?', *Industrial and Labor Relations Review*, 48/2: 293–304.

Touraine, A. (1955), *L'évolution du travail ouvrier aux usines Renault*. Paris: Centre National de la Recherche Scientifique.

Webb, S. and Webb, B. (1920), *Industrial Democracy*. London: Longman.

Williamson, O. E. (1975), *Markets and Hierarchies: Analysis and Antitrust Implications*. New York: Free Press.

Willman, P. (1986), *Technological Change, Collective Bargaining and Industrial Efficiency*. Oxford: Oxford University Press.

Zucker, L. (1986), 'Production of Trust: Institutional Sources of Economic Structure, 1840–1920', *Research in Organizational Behavior*, 8: 53–111.

7

Lack of Trust, Surfeit of Trust: Some Causes of the Innovation Crisis in German Industry

HORST KERN

Arguments which build on the notion of trust—or on parallel categories like 'networks of civic engagement', 'co-operation culture', 'social capital'—came into fashion some years ago. Often they associate good performance in the production of highly valued social goods with organizations that are blessed with a broad stock of trust. 'Innovation' is an example of a set of activities which trust organizations are said to perform well. Neotocquevillian currents in American social science exhibit this type of thinking as well as approaches to economic development which, more or less explicitly, rely on Alfred Marshall's idea of 'industrial districts'. It is my opinion that these arguments exaggerate the benevolent effects of trust too far and that the analysis of trust which they bring to the fore is sometimes rather misleading.

To point to Fukuyama's trust study (1995) would be to reason with too simplistic a case. But even such a complexly designed and brilliantly elaborated argument as that of Robert Putnam (1993) is not immune from such doubts. Certainly, Putnam recognizes that his main message—in organizations which are endowed with a solid base of 'civic engagement' life is easier, government is more efficient, economic progress is faster, education is better, anomie is less—is not compatible with Mancur Olson's observations (1982). As Olson had argued, well established economic and political organizations show some tendency towards inefficient cartellization. Having claimed in 1993 'the evidence and the theory of our study contradict . . . these theses' (Putnam 1993: 176) Putnam concedes in 1995 that further research is necessary in order to reconcile his results with the 'undoubtable insights' Olson offers (Putnam 1995: 76). Neither remark is satisfactory.

The weak point in Putnam's argument results from the theoretical framework with which he works, i.e. Coleman's concept of 'social capital'. According to Coleman social capital, as it exists in organizations with dense interpersonal relationships and with trust, 'is productive, making possible the achievement of certain ends that would not be attainable in its absence' (1990: 302). The root of this productive force is seen to reside in the fact that the human resources in a social organization which does have social capital are at the disposal of numerous actors and that these resources, precisely because they are used repeatedly, can display a rather high degree of

effectiveness (Coleman 1990: 399). As Coleman demonstrates with an example: the resource 'human capital of parents' encourages the production
of new human capital if it is actually accessable to their children. If the
family possesses social capital (e.g. if the parents are available for the kids
and care for them), the multiple utilization of this capital is guaranteed and
vice versa (Coleman 1988: 118, 119). Assuming the social environment of
the family embodies additional social capital (e.g. the kids attend school
together with others having the same religious background), parents can
influence their children all the more efficiently—or should one prefer: let
them all the more participate in their human capital?—simply by virtue of
the fact that within the parental group there is consensus on standards and
sanctions. Coleman associates such social capital with 'intergenerational
closure' (1988: 105–7) which, in his view, is reinforcing the production of
human capital.

Already at this point one gets a bit nervous. This assumption gives no
room to the trivial yet not irrelevant idea that the human capital passed on
to their young people by closed communities is often of a circular kind
which does not lead to anything better than the simple reproduction of the
capital stock already given. Is it, in our days, still necessary to insist on the
fact that human capital which deserves its name has to display the capability
to create something new and that this improvement occurs only if some
critical impulses are implanted in the cultural heritage? In other words, too
much trust in the familiar can lead to pretty unproductive views of the
world—and a dash of mistrust may reveal itself as being extraordinarily
productive. To be sure, it has not escaped me that Coleman adds to his
general idea of the productivity of social capital: 'A given form of social
capital that is valuable in facilitating certain actions may be useless or even
harmful for others' (1990: 302). But this qualification seems to be forgotten
when he elaborates his argument. The style he uses is sober. None the less,
the message which finally comes across sounds like high esteem, if not
romanticization, of high-trust communities.

Nobody can reasonably claim that the growth of human capital, learning,
or innovation can succeed in an atmosphere of mistrust. Experimenting,
which must be viewed as a prerequisite for such growth, depends on the
certainty among acting subjects that those mistakes and errors which serve
the experiment will gain applause instead of being turned into instruments
of opportunism. Within a social order whose institutions establish a general
supposition of trust, this certainty goes without saying. Boosted by such
basic trust, the actors can follow the risky path of exploration. However, it
needs some sensitivity to the inherent limitations or faults, in other words
some second thoughts or mistrust with regard to the actual functioning of
the order.

What follows is an attempt to check this line of reasoning by testing it in a case-study. The case I shall deal with is the innovation crisis into which German industry recently has plunged. In contrast to the 1980s, when many obervers still testified to German industry's innovative capacity, we currently hear much more critical talk. I shall focus on this change and explain it with an argument which has as its central building-block the notion of trust.

Economic innovation represents an excellent test case of the reach of trust theory. Normally innovation springs from collaboration between several knowledge bearers who succeed in matching their respective expertise to a new scheme which is able to serve a new economic function. The co-operation that nurtures such innovation is by definition an open, chancy business. For this reason it cannot be defined *ex ante* in all details, and it is all the more impossible to fix it meticulously in advance. When an actor merges with a partner because one can raise the knowledge needed for successful innovation only by means of that merger, nobody knows exactly where the collaboration will lead or end up. In this situation trust can work as a catalyst which ensures that such uncertainties do not veer towards risk aversion, i.e. to a behaviour which would damage innovation. Consequently a social environment which, either because of tradition or of shared culture, brings about trust should be very advantageous for innovation. Strong traditions, much trust, easy going innovations. The converse would also be true: where trust cannot flourish (or where it has been destroyed), innovation will not (any longer) take root.

Following this argument for solving my test problem (Why did German industry become a lame duck in innovation?) one would have to search recent German economic history for events which led to a loss of trust. I shall show that this search endeavour leads to positive findings and can indeed reveal some of the truth. But notice that this way one does not reach a complete understanding of our problem. Indeed we get the full picture only when we refine the theory of trust by including the idea that it is not always loss of trust that impedes innovation. Sometimes it is just the other way round, i.e. arranging oneself with given structures of trust, call it 'blind trust', can sometimes slow down innovation as well. This brings me to the conclusion that in these days trust, mistrust, and trusting are precariously coupled in German industry and that it is exactly from this entanglement that the innovation deficits spring.

I shall try to explain this position in two steps. The first step is to show that the erosion of the German industrial relations system is going to destroy 'background' trust which in turn makes innovation more difficult. This negative feedback primarily concerns one specific type of innovation, i.e. incremental innovations. The second step brings me to another type of innovation—basic ones. In that area one can also notice difficulties, but in this case they result from too much trust in inherited institutions.

1. LOSS OF TRUST IN INDUSTRIAL RELATIONS DAMAGES (INCREMENTAL) INNOVATIONS

To claim that German industrial relations are experiencing a period of shaken trust does not require much proof. Already in 1992/3 when a lot of firms responded to down-swing troubles by quick and brutal cuts of employees, anxiety spread. Later the growing debate on globalization accelerated the decline in trust. However far globalization may have advanced in reality (it is actually complicated to figure out how much of the globalization talk is justified by real economic internationalization), the increasing interconnection of economies is undoubtedly accompanied by the tendency for more production capacities (and since recently even R&D capacities) to move from Germany to foreign countries. External competitors gain larger market shares due to their growing capability to undermine the German exclusiveness in high quality segments by combining quality production with low cost. And German firms transfer increasing parts of their value chain across national borders in the desire to exploit external competitive advantages. These losses in capacity burden the German labour-market. Under these circumstances an essential ideological pillar of the German social model, i.e. the promise that everybody who demands a decent job can, in principle, get it, cannot be retained. Added to this is the fact that, in an increasingly global economy, delocalizing economic activities works like a stick in the creation of discipline. We have become used to a policy on the part of German employers which imposes rigorous concession bargaining by the mere threat to delocalize. Spectacular actions (like the recent suggestion of employers' associations to their member firms to ignore collective bargaining agreements which are still valid) are the tip of the iceberg. Especially in numerous everyday conflicts on the shop-floor, employees have been forced into concessions which spell the termination of a balance that, in former times, had been perceived as being guaranteed. Often these changes are portrayed as grassroots steps in collective bargaining (particularly by employers), and sometimes they are equated with the decentralization of the German industrial relations system which is indeed long overdue. Yet such comments misrepresent what is actually taking place, i.e. the erosion not to say destruction of an idea which is deeply rooted in the German understanding of a good firm, i.e. that firms, at least at the level of the shop-floor, have to be conceptualized as communities. The understanding that the plant is common ground for the employer and employees and that therefore the employer–employee conflict should temporarily be suspended on the plant level, gets damaged. It is evident that growing sections of the employers' camp have learnt to see the old pattern of reciprocal commitment, within which the plants had pacified the actions of both sides in the past, as unwanted in our days and they consequently withdraw their consensus from employees.

It is true, that economic globalization facilitates concession bargaining—a trend which we observe in a lot of industrialized countries. Nonetheless I see this development as being particularly problematic for Germany. In the German case the view of the plant as an area of collaboration mattered hugely. This community approach shaped the employer–employee nexus as a trust relationship, and it therefore shaped the norm of reciprocity which guided actors and actions within firms. All this supported the growth of the productive forces and thus contributed to the competitiveness of German industry. As trust now is fading, the entire construction of prosperity can fall to pieces. The two comments which follow may support such an understanding of the ongoing dynamics.

(a) Roughly speaking, we can differentiate between three categories of employees each of which is characterized by a very specific nexus between motivation, creativity, risk-taking, and trust (Marsden 1995: 68–9, 79–87). One extreme category is constituted by the low-skill/low-wage anybodies. Their situation disposes them towards instrumentalism. Due to a lack of better options they can be lured by any job offer as long as it gives them an income beyond the minimum social provision. Trust for them is neither necessary for accepting the work nor for performing it. On the opposite side of the range we see the high-skilled superprofis, i.e. free-lancing high-flyers who even attract risks without feeling the need to be hedged by guarantees. They reckon they can exploit the risks for their own purpose by means of their large expertise and superiority. For them to trust means simply to trust oneself. The middle position in between these two categories is filled by a third group, the skilled employees. Thanks to their skills they can contribute much to successful production if they put their potential into the service of innovation, and if it is also possible to motivate them to do so. In this they differ from the unskilled anybodies. On the other hand, they are (objectively and according to their self-image) less strong than the freelancers. They always bear in mind that in their case innovation could lead them to downgrading and downsizing (the very thing that brands them as real employees). In order to accept the role of fellow innovators it has to be plausible to them to believe in the goodwill of management. They must be sure that managers will not turn the situation against them should they become vulnerable in the unpredictable course of innovation. Knowing that institutions of one's own plant are so structured as to avoid conflicts may already foster this belief. From this knowledge employees can derive the trust that their support for innovation will not transform into harm and that they, as they commit themselves to the common good, will be accepted as important and responsible members of their organization. If and as long as these expectations of reciprocity are met (in some way), the firm gains, in the view of the third group, the quality of a community in which trust can feed innovation.

German industry, in contrast to American or British industry, relies on this middle group. For a long time it has focused on industries like machine-building, electrics, automobiles, and chemicals, i.e. on 'middle-range technologies' (Maurer 1994: 313). In such industries one finds a lot of skilled employees, be they craftsmen, experienced 'semi-skilled' workers, engineers, or well-trained clerks. Industrial structure, profile of the workforce, work rules, and competitiveness reinforce each other and create a virtuous circle of growth. Firms gain comparative advantages from further improvement of their (already fairly good) products and processes. The human capital embodied by the skilled employees is very well prepared for that type of innovation (i.e. for step-by-step innovations). On the one hand the industries owe their enduring top positions to the achievement of their workforce; on the other the prosperity of their sectors underpins the high status of the employees. The expectations of reciprocity can be fulfilled. This by itself strengthens innovation and so on.

But it is also true that the competitiveness of such a type of economy suffers and that its rank in world markets is lowered as soon as one of the partners plays up and turns a deaf ear to the other partner's expectations. One gets worried that this may be happening as a consequence of the behaviour exhibited by some German employers at the present time. Counteractions on the part of the skilled employees are inevitable, and the most natural type of counteractions is that they refuse to collaborate any longer. The end result is an innovation crisis as a consequence of the withdrawal of their commitment on the part of core workers.

(b) The trust structures in German industry are extraordinarily sensitive to the disturbances which have hit the pillars of the industrial relations system. In general, the trust of this type of skilled employee is not all that safe from erosion. Conceptualizing the plant as a community—and this is the concept we identified as a building-block of trust—must always resist the class logic that springs from the conflict between the interests of employees and employers. As the very existence of a class structure constantly conveys a message of confrontation and mistrust, trust needs a constant affirmation in order to avoid being denounced as fictitious. In the German industrial relations system the institutions of collective bargaining and codetermination have functioned as safeguards of trust. They have assured employees that in a decision on firm problems which affected them personally their voice would be heard ('stakeholder' constitution) and that matters were arranged according to the consensus principle upon which both classes had agreed for a defined time and on which one could depend. The social order founded on collective bargaining and codetermination has fostered a kind of general trust assumption which has allowed activities to happen even if there would be no immediate and certain payoff for employees. It was precisely this quality of the industrial relations system which has proved useful for innovation because it has encouraged skilled employees to shed their worries which in turn put them at ease when applying their expertise.

I am talking here in the imperfect tense because the system I have just described is almost gone. If a lot of German employers nowadays retreat from collective bargaining and codetermination, the whole edifice of trust could quickly collapse due to the symbolic appeal of the industrial relations system as a foundation of employees' trust. I leave open the question whether the Germans have already reached this point. At least we notice that uncertainty is rife among employees and that they feel that positions which have seemed very solid have become fragile. We notice too that today a lot of employees are less in tune with risk-taking than formerly— including risks wrapped in the relatively attractive package of an innovation. For why should they be committed to innovation when management utilizes the possibilities created by that very innovation unilaterally for downsizing and the cutting of labour cost? Who would work for innovation as long as one has to be concerned about one's own standing in the firm or even about one's job? Employees can no longer reject such questions, and hence the social climate in firms turns into one of mistrust—and into a reluctance to innovate. What has been up to now a comparative advantage of German industry, i.e. the capability to develop its core sectors continuously, is detrimentally affected.

With these remarks—all variations on the theme of 'loss of trust leads to difficulties with innovation'—the interaction between trust and innovation is not yet sufficiently illuminated. The road to lucidity is sometimes tricky. It is therefore unsurprising that the consideration which follows appears to go against the previous one.

2. DIFFICULTIES WITH (BASIC) INNOVATIONS THROUGH AN EXCESS OF TRUST

The more globalization undermines traditional locations, the more urgent becomes the search for compensatory activities. There arises a need for *basic* innovations, i.e. architectural inventions which have the potential for creating new products and new markets. By leaps in innovation the range of possibilities for future production is opened. Since the traditional markets have eroded, controlling basic innovations becomes a question of economic survival.

And this is the second burden which weighs heavily on the dynamics of German industry: producing basic innovations is the very weakness of the system. This shortcoming has been revealed by a series of studies (Audretsch 1995: 4; Maurer 1994: 315) and constitutes the reverse side of the strength of German industry in its classic core sectors. Lulled by the large batch of incremental innovations in the area of middle-range technologies, German industry has, for a long time, overlooked the utmost importance to global competition of basic innovations. This faulty programming has, once again, to do with the allocation of trust and mistrust. As before, a deficiency of trust is what disturbs the capabilities to innovate. But now the problem is the reverse of that dicussed above. Instead of lack of trust resulting from uncertainty, we now have too much trust (or call it too much attachment to the well-known), and this in turn is paralysing.

With regard to organizational capacities for basic innovation, the relevant research tells us that the ability to integrate knowledge across the boundaries between disciplines and firms is essential for success (Clark and Fujimoto 1991; von Hippel 1988: 6, 76–122; Henderson 1994: 608–11, 624–6). *Ceteris paribus*, basic innovation succeeds all the better the easier the knowledge, which so far was located in different places—in separate faculties or companies—can be combined. Integration competence is required, and it is just this which is scarce. The reason is that some central institutions of the German model are designed in a way so as to keep the interactions between different knowledge bearers, and correspondingly the articulation of the knowledge, on the relatively narrow tracks of the traditional organizational patterns. Trust in this context is a pull factor. Consider the functioning of (a) the German vocational training system, and (b) the networks between German firms.

Example (a). The vocational training system (particularly after its reform in 1986) has operated as the backbone of the German production model. The skilled employees are typically 'Berufsarbeiter', craftworkers. But no matter how much the occupational reform accentuated cross-sectional knowledge and social competence, the German 'Berufsarbeiter' are geared to the central area of their respective trade. They can develop their knowledge only with the support of others or, more precisely, only within the community of experts, i.e. within the trade. Only the combined experience of this community makes it possible for such workers to direct their stock of knowledge to changing purposes, bundle it in new manners, and learn by such tentative combinations. The price they have to pay for their relatively high problem-solving capacity therefore consists in fitting themselves into the vocational community. This fitting-in does some good in that it offers security, particularly because it ensures that, being confronted with a new task, every member will find supportive mates within the community. They all together have internalized the rules of collaboration and thus can trust each other. From this point of view trust invested in the trade actually makes it possible for the occupational expertise to be fluently discussed and shuffled around between colleagues. On the other hand, this trust restricts the discussions with regard to subjects and participants because it refers the craft people back to their craft. This adherance to the 'we-group' expresses itself in continuously claiming the privilege to act for the own trade ('exclusive competence') and in devaluing or underestimating external knowledge (Beck, Brater, and Daheim 1980: 81–7, 93, 176). Characteristic of the German understanding of occupational communities, such demarcations act negatively as soon as it comes to integrating knowledge for new tasks.

Example (b). The interfirm networks operate in a likewise contradictory fashion. A lot of German firms are embedded in stable networks which are partly organized and controlled by powerful final producers ('focal firms', cf. Döhl and Deiß 1992: 9; Sauer 1992: 58–65), but which partly also exhibit more balanced structures (that is why some observers call them Marshallian industrial districts; cf. Piore and Sabel 1984: 229–34). If, in order to create innovations, one firm must co-operate with others, because it gets the knowledge it needs only by means of such co-operation, well-worn networks work like a maelstrom, which seduces the firm to stick with intimate partners from within the network (cf. Grabher 1993: 23–6, 264–6). This inclination may be stronger in Germany than elsewhere, because the networks offer a lot in the German case. Yet for *radical* innovations such 'blind' preference for familiar types of collaboration is a hindrance. In this case the horizon of knowledge must really be pushed open. Then the adequate mode of integrating knowledge is not any longer the exclusive collaboration between close firms. Rather it extends over strangers if it is only outsiders who possess the wanted knowledge ('co-operation between rivals' (von Hippel 1988: 76)). As German firms find such 'away-game' collaboration as heavy going as their vocation-bound exployees do, they truly have a hard time with basic innovations.

So the need for basic innovations is confronted with dampening institutions. This is a finding which can certainly be read as support for the plea to break up trust structures. Indeed, the interaction patterns shaped by vocational orders and interfirm networks could profit from injections of mistrust. But notice that, especially when innovation is at stake, such a plea for mistrust cuts both ways. Mistrust-inducing interventions can abruptly change into total uncertainty which in turn will, by means of risk-aversion, actually counteract innovation. The trick would be to create 'targeted' uncertainties, to cut in small doses, and to cushion the cutback of trust on the one hand with trust-building measures on the other. Yet it is so hard to design and to implement such delicate manœuvres that German industry has failed to develop a proper line of handling thus far.[1]

3. CONCLUSION

In the German case, the collapse of background trust, as it derives from the erosion of the plant community, is an impediment to overcoming the innovation crisis I outlined at the beginning. The paradox of the story runs as follows. Actors in the plant do what would be necessary for more innovation—i.e. they become distanced from the patterns of knowledge exchange they are used to, and they start to experiment with nonfamiliar exchange modes—but actors need background trust to build on. On the other hand, the fact that this background trust does not exist any longer affects the actors in a manner which discourages and restricts them. Security precautions take the place of experimentations. Familiar things are certainly not given up—and consequently innovation seizes up. With this observation in mind we can run full circle. Testing the theory of trust in a case-study on innovation problems in German industry, we come up with the argument that the usual trust discourse invests too much trust in trust and pays too little attention to the unwelcome interventions of mistrust and blind trust.

NOTES

1. It seems reasonable to ask whether other industrial systems do better with the transfer of knowledge between strangers. An abridged version of my answers would be: (a) strangeness always burdens co-operation but does not exclude it principally (Axelrod 1984; Kreps 1990: 90–143); (b) examples of successful co-operation between strangers became known particularly in the US (Saxenian 1994: 29–57). Further systematic comparative research is needed in order to come up with better explanation for these differences.

REFERENCES

Audretsch, D. (1995), *The Innovation, Unemployment and Competitiveness Challenge in Germany*. WZB discussion papers. Berlin: WZB.

Axelrod, R. (1984), *The Evolution of Cooperation*. New York: Basic Books.

Beck, U., Brater, M., and Daheim, H. (1980), *Soziologie der Arbeit und der Berufe*. Reinbek: Rowohlt Verlag.

Clark, K. and Fujimoto, T. (1991), *Product Development Performance*. Boston: Harvard Business School Press.

Coleman, J. S. (1988), 'Social Capital in the Creation of Human Capital', *American Journal of Sociology*, 94 (Suppl.), 95–120.

——(1990), *The Foundations of Social Theory*. Cambridge, Mass.: Harvard University Press.

Döhl, V. and Deiß, M. (1992), 'Von der Lieferbeziehung zum Produktionsnetzwerk', in V. Deiß and M. Döhl (eds.), *Vernetzte Produktion*. Frankfurt/New York: Campus Verlag, 5–48.

Fukuyama, F. (1995), *Trust: The Social Virtues and the Creation of Prosperity*. New York/London: Free Press.

Grabher, G. (1993), 'Rediscovering the Social in the Economics of Interfirm Relations: The Weakness of Strong Ties: The Lock-in of Regional Development in the Ruhr Area', in G. Grabher (ed.), *The Embedded Firm*. London/New York: Routledge, 1–31, 255–77.

Henderson, R. (1994), 'The Evolution of Integrative Capability: Innovation in Cardiovascular Drug Discovery', *Industrial and Corporate Change*, 3/3: 607–29.

Kreps, D. M. (1990), 'Corporate Culture and Economic Theory', in J. E. Alt and K. A. Shepsle (eds.), *Perspectives on Positive Political Economy*. Cambridge: Cambridge University Press, 90–143.

Marsden, D. (1995), 'Deregulation or Cooperation? The Future of Europe's Labour-Markets', *Labour: Review of Labour Economics and Industrial Relations*, Special Issue, 68–91.

Maurer, R. (1994), 'Die Exportstärke der deutschen Industrie: Weltmarktspitze trotz technologischen Rückstands?', *Die Weltwirtschaft*, 3: 308–19.

Olson, M. (1982), *The Rise and Decline of Nations: Economic Growth, Stagflation, and Social Rigidities*. New Haven: Yale University Press.

Piore, M. and Sabel, C. (1984), *The Second Industrial Divide*. New York: Basic Books.

Putnam, R. D. (1993), *Making Democracy Work: Civic Traditions in Modern Italy*. Princeton: Princeton University Press.

——(1995), 'Bowling Alone: America's Declining Social Capital', *Journal of Democracy*, 6/1: 65–78.

Sauer, D. (1992), 'Auf dem Weg in die flexible Massenproduktion', in Deiß and Döhl (eds.), *Vernetzte Produktion*, 49–79.

Saxenian, A. (1994), *Regional Advantage: Culture and Competition in Silicon Valley and Route 128*. Cambridge: Cambridge University Press.

von Hippel, E. (1988), *The Sources of Innovation*. New York/Oxford: Oxford University Press.

8

Trust and the Transformation of Supplier Relations in Indian Industry*

JOHN HUMPHREY

1. INTRODUCTION

In the past decade, trust has surfaced as a critical issue in several strands of social science. Rapid industrial development in Germany, Japan, and Italy during the 1970s and 1980s gave support to the idea that economic development is facilitated when interorganizational relations are based on trust. In their different ways, the industrial districts of the Third Italy and Baden-Württemberg and the networks of firms organized by large enterprises in Japan have brought the issue of trust to the fore.[1] In the developing world, the issue has been discussed much less, but development agencies have begun to turn their attention to the question of the social conditions for economic development. In 1996, the World Bank set up a group to study the question of social capital, and a recent paper by Knack and Keefer (1996) explored the link between levels of trust and economic growth. Trust is emerging as the new 'missing factor' that explains why some countries develop rapidly and others lag behind. Societies that have higher levels of trust appear to grow faster.

The question of trust has emerged with particular force in the literature on business relationships, becoming an issue in studies both of horizontal relationships between firms (joint ventures, badging of products, and other forms of co-operation) and of vertical relationships between suppliers and their customers. Vertical relationships are the focus of this chapter. The more analytical literature often contrasts patterns of customer–supplier relations in high- and low-trust contexts. Sako (1992) examines patterns of supplier relations in the electrical industries of Japan and the United Kingdom, contrasting the closeness of ties in the former with arm's-length relations in the latter. Similarly, Lane and Bachmann (1996) explore supplier relations in Germany and the United Kingdom, highlighting the institutional and contextual factors that facilitate trust in the former and undermine trust in the latter. In both these studies, interorganizational trust is

* This work was carried out with support from the Department for International Development of the United Kingdom Government. This chapter draws from work on trust carried out with Hubert Schmitz and research on industrial restructuring in India undertaken with Raphael Kaplinsky. Both are colleagues at the Institute of Development Studies, University of Sussex. The author wishes to thank Reinhard Bachmann, Raphie Kaplinsky, Christel Lane, Mick Moore, and Hubert Schmitz for valuable comments on earlier drafts of this chapter.

seen to depend on institutions, practices, and expectations that support the trusting behaviour of any particular group of enterprises. Trust is sustained through the operation of multiple institutions, and it cannot be developed quickly.

In contrast to this, much of the more prescriptive, management-oriented literature suggests that close customer–supplier relations can be created if companies commit themselves to change. According to Womack, Jones, and Roos, 'the [Japanese] system replaces a vicious circle of distrust with a virtuous circle of co-operation' (Womack, Jones, and Roos 1990: 150). Western firms may have difficulties in changing their behaviour, but the difficulties mainly concern their understanding of the Japanese system and their reluctance to let go of established patterns of relationships. However, competitive pressures will force them to change. Once the supplier strategy is changed, its advantages will become apparent to all concerned. This view gives little importance to institutional and contextual factors in the determination of interorganizational trust, and by implication it suggests that trust can be developed quickly.

The importance of trust in customer–supplier relationships has become part of the new managerial orthodoxy. Suppliers have become 'partners', and they are 'an extension of the company'. There should be an identity of interest between the company and its suppliers. Co-operation pays. This orthodoxy has reached the developing world, even as elements of it are being questioned in the Industrially Advanced Countries. In India, business leaders are proclaiming the virtues of close relations between suppliers and customers based on trust. In June 1995 an article in the Indian magazine, *Business World*, with the heading 'Fewer Suppliers, More Friends' opened with the sub-heading: 'Companies are Cutting Down the Number of Suppliers and Forging Closer Ties with the Ones that Remain'. It went on to say:

Where once the relationship with their suppliers was one of indifference or of unabashed exploitation, it is now one of close co-operation. 'Business partner' is the term that companies now use to describe their suppliers.   (*Business World*, 14–27 June 1995)

Similarly, at the 1996 Quality Summit, organized by the Confederation of Indian Industry, a number of presentations by senior managers of prominent Indian companies stressed the importance of trust and co-operation in customer–supplier relations.

This concern with customer–supplier relations clearly derives from the pressures of economic liberalization. In India, the relatively sophisticated but inefficient industries built up behind protective barriers had developed long-term supplier relations, but the informational content and degree of co-operation tended to be low. Trade liberalization has suddenly and drastically exposed firms to new levels of competitive pressures. The widely diffused and accepted recipe for responding to this challenge involves internal restructuring using the principles of lean production and the development of new relationships with suppliers. However, the framework for intercompany relations has been one of low-trust or active mistrust. Awasthi, for example, has characterized the traditional approach to supplier relations in Indian manufacturing in terms of multiple sources, short-term contracts, choice based on cost, lack of trust and confidence and unhealthy cutthroat competition (1996: 464–6). Similarly, Holmström has referred to pervasive suspicion and exclusion of outsiders as characteristics of interfirm relations (1994: 4–5).

Discussions of trust in interfirm relationships have tended to focus on societies where trust relations are firmly embedded in institutional frameworks and established practices. Trust relations are sustained by institutional mechanisms and the 'taken-for-granted' nature of relationships. Firms in India are proposing to develop high-trust relationships in contexts where mistrust or a lack of trust has existed in the past, and the institutional support for trust is weakly developed. This suggests that two key questions should be asked. First, can the intention to create relationships based on trust be realized in India, where trust has not generally characterized interfirm relationships, and where the trust-building institutions and practices noticeable in both Japan (Sako 1992) and Germany (Lane and Bachmann 1996) are absent? This question is similar to the question raised by Sako and Helper, 'How can trust be created when there is none?' (1996: 2). Second, as firms in India attempt to restructure supplier relations along the lines of 'fewer and closer', is trust a part of the developing relationship?

These questions are explored in this chapter through a study of a large enterprise in the Indian electrical industry. This company was in the process of attempting to change its relationships with suppliers, particularly with its many small suppliers. Management characterized its strategy towards suppliers using terms such as stakeholders, trust, co-operation, and partnership. The development of supplier policy and practice was explored within the company, and the owners or managers of fifty suppliers to three plants were interviewed about their relationships with the company.[2]

The next part of the chapter discusses the concept of trust and the production of trust in interfirm relationships. Section 3 addresses the issue relationship between just-in-time production (JIT) and total quality management (TQM), and the development of closer relations with suppliers. These two sections lay the foundations for Section 4, which examines the restructuring of supplier relations in India.

2. THE MEANING OF TRUST

The many available definitions of trust have two core elements: an agent's acceptance of risk from the actions of others, and the expectation that the 'partner' will not take advantage of the opportunities opened up by the agent's acceptance of risk. One general definition of trust is provided by Baier, who defines it as 'accepted vulnerability to another's possible but not expected ill will (or lack of good will) toward one' (Baier 1986: 235).[3] This type of definition is often interpreted narrowly, and attention is focused on the problems of cheating and malfeasance—breaking explicit promises. However, two other types of trust are important in the context of supplier relations. First, there is trust in the ability of the supplier to fulfil commitments. Sako labels this 'competence trust' (1992: 37–8). Secondly, trust is involved when companies make investments in transaction-specific assets in the belief that: (i) the relationship will continue into the future even though no formal commitments can be made, and (ii) the partner will not take advantage of these investments and will behave responsibly when adaptations to contracts and relationships take place.[4] We will refer to this as 'goodwill trust', even though this falls short of the open-ended, moral commitment to which Sako refers. Both competence trust and goodwill trust involve a decision to make oneself vulnerable to the action of another because one has reasons for believing that the negative outcome will not materialize. Precisely because a judgement about the 'other' is being made, there would be cause for regret if the judgement turned out to be wrong (Luhmann 1988: 98).

The question of trust arises from the element of risk in economic transactions. Under perfect competition, economic exchanges do not involve risk. Agents can assume that contracts will be honoured, and risk is ruled out by the assumptions of candid rationality and perfect information. When these assumptions are abandoned, the questions of risk and trust arise. Entering into an economic exchange exposes the agent to risks arising from the action of others. If these risks are uncontrollable, then exchange is reduced, paralysed, or rendered costly by the need to take precautions. If the 'other' can be trusted, exchange is facilitated.

Beyond these basic points, however, there is considerable disagreement and confusion about trust. In this section, two issues will be addressed: (i) what constitutes trust? and (ii) how can interfirm trust be developed in situations where it is absent? The first question will be examined through a discussion of rational choice and shared meanings as bases for trust. The second will be examined through a discussion of personal trust.

2.1 Rational Choice and Calculative Trust

Trust is associated with risk-taking and the acceptance of vulnerability. This is most often discussed in the context of opportunism. Opportunists exist in the market and rational agents will take steps to avoid suffering from their opportunism.[5] Agents cope with opportunistic behaviour by calculating the pay-offs available to the potential partner from different courses of action. The only grounds for believing that the partner will not exploit the agent's vulnerability is the calculation that non-opportunistic behaviour will offer greater gains. Various means can be employed to compensate the agent for risk and to alter the pay-offs available to the partner. These include contractual penalties or increased monitoring of the partner's behaviour.

Sheppard and Tuchinsky characterize this situation as 'deterrence-based trust' (1996: 143). The agent trusts the partner not to cheat because the consequences of cheating have been made unattractive. The implications of this perspective are expressed most clearly by Coleman, who argues that 'the elements confronting the potential trustor are nothing more or less than the considerations a rational actor applies in deciding whether to place a bet' (1990: 99). This perspective is unsustainable. It reduces any sensible relationship with another firm to one of trust. Calculating risk on the presumption that the partner is likely to cheat if benefit can be gained from it would seem to be a good definition of mistrust. Williamson uses precisely this argument to suggest that most discussions of trust merely obfuscate calculative behaviour in the presence of opportunism, arguing that trust is 'irrelevant to commercial exchange' (Williamson 1993: 469).[6]

The discussion highlights two important issues. First, trust involves risk over and above what would be acceptable without it. As Luhmann argues, 'trust is only possible in a situation where the possible damage is greater than the advantage you seek' (Luhmann 1988: 98). Secondly, calculative trust assumes that the agent must be able to calculate the gains and losses of particular courses of action taken by the other. This presupposes not only calculative ability, but also an understanding of the other's ranking of gains and losses. This is not a simple process, and coming to understand and influence the other's preferences is an important element of trust, as will be seen below.

2.2 Shared Meanings

If Williamson sees calculativeness in economic life as making trust redundant, then the work of Luhmann adopts the opposite view: the impossibility of calculativeness makes trust essential. The complexities of social organization are so great that some assumptions about how people behave have to be made before calculations can be made. Social life (and the economic aspects of that life) is possible precisely because we take so much for granted: 'trust is produced among social actors when they hold shared beliefs and hence build up mutual expectations. This, as we have learned from Luhmann, makes the social world less complex and more predictable for actors' (Lane and Bachmann 1996). The basis for effective action is the shared meanings of actors.

This idea is often explained by using the analogy of traffic regulation. Hargreaves-Heap argues that a traffic rule such as 'give way to traffic coming from the right' helps generate information about other people's behaviour and makes calculation possible.[7] Furthermore, such shared rules are essential for calculation to take place in situations in which the behaviour of an agent depends on expectations about the behaviour of others. Shared meanings are essential for the constitution of social life. When Luhmann discusses the question of trust, he is really addressing the issue of how social life is possible at all. Some degree of predictability of behaviour is essential for interactions to be sustained. However, the existence of shared meanings does not by itself constitute trust in the way defined at the beginning of this section. Trust was defined in terms of an 'accepted vulnerability to another's possible but not expected ill will'. It would be perfectly possible for interactions to be based on the assumption of opportunism. As long as the actors shared the expectation that opportunism was the basic rule of the game, interactions would proceed in a predictable fashion. By themselves, shared meanings do not distinguish what we might consider high-trust and low-trust societies.

2.3 Personal Trust

We associate high-trust societies with the absence of opportunism. Agents are predictably non-opportunistic, in part because of the institutions which 'assume a "taken-for-granted" quality and thus provide shared cognitions to organisational actors' (Lane 1995: 274), and in part because there are mechanisms of various sorts which deter opportunistic behaviour. A number of studies of trust have emphasized the contrast between high- and low-trust systems of exchange. In the former, relations between agents or firms are supported by a broader framework of expectations and institutions that constrain behaviour. This framework may be formed by laws that regulate relations between firms, and/or by the activities of institutions such as trade associations and arbitration bodies (Lane and Bachmann 1996; Sako 1992: 158–72).

In her discussion of Japan, Sako demonstrates the importance of arbitration services in establishing a stable framework for relations between large and small firms (1992: 158–72). This is contrasted with the problems facing small firms in Britain because of late payment by large firms. Lane and Bachmann's study of supplier relations in Britain and Germany also argues that the legal and institutional frameworks existing in Germany reduce risk and uncertainty and make trust possible (1996: 6–10). First, they point to the role of law in Germany in regulating relations between enterprises. In Britain, for example, terms of payment are a frequent source of conflict and uncertainty in interfirm relations. Unregulated payment conditions both increase uncertainty for suppliers, raising their exposure to risk, and produce tensions that prevent close relationships developing. In Germany, terms of payment are regulated by law and institutional arrangements. This provides a stable relationship on which relations can develop (Lane and Bachmann 1996: 35–6). Second, trade associations in Germany play a role in standardizing relations in particular sectors—raising predictability and providing a clear framework for enterprises:

In Germany, Chambers of Commerce are statutory bodies with compulsory membership for firms within their sphere of influence. They execute quasi-political functions, such as issuing licences, settling disputes and advising banks on firms' creditworthiness, as well as providing collective support for smaller firms, such as assisting with export promotion or the provision of further training . . . Being part of this associational network encourages conformity to common norms and standards and thus reduces risk of individual failure. Reputations are more in the public domain and industry associations offer a forum for the exchange of information and the development of contacts. All these knowledge-generating activities reduce risk and are conducive to the development of a high level of trust in German business relations.   (Lane and Bachmann 1996: 24–5)

These institutions and practices support contractual trust and competence trust. At the same time, they establish the basis for goodwill trust by establishing a foundation for stable, long-term relationships regulated by shared meanings and the constraint of reputation.

However, the question remains of how to develop trust when such a stable framework of expectations and past behaviour is lacking. How can one decide who to trust in a situation in which one cannot rely on agents in general being trustworthy? Most answers to this question involve learning about the 'other' through repeat transactions. This by itself does not necessarily involve trust. One interpretation of the effect of repeat transactions on interorganizational relationships is that it merely alters the pay-offs to cheating. They offer a stream of future benefits that will be lost following opportunistic behaviour. A second perspective views repeat transactions solely as a means of building up information about a partner, but without any implication that trust will develop as a result. Sheppard and Tuchinsky suggest that repeat transactions merely enable agents to predict opportunism and guard against it (1996: 143). The other becomes more predictable, but not necessarily trustworthy.

However, repeat transactions may develop trust. Lewicki and Bunker use the concept of knowledge-based trust (discussed in more detail in Child, in this volume), employing the metaphors of courtship and gardening to capture this aspect of trust production:

The appropriate metaphor for knowledge-based trust may be from agriculture: Its development is more like 'gardening'—tilling the soil year after year. . . . In relationships, the parties cultivate their knowledge of each other by gathering data, seeing each other in different contexts, and noticing reactions to different situations.   (Lewicki and Bunker 1996: 121–2)

These metaphors capture at least two elements of the process of construct-ing personal trust which will be important for the study of supply-chain development in India. First, the partners test each other's trustworthiness by allowing opportunities to betray trust. The concept of knowledge-based trust is in many respects similar to Luhmann's concept of personal trust. Luhmann argues that a deepening of trust involves learning, and that 'such learning processes are only complete when the person to be trusted has had opportunities to betray that trust and has not used them' (1979: 45). Secondly, repeated interactions allow partners to understand each other's motives and priorities. One of the weaknesses of calculative and game-theoretical approaches to interorganizational transactions is that they assume an ability to calculate the pay-offs to partners of different courses of action. However, agents are boundedly rational and face different resource constraints. They have to make choices in uncertain conditions. Therefore, it is not possible to predict how a partner will behave merely through the calculation of alternative streams of benefits. Part of the process of building up trust involves finding out in practice about the strategies adopted by one's partners.[8] This is particularly important in situations where potential partners claim to be changing their behaviour, and where generalizations based on how firms have be-haved may no longer apply as external constraints and challenges change rapidly.

The development of knowledge-based trust is part of a three-stage pro-cess: from deterrence-based trust, to knowledge-based trust, and on to identification-based trust (cf. Child, in this volume, for a more extensive discussion). Identification-based trust arises when 'the parties effectively understand and appreciate each other's wants' (Lewicki and Bunker 1996: 122). In interfirm relationships there are two important aspects underpin-ning such trust. The first is the claim or recognition that the partners have common interests. Therefore, actions will be mutually beneficial, and the parties will have a strong interest in continuing and developing the relation-ship (which is restatement of Sako's notion of goodwill trust). The second is establishment of personal ties, or affect-based trust (cf. Child, in this volume), which reinforce organizational commitment through emotional bonds between agents.

The concept of personal trust has much in common with the notion of process-based trust developed by Zucker (1986). A theoretical discussion of the development of interorganizational trust based on this principle can be found in a simulation of trading strategies in a market characterized by information asymmetries. Kollock considers trading in two distinct types of market—for rice and rubber. Rice is a commodity whose value can be determined at the point of sale without difficulty. This facili-tates interaction between traders and the growth of spot markets. In contrast:

Rubber is an interesting commodity in that at the time of sale it is impossible to determine its quality. It is not until months later, after extensive processing, that the buyer can determine whether the grower took the extra time and expense to ensure a high-quality crop.   (Kollock 1994: 314)

This is a perfect recipe for market failure through 'prisoner's dilemma'— high quality would benefit all, but each seller has the incentive to cheat (defect) and each buyer should guard against this. In spite of this, the market has developed 'long-term exchange relationships between particular buyer and sellers. Within this framework it is possible for the growers to establish reputations for fairness and trustworthiness' (Kollock 1994: 314).

Kollock explains this pattern of exchange by constructing a simulation game to test the emergence of commitment in markets characterized by different information about the product. Groups of buyers and sellers engaged in repeated rounds of trading (up to twenty rounds) for two commodities—one like rubber where information asymmetries are high, and one where the value of the commodity is clear at the point of contract. Parties could make bids and offers freely, and they could decide whether to cheat or not. The aim was to maximize income by the (unknown) time at which trading finished. One key aspect of the game was that traders could choose with whom to trade, unlike most games where trades are random or the identity of the partner is not known. In the experiment, buyers and sellers moved to closer, process-based commitments when dealing in the commodity with greater uncertainty as to quality (Kollock 1994: 328–33). The buyers and sellers developed an understanding about how their partners behaved—finding out about their overall trustworthiness and their trading strategy. In successive rounds of the game, the traders could take risks (paying the price of good rubber without being certain that this would be provided) in order to isolate those partners who were willing to adopt a trading strategy based on the provision of high-quality rubber.

This process cannot eliminate the risks associated with trust. As Luhmann stresses, trust is always bound up with possibility of disappointment and regret. Just as contracts cannot specify all contingencies, so experience cannot provide either an infallible means of extrapolating behaviour into the future, or a test of behaviour under all possible circumstances. This problem is particularly acute when the behaviour of the partner is not constrained by institutional mechanisms or widely held expectations about acceptable behaviour. Even when it is so, the potential for disappointment remains. This is illustrated by Nishiguchi's account of the response to recession of an electrical plant in Japan. It cut the number of its subcontractors in half, causing severe problems for some of the subcontractors, which had made investments in transaction-specific assets (1989: 262–6). In this case the trust displayed by the subcontractors was misplaced.

They might have calculated that the dependence of the customer on them and the customer's long-term interests ought to have precluded such action, but they failed to anticipate either the external circumstance or types of calculation of gains and losses being used by the manager in the plant.

Given this inevitable uncertainty, the risks arising from the extension of trust must be limited by mistrust. Gambetta observes that 'we can circumscribe the extent to which we need to trust agents or cope with them in case of distrust' (1988: 220). The boundary of how far we are prepared to trust is defined by distrust. The development of personal trust gives agents a basis for trusting one partner rather than another and deciding what level of risk it is wise to incur or expect from others. As personal trust develops, risks are made acceptable by knowledge of the partner's aims and values, but at the beginning, the risks are high and investment may need to be made in order to develop the relationship. Establishing trust relationships has a start-up problem. Therefore, the containment of risk through formal means (contracts, penalties, etc.) may be used as a device not to reduce one's own exposure to risk, but to reduce the exposure of the partner in order to promote the initial investment in trust. This is particularly important where firms are trying to break with old patterns of relationships and establish new ones.[9]

3. TRUST AND COMPETITIVENESS

In the industrially advanced countries, the past two decades has seen a significant shift in the competitive environment facing enterprises. In fragmented and competitive markets, enterprises have sought to win customers by competing not only on price, but also on factors such as reliability, speed of delivery, product features, and innovation. In order to compete on these factors, firms in the West have looked to manufacturing techniques pioneered in Japan—just-in-time (within the factory) and total quality management. Once these principles are applied within plants, it becomes logical, even necessary, to extend them backwards to suppliers. Companies seeking to increase the reliability of their products and reduce the costs associated with poor quality can easily see the advantages of improving the conformance to standards of the products of their suppliers. Similarly, firms wishing to compete on the basis of rapid response to customer orders must be able to secure the same degree of rapid response from their key suppliers. The shift in supplier relations arises from the changing basis of competition. When firms competed on cost for market shares in largely standardized products, arm's-length contracting served to keep down costs. As firms compete increasingly on product reliability, speed of delivery, and speed of innovation, closer relations with suppliers are more effective.

Closer relations are held to promote greater efficiency through co-operation, but this creates the risk of opportunism. The exchange of information required to facilitate non-adversarial forms of price determination could be used by the more powerful party to force price reductions or be supplied to competing companies. Co-operation over design opens up the possibility of opportunism on both sides. If a contract for production is offered prior to the design co-operation, the supplier can exploit a guaranteed market. If no contract is offered, the buyer could take the knowledge gained in the design process to a competitor of the supplier. The most effective solution is for firms to develop a long-term co-operative relationship. There are powerful reasons for establishing co-operation, but serious obstacles have to be overcome as well. According to Sako, 'obligational contracting' (or Obligational Contractual Relations, OCR) makes these risks acceptable by establishing dense flows of information in both directions and establishing mutual transactional dependence. This is achieved through single or dual sourcing of parts, the dependence of the supplier on few customers, and the establishment of long-term relationships between firms through bidding processes which favour established suppliers.

Sako suggests that while both contractual trust and competence trust are involved in OCR, close relationships involving a high degree of transactional dependence are only sustainable because of goodwill trust: 'What underpins heavy mutual dependence as an acceptable, and even preferred, state of affairs is the existence of "goodwill trust". "Goodwill trust" is a sure feeling that trading partners possess a moral commitment to maintaining a trading relationship' (Sako 1992: 10). This leads to two questions. First, if transactional dependence and goodwill trust are intimately linked, which comes first? Secondly, is goodwill trust (or some approximation of it) possible without transactional dependence?

Both Dore and Sako view goodwill trust as arising from specific characteristics of Japanese society. Dore links it to the notion of benevolence (Dore 1983). Goodwill trust makes transactional dependence possible. It is, therefore, hard to transfer these relations to other societies. On the other hand, Nishiguchi argues that trust between customers and suppliers should be seen as the consequence of trading strategies which develop close relationships. He characterizes transactional dependence in supplier relations as a strategic option. It arises because the gains from improved supplier competence, mutual learning, and willingness to innovate far outweigh the losses and risks arising from restricting the supplier base. This assumption turns transaction costs economics on its head. Long-term co-operation leads to the creation of asset specificity, rather than vice versa (Nishiguchi 1989: 272). The dangers of opportunism and the problems associated with uncertainty are neither exogenous variables which determine forms of governance, nor cultural traits or habits determined outside the enterprise.

Rather, they are factors which can be controlled within on-going relationships. This makes Japanese-style supplier relations more replicable in other institutional environments.

Sako and Nishiguchi both associate trust with mutual dependence, even though they differ on the direction of causation. However, even leading Japanese firms have been reconsidering the extent to which such dependence is desirable in a more volatile environment. One leading Japanese electrical company prefers to have at least two suppliers for each product at its main Malaysian consumer-products factory, and for these suppliers not to sell more than 30 per cent of their output to it. It does not want the responsibility of dependent suppliers, and it wants to be free to seek out low-cost suppliers, even if this means switching suppliers more frequently than it has in Japan. It no longer encourages its Japanese suppliers to set up plants in overseas locations, because this would entail obligations that it no longer can afford to make.[10] This raises the possibility that 'close enough' relations can be developed, without a high degree of commitment but with the co-operation to achieve an efficient relationship.

If a high degree of mutual dependence is not the basis for trust, then the question of exposure to risk becomes particularly problematic for the weaker (usually smaller) partner in an exchange relationship. As Sydow (in this volume) observes, it is easier for the more powerful party in a relationship to be trusting. In the absence of a legal or institutional framework which might protect the interests of small firms, the question of limiting risk through distrust is one which India must address. With these considerations in mind, the following questions about trust and supplier development in India can be posed:

- Is it possible to develop trust in hostile institutional contexts, and can the question of mistrust be addressed by firms wishing to build up trust? Can trust be developed without transactional dependence?
- The reason for seeking closer relations is tied up with the achievement of particular goals, such as improving the quality of bought-out products or introducing new designs more rapidly. Does the usefulness of OCR depend on the particular competitive strategy of the enterprise or factory? Are Indian firms really seeking OCR?
- The driving force for changing supplier relationships is the changing nature of competition in the economy. Will the uncertainties of change undermine efforts to develop trust?

The transformation of supplier relations in India is still at an early stage. In order to answer these questions, the case of Indian Electricals will be examined, but mainly from the perspective of the factors driving change rather than the extent to which trust has been established.

4. TRANSFORMING SUPPLIER NETWORKS IN INDIA

In many developing countries, shifting customer–supplier relationships is a matter of urgency. Trade liberalization has suddenly and drastically exposed firms in formerly highly protected economies to new levels of competitive pressures. The shift in trade policy (i) increases the export-orientation of industry, encouraging firms to enter challenging new markets, (ii) makes imports more freely available in the domestic market, and (iii) encourages the formation of new competitors through Foreign Direct Investment.

In the period of protection, customer–supplier relations in India acquired certain distinctive characteristics. As is typical in developing countries, large firms often resolved supply problems through internalization, and the degree of vertical integration was high. Typically, firms purchased products from two types of supplier. On the one hand, raw materials, semi-processed products, and specialized inputs were purchased from large firms with a monopolistic or oligopolistic position in the market. These firms were protected by trade regulations and the Indian government's restrictions on internal competition. On the other hand, smaller, unsophisticated firms were used to complement production when necessary and as low-cost suppliers of non-critical parts. Policies to promote small-scale industries (SSIs) focused on the reservation of certain product lines, tax exemptions, and subsidies for firms under a certain size. This system created an SSI sector with large pockets of inefficiency, and at the same time, imposed penalties on firms wishing to grow. As a result, the main advantages offered by the SSI sector to large firms were low wages—under half of the level paid in the large-firm sector even when controlling for skill (Little, Mazumdar, and Page 1987: 254)—and flexible working.

Trade liberalization has upset these arrangements. In particular, the entry of new producers through foreign direct investment has begun to change the bases of competition in the domestic market. Firms in developed countries, whose standards of productivity, quality (conformance to standards), customer response, and innovation have been much higher, are beginning to compete with local producers. One clear example of the emergence of non-price competition would be washing machines: firms in this sector are now increasingly concerned with issues such as defects in the first year of operation. The leading domestic and transnational producers of white goods (fridges, washing machines, etc.) are targeting customer call-outs in the first year. This means working closely with suppliers. For example, a producer of washing machines found that electric-motor failures in the first month of use were damaging its reputation in the market. It worked closely with the supplier to identify the source of problems, examining the causes of defects at various stages of production and transport. Similarly, firms in India are beginning to compete on the basis of speed

TABLE 8.1. Supplier restructuring at Godrej Soaps, Bombay

Before supplier restructuring	After supplier restructuring
Multiple sources	Single sourcing
Short-term contracts	Long-term contracts
High inventory	Low inventory
Conflict	Co-operation
Delayed payments	Payment on time
Poor quality	Improved quality
Low trust	Risk-sharing and open books

Source: A presentation by the Senior Vice-President, Godrej Soaps, at the 4th Quality Summit organized by the Confederation of Indian Industry, in Bangalore, Nov. 1996.

of delivery and customer response, and this places greater demands on suppliers for timely delivery and rapid responses to changes in customer orders. Enterprises in India have begun to realize that the simultaneous achievement of the objectives of quality, cost, and delivery requires a transformation of both the internal workings of the firm and supplier and customer relations.

For these types of reasons, leading firms are emphasizing the importance of close relations with suppliers and advocating trust and mutual dependence. For example, the Senior Vice-President of Godrej Soaps, a company belonging to one of India's most important business houses, characterized the change in supplier relations at the company's Bombay plant in terms of a transition from arm's-length relationships to close relationships based on trust. The elements of this contrast are summed up in Table 8.1, which is based on the conference presentation. A similar message was given at the Quality Summit by the Deputy-General Manager at India's largest car producer, Maruti Udyog Ltd (MUL), who summarized the relationship with suppliers as follows:

The main elements of the customer–supplier relationship at Maruti have been: (i) long-term partnership approach with vendors based on mutual trust and fairness, (ii) continuous improvement of vendors. Vendors have been treated as partners of the company. They have been treated with respect, trust and fairness in a professional manner. (Dayal 1996: 452)

At MUL, 70 per cent of materials are shipped direct to the line without incoming inspection, and MUL works closely with its suppliers. It has achieved this through encouraging the formation of joint ventures between Indian and Japanese firms (suppliers to the majority shareholder, Suzuki) and establishing an industrial park for its suppliers close to the plant. Some major Indian components suppliers have built plants in the same area. MUL has been responsible for forty-five technical tie-ups between Indian firms and overseas partners. It has also emphasized prompt payment and financial support for suppliers, and even encouraged groups of small suppliers to work collectively towards ISO 9000 certification.[11]

Trust is clearly involved here. There is a high degree of transactional dependence between MUL and at least some of its suppliers. An 'open book' policy is in operation, and there is a high level of co-operation. However, this experience remains exceptional in India. MUL is a large and important company establishing new patterns of relationships for a new plant in the motor industry, the sector which pioneered obligational contracting in the West. A number of key suppliers have been formed from joint ventures with suppliers to the parent company in Japan. Maruti's strong growth over the last fifteen years, together with the protection afforded to Indian car producers, has provided its suppliers with advantageous trading conditions, although this will be changing. For most firms in Indian industry, the conditions for creating closer ties involving trust remain adverse. First, established firms have to break with past relations rather than build on them, given that these relations were often characterized by suspicion, arbitrary use of power, etc. Secondly, there are none of the legal and institutional frameworks that might support closer supplier–customer relations. Thirdly, while trade associations in Germany play a role in standardizing relations in particular sectors—raising predictability and providing a clear framework for enterprises—in India there are competing non-sectoral trade associations, and a division between those representing large firms and those representing small industries.

Set against these difficulties are the enormous pressures for improvement in performance and the widely advocated policy of supplier development. Firms which target quality, cost, and delivery as the key areas for improvement quickly realize that a considerable part of the quality and cost of the final product are determined by supplier performance. Similarly, enterprises targeting delivery times quickly find that supplier response is a key element in performance. Increasingly, firms are hearing the message that closer relations based on trust can resolve supplier problems and improve overall performance.

The potential and limitations of new approaches to supplier development in India emerge clearly during a study of 'Indian Electricals', a large company in the electrical industry. By Indian standards, this was a large, diversified company. In 1995 and 1996, the processes of internal restructuring and supplier development were studied in detail at three plants: a plant producing ceiling and table fans, a plant making medium-sized electric motors, and a plant making low-tension switchgear.

The firm had set about transforming relations with its suppliers as part of a strategy aimed at transforming itself into a world-class company. The company had long worked with the arm's-length supplier relations typical of Indian industry. While it had worked with many suppliers for a long time, the relationships were not close. Supplier quality was low, delivery schedules poorly adhered to and exchange of information very limited. Long-term relationships were more an indication of the slackness of a protected economy than a sign of mutual commitment. But as the company began to pursue just-in-time and total quality management programmes within its plants, the need to change relationships with suppliers became apparent. As quality and speed of response to customers became more important, supplier shortcomings became more evident.

The study focused mainly on the company's smaller suppliers. Indian Electricals had limited influence on the large suppliers of commodity items such as steel bars, aluminium, copper and copper wire—the basic elements for electrical products. Supplier restructuring was focused mainly on firms which supplied items such as castings, pressed and machined metal parts, windings and fabricated items. Many of these firms were small. In the past, the company's policy had been to maintain various suppliers for each product, negotiating prices down in a typical ACR style. While the company had tended to maintain long-term relationships with its suppliers (60 per cent of the sample of fifty suppliers had supplied the company for more than a decade), they could not rely on stable orders or predictable demand. Critical processes were kept in-house, and design work was mainly carried out in-house, too. Suppliers were often used to supplement in-house production, and their main advantages were flexibility and low wage costs. Communications between the company and its suppliers were poor, and the company had a bad reputation for late payment and extended credit periods, paying its bills with notorious delay. In return, the company received poor quality products, partly because the small suppliers did not have quality systems, and partly because the suppliers reduced costs by cutting corners and saving on materials. For example, the practice of firms contracted to wind motors saving copper by reducing the number of windings below specification was said by managers to have been widespread. For both large and small suppliers, quality was controlled by in-coming inspection, but inadequacies in this system meant that final quality was often compromised. Indian Electricals developed a corporate-wide programme for supplier restructuring, which involved two key elements:

- Cutting back the number of suppliers. At the fans plant, the number of suppliers was reduced by a third, and at the switchgear plant by more than half. The company did not have a policy of single sourcing. Poor infrastructure and industrial relations problems made the company wary of relying on just one supplier, but a corporate policy of dual sourcing for each part, with one further possible supplier in reserve, still left ample room for a considerable reduction in supplier numbers.

- Establishing closer and more co-operative relationships with the suppliers which remained. Suppliers were to be viewed as stakeholders or partners.

The main reason for this change was undoubtedly quality. Indian Electricals, in common with many other firms in India, had for many years accepted a high level of defective parts. The concern for quality, which had been reflected in changes in production and inspection practices within plants, was extended to suppliers. The focus was very much on the smaller suppliers, because these were disproportionately the source of problems. Visits by managers from materials management and quality assurance became more common. The company began to specify basic quality systems for these suppliers, based loosely on ISO 9000 procedures. It also supplied process sheets, which specify the sequence of actions to be followed by workers in the suppliers. It insisted increasingly on regular calibration of gauges and measuring equipment, and in a few cases provided the equipment required. In all three plants, communications became more intense. Forty per cent of the supplier sample were visited at least once a week by someone from the materials department, and 45 per cent by someone from the quality assurance department. This change in policy may have had some impact on quality, although not as much as might have been expected. Two-thirds of the suppliers had reduced the level of incoming defects in the three years up to the end of 1996, while in one-third defect levels had increased.

Quality was not the only motivation for supplier development, and in one of the three plants studied more profound changes in supplier relations resulted from the pursuit of improved delivery schedules. The switchgear plant had targeted speed of delivery as the key factor for gaining market share and profitability in a market in which products could only be made to order. It realized that reducing response time for the assembly of customized products with a high degree of variability would require much more effective integration of suppliers. Accordingly, management reorganized its seventy small, local suppliers in two tiers. The first tier, consisting of fifteen suppliers, not only took responsibility for organizing the rest, but also began to deliver completed sub-assemblies to the plant on a *kanban* basis. These fifteen suppliers were chosen for their greater technical competence, and their ability to manage the relationship with Indian Electricals. All but one of these suppliers were located within 10 kilometres of the plant, and they received more frequent visits than suppliers at other plants. The pursuit of delivery time had a more direct impact on suppliers than did quality. Quality could be secured by end-of-line inspection at the supplier. The delivery response requirements at the plant could only be achieved by the reorganization of work at the suppliers and a much closer integration of supplier and customer production schedules.

Indian Electricals was pursuing the new orthodoxy of 'fewer and closer', but to what extent was trust involved in this transformation, and was the trust the same for suppliers as for the customer? The questions of competence trust and goodwill trust will be considered, with contractual trust being viewed as an enabling factor.

4.1 Competence Trust

The driving force behind the supplier development programme at corporate level was competence trust. The aim was not to develop highly skilled small suppliers. In all three plants, in fact, managers argued that the production of critical parts ought to remain in-house.[12] However, the company did wish to greatly improve the level and consistency of quality for all its parts, including the most unsophisticated. The element of risk for the company was, first, that it was willing to invest resources, particularly management time, into these suppliers, and the return on this investment depended on the suppliers' willingness to make similar efforts and the continuation of the relationship. In two of the three plants studied, a few suppliers had begun delivering direct to the line without passing through inspection, and this greatly increased the vulnerability of the company to inconsistent quality. This clearly indicates a considerable extension of competence trust compared to past practices. The company's vulnerability was limited by its increased knowledge of supplier quality systems, the improved basis for supplier selection, and the fact that many of the parts being delivered without inspection could be produced by other companies. The suppliers needed to maintain quality in order to retain the contract.

The vulnerability of the switchgear plant related less to quality than to delivery. The development of just-in-time delivery based on a *kanban* system made the plant highly dependent on the ability of its suppliers to meet their schedules. This dependence was further increased by the transfer of sub-assembly work to the first-tier suppliers. The plant produced to order, and its ability to meet delivery schedules (the key factor for market success) depended on the performance of the first-tier suppliers and their relationships with the second tier. The high level of integration between the plant, these suppliers and the second-tier suppliers meant that they could not easily be replaced by others. In this case, the degree of vulnerability of the plant, and hence the level of Indian Electricals' trust in its suppliers was considerably higher than in the other two plants.

For the suppliers, the development of competence trust does not appear to increase vulnerability. Certainly, the suppliers must invest in the relationship with the company, and they must learn to work the quality systems required. However, they gain from the technical inputs offered by the company, particularly as these create general competencies that can be used for other companies. If the gains from collaboration are transportable, then the risk is negligible.

4.2 Goodwill Trust

If the risks and the need to trust were predominantly on the side of Indian Electricals in the case of competence trust, the opposite was true with respect to goodwill trust. For the company, the reduction in the number of suppliers made it vulnerable to disruption in supply in the short term. A key supplier might well provide more than half the input of a given product. However, the risk of opportunism on the part of suppliers was low. Corporate policy was to maintain two active suppliers and a third accredited supplier in reserve. In addition, many of the parts supplied were technically unsophisticated, and in some cases the company could also produce the parts in-house. Any attempt by suppliers to exploit the position would lead to substitution. More important for the company, was the investment it was making in communication and technical support. Considerable efforts were being made to build up the competence of suppliers, and the returns on this investment depended on continued supply.

The problem of goodwill trust was more serious for the suppliers. Three issues arose. First, there was the question of supplier dependence. Although corporate policy was for suppliers not to sell more than 40 per cent of their output to the company, small suppliers were already often highly dependent. Just under half (48 per cent) of the supplier sample sold at least half of their output to Indian Electricals, and one-third depended on it for at least 80 per cent of their sales. Secondly, there was the question of the extent to which suppliers should go along with the company's discourse about growing together and developing the quality of the relationship. This would require increased effort and investment. Thirdly, there were long-term consequences of closer relations. The suppliers were already subject to pressure for better quality and more frequent deliveries. The next step was for the suppliers' cost base to be improved. Indian Electricals was hoping to send engineers to its suppliers to improve their production processes, but this was potentially a source of conflict and mistrust. While Nishiguchi observes that longer-lasting cost reductions can be achieved by what he terms a 'problem-solving' approach rather than a 'bargaining' approach (1989: 279–83), the suppliers were unsure how these gains would be distributed. They needed to decide how much they were prepared to trust the company before they allowed access to information which might be misused. The development of personal trust based on experience and knowledge of the customer seems to depend on four factors: the previous pattern of relationships, the factors underlying the relationships between the company and its suppliers, the way in which the company handled its suppliers, and the strategy used to develop trust. The outcome in two plants with contrasting experiences will be considered here.

The worst outcome was seen at the factory producing ceiling fans. This plant had had poor relationships with its suppliers, and it had made the position much worse by responding to a cash-flow crisis by delaying payments to suppliers. The company as a whole had a reputation for poor payment terms and late payment, but the fans plant had exacerbated this, just at the point when it was proclaiming a new attitude to suppliers. Interviews with suppliers showed just how much this undermined trust. Delays in payment caused particular problems for small firms, and they were greatly resented. It would be a considerable risk to make new investments on the promise of expanding output when the company could not even make payments on time.

The suppliers were in a vulnerable position. Most of them made parts which could be produced by other firms. The fans market was subject to fierce price competition, and all of the major producers were losing money. Inevitably, this put pressure on costs, and more suppliers to the fans plant than to the other plants complained about pressures for price reductions. It is not surprising, therefore, that attempts by management at the plant to involve suppliers in cost reduction exercises were viewed with some suspicion. The pressure for 'open books' was threatening.

Similarly, it is not surprising that some smaller suppliers feared that Indian Electricals would appropriate what few secrets they had and pass them on to competitors. Their 'secrets' would be easily appropriable. The only exceptions to this generalization supplied products requiring specialist expertise, such as castings. In other words, the suppliers were willing to work more closely with Indian Electricals, but they clearly mistrusted the company. This mistrust had good grounds. The suppliers were vulnerable because they mostly offered unsophisticated products. They were being asked to trust the company, but the company's past behaviour did not justify trust being extended and the main visible difference was only the discourse of partnership.

At the fans plant, the dangers were particularly stark. The plant's survival did depend on reducing costs, and improving the cost base, and the quality of the suppliers was part of this process. However, the long-term future of the plant was in doubt. It was producing a cost competitive product in a high-cost location, and the company had already opened new factories in a low-cost area. Similarly, it had begun to source parts from 500 kilometres away, seeking out even lower-cost suppliers for high value-to-weight components. The future of the plant was uncertain. In any other country, it would have been closed or switched to alternative production. The suppliers had every reason to be wary.

To break this impasse the company needed to show concrete changes in behaviour, but there was little evidence that the fans plants was capable of demonstrating a change in behaviour. While management offered some technical support and many soothing words, it undermined its efforts by its failure to address the crucial problems. The suppliers were particularly resentful of poor payment terms. They were also greatly inhibited by erratic and unstable order quantities. This raised costs and often led to excess stocks being held. In extreme cases, management would cancel orders at short notice, leaving suppliers with useless stocks. The plant seemed incapable of doing anything about this, which would require more competent production planning and control. It seemed unwilling to tackle the first problem, sacrificing supplier confidence in order to reduce its own interest payments.

The fans plant is an extreme example of the failure to create trust. At the opposite extreme was the switchgear plant, where concrete changes in supplier relations were most evident. The plant had a network of small suppliers in the locality, set up following its establishment in 1980. These suppliers were the focus of the new supplier strategy. This strategy was founded on the restructuring of the suppliers into two tiers and the development of a *kanban* system for controlling supplier production. The first-tier plants were responsible for co-ordinating the second tier. This, in itself, gave them a more secure position, as they now had a strategic role. It also demonstrated the trust the company had in them. The plant had targeted customer response time as its key competitive edge, but it had reduced stocks and become dependent on the rapid response of the first-tier vendors. However, the plant's management also needed the question of trust directly. First, the company was demanding considerable changes in work patterns at the suppliers (the *kanban* system). It also wanted to ensure continuity of management, and insisted on a technically qualified person being available in the plant in the owner's absence. Secondly, the plant had ambitious plans for expansion. If it was to move to single or dual sourcing and greatly expand output, the local suppliers would need to greatly increase their shipments to the plant. This would mean investing heavily in new capacity and/or increasing their dependence on the plant. The discourse of management clearly appealed to identification-based trust. Suppliers were referred to as partners, and the goal would be to grow together. However, talk is cheap, and similar discourses were visible at the other plants. To persuade the suppliers to make changes in organization and new investments, the plant's management had to convince the suppliers that they could be trusted to maintain the policy and provide a fair deal in the long term.

The first-tier suppliers were given a special name, the 'Silver Club', and were the focus of specific attention. Visits from plant management to the Silver Club suppliers were significantly more frequent than to other suppliers at the same plant and the other plants. These types of personal contacts are important in establishing trustworthiness. They are related to the notion of affect-based trust discussed above. The *kanban* system itself might contribute to this process if it established good and constructive channels of communication between plant managers and suppliers. However, the plant's management still faced the 'start up' problem mentioned in Section 2. They wished to move quickly, but trust develops slowly, and some incentive to take the first steps of risk exposure had to be made. Management at the plant saw the renegotiation of supplier contracts as an important element in these efforts, and in 1995 it began to discuss new draft contracts with suppliers. These were oriented towards risk reduction. They emphasized the importance of a long-term relationship and explored the possibility of making the company pay for parts ordered but later cancelled. Implicit in this contract was the issue of late payment, which was generally a problem at the company. In this case, management viewed the formalization of contracts as a means of promoting trust where it had not existed before. Contractual clauses which put greater obligations on the customer to pay promptly and to accept goods which have been ordered provide protection to small firms whose larger customers have not shown benevolence in the past.[13] At the same time, they act as a demonstration of goodwill and good faith. The company's credibility is established by offering concrete improvements in the short term.

This was an important start for a plant's supplier strategy. Once this first step is taken, then the process of developing knowledge-based and identification-based trust can be put in place. Similarly, the interactions developed through the programme should reinforce personal ties between managements at the customer and the suppliers. However, the acid test of trust will be when the opportunity of betrayal is available and attractive, but not taken. At some point in the future, management might encounter a situation where some benefit might appear to arise from the betrayal of trust. When this opportunity is forgone, the suppliers' trust will be shown to be well-founded.

4.3 Trust and Uncertainty

The negotiations of new contracts and the provision of technical assistance are not a substitute for personal trust. They merely limit risk and demonstrate good faith while relationships are built up. Both the company and its suppliers need time to see how the new strategy would work out in practice, not only because of the risk of bad faith, but also because of uncertainty about policy and the external environment. First, neither the company nor the suppliers could be sure how declarations would be translated into practice. At the beginning, the company's policy was not fully defined and stable. There were clear differences in practice and in statements of policy about single sourcing and dependence of suppliers on the company, for example. Corporate policy favoured dual sourcing and limited supplier defendants, but at plant level, various policies were being pursued, including dedicated suppliers and single-sourcing. In addition, plants were subject to various contradictory pressures, including cost pressures. These could lead to exploitation of dependent suppliers or supplier switching.

Secondly, the company's supplier strategy was largely a response to the supply conditions in the Indian economy at the time. Suppliers were poor, and the only way to improve them was to invest in upgrading. But, at some point in the future, the level of competence among small- and medium-sized enterprises might well rise, obviating the need to develop close relationships in order to secure adequate quality.[14] Thirdly, most of the small suppliers lacked technical competence, and they could offer little in the way of design inputs or problem-solving capabilities. If new companies with these capabilities were to develop in India as a result of the change in competitive climate, the established suppliers might be marginalized.[15] To the extent that the achievement of competence trust was limited to a low level of competence, it would not necessarily create goodwill trust.

Finally, liberalization continues to create uncertainties. Managers have to plan in an uncertain and rapidly changing environment. Nothing is fixed, and this limits the predictability of relationships. This can be seen as a reason for developing trust. Reducing controllable uncertainties in interfirm relationships enables companies and their managers to confront these broader uncertainties. However, the bases for trust can be undermined by such uncertainties, too. The uncontrollable uncertainties increase the level of risk arising from trust. In particular, new competitive conditions might change the bases on which the company remained competitive, altering its relations with suppliers in quite radical ways.

5. CONCLUSIONS

It is widely acknowledged that interfirm relationships based on trust can be a source of competitive advantage, and this is particularly evident for companies that are developing just-in-time and total quality management systems. Much of the analysis of trust relations has focused on those countries where trust has a systemic character. Patterns of interfirm relationships are well established and embedded in institutions that both regulate behaviour and give trust a taken-for-granted aspect. However, business fashion and competitive pressures are pressuring companies to restructure supplier relations even when the institutional context is unfavourable. This restructuring is particularly important for those developing countries whose economies are making a relatively rapid transition from being protected and inward-oriented towards being increasingly competitive and internationally oriented. Firms in these countries cannot wait for an institutional framework to develop. They must do all they can to improve supplier relations and competitiveness. The development of closer relations with suppliers involves increased vulnerability to the actions of others, and trust makes this risk acceptable.

The concept of personal trust allows a better understanding of the processes of trust construction between firms in adverse environments. Trust has to be constructed slowly through a process of mutual learning. In India, there are clear signs that firms wish to develop closer relations. The basis for these relations is neither a high degree of mutual dependence nor the presumption of benevolence on the part of the large customer. The development of personal trust does allow closer ties to be sustained, even though they imply greater vulnerability to opportunistic behaviour. However, there were clear limits to the granting of trust. To some extent, this was a structural problem. The pursuit of improved quality did not necessarily make suppliers indispensable to the customer, and this left them vulnerable to substitution. The issue of reducing risk for suppliers and promoting trust only emerged at the plant which had developed just-in-time delivery. At this plant, management was actively seeking to renegotiate contracts as a means of establishing a basis for closer relations. While in the longer term the relationship itself would provide the basis for trust, in the early stages of the new relationship better contracts for suppliers reduced their exposure to risk and acted as a demonstration of good faith.

Firms in developing countries can neither hope to create the institutional framework that regulates interfirm relationships in Germany, nor create the supplier structures seen in Japan. Even if they wanted to do so, this might well be inappropriate for the competitive conditions prevailing in countries such as India. Therefore, Indian companies must be wary of trying to imitate patterns of supplier relations in those two countries. They must look behind the recipes and imaginatively recreate what they find so that it works in a very different environment. This re-creation must consider not only the end-point of the journey towards increased trust, but also the stages through which trust relationships must pass as they are constructed.

NOTES

1. See, for example, Williamson (1993) on transaction costs economics, Putnam (1993) and Piore and Sabel (1984) on Italy, Semlinger (1995) on Baden-Württemberg, and Dore (1983) and Sako (1992) on Japan.

2. Most of the interviews were carried out by Indian researchers, who spoke English or the local language as seemed appropriate for each interview. The author and Raphael Kaplinsky also visited some of these suppliers.
3. Cited in Meyerson, Weick, and Kramer (1996: 170).
4. This second aspect of trust is wider than Sako's definition of contractual trust, but not as broad as her definition of 'goodwill trust' (Sako 1992: 37–9). The idea of responsible behaviour at the point of adaptation of contracts to changing market circumstances is presented by Williamson (1979: 241), although he regards relying on such behaviour as foolhardy.
5. For this argument to hold, it is not necessary to assume that all potential partners will act opportunistically if it were profitable to do so. It is merely necessary to assume that it is not feasible to determine *ex ante* who will act opportunistically and who will not: 'It is not necessary that all agents be regarded as opportunistic in identical degree. It suffices that those who are less opportunistic than others are difficult to ascertain *ex ante* and that, even among the less opportunistic, most have their price' (Williamson 1979: 234).
6. For a lengthier discussion of these issues and their relevance for economic development, see Humphrey and Schmitz (1996).
7. Cited in Furlong (1996: 15). Luhmann himself uses the traffic analogy (1979: 24).
8. In the case of the Rover–Honda partnership, the unfriendly divorce was a shock to Honda not because it had miscalculated the potential benefits to Rover's parent of a split, but rather because Honda was working on a different set of business calculations altogether, oriented towards long-term growth, commitment to all stakeholders etc. Similarly, trading can allow companies to work out the bases of calculation of their partners.
9. On the 'start up' problem in the case of trust-based co-operation between small enterprises, see Semlinger, 1995: 274.
10. This information comes from interviews carried out by the author with managers of the company at the Malaysian plant and at the international headquarters in Japan.
11. This information is taken from a presentation by R. Dayal, Deputy-General Manager MUL, at the 4th CII Quality Summit, see Dayal (1996). Interestingly, MUL has drawn back from single sourcing of parts because of the uncertainties of production in its suppliers.
12. Similarly, an important order from a leading Japanese firm was conditional on no parts being brought in from outside. The Japanese customer did not trust supplier quality.
13. On the question of the role of benevolence in relations between large and small firms in Japan, see Dore (1983).
14. These suppliers were producing very simple products, such as machined shafts. In Japan these might have been made by second- or third-tier suppliers, which would not enjoy the same close relationship with the final customer.
15. This process is evident in Japan in the 1990s. See, for example, Ikeda and Nakagawa on the restructuring of supplier relations and the elimination of less technically competent suppliers at Hitachi Automotive Products (1996).

REFERENCES

Awasthi, S. (1996), 'Partnership for Progress', paper presented at the 4th Quality Summit: 'Quality in a Competitive Environment', Bangalore, India.

Baier, A. (1986), *Postures of the Mind*. Minneapolis: University of Minnesota Press.

Coleman, J. S. (1990), *Foundations of Social Theory*. Cambridge, Mass.: Harvard University Press.

Dayal, R. (1996), 'Managing Customer–Supplier Relationships', paper presented at the 4th Quality Summit: 'Quality in a Competitive Environment', Bangalore, India.

Dore, R. (1983), 'Goodwill and the Spirit of Market Capitalism', *British Journal of Sociology*, 34: 459–82.

Furlong, D. (1996), 'The Conceptualisation of "Trust" in Economic Thought', *IDS Working Paper*, 35, Brighton: Institute of Development Studies.

Gambetta, D. (1988), 'Can We Trust Trust?', in D. Gambetta (ed.), *Trust: Making and Breaking Co-operative Relations*. Oxford: Blackwell, 213–37.

Holmström, M. (1994), 'A Cure for Loneliness? Networks, Trust and Shared Services in Bangalore', paper presented at Workshop on 'Industrialization, Organization, Innovations, and Institutions in the South', Vienna.

Humphrey, J. and Schmitz, H. (1996), 'Trust and Economic Development', *IDS Discussion Paper*, 355, Brighton: Institute of Development Studies.

Ikeda, M. and Nakagawa, Y. (1996), 'New Styles of Rationalisation in the Japanese Auto Industry After Extreme Appreciation of the Yen', paper presented at 4th GERPISA International Auto Industry Workshop, Paris.

Knack, S. and Keefer, P. (1996), 'Does Social Capital Have an Economic Payoff? A Cross-Country Investigation', mimeo, University of Maryland and The World Bank.

Kollock, P. (1994), 'The Emergence of Exchange Structures: An Experimental Study of Uncertainty, Commitment and Trust', *American Journal of Sociology*, 100/2: 313–45.

Lane, C. (1995), 'The Social Constitution of Supplier Relations in Britain and Germany', in R. Whitley and P. H. Kristensen (eds.), *The Changing European Firm*. London: Routledge, 271–304.

——and Bachmann, R. (1996), 'The Social Constitution of Trust: Supplier Relations in Britain and Germany', *Organization Studies*, 17/3: 365–95.

Lewicki, R. and Bunker, B. (1996), 'Developing and Maintaining Trust in Work Relationships', in R. Kramer and T. Tyler (eds.), *Trust in Organisations*. Thousand Oaks, Calif.: Sage, 114–39.

Little, I. M. D., Mazumdar, D., and Page, J. (1987), *Small Manufacturing Enterprises: A Comparative Study of India and Other Economies*. Oxford: Oxford University Press.

Luhmann, N. (1979), *Trust and Power*. Chichester: Wiley.

——(1988), 'Familiarity, Confidence, Trust: Problems and Alternatives', in Gambetta (ed.), *Trust: Making and Breaking Co-operative Relations*, 94–107.

Meyerson, D., Weick, K., and Kramer, R. (1996), 'Swift Trust and Temporary Groups', in Kramer and Tyler (eds.), *Trust in Organisations*, 166–95.

Nishiguchi, T. (1989), 'Strategic Dualism: An Alternative in Industrial Societies', Ph.D. thesis, Oxford.

Piore, M. and Sabel, C. (1984), *The Second Industrial Divide: Possibilities for Prosperity*. New York: Basic Books.

Putnam, R. (1993), *Making Democracy Work: Civic Traditions in Modern Italy*. Princeton: Princeton University Press.

Sako, M. (1992), *Prices, Quality and Trust*. Cambridge: Cambridge University Press.

—— and Helper, S. (1996), 'How Does Trust Improve Business Performance?', paper presented at 8th International Conference of the Society for the Advancement of Socio-economics, Geneva.

Semlinger, K. (1995), 'Public Support for Firm Networking in Baden-Württemberg', in L. E. Andreasen, B. Coriat, F. den Hertog, and R. Kaplinsky (eds.), *Europe's Next Step: Organizational Innovation, Competition and Employment*. London: Frank Cass, 271–85.

Sheppard, B. and Tuchinsky, M. (1996), 'Micro-OB and the Network Organisation', in Kramer and Tyler (eds.), *Trust in Organisations*, 140–65.

Williamson, O. E. (1979), 'Transaction-cost Economics: The Governance of Contractual Relations', *Journal of Law and Economics*, 22: 233–61.

—— (1993), 'Calculativeness, Trust and Economic Organization', *Journal of Law and Economics*, 36: 453–86.

Womack, J., Jones, D., and Roos, D. (1990), *The Machine That Changed the World*. New York: Rawson.

Zucker, L. G. (1986), 'Production of Trust: Institutional Sources of Economic Structure, 1840–1920', *Research in Organisational Behaviour*, 8: 53–111.

9

Trust and International Strategic Alliances: The Case of Sino-Foreign Joint Ventures*

JOHN CHILD

1. INTRODUCTION

It is evident that co-operation, both within and between enterprises, is becoming more crucial for their success (Smith, Carroll, and Ashford 1995). Co-operation between firms continues to grow, manifested both in close and integrated relationships between manufacturing firms and their suppliers (Lane and Bachmann 1996) and in more comprehensive strategic alliances between companies (Bleeke and Ernst 1993).

Strategic alliances can take a number of forms, ranging from the total integration of partners via mergers between them, through joint ventures, to more loosely constituted arrangements such as consortia and collaborations (Lorange and Roos 1992). The likely degree of permanency of alliances tends to decrease as one moves through this range of alternatives. Alliances are normally established by their partners with a number of objectives in mind, prominent among which are the sharing of risk in complex and/or high technology projects, the transfer of technology and other forms of knowledge, the facilitation of entry into new markets, and the strengthening of a strategic position within an existing market.

Since the mid-1980s, there has been a rapidly growing number of international strategic alliances (ISAs). They have become the major vehicles for the foreign direct investment (FDI) made by international companies from one country to another. The greater proportion of FDI flows between the developed countries which constitute the so-called 'Triad' of North America, Western Europe, and Japan. Since the beginning of the 1990s, however, the share of world FDI originating from the East Asian 'Newly-Industrialized Countries' (especially South Korea, Singapore, and Taiwan) has increased, while the share of FDI inputs to developing countries has also been increasing. Today, China is by far the largest developing country host for FDI and, indeed, has become the second largest recipient of FDI in the world (UNCTAD 1997). In the so-called 'Emerging Economies' like China, international joint ventures are the most common basis on which co-operation between host country and foreign partners is established, with

* The author wishes to thank Sally Heavens, Christel Lane, Guido Möllering, and Yanni Yan for their very helpful comments on an earlier draft of this chapter.

FDI usually being incorporated into the equity of such ventures (Child 1994).

Strategic alliances depend for their very existence on the establishment of effective co-operation between the partners. This is certainly the case with joint ventures to which two or more partners contribute capital, and normally allocate or appoint staff to work together in managing the ventures. Joint ventures are often constituted as newly-founded 'hybrid' organizations (Borys and Jemison 1989), though they can also take the form of an agreed exchange of shares between the partners rather than the creation of a new company with its own legal identity.

Co-operation within ISAs involves mutual reliance and requires trust to succeed.[1] For as Smith and his colleagues (1995: 10–11) note, 'although research has identified many determinants of cooperation, virtually all scholars have agreed that one especially immediate antecedent is trust'. When, in the case of equity joint ventures, the partners sink specific assets into them, they incur additional risk. Developed/developing country joint ventures normally involve a greater investment of specific assets by the developed country partner(s) than by the developing country host partner(s), and in this way the former bear the greater risk. One of the hybrid characteristics of alliances arises from the paradox that they often combine elements of co-operation and competition, or at least the attempt to formulate common goals on the basis of not wholly complementary objectives (cf. Hamel 1991). The combination of mutual reliance between alliance partners with residual or potential elements of competition or conflict between them can set up a game theoretic dynamic that adds to the risk and precariousness of the co-operation. Trust between the partners is required to help overcome this threat, yet at the same time the source of the threat inhibits the development of trust. The reality of this dilemma would appear to be borne out by surveys which suggest that between 40 and 50 per cent of strategic alliances fail within five years (Bleeke and Ernst 1993).[2] It also accounts for the sentiment expressed by a recently retired senior executive from a firm whose success is based partly on its ability to form and sustain joint ventures and other forms of strategic alliance, quoted by Spekman and his colleagues (1996: 346):

If you have a choice, don't do them . . . Strategic alliances take up an inordinate amount of management time, energy and attention. It would be best to look for other ways to do business. I really mean it.

The fundamental necessity for trust in strategic alliances has been recognized in the literature on the subject (e.g. Faulkner 1995), but it remains both theoretically and empirically underdeveloped. The association between alliance partners takes on a network character, and indeed may form part of a more extensive business network. As Creed and Miles (1996: 30) comment, 'both across the firms within a network and within the various network firms, there is little choice but to consider trust building and maintenance to be as essential as control system building and maintenance are viewed in the functional form'. Moreover, increased trust between alliance partners promises an economic pay-off for each. If they can develop mutual trust, this should reduce the negative effects of bounded rationality, specific investment in the alliance, and opportunism which would otherwise arise, and so reduce transaction costs (Chiles and McMackin 1996).

The establishment and maintenance of trust within relationships between the partners and their staffs in international strategic alliances present a special challenge because these cross the boundaries of the cultural and institutional systems which importantly support trust through the sharing of a common social identity, norms of conduct and institutional safeguards such as the law. The fact that ISA partners as a result follow different assumptions of 'what can be taken for granted' places particular difficulties in the way of creating trust-based relationships between them, over and above the tensions which might be expected to arise within strategic alliances in general, due to their hybrid nature.

One of the more challenging cases for establishing trust arises with alliances between Chinese and Western partners which, as already noted, have come to occupy a highly significant place within international business and investment. Despite the less than perfect homogeneity among Western countries in the way they socially constitute and support trust relations (cf. Lane and Bachmann 1996), China contrasts sufficiently in its cultural and institutional foundations with both North America and Western Europe as to present a particularly interesting comparison as well as a challenge for management policy. It will be argued in this chapter that the problematic for trust in Sino-Western joint ventures derives in large measure from China's social environment, which is highly complex and hence uncertain from a Western perspective.

Within the broad category of ISAs, this chapter focuses on the case of Sino-foreign joint ventures. It proceeds in the following way. The next section considers different conceptions of trust in relation to the development of co-operative relationships. The analysis is then applied to the process of ISA development. Having laid down this framework, the two following sections examine the social constitution of trust within China and the problematic this presents for Sino-foreign joint ventures.

2. TRUST AND CO-OPERATIVE RELATIONSHIPS

The many definitions of trust which have been offered tend to agree that the concept denotes the confidence of a person, group, or organization relating or transacting with another under conditions of some uncertainty that the other's actions will be beneficial rather than detrimental to it (cf. Gambetta 1988, McAllister 1995, Kramer and Tyler 1996). Trust is risky, virtually by definition because, without some uncertainty regarding the outcome of the relationship or exchange, it would not come into play. The trustor's expectations about the future behaviour of the trustee may turn out to be incorrect, possibly due to unfamiliarity with the trustee or the absence of social mechanisms to contain the risk (Lane and Bachmann 1996: 368). This conditional nature of trust has given rise to enquiry into the grounds on which trust might develop and the foundations on which it can rest.

This enquiry has produced three insights which are particularly relevant to an understanding of co-operative relationships, and hence to those within ISAs. The first is contained in the distinction between calculation, cognition, and normative identification as bases for trust. The second is an appreciation that co-operative relations can develop over time and that this development may be associated with the deepening of trust based on an evolution of its foundations. The third is a recognition that trust is socially constituted, in that it tends to be strengthened by cultural affinity between people and can be supported by institutional norms and sanctions. The first two of these insights contribute to an understanding of co-operation between alliance partners in general, including those engaged in purely domestic alliances, while the third insight is of particular importance for the case of international alliances.

2.1 Calculative, Cognitive, and Normative Trust

In the Introduction to this book Lane identifies three perspectives on the basis of trust. The first is *calculative trust*, namely that 'trusting involves expectations about another, based on calculations which weigh the cost and benefits of certain courses of action to either the trustor or the trustee'. Lewicki and Bunker (1996) argue that this form of trust is based on the assurance that other people will do as they say because the deterrent for violation is greater than the gains, and/or the rewards from preserving trust outweigh any from breaking it. 'In this view, trust is an on-going, market-oriented, economic calculation whose value is derived by determining the outcomes resulting from creating and sustaining the relationship relative to the costs of maintaining or severing it' (Lewicki and Bunker 1996: 120). Trust based on calculation clearly depends on an availability of relevant information, and in practice there may be significant limits to this. Indeed, some critics of the calculative view of trust have argued that it is when relationships or transactions are initiated under conditions of information *uncertainty* that trust in the proper sense come into play (Lane 1997).

Trust based upon calculation is likely to apply particularly to relationships which are new and hence can only proceed on the basis of institution-alized protection (incorporating deterrence) or the reputation of the part-ner. It may also be the only form of trust which can apply to arm's-length and hence impersonal economic exchanges. However, if those exchanges become recurrent, such as with repeat mail-order business, then another form of trust may also emerge. This is based on increased mutual knowl-edge among the partners, which nurtures the realization that they share relevant expectations. As we note below, calculation-based trust is very relevant to the formation phase of ISAs, though its withdrawal can also undermine the mutual confidence of partners who have developed other bases for trust as well.

A second potential basis for trust lies in the sharing of cognitions, includ-ing common ways of thinking, between the parties concerned—*cognitive trust*. This sharing of cognitions provides a basis for understanding the thinking of a partner and for predicting that person's actions. Clearly, some cognitive sharing is necessary for a calculative basis of trust to come into play, but common cognitions provide the further reassurance that one can now reasonably predict other people on the basis of shared expectations. One can normally only be sure of sharing ways of thinking with others by getting to know them well enough, and an aspect of cognitive trust is what Lewicki and Bunker have termed 'knowledge-based trust'. Knowledge-based trust 'is grounded in the other's predictability—knowing the other sufficiently well so that the other's behaviour is anticipatable. Knowledge-based trust relies on information rather than deterrence' (1996: 121). The assumption of rationality contained in the calculative view of trust is re-laxed somewhat in cognitive trust, because the trust here is founded upon both the security and comfort that the partner is well-understood and is known to share important assumptions.

A third view of trust is *normative trust*, which depends on people sharing common values, including a common concept of moral obligation. As Lane points out, common values and norms of obligation can develop in a long-standing relationship where trust was originally created in an incremental manner. Normative trust is likely to find a parallel at the more interpersonal level, in what Lewicki and Bunker (1996) call 'identification-based trust'. This 'trust exists because the parties effectively understand and appreciate the other's wants; this mutual understanding is developed to the point that each can effectively act for the other' (p. 122). If friendship develops within a long-term relationship, the emotional bond thereby introduced is likely to provide a mainstay for identification-based trust, because it enables a per-son to 'feel' as well as to 'think' like the other (p. 123). The presence of affect is also likely to encourage people to place themselves voluntarily within the powers of another—this is what Brenkert (1997) calls 'the Voluntarist view' of trust.

Running somewhat parallel to this threefold distinction between calculative, cognitive, and normative trust is the broader distinction, made by McAllister (1995) among others, between cognition-based and affect-based trust. Trust that is cognition-based rests upon the knowledge people have of others and the evidence of their trustworthiness: 'available knowledge and "good reasons" serve as foundations for trust decisions' (ibid. 26). McAllister points out that previous organizational researchers have assumed competence, responsibility, reliability and dependability to be important sources of cognition-based trust. Brenkert (Chapter 10, in this volume) identifies a 'predictability view', which holds that trust denotes the extent to which one can predict that the person being trusted will act in good faith. While Brenkert argues that such prediction rests on 'a belief that one person has about another', this is consistent with the concept of cognition-based trust because the belief almost certainly rests on a degree of knowledge about the other person which is taken to constitute 'good reasons' for trust, however limited and imperfect that knowledge might be.

By contrast, affect-based trust, according to McAllister (1995: 26), is founded on the emotional bonds between people. These bonds express a genuine concern for the welfare of partners, a feeling that the relationships have intrinsic virtue, and a belief that these sentiments are reciprocated. In other words, they incorporate an identification with the other person's wishes and intentions. Affect-based trust is clearly a form which is most likely to develop and deepen through fairly intensive relating between people on a person-to-person basis over quite a long period of time. As such, it is facilitated by the ability to communicate well and to avoid, or quickly clear up, misunderstandings. So mutual knowledge and the sharing of information between the people concerned remain essential conditions. Cultural and associated language differences tend to impede communication and easy understanding, and may therefore stand in the way of affect-based trust. Perceived conflicts of interest will also make it hard to develop or maintain this kind of trust. In ISAs, affect-based trust and co-operation will therefore be difficult to achieve, and if they emerge at all this is only likely after the alliance has been operating successfully, and up to the partners' expectations, over a period of some years.

The distinction between cognition and affect in trust-based co-operative relationships suggests that these are likely to form on the basis of essentially cognitive considerations, including calculation, but that as the relationship matures it may increasingly incorporate affect through the development of friendship ties.

2.2 Development and Deepening of Trust-Based Relations

The second insight which it is appropriate to apply to ISAs is that co-operative relations can develop over time, supported by a corresponding evolution of trust. As Smith, Carroll, and Ashford (1995) note, several writers have suggested that co-operative relationships develop through a number of stages. There are feedback loops in this process whereby the partners evaluate their experience and decide whether to continue their co-operation and, if so, in what form (Ring and van de Ven 1994). The distinction between calculative, cognitive, and normative trust opens a window on the way that the evolution of trust is integral to this dynamic process of evolving co-operation.

In this vein, Lewicki and Bunker propose a model of 'the stagewise evolution of trust' in which 'trust develops gradually as the parties move from one stage to another' (1996: 124). They argue that trust first develops on the basis of calculation. This is the stage at which people are prepared to take some risk in entering into dependence on others because they are aware of some institutional safeguards or deterrents against reneging. For some relationships, trust may remain of this kind and at this level, as in repeated but arm's-length transactions between people. Lewicki and Bunker suggest that many business and legal relationships begin and end in calculative trust.

If calculative trust activities serve to confirm the validity of the trust and thus encourage repeated interaction and transaction, then the parties will also begin to develop a knowledge base about each other. This generates the conditions for a transition to cognitive trust. This is the stage in a relationship at which a person feels comfortable with a partner in the knowledge that he or she has proved to be consistent and reliable, and that the partner shares important expectations about the relationship. As a result, the partner is proving to be predictable. In this way, the parties' experience of a calculative trust relationship (i.e. feedback) is critical for their willingness to undergo the shift to cognitive trust. If the feedback is negative, and trust is broken, they will probably move to terminate the relationship. Even short of fracture, if the experience of relating on a calculative basis is not strongly positive, or if the relationship is heavily regulated, or if the interdependence of the partners is heavily bounded, they will have little cause to develop cognitive (knowledge-based) trust.

A further transition may come when normative trust builds on the depth of knowledge which the parties have acquired of each other and on the mutual confidence they have developed. These outcomes from the relationship may encourage the parties to identify with each other's goals and interests. A certain amount of mutual affect will probably now enter into the relationship, so that this stage is typically one at which the partners have become friends. Lewicki and Bunker believe, however, that whereas stable cognitive ('knowledge-based') trust characterizes many relationships, trust based on shared values and identification may be less common especially in business or work transactions where some difference of interest is usually inherent in the relationship.

Certain specifics of Lewicki and Bunker's model may require modification. It does not, for instance, appear to allow for the possibility that, in the absence of effective external institutional guarantees, it may be necessary to develop a degree of cognitive trust alongside that based on calculations about the deterrents and motivations which the other party perceives to apply to the relationship. Otherwise an adequate foundation for the calculation will not exist. Nevertheless, it will become apparent that the evolutionary model of trust advanced by these authors can contribute in a very significant way to an analysis of ISA formation and development.

2.3 The Social Constitution of Trust

The third insight is a recognition that trust is socially constituted, in that it is necessarily realized, and strengthened, by social interaction, cultural affinity between people and the support of institutional norms and sanctions. Zucker (1986) argues that trust is socially produced through three main modes, of which the latter two have their bases in socially constituted entities. The first mode is one in which trust develops on the basis of the experience of past exchange or the expectations attached to future exchange. Production of trust in this mode arises through the mutual reinforcement of investments in trust and the quality of the co-operation associated with it, and is consistent with the process of developing and deepening trust-based relations noted above. The second mode is based on the sharing of common characteristics, such as ethnicity and culture. The third mode is one in which formal institutional mechanisms provide codes (as in medicine) or guarantees (as in financial supervision) that transactions will take place as promised.

With respect to the second of Zucker's modes, co-operation is likely to be easier between people who have the same cultural norms, for a number of reasons. People are more likely to trust those who share the same values, because this establishes a common cognitive frame and promotes a sense of common social identity which has a strong emotional element. Differences between cultures in language, symbolism, and meaning can make it very difficult to find a common cognitive basis from which trust can first develop. In respect of institutional supports, it will be easier for trust-based relationships to develop if the risks involved are reduced by institutional mechanisms such as an effective law to enforce contracts and/or a strongly developed moral opprobrium for any violation of the social norms applying to trust. The presence of social and cultural norms which attach a value to trust, define the circumstances under which it should be honoured, and justify sanctions for violation, indicate the extent to which trust is a socially constituted phenomenon (cf. Lane and Bachmann 1996). While this social constitution can support trust-based co-operation within the boundaries of a given social unit, such as a nation and to a lesser degree an organization, it clearly presents problems for relationships which cross these boundaries. Those in a domestic strategic alliance cross the boundaries of organizations as social units, whereas those in an international strategic alliance cross both national and organizational boundaries. The development of trust-based co-operative relationships within ISAs is therefore a major challenge, especially in the case of alliances between partners from a developed and a developing society. In this case, the partners involved do not share common cultural characteristics and they cannot rely upon the same system of institutional support, except to the extent that international trade law and arbitration procedures have effect. This means that the development of trust in ISAs will depend heavily upon the process mode of its production, namely the way that their relationships are established and managed.

3. TRUST AND THE PROCESS OF INTERNATIONAL STRATEGIC ALLIANCE DEVELOPMENT

There is considerable agreement among writers on strategic alliances that their development can be broadly divided into three phases: formation, implementation, and evolution (Lorange and Roos 1992). Formation is the phase during which the future partners conceive an interest in the possibility of forming an alliance, select potential partners and negotiate an agreement (usually a contract). Implementation is the phase during which the alliance is established as a productive venture and people are appointed or seconded by the partners, systems installed, and operations commenced. Evolution refers to the ways in which the alliance develops further following its establishment.

Early in the formation process, the future partners will have come to the conclusion that they favour an alliance out of a range of possible alternatives. For example, if one partner's purpose is to enter a new market, it has a range of possibilities for accomplishing this objective: these include exporting into the market using local agents, licensing technology to a local producer, forming an alliance with a local firm (in the form of a collaboration, equity joint venture, or merger), and setting up a wholly-owned subsidiary (Root 1994). The choice between these alternatives is likely to be informed by the partner's strategic intentions and previous experience of managing different forms of market entry. It will rest almost entirely on calculation concerning the relative costs and benefits of each alternative. At this stage, the calculation has to rely primarily upon business intelligence.

If it is decided to explore the possibilities of forming an alliance, the selection of a partner is also likely to be based importantly upon calculation. During this phase, potential partners are identified and their mutual interest grows sufficiently for them to start exchanging information directly rather than using business intelligence. In principle, the potential partners try to find out as much as they can about each other and then compare the information obtained against a range of selection criteria in order to assess the degree of strategic fit between themselves (Geringer 1991; Faulkner 1995).[3] In reality, however, information about prospective partners will be limited, especially that relating to their internal cultures, competences, and values. This means that judgements will have to be made on the basis of the partners' reputations, including those for trustworthiness. This 'information stage' (Möllering 1997), during which the prospective partners try to find out as much as possible about each other, will normally precede their entry into negotiations on a contract. In learning about the other, the partners are also 'getting to know' each other. If, as is usually the case, the process takes the form of deepening personal contacts between the limited number of people who are actively pursuing the contacts between partners, then incrementally by 'small steps' (Smitka 1994) bonds will form between them. These bonds will be nurtured by mutual knowledge, and possibly by the emergence of some mutual affect.

While the information stage of alliance formation is ostensibly aimed at establishing the nature and degree of 'strategic fit' between potential partners, in the case of a putative *international* strategic alliance the nature of cultural differences between them will also become evident. Cultural differences could inhibit the development of mutual understanding and trust and, if this were to outweigh its counterpart (namely the facilitation of cultural integration through the development of calculative and cognitive bases for mutual trust), then the process of moving towards a formal agreement would be jeopardized. This is a quite realistic possibility when alliances are being discussed between partners from societies which are culturally and institutionally disparate. Particularly at the stage of forming an international alliance, it is not possible to treat strategic fit and cultural fit separately and sequentially, because the exchange of information during this phase depends on an initial development of trust which, in turn, depends on how the relations between the partners are affected by their cultural distance (Möllering 1997). Once the calculative basis for the alliance has been agreed, it may become more feasible to work systematically towards a resolution of the operational problems which continue to result from the cultural differences between the partners (Child 1994).

The process of information gathering, if sustained, will move into one of negotiation. Negotiation hammers out a calculative framework for the 'strategic fit' and the mix of commitments and safeguards embodied in an alliance contract. It also provides an opportunity for the parties to establish a level of comfort for future co-operation based on a deepening of their mutual knowledge. In other words, in so far as the agreement to co-operate is one to establish a mutual dependency between the partners but, where considerable uncertainty remains, it is an act of trust based primarily upon calculation. While the calculus will take account of legal and other institutional safeguards, it is also likely to be informed by the direct knowledge the partners have gathered about one another.

Smitka (1994: 93) uses the term 'contracting' to refer to the negotiation of, and agreement upon, mutual obligations between potential partners, or 'the framing of the environment for transactions'. The value of this term lies in the way it directs attention to the process of negotiating and agreeing the terms of an alliance relationship. Nor is it assumed that the outcome is all captured in the terms of a formal contract *per se*, which is signed at a particular point in time and supposed to define the relationship thereafter. In other words, 'contracting' may well continue after a formal alliance contract is signed and, as we shall see in the case of Sino-foreign alliances, the expectations of Western and non-Western partners can differ considerably on this point. Different expectations on this issue constitute one of the most significant threats to trust between the partners, because from the Western perspective they can readily be interpreted as signs of the other partner's bad faith on the fundamentals of the alliance.

Following the establishment of a strategic alliance, with the allocation of capital and other resources to it, there is a phase of implementation during which it is commissioned as a productive venture. During implementation, people are appointed, technology and systems installed, and operations commenced. Implementation is of crucial importance for the quality of co-operative relations within the alliance. The people appointed to work together may or may not possess the necessary technical competences for the alliance to succeed, and this is equally the case with their cultural competences. If these competences are lacking and, as a result, the alliance founders, the underlying calculus for the alliance can no longer remain valid. The systems which are installed are also very significant, particularly those for control and information reporting, because these can determine the quality of knowledge that is available to each partner. For example, if one partner's systems for accounting, marketing, operational and technical information reporting are installed in a joint venture, this adds to the quality of the knowledge available to that partner, but not necessarily to the other. The first partner enjoys a potential for cognitive trust to mature which may be denied to the other. Similarly, if the personnel appointed to work together within the alliance are insensitive to each other's cultures, the likelihood of their achieving a close co-operative relationship on an integrated basis will be diminished and the most that can achieved may be a sub-optimal segregation between spheres of activity and influence (cf. Child and Markóczy 1993, Tung 1993).

If difficulties such as these can be avoided or overcome, and if the alliance proves to be an economic success, it is likely to mature into an organization with an increasing sense of its own identity and culture. Unless the alliance is established for a one-off or temporary purpose only, or as a stepping-stone for one partner to absorb the other, the partners may well not place

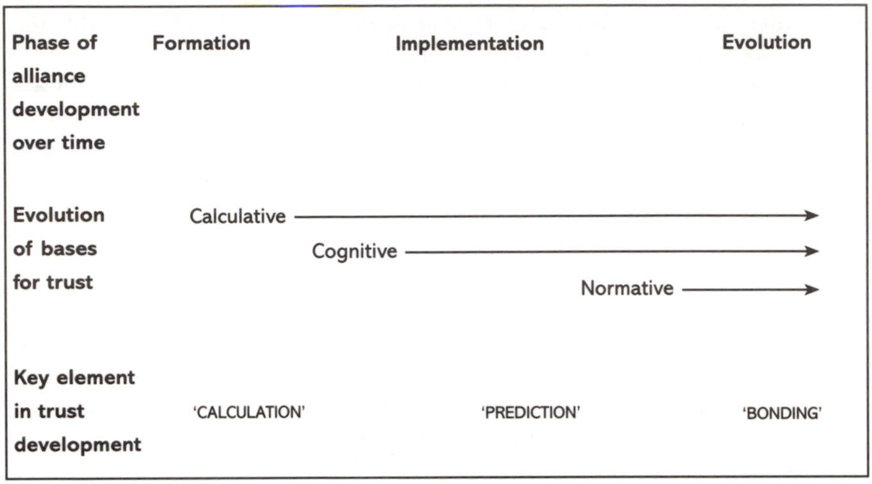

Phase of alliance development over time	Formation	Implementation	Evolution
Evolution of bases for trust	Calculative ———————————————————→		
		Cognitive ———————————————→	
			Normative ————————→
Key element in trust development	'CALCULATION'	'PREDICTION'	'BONDING'

FIG. 9.1. Phases of alliance development and the evolution of trust

any time limit upon its potential life. The very success of an alliance will tend to encourage the partner/parent companies to grant it an increasing measure of autonomy, and also provide the management of the alliance with the legitimacy to take its own decisions (Lyles and Reger 1993). This evolutionary process permits stable, on-going relationships to develop, relationships both between people in the partner organizations who have a responsibility for (or interest in) the alliance and between people working on an everyday basis in the alliance's own organization. They are in a position to accumulate knowledge about each other, and this tends to reinforce the relationship. Moreover, the success of the alliance in meeting partner interests also preserves that basis for their relationship which lies in calculation. As relationships develop over time within the context of a successful collaboration, so there is a natural tendency for those concerned to identify increasingly with one another's interests as well as for emotional ties to grow. In this way, 'bonding' can form between partners, which Faulkner (1995) has identified as being, in turn, a significant requirement for alliance success. Thus a virtuous cycle may be established, which reinforces both trust and the co-operation which it nurtures. This cycle can, of course, be broken and reversed, as we note shortly.

Figure 9.1 summarizes the co-incidence between strategic alliance development and the evolution of trust-based relationships, which has been analysed in this section. The figure draws upon the threefold distinction of calculative, cognitive, and normative-based trust.

It is important to make two further observations in connection with this analysis. First, in reality there will be only certain individuals relating across the boundaries of co-operating organizations. Their role in promoting trust between the partner organizations is therefore a key one, and the trust that can be said to exist between the organizations will to a large extent come down to the quality of mutual trust which exists between those individuals. This recalls that trust is actually an interpersonal phenomenon, upon which the quality of interorganizational relations is founded. The organizational members upon whom interorganizational co-operation depends can perhaps be best labelled 'trust guardians'. The contribution that these trust guardians make to interorganizational co-operation is likely to be a function of (a) the mutual trust they have developed, (b) the influence they enjoy within their respective organizations, and (c) their numbers in each organization.

It follows that if there is a frequent turnover of the personnel allocated by the partners to an alliance, the opportunities for developing trust-based co-operation between them will be diminished. Overseas tours of duty for the personnel of a foreign ISA partner are often limited in duration, especially when the other partner is located in a developing country with 'hardship' conditions attached. We shall see that this is a factor inhibiting the development of trust in Sino-foreign joint ventures, especially within the context of a local culture which attaches high value to transactions based upon personal relationships.

The second observation concerns the vulnerability of trust-based co-operation within strategic alliances. As noted earlier, alliances between firms are based on co-operation between partners whose interests do not usually wholly coincide and who, in the case of horizontal alliances, could become competitors at a future point in time. The multi-stage model of trust evolution points to the danger of collapse in an alliance relationship at any stage of its development if the previous bases of trust are withdrawn. In business relationships, given the financial expectations of owners and external stakeholders, bonding cannot sustain trust if one or both of the partners conclude that the calculative or cognitive basis of their co-operation has disappeared. Equally, if a problem arises in the basis for a higher level of trust development, such as the emergence of a personal antipathy, it may prove necessary to return to previous foundations for the relationship in order to rebuild it. For instance, if a personal dislike arises between two interorganizational trust guardians, it may still be possible to rescue the relationship between the organizations themselves through their leaders recognizing that it continues to retain a basis in mutual economic benefit. A hierarchy of foundations for trust and co-operation is, in effect, being posited here with calculative trust at the base, cognitive trust in the middle, and normative trust at the apex.

4. TRUST IN CHINESE SOCIETY

Trust in Chinese society presents a paradox. For it is a society in which trust-based relationships within defined local groups, especially the family, assume very considerable importance as a means to protect people against the high level of opportunism, and hence low trust, that prevails within the country as a whole. It provides a clear illustration of the argument that 'trust begins where rational prediction ends' (Lane 1997: 5), and that trust within a secure in-group becomes more important the lower the level of external rationality.

The historical sources of this low trust within Chinese society lie in the capriciousness of imperial rule, the chaos and exploitation which accompanied its periodic breakdown, the lack of clear ownership rights, and the Confucian injunction to place loyalty to one's family (especially the father) above that to society.

The government of imperial China has been described as 'a relatively small, highly centralized body that floated on a sea of isolated peasant communities' (Rodzinski 1984: 48). While the imperial bureaucracy did not normally extend down beyond district capitals, the state could nevertheless arbitrarily intervene in people's lives for financial or military purposes. As Fukuyama (1995: 87) notes, the Chinese state provided few social services in return for its demands despite the injunctions of Confucius concerning the obligations of the paternalistic Emperor:

In traditional China, there were no established property rights. Through much of Chinese history, taxation was highly arbitrary; the state subcontracted tax collection to local officials or tax farmers, who were free to set the level of taxation at whatever the local population could endure. Peasants could also be drafted arbitrarily for military duty or to work on public works projects.

The threat of disorder arose from a combination of natural and official capriciousness. For example, Seagrave, in his study of the overseas Chinese, notes how mass emigrations from South China were caused by invasion from the North, imperial repression and taxation, and natural calamities both local and in the North. The latter led to further pressures from a movement of population southwards. The result, as Seagrave put it, was that 'to the ordinary Chinese, . . . chaos is always just around the corner' (Seagrave 1995: 183).

The institutional environment in China has provided few guarantees against the betrayal of trust. Historically, the Chinese have not been protected by a legal system that was independent of the state and supreme in its own right. In the absence of a codified commercial law, merchants and producers were at the mercy of a system in which imperial officials and their acolytes could exercise arbitrary power through taxes, licensing fees, and restrictions on trade and travel. Even today, despite continued legal reform since 1979 which has begun to evolve a distinct body of legal rules and institutions, evidence suggests that the law in China remains 'a tool of state administration and always within close reach of the Chinese Communist Party' (Lubman 1995: 2). Thus little progress has been made in the effective ability of China's laws to provide a means of controlling official arbitrariness (ibid. 11).

The limited development, even today, of institutional guarantors for economic transactions in China means that economic actors within the system, both Chinese and foreign, face considerable complexity and hence uncertainty. In order to appreciate the nature of this complexity, and the context it creates for Sino-foreign business relationships, it is useful to refer to the distinction which Gell-Mann (1995) draws between two types of complexity. These are 'crude complexity' and 'effective complexity'.

Crude complexity is a function of the number of elements in a system and the number of connections between them. It is in these terms that most management and organization theorists have referred to 'complex' organizations and 'complex' environments. Crude complexity has been increasing in all societies along with the explosion of information and the differentiation of occupations, organizations, and countries themselves. Modern information sources and technologies now provide considerable assistance towards coping with this kind of complexity, which does not therefore in principle pose a major problem for relationships between firms. Effective complexity, by contrast, is a function of the irregularity and hence unpredictability of a system of elements and relationships. Some management theorists have referred to this type of complexity in terms of 'variability' or 'turbulence' in organizational environments. It is a much more potent source of uncertainty and poses a correspondingly greater degree of risk for those engaged in business relationships.

The Chinese environment embraces both types of complexity, but it is the considerable presence of effective complexity that generates potential problems for trust-based relationships. The existence of different business systems (state-controlled, collective and private, with different levels of sector marketization), many contrasting regions and generational differences are all aspects of China's crude complexity. The challenges they present for foreigners are those initially of understanding the phenomenon and then taking account of the additional complications it poses for decision-making. However, once recognized and understood, it is possible to assess their implications with reasonable certainty.

Other characteristics of the Chinese context, on the other hand, generate effective complexity in the system, and this poses far greater difficulties for those engaged in economic relationships. These include the close involvement of government agencies in business affairs, continuing political uncertainties, and the persistence of resource limitations. Governmental bodies are heavily involved in land use, labour administration, banking, and licensing. Laws and regulations are formulated centrally but administered locally, thus giving rise to ambiguity as to who is 'the government'. Another area of ambiguity is the ownership status of state-owned enterprises and the property rights the state enjoys over them. Despite the objectives of the economic reform, many state and collective enterprises are beholden to governmental bodies, especially for working capital and the enforcement of transactions. This dependence can extend to the joint ventures they form with multinational companies.

Areas of political uncertainty include the lack of transparency of many Chinese laws and/or their uncertain enforcement, as is the case with intellectual property rights. Local governmental agencies have powers to interpret regulations, issue licences and impose taxes, which furnish ample scope for negotiation and corruption. The way that agreements are interpreted can depend on the influence or autonomy that the Chinese partner enjoys with higher authorities. The signing of a formal contract does not guarantee the end of uncertainty or even the conclusion of negotiation. Murray (1994: 161) quotes a foreign businessman on this problem:

The political element cannot be ignored. You may open your business in an aura of rosy optimism and all seems to be going well. Then, you're back in Britain or the US or whatever, and suddenly it's becoming increasingly difficult to get anything out of your Chinese partner; communications break down; you don't really know what is going on and everything begins to get woolly and cloudy. The reason may be that the power the local guy had enjoyed previously has been rescinded. He no longer has the power to act as the centre pulls in the reins. He has to hedge and pull in his horns. No amount of waving contracts under his nose is going to make the slightest difference.

Moreover, the attitude and flexibility of government bodies can vary between different locations. At the time of writing, government policies towards foreign investing companies are becoming more directive, and it is known that in some sectors such as automotive it is the government's intention eventually to reduce China's reliance on co-operation with foreign companies. This generates uncertainty about the authorities' long-term intentions.

On the resource side, there continues to be a shortage of two key business resources, namely domestic working capital (much of it being administratively redirected to prop up ailing state-owned enterprises), and high quality, well-trained managers. When neither the availability of working capital nor the loyalty of key local managers can be taken for granted, significant elements of uncertainty are injected into the business environment. Infrastructural limitations, especially in the transportation of goods, add another source of uncertainty. These uncertainties increase the temptation to act opportunistically; for example, to renege on an employment or supply contract in order to take advantage of available economic rents.

The wide range of unethical behaviours which the Chinese categorize as 'corruption' not only create great uncertainty in business relationships, but also undermine the development of trust. The problem is recognized at the highest level. Premier Li Peng, addressing the National People's

Congress in March 1994, stated that the struggle against corruption 'is a matter of life and death for the nation' (quoted by McDonald 1995: 175). There are several specific practices which are quite common, and which are particularly inimical to the establishment of trust. One is product piracy, including the illegal use of their foreign partners' brand names by Chinese enterprises. The Chief Executive of a global US household goods company told the writer that this was the single greatest problem his firm faced in China. Another is embezzlement, a problem which has led many foreign companies to insist that they control the appointment of chief financial officers for their China joint ventures. A third practice, and probably the most common, is that of bribery. Bribery, of course, implies the threat of non-co-operation or even reneging on agreements if side-payments are not made.

The basic logic by which the Chinese economic system is ordered has idiosyncrasies which also engender uncertainty for foreign companies. The system is characterized by low levels of codification, so that transactions are subject to tacit and implicit conditions (Boisot and Child 1996). The interpretation of the terms of transacting, and reliability of transactions, depend on personalized criteria and understanding which can readily give rise both to a distortion of economic rationality and to corruption. The investment in cultural sensitivity required, and of time to develop the necessary relationships, are themselves not easy to ascertain in advance, and this adds yet further uncertainty. As noted, the law in this milieu has limited coverage and is itself subject to uncertain interpretation.

The combination of external arbitrariness and effective complexity, with the emphasis which Chinese Confucianism placed on filial loyalty and family relations, has led to the family becoming the primary locus of trust and protection against outside threat. As Redding (1990: 66) puts it:

The key feature [of trust in Chinese society] would appear to be that you trust your family absolutely, your friends and acquaintances to the degree that mutual dependence has been established and face invested in them. With everybody else you make no assumptions about their goodwill . . . To know your own motives well is, for the Chinese more than most, a warning about everybody else's.

As Redding goes on to note, connections between family and other units of shared identity are necessary for their survival, or indeed prosperity. These connections become strongly bonded through *guanxi*, and networks grow on this basis.

Thus specific trust-based relationships in China fall into two categories, and the basis for the trust is different within each of these categories. The first comprises the extended family, and to a lesser degree relationships stemming from a common formative experience in home town and school, all of which provide for group loyalty and shared identity. This trust is based upon blood and upbringing, and it often takes on fief-like qualities. The foundations of trust within these close social units are those of identification and affect. The Chinese family business, which culturally is the typical economic unit, exemplifies this form of trust-based governance of economic activity (Redding 1990).

The second category is the network, which can sometimes be quite extensive, taking on clan-like qualities (Boisot and Child 1996). Trust within Chinese networks is based on what the Chinese know as *guanxi*. *Guanxi* refers to the credit which a person or a group has with others, based on the giving of assistance or favours, or deriving from personal recommendations. It is significant within work units, and even more so for the development of interorganizational relations in which the actors have no other foundation on which to establish trust in a society where institutional guarantees and protection are weak. There is a risk involved in offering the favours through which it is hoped to build up *guanxi*, and trust within Chinese networks therefore has an important basis in calculus. The main guarantee against lack of reciprocity lies in the strong social norms by which the acceptance of favours places an obligation upon the recipient.

Trust-based relationships are particularly significant modes of economic transacting in China because of the weak institutional sanctions against reneging on commitments. Both shared social identity and *guanxi* can provide the foundations for long-standing relationships which govern business transactions and upon which transactional networks are built. To an important extent, transactions within the Chinese business system are governed by the relatively tacit norms and expectations which accompany these trust-based relationships, rather than by the more codified rules characteristic of transactions regulated either by hierarchical rules or by laws of contract applied to market dealings (Boisot and Child 1996). This is the case even within the ostensibly bureaucratic PRC state-owned enterprise, where key norms of conduct are implicit and where strong fief-like loyalties exist around key office-holders (Child 1994).

It is clearly not easy for a foreign company to enter into such relationships. It is virtually impossible to enter into the first category based on family or other groupings with a strong shared identity. It is also very difficult to gain acceptance as part of what are often long-established clan-like networks. This means that there are two main alternatives which a foreign firm can adopt in the attempt to cope with the high level of complexity and weak institutional context. Each implies that co-operative relationships between Chinese and foreign partners will be established on a different basis.

The first alternative is an attempt to 'reduce' complexity through imposing routines and standards upon business in China. This imposition is, in effect, an attempt to compensate for institutional support, and it may follow both external and internal routes. The external route includes measures such as lobbying foreign governments to pressure China into creating a more codified environment, especially via legislation and its effective enforcement, deploying big corporate guns to negotiate Chinese institutional tolerance of the foreign investor's intentions, and using the Chinese need for technology and finance as bargaining levers. The external route amounts to an attempt to enact the environment so as to create more favourable conditions for internal measures to reduce complexity. The internal route includes the importation of standardized systems (accounting, quality, production, HRM, and so forth) which enforce predictability onto Chinese behaviour and lock the China venture into the MNE's global network, the establishment of control over personnel selection so as to recruit employees, preferably young people, who are 'untainted' by Chinese work and institutional norms, and a reliance upon a combination of training and attractive rewards to mould Chinese workplace behaviour.

This approach relies on the rapid establishment of codified structures and systems, and those adopting it are prepared to experience short-term costs in the process. For it tends to involve a heavy presence of expatriates in the early life of the Chinese affiliate and there can be considerable conflict as the foreign parent company's structures and practices are applied. The intention is to replace expatriates with 'home-grown' Chinese managers who can run and accept foreign systems as soon as they can be found and trained. There is some doubt, however, whether the early replacement of expatriates is going to be possible under this approach. One of the reasons for this is that the approach bases co-operative relationships between the Chinese and foreign parties almost entirely upon calculation. As such it is likely to engender only the most basic level of trust and co-operation between the partners; we may call this the 'low trust option'. The primary basis of the relationship lies in the promise of favourable rewards to the Chinese partner, in terms of dividends, employment, and technology transfer, and to individual Chinese employees in terms of high levels of personal income. There is no doubt that this buys co-operation, but only up to a point and not on a basis of a commitment to the joint enterprise. It is not surprising therefore that many foreign managers complain about their partners' instrumental, even underhand, attitude towards the protection of resources such as technology transfer and brand equity, as well as about the difficulty of retaining good Chinese managers.

The second approach to dealing with the complexity of the Chinese system is one of using local Chinese capabilities to 'absorb' it. Again, there are both external and internal routes to doing this. The external one includes the selection of Chinese partners who have institutional influence, and allowing them to handle the external complexity which derives mainly from the bureaucracy and its manifestations of arbitrary behaviour. The internal route may include several measures. First, an involvement of Chinese managers in the decision processes of joint ventures or subsidiaries, and appealing to the venture's collective identity in so doing. Second, adapting procedures to suit the local context, though retaining reporting systems which are compatible with those of the foreign investor. Third, developing long-term relationships through frequent contact between Chinese and foreign board members, a planned programme of visits between foreign and Chinese executives, relatively lengthy assignments of foreign executives to China joint ventures, and emphasizing the need for cultural sensitivity.

This second approach attempts to absorb complexity in the Chinese context by giving primacy to establishing a system of relationships both within and outside the business venture. It is prepared for this to take some time to develop (a matter of years rather than months). In terms of Figure 9.1 above, this policy is one directed at placing co-operation on a more extensive basis than mere calculation. It involves the development of both mutual cognition (knowledge and understanding) and normative identification as supports for trust between the partners and their people. We may therefore term this 'the high-trust option'. It is an approach which appears to lay a sounder basis for Sino-foreign joint-venture development, especially when the foreign partner does not possess overwhelming technological, brand, or financial advantages (i.e. when its power to bargain on the basis of offering a favourable calculus is limited). This conclusion is in line with that of research into joint ventures in other developing countries with a low institutional support for trust (Beamish 1988).

5. THE PROBLEMATIC OF TRUST FOR SINO-FOREIGN JOINT VENTURES

Two broad options have been identified for addressing the high level of 'effective complexity' in the mainland Chinese environment. One involves the attempt to establish co-operation with local partners primarily on the basis of calculation and foreign control. The other involves an attempt to deepen the co-operation further, by building it upon a more developed level of mutual trust. This section explores these two broad options further, drawing upon case-study experience, and using the analytical framework of alliance development and trust evolution presented earlier (see Fig. 9.1).

Two sources of information are utilized. First, the author and his colleagues have over the past six years conducted several studies into the management of Sino-foreign joint ventures, and there is work still in progress (Child *et al.* 1990, Child 1994; Child, Yan, and Lu 1997; Lu, Child, and Yan 1997). While this research has not been directed explicitly at the issue of trust, it has been in part concerned with the quality of Sino-foreign

partner relationships. Second, other cases and accounts of experience provide valuable evidence on which to draw (e.g. De Keijzer 1992, Newman
1992, Murray 1994, Yan and Gray 1994, 1996).

5.1 The Low-Trust Option

The low-trust option for foreign joint-venture partners in China is to use
their financial and technological advantage to reduce dependence on the
Chinese partner. This means securing management control of the joint
venture and dealing with key external institutional bodies directly. It is a
policy currently being pursued by many Western multinationals and is,
indeed, advocated by leading consulting organizations such as McKinsey's.
Thus, Meier and his colleagues—in McKinsey's Hong Kong office—have
argued that, given its size and reputation, the multinational is in a better
position than its local partner to deal directly with 'the complex, often
confusing web of government entities that approve and facilitate business
development—especially in highly regulated sectors such as telecommunications and energy' (Meier, Perez, and Woetzel 1995: 21). A strong, co-
ordinated approach by the foreign company will, in their opinion, reduce
the risk of the Chinese authorities playing off one of its business units
against another. Moreover, most Chinese partners suffer severe financial,
managerial, and technological disadvantages. This has led many multinationals to reconsider their role and adopt a more hands-on approach to joint
venture management: 'to play a more active role in JV management, MNCs
are seeking overt equity control, deploying expatriates in key venture management positions, and controlling financial and information systems
directly' (ibid. 27).

In joint ventures where the foreign partner contributes most of the key
resources, has built a greenfield facility rather than relying on its partner,
and has its own influence with governmental authorities, the level of dependence on the local Chinese partner can be quite low. As a result, it does
not need to place more than a limited amount of trust in that partner. In
such cases, taking on a local partner is more a necessary key to official
approval of entry to the Chinese market than to anything else. In high-
technology sectors, foreign firms have already secured dominant positions
vis-à-vis domestic competitors, and their reliance on local partners for
tangible or intangible resources has become relatively small. For example,
by early 1996 major multinationals, most of them working through joint
ventures, had already secured 80 per cent of car sales, 90 per cent of PC
sales, and almost 100 per cent of telecom equipment sales within China
(*Business Week* 1996).

A joint-venture co-operation of this kind is asymmetrical in terms of the
partners' power and control (cf. Hardy and Phillips 1997). As such it involves greater commitment of trust on the Chinese side than on the foreign

side. There has been an unmistakable trend over the past ten years or so towards an increase of joint-venture equity share and assumption of managerial control by foreign partners (Child, Yan, and Lu 1997). This has amounted to a relinquishing of power by the Chinese partner in return for evidence of the foreign partner's trustworthiness. Several factors contribute to the Chinese partner's willingness to accept an asymmetrical co-operative relationship. All depend on the generation of confidence that the foreign partner will deliver on the explicit and implicit calculus underlying the relationship.

One factor is the foreign company's reputation, based on its global scope and size, its history and the image which attaches to its name. Most multinationals clearly enjoy a high reputation on these grounds. This reduces any concern that the foreign company may be a 'fly-by-night' partner, that it might renege on its commitments, or become bankrupt. Multinational enterprises were generally introduced to their first Chinese partners by government ministries and sometimes senior Chinese politicians, and this added to the confidence in their reliability. Once established in China, making an obvious contribution to the country's economic and technological development, and having demonstrated its ability to generate profits, a foreign multinational's reputation becomes indisputable, and such high-level introductions are no longer a necessary basis for establishing new joint ventures.

Another factor which adds to a Chinese partner's willingness to yield managerial control to the foreign partner is its belief in the latter's competence. This competence is most clearly manifested in technology and managerial expertise, and the transfer of these capabilities is the main rationale for the Chinese government to favour the linking of inward FDI to the joint-venture form. It has become evident that the influence enjoyed by the foreign partner in the operation of Sino-foreign joint ventures results significantly from the tangible evidence of its competence through the continuing provision of resources such as know-how, specialist services and training over and above what is contractually laid down (Child, Yan, and Lu 1997). This influence derives directly from the foreign partner's competence as well as from the goodwill and commitment to the partnership that it indicates.

A third element in the calculus for the Chinese partner, which depends on the first two, is the prospect of sharing in a favourable profit stream. Local partners have generally benefited financially from their joint ventures and, in so far as the majority of them, as state- or collectively-owned enterprises, are beholden to higher governmental authorities, this has elicited official acquiescence in foreign business leadership as well. Indeed, the position has sometimes been reached in which the foreign partner has totally bought out an ailing state enterprise partner, so relieving the relevant government authority of a financial and social burden.

The 'low-trust' option thus provides for an acceptance by Chinese partners of foreign leadership on the basis of a calculus which takes account of reputation, competence, and financial return. Foreign investing companies may not, however, perceive that a comparable calculation can be made with respect to their local partners, and this is a prime motivation for their assumption of increasing control. Even if a co-operative relationship is successfully sustained on this basis, it may carry forward sufficient underlying cultural tension to prevent the further development of trust. One of the complaints that many Chinese joint venture managers have made to the writer and his colleagues is that they are excluded from sharing in business and technical information by their foreign counterparts, thus reducing the chances that the shared knowledge-base for cognitive trust will develop. They also complain that, with short-term expatriate assignments, it is very difficult to get to know foreign managers well, let alone to develop a social relationship with them which could lead to bonding. For their part, most foreign managers in China live in their own special housing areas and do not socialize with their Chinese colleagues.

It is quite usual in joint ventures where the foreign partner pursues the low-trust option, and hence opts to compensate through exercising strong control, to find that it also attempts to suppress culturally rooted Chinese norms. This makes it even more difficult for trust between the partners to develop beyond the calculative stage. Foreign multinational partners do not, for instance, normally consider *guanxi* and face-saving to be acceptable norms of business practice. Within joint ventures the exercise of *guanxi* may require favouritism in the selection of new employees or in the allocation of contracts for supplies, and it may embrace what foreigners regard as corruption. Foreign managers generally see their role as being to introduce management expertise into China joint ventures, which does not allow for informal local practices such as these. Some Western management practices can themselves make for difficulties in establishing relationships with Chinese partners or their staff. These include confrontation during meetings (leading to loss of face by Chinese participants) and insistence on Chinese managers assuming individual responsibility for actions which exert pressures on Chinese staff.

5.2 The High-Trust Option

The high-trust option for foreign investors in China is to rely on the Chinese partner to cope with significant aspects of the complex environment, be they relations with governmental authorities, access to the market, or management of the workforce. The foreign company may not have the reputation, internationally known brand or technology, or the resources to take on such activities without local support. This means that it depends heavily on finding the right Chinese partner whom it can trust to deliver these requirements.

The first stage of a high-trust strategy by the foreign partner therefore requires a mutually acceptable calculus for the co-operative relationship to be established. If this cannot be reached or later fails, the co-operation will almost certainly be terminated. For unlike the low-trust option, there is really no alternative open to the foreign partner because its degree of dependence rules out going it alone or relegating the Chinese partner to a subsidiary role. If, on the other hand, the requirements for the calculative stage can be met, the high involvement of the Chinese partner makes it quite probable that the relationship can move onto a deeper foundation. In other words, the high-trust strategy will accord a significant role in joint-venture policy-making, as well as operational management, to the Chinese partner, and this may well be substantiated by that partner having an equal or even majority share in the joint-venture equity.

A medium-size British company, which established a joint venture in Shanghai in 1995, illustrates the threat to the co-operation which arises if the Chinese partner cannot satisfy the calculative criteria necessary in the first stage of even a high-trust strategy. The groundwork for this strategy was laid down by the UK company's chief executive who, prior to seeking a joint venture, had spent ten years regularly visiting China to trade and to assess the market, sources of supply, and so forth. He had been trading in the East Asia region for some twenty years before that. He was therefore by no means unfamiliar with Chinese business or cultural norms. Moreover, he investigated five potential partners before deciding on the one in Shanghai. One of his main considerations in making that choice was the quality of the Chinese management and the confidence it inspired in him. As he said, 'I liked the idea of having a strong partner [and] of having someone as a partner who wasn't in the business that we were in because then he didn't come with any baggage or any prejudices. . . .' This sense of confidence was particularly important because this was the first foreign joint venture (as opposed to trading relationship) that his company has undertaken. In fact, by the close of the negotiations, the UK chief executive had established a good personal relationship with the director of the Chinese enterprise. Despite its partner's lack of involvement in manufacturing, it was a municipal government customer for the UK company's products, and the British understanding was that in entering the joint venture it would depend heavily on the Chinese partner, not only to deliver basic facilities and handle relations with the city authorities but also introduce customers to it.

Things started to go wrong when the joint venture entered its implementation phase. There were several reasons for this, but a major factor lay in the inability of the Chinese partner to meet the calculative expectations of the British company. The partner met these very well in terms of the quality of the site and building that it secured for the joint venture. However, the UK company had also expected its Chinese partner to deliver customers to the joint venture through its connections in the Shanghai region. This is an expectation which puzzles the observer because the partner had entered the joint venture primarily as a supplier of land and factory premises, with no experience of the sector. In the event, it failed to deliver the customers. Further misunderstandings arose because of the Chinese partner's inexperience in the sector. For example, the British-appointed joint-venture general manager (who had previously been the company's production manager with no prior experience of working abroad) expressed a complete loss of trust in his counterpart (the Chinese deputy general manager) because the latter had given him incorrect information as to local wage rates. The British manager saw this as a deliberate deception in order to wrest unnecessarily high-wage payments from the joint venture, whereas it probably arose because the local partner did not have any better information.

There was insufficient reciprocal partner competence built into the relationship to create a sense of trustworthiness in the foreign general manager's eyes. The situation was exacerbated by his own lack of relevant cultural experience, his inability to speak Chinese, and the ghetto mentality which he consequently developed. As the joint venture continued to perform well below capacity, having only overseas orders diverted to it by its UK parent company to work on, pressures from both partners mounted on its general manager. To make matters worse, his own UK boss continued to visit the director of the Chinese parent organization. These visits sustained a close relationship at this higher level, which served to imply that problems lower down were the personal fault of the general manager. They also tended to encourage a by-passing of his authority by Chinese joint-venture managers who perceived that they could get a response more to their liking by channelling issues up to the UK partner's chief executive via their own external Chinese hierarchy rather than through the joint venture's. This, of course, further reduced the trust which the foreign general manager could place in his Chinese colleagues, since he perceived that they were in this manner attempting to undermine his authority.

There are, on the other hand, examples of successful high-trust strategies among Sino-foreign joint ventures. One of the earliest joint ventures in the field of telecommunications was formed in the 1980s between a European and a Chinese state-owned enterprise, with the foreign partner taking a minority equity share. The foreign partner was highly dependent on its counterpart for marketing, with most of the joint venture's output being purchased by municipal and other PTT bodies. The Chinese partner was similarly dependent upon the advanced technology brought to the joint venture by the foreign company. This complementarity provided the basis for an effective economic calculus, providing for a 'win-win' situation, especially as the joint venture was the first foreign entry into the Chinese market. After an initial start-up period, the joint venture has been consistently profitable and expanded to become the fifth largest Sino-foreign joint venture, by sales, in 1996. It is regularly cited by the Chinese authorities as a model of its kind. It went on to establish a further joint venture with a local partner which took a majority equity share, and which now supplies it with components. The first joint venture has a foreign general manager but all the other senior managers are Chinese. The offspring joint venture is under entirely Chinese management with the exception of one joint deputy general manager.

The original joint venture was initially established on the basis of a favourable calculus. This calculus was reached after a ten-year period of very thorough familiarization and search by the foreign partner. Since its formation, the relationship has progressively deepened on the basis of open communication with, and participation by, the Chinese partner and managers. The Chinese authorities have for their part become increasingly open to the foreign side and supportive of the joint venture. Mutual confidence has thus developed through the sharing of knowledge. Moreover, the joint venture's foreign general managers have had relatively long contracts and so been able to develop personal relationships both with their Chinese joint-venture colleagues, and also with people from the Chinese partner and the PTT ministry officials at local and central levels to whom the partner reports. The level of trust that has been achieved in this case is regarded as exemplary by the Chinese authorities. That trust is reinforced by this normative approval as well as by the joint venture's economic success.

Another example of a successful high-trust strategy is provided by a major glass-manufacturing joint venture. This was established after several years of negotiation. The two foreign partners took up a 25 per cent equity share (the minimum permitted by Chinese joint-venture regulations), though only one was an active partner. The active foreign partner supplied its advanced glass-making technology on a royalty basis; it also provided the first joint-venture general manager and a considerable amount of technical and managerial training. The Chinese partner provided the rest of the management, and the venture is today wholly Chinese-managed. The initial calculus was that the active foreign partner would benefit from technology transfer with minimum investment risk exposure, while relying on the main Chinese partner to develop the market. Since the technology royalty was based on sales, there would be a direct gain from market development. The Chinese partners, who were a mix of government investment trust, construction industry bureau and state enterprise, would through the joint venture promote the technological upgrading of the domestic glass industry and benefit financially from the construction boom in their country.

The main foreign and Chinese partners have maintained close relations, which were augmented by extensive training provided by the foreign side. The foreign partner has never sought to dominate the joint venture and, when the first foreign general manger had completed his term of office, he was succeeded by the then Chinese deputy general manager who continues to head the joint venture. The Chinese management team have been highly successful in developing both the domestic Chinese market as well as sales in other East Asian markets which the foreign company had considered too difficult to enter. The partners' senior managers enjoy a high level of mutual respect, a symbol of which is the award of a medal to the first (foreign) general manager by the local municipality on his retirement in 1996. Another indication of the trust which has developed is the fact that this joint venture has joined its foreign parent in forming further joint ventures in China. The relationship has deepened, on a knowledge-sharing basis, through the continued technological support offered by the foreign partner and through the full access to the joint venture which the majority Chinese partners have always accorded to it. It has also become highly personalized over the course of some ten years, through a close bond between the original general manager and his then deputy, who are also directors of the joint venture. Interestingly, this bond developed despite the fact that neither has a good command of the other's language.

Other successful high-trust strategies pursued in Sino-foreign joint ventures are now recorded in the literature. Two examples are the Nantong Cellulose Fibers Company (Newman 1992) and the Guangzhou M.C. Packing Group (Shenkar and Nyaw 1994). In both cases, the foreign side held a minority equity share and had to enter into a considerable commitment of trust in their local partners. The outstanding success of both joint ventures has been largely attributed to the quality of co-operation between the partners (see also Yan and Gray 1996). 'The relationship between the partners had to move from suspicious bargaining to a mutual concern with finding practical ways to cooperate that would assure the economic soundness of the new venture' (Newman 1992: p. ix); 'Key factors for success include . . . above all, cooperation between foreign and Chinese partners' (Shenkar and Nyaw 1994: 281)

Several factors appear to favour success in a high-trust strategy. It is extremely important to get the basic calculus right, through careful planning. This planning takes time and thus provides an opportunity for a degree of mutual confidence and respect to develop between the main negotiators. Even so, as Newman argues, it may be necessary for 'boundary-spanners' with experience of both cultures and institutional systems to facilitate the process and remove blockages. In the case of Sino-foreign joint ventures, two other features may be required to realize the calculus. First, the partners must possess the competence to deliver on their promises. Second, the support of the relevant government authorities is generally essential in an institutional environment such as China where government agencies retain considerable powers over the conditions of doing business, including the granting of licences.[4]

When the joint venture moves into its implementation stage and evolves from that, open communication, a willingness to consider mutual interests, and close relations between key managers in the partner companies all appear essential for the quality of co-operation to take on elements of cognitive and then normative trust. These relationships must, in China, embrace key actors in external institutional bodies. Whereas foreign companies taking the low-trust option may opt to cultivate these external relations directly themselves, a high-trust strategy will work through and with the Chinese partners on this count. Another supporting factor which has been found to be significant is the willingness of the foreign partner to demonstrate a long-term commitment to the joint venture, and to the Chinese partner, through a continuing provision of resources on non-contractual terms.

Although we have adopted a contingency approach in suggesting that preference for one or other of the two trust options may derive from the balance and nature of inter-partner dependencies, this should not be taken to imply that differences or inequalities in partner competences and resources cannot be reduced through mutual co-operation and learning, nor that these will necessarily inhibit the development of high trust on both sides. The analysis summarized in Figure 9.1 implies that, so long as a successful calculative basis for co-operation can be maintained, trust between the partners in an ISA can build further upon a growing sharing of cognitions and perhaps upon the development of normative and affective bonding.

Moreover, after the successful implementation of a trustful alliance, future projects between the same partners are likely to be greatly facilitated. In view of the fact that smaller projects are generally easier to implement, and involve less risky sunk investment, the strategy of 'begin gradually' (Smitka 1994: 98) with a small project before committing to bigger ones recommends itself as a path towards building co-operation soundly on the basis of growing trust.

In the long run it is the high-trust strategy that will probably secure a firmer basis for business co-operation in the Chinese context. Enlisting as it does the active co-operation of both partners, this option is more aligned with China's fundamental policy objectives of developing local technological and managerial capabilities, and with foreign companies' objectives of learning how best to produce and market in China. Working as it does through Chinese networks and longer-term relationships, the high-trust strategy is also more in tune with underlying Chinese cultural preferences. While a low-trust strategy may offer superior economic returns to the partners in the shorter term, it may seriously impede the development of the Chinese partner's business and managerial acumen on which a reversal of the policy in the longer term will depend.

NOTES

1. See the Introduction to this book for a discussion of the meanings which have been attached to the concept of 'trust'. Some of these will be incorporated into the analysis presented in this chapter.
2. These percentages are inflated by the fact that some alliance 'failures' are not necessarily to be judged as such; for instance, when the partners agree to part amicably or when one partner agrees to its share being bought out by the other.
3. The notion of 'strategic fit' refers to the extent to which the alliance partners have complementary objectives for entering into an alliance and can provide complementary resources to that alliance.
4. The failure in 1989 of the $US256 m. joint venture Ramada Renaissance Hotel in Guilin was largely due to a lack of support from the local government which in turn undermined the commitment of the Chinese partners to the project.

REFERENCES

Beamish, P. W. (1988), *Multinational Joint Ventures in Developing Countries*. London: Routledge.

Bleeke, J. and Ernst, D. (1993) (eds.), *Collaborating to Compete*. New York: Wiley.

Boisot, M. and Child, J. (1996), 'From Fiefs to Clans and Network Capitalism: Explaining China's Emerging Economic Order', *Administrative Science Quarterly*, 41: 600–28.

Borys, B. and Jemison, D. B. (1989), 'Hybrid Arrangements as Strategic Alliances: Theoretical Issues in Organizational Combinations', *Academy of Management Review*, 14: 234–49.

Brenkert, G. G. (1997), 'Trust, Morality and International Business', in C. Lane and

R. Bachmann (eds.), *Trust Within and Between Organizations*. Oxford: Oxford University Press.

Business Week (1996), 'Global Tremors from an Unruly Giant', 4 Mar., 1–5.

Child, J. (1994), *Management in China during the Age of Reform*. Cambridge: Cambridge University Press.

——and Markóczy, L. (1993), 'Host-Country Managerial Behaviour and Learning in Chinese and Hungarian Joint Ventures', *Journal of Management Studies*, 30: 611–31.

——Yan, Y., and Lu, Y. (1997), 'Ownership and Control in Sino-Foreign Joint Ventures', in P. W. Beamish and J. P. Killing (eds.), *Cooperative Strategies: Asia Pacific Perspectives*. San Francisco: New Lexington Press, 181–225.

——Boisot, M., Zhaoxi, L., Ireland, J., and Watts, J. (1990), *The Management of Equity Joint Ventures in China*. Beijing: China-European Community Management Institute.

Chiles, T. H. and McMackin, J. F. (1996), 'Integrating Variable Risk Preferences, Trust, and Transaction Cost Economics', *Academy of Management Review*, 21: 73–99.

Creed, W. E. D. and Miles, R. E. (1996), 'Trust in Organizations: A Conceptual Framework Linking Organizational Forms, Managerial Philosophies, and the Opportunity Costs of Controls', in Kramer and Tyler (eds.), *Trust in Organizations*, 16–38.

De Keijzer, A. J. (1992), *China Business Strategies for the 1990s*. Berkeley: Pacific View Press.

Faulkner, D. O. (1995), *International Strategic Alliances: Co-operating to Compete*. London: McGraw-Hill.

Fukuyama, F. (1995), *Trust: The Social Virtues and the Creation of Prosperity*. London: Hamish Hamilton.

Gambetta, D. (1988), 'Can We Trust Trust?' in D. Gambetta (ed.), *Trust: Making and Breaking Cooperative Relations*. Oxford: Blackwell, 213–37.

Gell-Mann, M. (1995), *The Quark and the Jaguar: Adventures in the Simple and the Complex*. London: Abacus.

Geringer, J. M. (1991), 'Strategic Determinants of Partner Selection Criteria in International Joint Ventures', *Journal of International Business Studies*, 22: 41–62.

Hamel, G. (1991), 'Competition for Competence and Inter-Partner Learning within International Strategic Alliances', *Strategic Management Journal*, 12: 83–103.

Hardy, C., Phillips, N., and Lawrence, T. (1997), 'Overcoming Illusions of Trust: Toward a Communicative Theory of Trust and Power', in C. Lane and R. Bachmann (eds.), *Trust Within and Between Organizations*. Oxford: Oxford University Press.

Kramer, R. M. and Tyler, T. R. (1996) (eds.), *Trust in Organizations: Frontiers of Theory and Research*. Thousand Oaks, Calif.: Sage.

Lane, C. (forthcoming), 'Introduction', in C. Lane and R. Bachmann (eds.), *Trust Within and Between Organizations*. Oxford: Oxford University Press.

——and Bachmann, R. (1996), 'The Social Constitution of Trust: Supplier Relations in Britain and Germany', *Organization Studies*, 17: 365–95.

Lewicki, R. J. and Bunker, B. B. (1996), 'Developing and Maintaining Trust in Work Relationships', in Kramer and Tyler (eds.), *Trust in Organizations*, 114–39.

Lorange, P. and Roos, J. (1992), *Strategic Alliances: Formation, Implementation, and Evolution.* Oxford: Blackwell.

Lu, Y., Child, J., and Yan, Y. (1997), 'Adventuring in New Terrain: Managing International Joint Ventures in China', *Advances in Chinese Industrial Studies*, 5: 103–23.

Lubman, S. (1995), 'Introduction: The Future of Chinese Law', *China Quarterly*, 141 (Special Issue on 'China's Legal Reform'), 1–21.

Lyles, M. A. and Reger, R. K. (1993), 'Managing for Autonomy in Joint Ventures: A Longitudinal Study of Upward Influence', *Journal of Management Studies*, 30: 383–404.

McAllister, D. J. (1995), 'Affect- and Cognition-based Trust as Foundations for Interpersonal Cooperation in Organizations', *Academy of Management Journal*, 38: 24–59.

McDonald, G. (1995), 'Business Ethics in China', in H. Davies (ed.), *China Business: Context and Issues.* Hong Kong: Longman, 170–89.

Meier, J., Perez, J., and Woetzel, J. R. (1995), 'Solving the Puzzle: MNCs in China', *McKinsey Quarterly*, 2: 20–33.

Möllering, G. (1997), 'The Influence of Cultural Differences on the Establishment of Trust between Partners in International Cooperation', unpub. paper, Judge Institute of Management Studies, University of Cambridge, Jan.

Murray, G. (1994), *Doing Business in China.* Folkestone, Kent: China Library.

Newman, W. H. (1992), *Birth of a Successful Joint Venture.* New York: University Press of America.

Redding, S. G. (1990), *The Spirit of Chinese Capitalism.* Berlin: De Gruyter.

Ring, P. S. and van de Ven, A. H. (1994), 'Developmental Processes of Cooperative Interorganizational Relationships', *Academy of Management Review*, 19: 90–118.

Rodzinski, W. (1984), *The Walled Kingdom.* London: Fontana.

Root, F. R. (1994), *Entry Strategies for International Markets.* New York: Lexington Books, rev. edn.

Seagrave, S. (1995), *Lords of the Rim.* London: Bantam Press.

Shenkar, O. and Nyaw, M.-K. (1994), 'How to Run a Successful Joint Venture in China', *Advances in Chinese Industrial Studies*, 4: 273–83.

Smith, K. G., Carroll, S. J., and Ashford, S. J. (1995), 'Intra- and Interorganizational Cooperation: Toward a Research Agenda', *Academy of Management Journal*, 38: 7–23.

Smitka, M. J. (1994), 'Contracting without Contracts', in S. B. Sitkin, B. Sim, and R. J. Bies (eds.), *The Legalistic Organization.* London: Sage, 91–108.

Spekman, R. E., Lynn I. A., MacAvoy, T. C., and Forbes, T. III. (1996), 'Creating Strategic Alliances which Endure', *Long Range Planning*, 29: 346–57.

Tung, R. L. (1993), 'Managing Cross-National and Intra-National Diversity', *Human Resource Management*, 32: 461–77.

United Nations Conference on Trade and Development (UNCTAD) (1997), *World Investment Report 1997.* New York: United Nations.

Yan, A. and Gray, B. (1994), 'Bargaining Power, Management Control, and Performance in United States–China Joint Ventures: A Comparative Case Study', *Academy of Management Journal*, 37: 1478–517.

————(1996), 'Linking Management Control and Interpartner Relationships with Performance in US–Chinese Joint Ventures', in J. Child and Y. Lu (eds.), *Management Issues in China: International Enterprises*. London: Routledge, 106–27.

Zucker, L. G. (1986), 'Production of Trust: Institutional Sources of Economic Structure, 1840–1920', *Research in Organizational Behavior*, 8: 53–111.

10

*Trust, Morality, and International Business**
GEORGE G. BRENKERT

1. INTRODUCTION

The expanding globalization of business brings with it the increased importance of answers to a host of crucial moral issues. We need solutions to questions concerning when workers in developing nations are being exploited, which dangerous products should not be shipped across national borders to be sold, and when the offer of cash or gifts amounts to bribes by members of another society. Ethical guidance is needed for the managers of multinationals concerning transfer pricing, the use of child labour, and attempts to develop economically people living in tribal conditions. And moral direction is required for those considering the development of large industrial plants, electrical plants, dams, etc. in developing nations.

However, such solutions and guidance will be of little value if those who propose them do not take into account the relations of trust (and distrust) which exist between individuals and firms doing international business. Though the role of trust has been examined recently from a number of directions, e.g. its role in the production of national prosperity (Fukuyama 1995); in competitive advantage (Barney and Hansen 1994; Jones 1995); and even as part of morality itself (Hosmer 1995), it has not, as far as I know, been considered in the context of the moral issues which arise between participants in the globalization of business. The following chapter seeks to redress this condition. It maintains that trust is one of the important background conditions for answers to moral problems of international business. As such, the central aim of this chapter is to spell out the nature and conditions surrounding trust, as well as some of the obstacles to the formation of trust between international agents. More generally, this paper is an exploration of trust and its relation to morality on the international level between commercial agents.

Accordingly, this chapter begins by briefly identifying several different senses of trust that are invoked in the literature relevant to international business and ethics. It argues that only one of these senses of trust is appropriate for issues of business ethics. Next it identifies three morally crucial contexts in which trust plays different roles in business relationships.

* I am indebted to the comments of Ken Alpern, Reinhard Bachmann, Robbin Derry, John Dienhart, Daryl Koehn, and Christel Lane on earlier versions of this chapter.

These different kinds of trusting relationships are essential to moral business. Trust, in this sense, is a necessary condition for an international business morality. This is not surprising. In the international, as well as the national and local, setting 'conditions of trust sustain the *contexts* in which moral principles achieve their concrete embodiment' (King 1988: 475).

I then specify several conditions for each kind of trust and note some difficulties which arise for the development of trust within international contexts. These difficulties must be met by a variety of responses, which are only briefly referred to here. The chapter proceeds to identify morally important features of trust and some of the implications of these features for an international business morality. This leads to the final interesting consequence that by focusing on trust an international business ethics might be developed from the bottom up, rather than imposed from the top down. This could have welcome implications both for business and an international business ethics.

2. THE NATURE OF TRUST

At the outset it is appropriate to note several different understandings of trust which have been used in the literature. They may be characterized as the *Attitudinal*, *Predictability*, and *Voluntarist* senses of 'trust'.

The *Attitudinal* understanding of 'trust' is used in a wide variety of discussions. It is captured by such statements as the following: 'Trust is the mutual confidence that no party to an exchange will exploit another's vulnerabilities' (Sabel 1993: 1133); and trust is 'a relatively informed attitude or propensity to allow oneself and perhaps others to be vulnerable to harm in the interest of some perceived greater good' (Michalos 1990: 619). Finally, trust has also been conceptualized as 'the willingness of a party to be vulnerable to the actions of another party based on the expectation that the other will perform a particular action important to the trustor, irrespective of the ability to monitor or control that other party' (Mayer, Davis, and Schoorman 1995: 712). On this *Attitudinal* view, trust is not simply a belief or cognitive state. Rather it involves an attitude, disposition, or inclination to act in certain ways in light of various beliefs one has both about oneself and others. Typically these beliefs concern one's own vulnerability and the restraint the trusted agent is prepared to exercise not to take advantage of that vulnerability.

The *Predictability* view claims that 'trust' is to be interpreted as 'the extent to which one person can expect predictability in the other's behavior in terms of what is "normally" expected of a person acting in good faith' (Gabarro 1978: 294). Similarly, Gordon Tullock has suggested that 'trust' means 'being able to predict accurately the behavior of the person trusted' (Held 1968: 156; emphasis deleted). Finally, Dasgupta uses 'trust' in 'the sense of correct expectations about the *actions* of other people that have a bearing on one's own choice of action when that action must be chosen before one can *monitor* the actions of those others' (Dasgupta 1988: 51).

On this view, trust is simply a belief that one person has about another. Sometimes this is formulated in terms of an ability to predict certain behaviours. At other times, it is developed in terms of expectations one might have about the predictability of others' behaviour. Of course, expectations might be viewed as a kind of attitude or disposition one has. But the emphasis here is on the predictability of the behaviour of someone else. When Dasgupta speaks of the correct expectations about the actions of others, there appears to be little emphasis on attitudes or dispositions. This is compatible with beliefs that one party has about the actions of other parties.

The *Voluntarist* sense of 'trust' is less frequently held, but has received prominent defence. It is found in such statements as: 'To trust another is to voluntarily make oneself vulnerable with respect to some good, having been led to believe by the other's actions toward one that no loss or harm will come to one as a result' (Thomas 1989: 181). Annette Baier suggests that 'trust . . . is letting other persons (natural or artificial, such as firms, nations, etc.) take care of something the truster cares about, where such "caring for" involves some exercise of discretionary powers' (Baier 1995: 105). Baier notes that this model of trust is based on an 'entrusting' view from Locke (Baier 1995: 101). Similarly, D. O. Thomas has claimed that 'trust involves commissioning a person to do something, investing them with a charge or a responsibility' (Thomas 1978: 91).

On the *Voluntarist* view, trust involves various actions voluntarily or freely undertaken whereby one places oneself, or what one cares about, within the powers of another who, but for their good will, might impose harm upon oneself or those things one values. Trust here consists not in a prediction or an attitude that one person has towards others, but rather in the voluntary action of placing oneself in the hands of another. Baier maintains that such an account of trust is desirable since it may be applied not simply to articulate and equal adults, but may also be applied to individuals who exist in relations in which there are significant power disparities. Accordingly, this voluntarist account supposedly may also account for cases in which subordinates trust superiors and infants or children trust adults, even though those doing the trusting have few beliefs, expectations, or informed attitudes towards their superiors or adults. Indeed, proponents of this view may emphasize that some form of trust must be innate, since people (adults or children) may spontaneously and freely trust another being without any reflections on or judgements about the other (Baier 1995: 107). It is the commitment, conveyance, or bestowing, i.e. the entrusting, of oneself to another that is the focus of this view. In short, the *Voluntarist* view focuses on the action that takes place in trust; the *Attitudinal* view looks to the dispositions or attitudes to behave in certain ways; and the *Predictability* view concentrates on the predictions one has about the behaviour of those who are trusted.

Now since we are interested in a notion of trust as it might function in international business relations (and hence as it might constitute part of the background conditions for a morality to which international business might turn), I contend that we should reject the *Predictability* and *Voluntarist* views of trust.

The *Predictability* view is inappropriate for several reasons. First, a business or an individual may be able to predict the behaviour of another firm, and undertake with it various mutual activities or exchanges, but still not trust the other firm (cf. Thomas 1989: 178f.). Just because we can accurately predict that firm XYZ will share a particular technology with our firm, it does not follow that we thereby trust XYZ either in their performance of that act or more generally. We may. We may not. Second, questions of trust frequently arise in contexts when we cannot accurately or definitely predict the behaviour of others, rather than in those contexts when we can. If I can accurately predict your behaviour, it would seem that there is no need for me to trust you. On the other hand, if I cannot predict your behaviour and do not have the means to ensure that your behaviour must take certain forms, then I might seek to defend myself against you, flee from you, or (possibly) trust you. In short, trust involves some form of uncertainty or risk in the attitudes and behaviour of one party towards another party. Third, suppose that one agent could roughly predict the behaviour of another agent. This may serve as one reason, among others, for the former to trust the latter. But then the predictability is a *reason* for trusting, rather than the trust itself. Accordingly, predictability and trust are two different things. This does not imply that predictability is not important in the determination of whether to trust. It does mean that predictability cannot be equated with, or is not sufficient for, trust as it may be sought in business relations. Further, it may not, on some occasions, even be necessary. There may be situations in which one person cannot accurately predict another person's behaviour, but may still trust the other person for different reasons. Accordingly, we will have to consider below what role predictability may play in the justification, development, and maintenance of trust. Finally, none of the preceding is to say that we do not use the word 'trust' in the manner which the *Predictability* view suggests. We might say, for example, that we trust that Indian visitors to our home will like a curry meal. There may be little doubt in our minds about this. They haven't had any curry for weeks. We know that they eat curry in India. We confidently predict that they will enjoy this curry meal. To speak of trust in such circumstances is simply to speak of a prediction one believes one is entitled to make on the basis of some body of information. My argument above is not that we may not speak in this way. Rather, it is that this view of trust is less relevant than the *Attitudinal* view for discussions of (international) business for the above reasons. It is not the *Predictability* view that exercises people when they seek to trust their business associates.

It is also mistaken for present purposes to adopt the *Voluntarist* view of trust. Trust is not simply letting someone else take care of something one cares about, since a business might do this and still be able to monitor and oversee each aspect of that person's caring (*contra* Baier). Further, trust is more than simply voluntarily making oneself vulnerable to another with respect to some good (albeit on the basis of a belief, due to the other's actions toward one, that no loss or harm will come to one as a result), since I might let someone take care of something I care about but do this out of a sense of obligation, fear, or social embarrassment of doing anything else, while, at the same time, remaining quite worried about the results. In addition, though the action of placing oneself, or what one cares about, in the hands of others is an important part of trust, this seems only a part of a broader understanding of trust that encompasses one's ongoing prepared-ness to do so. This broader attitude or disposition involves various beliefs, values, and expectations which are part and parcel of the trust one may be willing to extend to another person or firm. Finally, the *Voluntarist* view of trust is an account which is more designed to capture the nature of trusting relations between individuals rather than organizations, and between a wide variety of individuals, e.g. infants, children, and parents, rather than participants in the marketplace. As such, it encompasses instances of trust in which trust does not need to be won, but simply exists in some innate fashion (Baier 1995: 107). Again, though we may be willing to speak of trust in such circumstances, this kind of trust is less relevant to the trust that businesses seek between themselves when they do international business.

Accordingly, if we are to consider the role of trust for an international business ethics, we should adopt the *Attitudinal* sense of 'trust'.[1] However, the nature of this form of trust needs further specification.

3. TRUST AND MORALITY

There are several important characteristics of this form of trust which influence the role it can play in international business relations.

First, trust is not a principle, let alone a moral principle, but an attitude or disposition to behave and respond in certain ways, namely to accept certain risks of harm or injury from another agent on the basis of a belief (for which there is some degree of uncertainty) that the other does not intend to do harm to one (or those one cares about), even though he/she could (cf.

Solomon 1992: 213). It is not surprising then that Rawls calls trust a natural attitude (Rawls 1971: 497). Solomon calls trust a business virtue, due to its dispositional nature and that it involves acting in admirable ways (Solomon 1992: 107 f.).

Held denies that trust is, as such, a virtue. Her reason is that trust may be misguided, misplaced or foolish (Held 1984: 65). However, this reasoning would have the unfortunate consequence of excluding not only trust, but other dispositions such as courage and loyalty, from being virtues. But surely courage and loyalty, as well as trust, are virtues even when they are misdirected. We must simply allow, in response to Held, that there may be courageous enemies, employees loyal to corrupt bosses, and managers who foolishly trust those who deceive them. Nevertheless, we speak intelligibly of the courage, loyalty, and trust of these individuals. Depending upon the context, these ordinarily exemplary ways of getting along with other people may lead to harm, and destruction of social harmony (cf. Solomon 1992: 108, 192). What this points out is that trust is not necessarily the same thing as morality or moral action. Though trust is essential for moral relations, this does not imply that all instances of trust are moral occasions.

Second, trust involves a commonality of values or aims (real or perceived) in terms of which the trust relationship is built. This commonality need not be complete or even extensive. People with very different values can trust each other. Still, there must be some common aims or values in light of which the trust relationship is established and maintained. Such values might include those of consistency, non-maleficence, certain forms of expertise, as well as appreciation of similar activities and forms of success. In short, both moral and non-moral values and aims might be part of this commonality. The role of these common values and aims is to foster the development of trusting attitudes inasmuch as they may give one reasons to believe that the trusted party will not act contrary to, or harm, vulnerable interests one deems important. Such reasons may take the form of various explicit expectations or predictions of the other's future behaviour. They may also take more implicit intuitive forms of confidence in the trusted individual. Her wants are compatible with ours; they value the same things we do; we enjoy a strong sense of mutual sympathy. In these situations, we may trust each other, not because we are thinking about predicting future behaviours, but because we are responding to present mutual connections.

Due to these common values or aims there is, then, a form of mutuality in any trusting relationship. Unfortunately, this mutuality is confused by some with the view that trust involves a mutual confidence in each other (cf. Sabel 1993; Barney and Hansen 1994). But this latter form of mutuality, i.e. 'mutual confidence', is not necessary for trust, since one agent may trust another, without that trust being reciprocated. Thus, Barney and Hansen are mistaken to adopt Sabel's view that 'trust is the *mutual* confidence that no party to an exchange will exploit another's vulnerabilities' (Barney and Hansen, 1994: 176; my emphasis). Nevertheless, even when only one member of a dyad trusts the other, if there were not some common values or aims there would not be trust.

This mutuality of values may also explain why the trust people have in each other is not simply an economic calculation. When people trust, in light of shared values, their trust involves a mutual affirmation or identification with the agent trusted through these common values or aims. As such, their trust grows out of this mutuality of values, rather than an economic calculation.[2] It is not surprising, then, that others have noted that, when one trusts, the loss that one may suffer through harm from the trust not being fulfilled is greater than the gain one might obtain by not trusting. This is an expression of the fact that the trust involved is not simply an instance of economic rationality (Hosmer 1995: 381).[3] However, one might also anticipate that the gain one (or both individuals) will receive if the trust is kept is greater than if there had been no trust at all. We need not deny that there may be economic (or other) gain through trust.

Third, trust may involve judgement in at least two ways. On the one hand, one may make certain judgements about the trustworthiness of someone else. And this may play an important role in entering a trusting relation with that other individual or firm. On the other hand, trust involves allowing some discretion on the part of the person or agent trusted. Thus, Baier comments that '. . . to trust is to give discretionary powers to the trusted, to let the trusted decide how, on a given matter, one's welfare is best advanced, to delay the account for a while, to be willing to wait to see how the trusted has advanced one's welfare' (Baier 1995: 136). That is, each member of the relation is granted some leeway to make various judgements and decisions which are not themselves prescribed by a contract or other set of rules. Rather, the goodwill and intentions of each member is assumed. It is assumed that they will competently make certain judgements as to what is to be done for the well-being of both parties in the relationship.

Fourth, trust must be distinguished from trustworthiness. Trust is an attitude or disposition to place oneself under certain circumstances in a situation where one is vulnerable to harm which may come from others on whose goodwill one depends. As an attitude or disposition, trust tends to be open-ended; it need not be specific to a particular, single situation. Hence, it tends to concern longer-term relationships than simply brief, limited ones. The temporal extendedness of trust variously depends upon a number of factors, including the mutuality of the interests that bring those that trust together, the degree and kind of trust, the non-violation of vulnerabilities, and the continuing fulfilment of the conditions of trust.

Trustworthiness, however, is not an attitude, but the evaluative appraisal that an individual is worthy of trust, i.e. that another person might reasonably place his or her trust in that individual. As such, trustworthiness cannot be equated with an individual (or firm) being one that others ought to trust (cf. Horsburgh 1962: 28) or with simply not being opportunistic (Jones 1995: 421). The fact that a person or business is trustworthy does not imply that others ought to trust them, since other firms or people may have no reasons to form a relationship with them at all. Further, if 'opportunism' is understood as 'pursuing self-interest with guile', then a person might not be opportunistic and still not trustworthy. This might occur when a person wished only the best for someone else, but could not be considered trustworthy because he was incompetent, not able to keep promises, or unwilling to listen to what others really wanted. Instead, one's trustworthiness betokens the reasonableness with which others might trust one. Accordingly, trustworthiness relates both to the qualities of the person or organization to be trusted, as well as to those doing the trusting. Relevant conditions regarding the former are discussed below. With regard to the latter, to make appropriate determinations they must have a certain amount of knowledge about the other person and the circumstances within which the question of trust arises. The limiting case of such trust, when an individual has virtually no knowledge, is what we call 'blind trust'. More generally, one's preparedness to consider another person or organization trustworthy will depend on the level of confidence one has that the trusted individual will not harm one's interests, the degree of vulnerability to which one is prepared to expose oneself and the value one places upon the interest which is vulnerable. Thus, I will look for greater trustworthiness in a person who asks to borrow my car, than from a person who asks to borrow my pen. I will also demand greater trustworthiness from someone to whom I am considering revealing my innermost secrets, than from a person to whom I may disclose what I read last week.

Fifth, the conflicted relation of trust to morality deserves notice. On the one hand, trust is widely accepted as an important value. Part of the importance of trust is that it is valued by individuals and cultures around the globe even though they are divided on a variety of other values and principles. For example, Puffer and McCarthy note that 'maintaining trust' is one value which both Americans and Russians share and on which they can build mutual relationships (Puffer and McCarthy 1995: 35). In contrast, they claim, 'maximizing profits' though viewed as ethical in the USA is considered unethical in Russia, whereas 'price fixing' is deemed to be unethical in the USA but ethical in Russia (ibid. 35). However, 'maintaining trust' is ethically esteemed by both societies. This result may well be replicated with other countries (e.g. Japan). Thus, trust may constitute a common value to which people and organizations across different cultures may (and must) appeal.

This is not to say, however, that certain instances of trust may not serve immoral ends. When some are able, because they trust each other, to engage in an enterprise that dumps toxic chemicals in the ocean, overbills a government, colludes against other firms, or misappropriates funds intended for villages affected by their manufacturing plants, then immoral ends are served. Accordingly, Baier comments that 'there are immoral as well as moral trust relationships, and trust-busting can be a morally proper goal' (Baier 1995: 95). Consequently, trust is not an unconditional value. Its value in particular instances depends upon the context within which it is exercised. If trust is employed concerning morally worthy projects, then such trust is valuable. On the other hand, when it is formed around morally unworthy projects trust may lack moral value. Without a good will, as Kant might say, trust can be extremely bad or harmful. What this implies is that trust cannot be a sufficient condition for moral business relations, though it is a necessary condition. As we shall see below, trust involves various forms of interaction which are essential to moral systems and upon which a business ethics may draw. Consequently, it is mistaken to think that trust has no relation to morality or ethics at all because it does not guarantee moral action. People may dispute over whether a glass of water filled to the middle is half empty or half full, but it would be hasty for those who decide it is half empty to proceed to conclude that there is no water in the glass at all.

Still, it would appear that trust is not simply something of instrumental value, but also of intrinsic value. Trust is like courage in that even when it occurs in conjunction with immoral ends we can appreciate the value of the trusting (or the courage) itself. Trust, in this sense, is a kind of attitude and behaviour which is distinguishable from instances in which people are unable or unwilling ever to render themselves vulnerable to others, as well as those who recklessly place themselves in the hands of others. The former end up recluses, isolated from others. In the latter case, when people simply place themselves in the hands of others, who are utterly untrustworthy, their trusting may be valuable in itself, even though due to their naivete their trusting behaviour may also be viewed as a case of foolhardiness and recklessness.

It follows that the tendency of Jones, Hosmer and others to equate trust and morality must be rejected. A firm which contracts with suppliers on the basis of mutual trust and co-operation need not be a moral firm (cf. Jones 1995: 422). Similarly, Hosmer's recent definition of trust as 'the expectation by one person, group, or firm of ethically justifiable behavior . . . on the part of the other person, group, or firm in a joint endeavor or economic exchange' must also be rejected (Hosmer 1995: 399). First, this moralization of trust excludes by definition what we know otherwise about trust, i.e. that trust may undermine morality (cf. Hosmer 1995: 399). Though trust in another person or institution may be important, such trust may also be the basis for immoral behaviour. Presumably even thieves may trust each other.

Further, moralized accounts of trust do not allow for situations in which one person or group trusts a second person or group, which has not, however, accepted any duty toward the first person's or group's interests or rights (cf. Hosmer 1995: 393). And yet surely this may happen when the people of a community trust a multinational company (MNC) which has established a manufacturing plant in their community, but which is not prepared to accept the broad implications of the trust which those individuals have placed on it. Accordingly, trust does not characterize the mutual relationship, i.e., 'the mutual confidence', of those who trust, but rather the individuals engaged in that relationship. And, it may pertain to only one of the members of a relationship involving trust.

Finally, the role that trust plays within a competitive system such as the market-place is different from the role it plays in ordinary life. For example, Horsburgh claims that, in ordinary life, anything which tends to give strong support to other moral agents will often be obligatory. Now though there is no prima facie obligation to trust one another, since trust is one of the most important ways in which one individual can give moral support to another, it is often one's duty to trust others, including those whose past conduct makes it seem probable that one's trust will be abused (Horsburgh 1960: 354). However, this duty does not seem appropriate in the market-place. Individuals do not have an obligation to trust the businesses or corporations they deal with in the market in order to give them moral support. And corporations don't have an obligation to trust unspecified others as a means whereby to help support them. They may have some obligation to be trustworthy, particularly with regard to stakeholders, however it is not obvious that they have obligations to engage in trust relations with other individuals simply on the basis that it might help them.

In fact, there appears to be some tension between market competition and trust. When we engage in tough competition I try to figure out your weaknesses and attempt to exploit them. Within the rules of the market, this is legitimate. However, I must also be able to trust that you will not exploit certain other weaknesses or vulnerabilities I have (e.g. you won't shoot me to get my customers). Thus, Gambetta comments that 'even to compete, in a mutually non-destructive way, one needs at some level to *trust* one's competitors to comply with certain rules' (Gambetta 1988: 215). But there is always a risk here that a highly competitive firm will take advantage of certain vulnerabilities which no one else has exploited before and concerning which the law is silent and morality unclear. Thus, we may fear that trust and competition conflict and that competition may undo trust. This is not necessarily the case, as we will see. In the next section, I shall adopt the view some have defended that trust of others may provide certain firms with a competitive advantage over others. However, within the market, trust will require special efforts and commitments which it does not necessarily require in ordinary life.

Thus, we must look closely at the role trust plays in the market-place, as well as in an efficacious and stable international business morality. It is clear from the preceding that trust is both important to business morality and, at the same time, at odds with certain aspects of the competitive market-place.

4. TRUST WITHIN THE BUSINESS CONTEXT

We may portray the role of trust within business by distinguishing three different forms of trust. These are distinguished in terms of the particular contexts in which trust functions. Accordingly, we may distinguish *basic trust*, *guarded trust* and *extended trust*. A complete account of trust and of business ethics needs to address these forms of trust.[4]

Basic trust is the trust that individual agents have that other moral agents, with whom they have only impersonal, systematic relations, will act in certain kinds of standard ways not to take advantage of their vulnerabilities. This is a general form of trust which might be said to be 'coextensive with the very existence of a social order' such as the market or morality itself (Gellner 1988: 142; Thomas 1978: 90). Sabel speaks of such trust as being a precondition of social life (Sabel 1993: 1136). Thus, DeGeorge comments that 'if there were not some minimum level of trust between buyer and seller on the international level, just as on the national level, business transactions would prove impossible' (DeGeorge 1993: 21). And Baier says that '. . . as anything more than a law within, [morality] itself requires trust in order to thrive . . .' (Baier 1986: 232). Accordingly, trust is a background condition, or part of the background environment (Dasgupta 1988: 49; DeGeorge 1993; Brenkert 1994). In this sense of trust, we must trust strangers. Hence this is an underlying, impersonal, and systematic form of trust, which occurs between participants or members of a social system or institution.

So understood, basic trust differs from the 'goodwill trust' that Sako identifies. 'Goodwill trust' holds between specific individuals and requires that a person be 'dependable and can be credited with high discretion, as he can be expected to take initiatives while refraining from unfair advantage taking' (Sako 1992: 452–3). Basic trust is a background form trust for this more specialized case of trust. If we did not regularly trust in this basic manner, but distrusted each other or doubted each other's sincerity, co-operation, and good intentions, more elaborate forms of trust would be difficult if not impossible. It is in this sense then that H. B. Acton is said to have held that 'trust and mutual confidence are the norm in social life, and that deception and wrong-doing are to be regarded as abnormalities' (Thomas 1978: 90). This does not mean that social life cannot tolerate distrust. However, as D. O. Thomas argues, 'the more violations of trust there are and the greater the reluctance to trust, the more impoverished does social life become and the fewer the benefits that men derive from it' (Thomas 1978: 92). Basic trust need not be, and most generally is not, articulated or made explicit. However, when it is violated, those involved are made painfully aware that they had indeed trusted that the violator would not act in the way in which he/she did. Basic trust within the market system assumes that others will play by recognized, generally accepted rules, customs, or standards, not that they won't use those rules and their abilities to try to get an advantage over one's firm.

Guarded trust is necessary when agents invoke various explicit contracts to protect their vulnerabilities and specify penalties for injury to those vulnerabilities and their interests. Trust is required here to maintain the relation in the face of unclarities and uncertainties in contracts. 'In fact no contract, even if it is scrutinized by sharp lawyers, can detail every eventuality, if for no other reason than that no language can cope with unlimited refinement in distinguishing continuities. Trust covers expectations about what others will do or have done . . . in circumstances that are not explicitly covered in the agreement' (Dasgupta 1988: 52–3). Thus, guarded trust makes contracts possible. As such, it is singularly important for business. Sako refers to this as contractual trust, i.e. when each partner adheres to agreements and keeps promises (Sako 1991, 1992). However, 'guarded trust' does not require, as does Sako's contractual trust, that those who engage in this form of trust are involved in 'upholding a universalistic ethical standard, namely that of keeping promises' (Sako 1992: 451). Of course, they might be doing this. On the other hand, they might be appealing to some other moral standard(s) or simply to some non-moral values or aims which motivate and justify their maintenance of the contract. Sako's view overly moralizes this form of trust. Barney and Hansen refer to this trust as 'Semi-strong form trust'. When significant exchange vulnerabilities exist, but the parties can protect themselves through various governance devices, semi-strong trust can exist (Barney and Hansen 1994: 177). Both market-based and contractual governance devices are relevant to guarded trust (ibid. 178).

In contrast to basic trust, guarded trust holds only between those firms and individuals who set up specific contracts and monitoring practices. Hence it is limited in time. In addition, the monitoring devices and restricted range of guarded trust limit the flexibility of the partners and involve various transaction costs. Do such contracts, monitoring devices and sanctions render guarded trust irrelevant? Some have claimed that trust is incompatible with sanctions, contracts, etc. D. O. Thomas says that '. . . trusting someone to do something does, logically, exclude sanctions . . .' (Thomas 1978: 91). Accordingly, he claims that 'the risks we run [with trusting] are those that come from denying ourselves the use of sanctions and from sacrificing the benefits that come from the kind of conformity that sanctions can produce' (ibid. 100).

This view is, however, mistaken. Trust may involve sanctions in various ways. For example, I may trust my friend to do something, understanding that if he breaks my trust other people will be prepared to condemn him, reluctant to accept him as a friend, or to trust his word. These are real sanctions in the background of our trust. These are compatible with trust since they do not remove all uncertainty or my vulnerabilities. Still, they provide a context within which I may trust. In business contexts, this background framework may further include legal sanctions and standards formulated by trade associations which together may promote long-term relations in which trust might develop (Arrighetti, Bachmann, and Deakin 1997). What would be incompatible with trust would be an individual or a firm surrounding the performance of an action by another firm it claimed to trust with a complete, detailed, and significant set of sanctions, e.g. the firm claims to trust another firm with some confidential information, but clearly indicates that others will monitor each step of its use of that information and that any misuse will result in significant monetary penalties.

Extended trust involves firms and individuals acting to trust one another beyond basic and guarded forms of trust. It develops within special relations which involve trusting other firms and individuals when contracts and monitoring devices have been significantly reduced. It is in this sense of trust that we are taught as children not to trust strangers, but only certain special individuals. Extended trust requires that firms and individuals expose their vulnerabilities to one another when there is clear uncertainty and risk that harm could come to the firm, or individuals in the firm, from those who are trusted. It is part of an ongoing relationship which is not necessarily temporally limited to a particular contract, but arises out of the value structures of the firms which permit this greater exposure of each firm's vulnerabilities to the other firm so as to create a relation which is mutually desired. To the extent that firms and individuals can trust in this manner they will be able to act with greater flexibility and freedom in their relations with those whom they so trust (cf. Barney and Hansen 1994; Jones 1995). This relation may exist not only between firms, but also between firms and their stakeholders (e.g., employees, stockholders, and members of the community). Jones and Sako have both called attention to this broader role for trust. Sako calls it 'goodwill trust'. However, Sako's 'goodwill trust' involves the expectation that one's trusted partner is 'committed to take initiatives (or exercise discretion) to exploit new opportunities over and above what was explicitly promised' (Sako 1992: 453). Extended trust is compatible with such an expectation, but does not require it. Business firms might share a relation of extended trust but not expect each other to 'exploit new opportunities'.

They may also be content to do business outside the limits of guarded trust. Extended trust, then, differs from guarded trust in the significant reduction of monitoring devices, formal contracts and special sanctions that are required for guarded trust, as well as in its dependence on the value structures of the participants which permit greater openness to each other through their restriction of their self-interested actions (cf. Barney and Hansen 1994). Those who trust in this extended fashion may well go on to engage in special initiatives. But firms may also engage in extended trust relations with each other without each partner doing so. It would be sufficient that they engage in various forms of exchange and interchange within a present set of activities, which lack the protections of contracts, monitoring devices, etc.

Accordingly, basic trust and guarded trust are important for sustaining the social, economic, and moral systems within which business acts. Without these forms of trust, these systems would collapse. Extended trust is important for the flexibility and independence which it may afford particular businesses which can engage in it as well as for the morally richer relationships which it permits. In addition, one might maintain that if there is extended trust between a firm and its subsidiaries, then the subsidiary will be allowed to make a wider range of decisions involving product differentiation, etc. which permits a fuller moral agency of the subsidiary. If we assume that, all things being equal, a person or group which is accorded full moral agency will respond favourably, then we might expect not only a higher level of morality, but also greater efficiency from such a unit. Consequently, a business ethics which does not take these forms of trust into account or provide for their development cannot be complete or a sustainable business ethics. However, since trust may also be involved in nefarious relationships, we must now look more closely at trust within the context of an international business morality.

5. TRUST AND INTERNATIONAL BUSINESS

Different conditions are required to produce each of the preceding forms of trust. By considering these conditions, we may also see the problems which trust faces within an international business context. We can also identify difficulties which an international business ethics must confront.

Basic trust rests upon two underlying conditions: (a) the commonality of motives associated with mutual acceptance of common basic norms, values, and customs; and (b) the consistency of behaviour of those acting on those motives. Individuals tend to trust each other the greater the similarity and mutuality of their motives, values, and ends. Accordingly, basic trust rests on several assumptions: that others do not have motives to harm them; that if they do have such motives, they have other overriding motives which keep the former in check; or, finally, that if they have motives which may lead to their harm, these motives are exercised within certain widely recognized and accepted forms of behaviour such that they may be anticipated or avoided. Consequently, if one business simply out-competes another business, this is not a reason to abandon one's basic trust in the market system or in other individuals more generally.

The consistency of the behaviour of others is also crucial for basic trust. Obviously, in cases of trust, there is uncertainty by the nature of the case. However, if an individual or firm acted simply arbitrarily or inconsistently, it would not be one that would readily be trusted. It is for this reason that reputation is also so important in establishing the trustworthiness of a firm or individual (Dasgupta 1988).

Guarded trust requires both of the preceding two conditions regarding common motives and consistency of behaviour, as well as knowledge of the competence of the other party, i.e. that the other party is capable of carrying out the contract. If a firm is prepared to commit itself to doing certain things, but is perceived not to be able or competent to do those things, then trust is less likely in such cases. Such competence might include categories which Gabarro has identified: (a) functional or specific competence: competence in the specialized knowledge and skills required to do a particular job; and (b) interpersonal competence: people skills and knowing how to work with people (Gabarro 1978).

Finally, extended trust requires the preceding three conditions (common motives, consistency of behaviour, and acknowledged competence) as well as a fourth condition, openness. Individuals or firms may engage in extended trust depending upon whether each is prepared to open up to the other so as to reveal private or confidential information. Openness may also involve being physically available to the other, e.g. opening the doors of one's plant to the trusted partner. Finally, openness may involve levelling with another, as well as not creating or permitting misleading expectations to be generated in the other (cf. Gabarro 1978).

Thus, as we move from simpler to more complex forms of trust, the conditions required for earlier forms of trust are added to those required for later forms of trust. Extended trust, the most developed form of trust, requires commonality of motives (or ends), consistency of behaviour, acknowledged competence, and openness.

It is immediately obvious that the creation of morally worthy trust within international contexts faces special problems that it does not face on the national level. A partial list of obstacles includes the following:

1. Values and motives may differ dramatically. For example, attitudes towards and evaluations of individualism, uncertainty, and aggressive com-

petition may impede trusting relationships (cf. Hofstede 1979).[5] It is not surprising then that it is frequently claimed that trust is more likely to be developed in circumstances where there is a common history, belief in the same god, and dedication to the same political ends (Sabel 1993: 1135). Thus Shell comments that 'similarity of backgrounds and tastes also helps smooth the way to trusting relations' (Shell 1991: 258). And Baier agrees that 'awareness of what is customary . . . affects one's ability to trust' (Baier 1986: 245). Since it is not possible internationally, to rely on joint customs, traditions, language, or histories, much of the common basis upon which trust may develop within a national culture is missing. In addition, similar institutions and social structures such as those regarding property also help in the production of trust. But where there exist significant differences, for example, over intellectual property, obstacles to trust will again be perceived.

2. Ethnocentric and egocentric tendencies will also impede trusting relations internationally. For example, the tendency of an egocentric fairness bias, 'which is a tendency for people to see arrangements that favour themselves over others as fairer than arrangements that favour others' will acerbate other ethnocentric biases (Michalos 1990: 624; Messick *et al.* 1985).[6] Michalos notes studies which show that 'most people think most [other] people are not as nice as they are themselves and, therefore, cannot be trusted to behave as well' (Michalos 1990: 627). These tendencies will be particularly acute internationally, where people look, talk, and behave differently.

3. Due to past colonialism and imperialism, past histories may stand in the way of trusting relationships. Further, due to racism (or suspicions of racism) trusting relations will also be hampered. Similarly, different economic histories of capitalism, socialism, and communism will also play a role in restricting such trusting relations between various MNCs and Third World Nations. In addition, some cultures may have different tolerances for inconsistency, standards for competence, and different time frames within which performance of various activities may be expected.

4. Finally, individuals in some cultural contexts might find it more difficult to be open in the same manner as those from other cultures. Their concern might not be with openness so much as not hurting another's feelings or with, perhaps, saving face and not embarrassing themselves or others. When circumstances exist in which these different responses arise, the trust between partners might be jeopardized. One member of the relation might feel that he or she can never 'really' know what the others are thinking, because they will not speak their minds. Similarly, if Fukuyama is correct, the social structures within societies differ with respect to the extensiveness of trust which members of those societies may 'naturally' engage in. These differences will also inhibit the development of trusting relations both within certain societies and between societies.

In short, the obstacles to trust within an international market are substantial. Further, these are also obstacles to the ready acceptance of, and adherence to, systems of international business ethics. Suppose, for instance, that we distinguish between ethics, as a theoretical statement of principles, rules, values, and ideals by which individuals, business, and countries ought to live and act, and morality which (for present purposes) we may take to be an embedded or lived form of an ethics. As such, a morality (or an embodied ethics) must be capable of being taught and communicated to others; it must not be radically inconsistent; it must have forces which lead to its renewal; it must be something that can be stable. If we are to speak of an international business ethics, then surely we seek an ethics that can be a morality. But to speak of such an ethics as being a morality, we must seek to identify the conditions for this transformation of the theoretical into the practical. Trust, as we have seen, is one of these conditions.

Hence, any international business ethics which does not give significant place to the commonality of values or motives, consistency of behaviour, reputation, competency determinations, and openness will be an ethics which does not allow for basic conditions which promote its own stability and efficacy as a morality. It is these factors which the preceding identifies as necessary conditions for the various forms of trust. And these forms of trust are crucial as background or supporting conditions for the development and maintenance of morality. Without them an international business ethics will not become a morality.

Now the obstacles to trust can be met only gradually and incrementally. The instruction of managers and participants in international business in ethics will be important (Noreen 1988), but clearly not be sufficient. Instead, a complicated pattern of interaction among individuals, firms, industries, international organizations, and governmental structures and mechanisms will be required to overcome the obstacles briefly noted above. They will require various trust-enhancing mechanisms including the law, trade associations, various third parties, and the like (Arrighetti, Bachmann, and Deakin 1997). Periods of adjustment with gradual increments of trust formation are obviously required. This will involve confidence-building measures (Bluhm 1987). For example, extended trust might be enhanced by an exchange of personnel at home and abroad so that all sides may keep in touch and different interpretations or understandings are recognized. Guarded trust will be enhanced through various market-based and contractual governance devices (Barney and Hansen 1994). Basic trust will be enhanced by other background institutions, frequency of contact, etc. Accordingly, we must look to both informal and formal means to overcome obstacles to trust.

What this suggests is a shift in the practical basis for business morality as we move from the national to the international arena. We move from a basis which includes common histories, customs, languages, etc. to more external and formal mechanisms (Sellerberg 1982). On this view, personal relations continue to be crucial for international trust, since it is the individuals from different businesses and cultures who gain knowledge of and form trust with each other. It is for this reason that business executives travel with the presidents, prime ministers, and commerce secretaries of their national states. 'Face-to-face interaction with very senior people . . . [overseas and in the company of national leaders] sends a powerful symbolic message. It helps establish trust.'[7] This implies the importance of the time and circumstances to allow such relations to develop. Still, inter- and intrainstitutional structures are required to support and sustain such personal trust, as well as to create forms of trust which are not simply personal, but organizational or institutional, and which would lend their support to an international business morality (Dodgson 1993; Zucker 1986).

6. MORALLY RELEVANT FEATURES OF TRUST

Finally, though specific cases of trust are not necessarily moral, the fact that firms and people can and do trust in the preceding ways means that something morally important happens in trust. This 'something' is that trust goes beyond simple self-seeking behaviour. This is not to deny that individuals and firms form various relations involving trust for self-interested reasons. Obviously they do. However, it does not follow from this, when these relations include the different forms of trust distinguished above, that these forms of trust can be understood *simply* in terms of self-interest. They cannot. Self-interest may be the occasion for seeking or desiring relations with some other person or firm which require trust. Further, one's self-interests may also be met through those trusting relations. But, again, this does not imply that such trust does not include features important for morality. It is an overly rigorous, if not misguided, morality which demands that self-interest and morality be wholly separate. Still, self-interest does not itself provide an account of the nature or justification of the trust they may develop between individuals and firms. For this, we have seen that (depending upon the kind of trust) we must look to one's preparedness to refrain from taking advantage of another's vulnerabilities or weaknesses, the consistency of one's behaviour, the appropriateness of one's competencies, and one's readiness to be open regarding knowledge of one's self or firm to others. All these conditions may restrict action on behalf of one's self-interests. Further, social (and industry) norms and expectations, which are part of the commonality of values and beliefs crucial to trust, play a role in constituting forms of behaviour, as well as individuals and firms themselves, which are not simply self-seeking. Finally, in trust there is a consideration of the interests of others, beyond one's own present interests. There are, that is, various inherent aspects of trust which might be exploited to promote moral forms of trust. I wish to explore these in the following.

First, to the extent people mutually and consciously trust each other (for example, especially in guarded and extended trust), they must be in communication with, and have a mutual understanding of, each other. They must seek and share knowledge about each other as well as make judgements about the fitness of each other. As we have seen, this mutual understanding involves knowing and assessing each other's motives, consistency, competency, and openness. Such knowledge of others (and oneself) has, traditionally, been held to be important for morality.

Second, trust involves a morally significant exposure of oneself to others in that one bares one's vulnerabilities to them. With mutual trust there is a sharing of vulnerabilities. In this manner a dependence (possibly a mutual dependence) is developed whereby one is expected not only not to harm the other but also to act in ways which promote the well-being of the other. That one is prepared to act in these ways and thereby create certain expectations about the future behaviour of those who are trusted may open firms and individuals up to other more obviously moral relations. For example, to the extent that one trusts others one treats them 'as being able and willing to act in accord with the rules without inducement or threats' (Thomas 1978: 92). Accordingly, Thomas has claimed that trust is involved in respecting the moral dignity of each person. As such, trust creates a potential for morality between those who share in the trust.

Third, trust involves the restriction of self-interested behaviour so that the interests of others are not harmed, and may be promoted, even though doing so might not be in one's immediate self-interests. This may involve various preventative forms of behaviour as well. For example, to the extent that individuals share such a relation they do not manipulate each other '. . . by deliberately raising false expectations in them about how one will respond to something one wants them to do' (Baier 1995: 134).[8] Similarly, they '. . . take due care not to lead others to form reasonable but false expectations about what one will do, where they would face significant loss if they relied on such false expectations' (ibid. 134). Finally, they '. . . take steps to prevent any loss that others would face through reliance on expectations about one's future behavior, expectations that one has either intentionally or negligently led them to form' (ibid. 134). In short, those engaged in trust relations avoid certain standard negotiating tactics which result in zero-sum games with one's negotiating partner.

Fourth, mutual trust involves a reciprocity between members of the trusting relation which fosters their autonomy. Guarded and extended trust relationships usually only develop slowly, after initial experiences and probing of each other's intentions and reliability. When the other responds positively and in a trusting manner, one may oneself (further) respond in a positive and trusting manner. As such relationships develop, particularly extended ones, it may be that something one does may give the other a one-sided benefit, which one then trusts he or she will not take advantage of. It may even occur that the trust one has bestowed on another is not fulfilled, or not fulfilled in the manner expected. This need not result, however, in a 'tit-for-tat' response, if the trust relationship is healthy and firm. Indeed, when there is trust, each party to the relationship will allow the other a wider range of decisions and actions than when distrust characterizes their relationships. If we may then assume that morality is bound up with some form of autonomy or self-determination, trust will promote the realization of this basic condition for morality. In this way, trust is not indifferent to morality, but is positively linked with it. This is in harmony with the connection Horsburgh draws between trust and moral agency in his view that for a person to be a moral agent he or she cannot hold an attitude of systematic and pervasive distrust toward all other people (Horsburgh 1960: 354).

Hence, at least four morally significant phenomena are inherently linked with trust: (a) communication of self-understanding to others; (b) the voluntary exposure of one's vulnerabilities to others; (c) voluntary restriction of self-interested behaviour; and (d) a reciprocity which fosters autonomy. These inherent features of trust are central to morality as well and, hence, link these two concepts.

It is in this sense, perhaps, that we should understand Gewirth's claim that 'a principle of mutual trust' is 'the moral principle which is at the basis of a civilized society' (Gewirth 1982: 185). I think that Gewirth clearly overstates the moral nature of trust. Trust may also exist, as we have seen, between corrupt parties. Further, Gewirth is mistaken to link the principle of mutual trust with that of 'mutual respect for certain basic rights' (ibid.). We may speak about such moral relations without necessarily introducing the notion of rights. Gewirth's view moves the notion of trust from one concerning relations to one concerning rights, rules, and obligations. Feminists might object that this replaces a care-based ethic with a rule-based ethic. However, in the sense developed in the preceding paragraphs, Gewirth's reference to the basic importance of trust is surely correct.

This account of trust has a wide range of implications for international business. I will mention only a few.

1. First, it has been argued, convincingly I believe, that firms of integrity have obligations to go beyond a moral minimum to fulfil various positive obligations and ethical ideals whether in their home countries or in their host countries (DeGeorge 1993). These include fulfilling various obligations to be charitable, promote the working conditions of their employees, etc. Now such activities will be enhanced, if not made possible,

to the extent that trusting relationships are developed between the firm and those who are to be the recipients of these activities. Indeed, such trusting relationships may be involved in differentiating paternalistic behaviour on the part of the firm from behaviour which is received as genuinely helpful. Thus, the greater the level of trust, the more likely that firms will be able to engage in the full range of activities whereby they are businesses of integrity, rather than businesses simply meeting some minimal standards.

2. Second, the nature and extent of moral guidelines which international businesses require will depend upon the extent and levels of trust which are generated among the participants in the particular moral arenas in which they are engaged. Thus, the greater the level and extent of trust, the more it will be morally acceptable to leave ethical determinations to those businesses, their subsidiaries, and the communities involved. On the other hand, interactions between members of societies with low levels of trust may be expected to produce greater moral dissonance than those in which the levels of trust are high. Such moral dissonance may require the greater moral guidance of explicit rules, principles, and guidelines, as well as protections from various monitoring agencies.

3. Finally, though trust cannot be the sole touchstone for international businesses which would act morally, the inherent features of trust noted above as morally significant might serve not only as (part of the) practical and effective basis for an ethics, but also for (part of) the basis upon which the norms of an international business ethics might themselves be developed and justified. The moral test of such norms would be based upon the extent and level of the trusting relationships from which such norms were derived. Thus, those ethical norms which derived from a broad range of trusting relationships (i.e. basic, guarded, and extended trusting relationships) which were also extensively held (i.e. across all the communities and individuals affected) would have a prima facie moral acceptability to them. This might be part of a bottom-up ethics, rather than a top-down ethics. It would be an ethics with a strong endogamous component, rather that one fundamentally exogamous. Such an ethics would begin with the urgent need of individuals and firms to do business with each other, with communities and governments, and the trust which is necessary for these relationships. Out of these bilateral and multilateral relationships of various organizations and institutions would develop the effective morality from which an international business ethics might be abstracted. This can be viewed as an elaboration on the comment by Luhmann that 'the necessity of trust can be regarded as the correct and appropriate starting point for the derivation of rules for proper conduct' (Luhmann 1979: 4).

This is not to say that the ethical environment within these organizations and institutions would not have to be strongly supported by their top executives and leaders. It is also not to say that there would not need to be strong international monitoring organizations which would work to foster international business morality. In this sense, morality within organizations requires strong 'top-down' ethical support. However, the preceding is to say that the norms which might be supported and imposed in those cases would arise out of the characteristics of the trusting relations which these organizations develop, rather than be derived from various philosophical constructions such as hypothetical contracts and abstract universal rights. Such a morality would have an inductive, rather than a deductive, nature.

7. CONCLUSION

Trust has been both oversold and underbilled in current discussions of international business. Its value extends beyond the prudential or self-interested value for individuals and firms which has been frequently portrayed. However, it is too much to identify trust with morality itself. Those who trust might still harm others. Thus, trust is not the final solution to moral questions.

In seeking to understand its nature and relation to an ethics of international business, I have argued that the *Attitudinal* view of trust, rather than the *Predictability* or *Voluntarist* views, is the proper one. In its *Attitudinal* form, trust plays a crucial role in three crucial kinds of instances: basic trust, guarded trust, and extended trust. Each of these kinds of trust requires various conditions to develop. Thus, basic trust requires conditions surrounding the commonality of motives and consistency of behaviour of individuals or firms. Guarded trust requires conditions concerning motives, consistency, and competence. And extended trust requires conditions involving motives, consistency, competence, and openness.

However, given the international setting within which these conditions must be fulfilled, various obstacles arise which don't arise (or do so to a much lesser degree) within a particular culture or society, e.g. problems of knowledge and interpretation of the motives and values of others, differences of motives and values, egocentric, and ethnocentric tendencies, etc. This is the truth behind those who challenge the role of morality in international business. These obstacles will have to be met with a variety of formal and informal mechanisms about which it is difficult to generalize. Still, out of the nature of trust we can draw certain conditions for morally worthy trust. If these conditions were broadly extended we might have part of a basis for an international business ethics which would arise from the bottom up, rather than be imposed top down.

NOTES

1. Hereafter, instead of speaking of '*attitudinal* trust,' I will simply refer to 'trust', by which I will understand its *attitudinal* variety.
2. Ken Alpern has urged on me the importance for trust of the notion of the affirmation of the other.
3. Hosmer is drawing on Deutsch 1958. See Luhmann: 'Trust therefore always bears upon a critical alternative, in which the harm resulting from a breach of trust may be greater than the benefit to be gained from the trust proving warranted' (Luhmann 1979: 24).
4. Others also draw distinctions among different kinds of trust. Among such accounts are: Barney and Hansen (1994), Sako (1991, 1992), L. Thomas (1989), and Zucker (1986). I believe that my account is importantly different from each of these accounts and serves different purposes than those authors sought to address in their accounts.
5. Hofstede measures the value differences between cultures in terms of a Power Distance Index, an Uncertainty Index, an Individualism Index, and a Masculinity Index (Hofstede 1979).
6. Liebrand, Messick, and Wolters (1986) show that 'these fairness biases have transcultural generality' (p. 602).
7. The quotation is from Robert Bontempo, Associate Professor of International Management at Columbia University Business School. He was cited by Alex Markels, Joann S. Lublin, and Phil Kuntz, in 'Why Executives Tour World With Politicians', *Wall Street Journal* (4 Apr. 1996), B1.
8. I cite this and the following two passages from Baier, who is rephrasing the work of Thomas Scanlon on promises and the expectations that promises may set up in others (cf. Scanlon 1990).

REFERENCES

Arrighetti, A., Bachmann, R., and Deakin, S. (1997), 'Contract Law, Social Norms and Interfirm Cooperation', *Cambridge Journal of Economics*, 21: 171–95.

Baier, A. (1986), 'Trust and Antitrust', *Ethics*, 96: 231–60.

——(1995), *Moral Prejudices*. Cambridge, Mass.: Harvard University Press.

Barney, J. B. and Hansen, M. H. (1994), 'Trustworthiness as a Source of Competitive Advantage', *Strategic Management Journal*, 15: 175–90.

Bluhm, L. H. (1987), 'Trust, Terrorism, and Technology', *Journal of Business Ethics*, 6: 333–41.

Brenkert, G. (1994), 'The Importance of the Structural Features of Moral Systems for International Business Ethics', *Proceedings of the Fifth Annual Meeting of the International Association For Business and Society*, 101–6.

Dasgupta, P. (1988), 'Trust as a Commodity', in D. Gambetta (ed.), *Trust*. Oxford: Blackwell.

DeGeorge, R. (1993), *Competing With Integrity In International Business*. New York: Oxford University Press.

Deutsch, M. (1958), 'Trust and Suspicion', *Journal of Conflict Resolution*, 2: 265–79.

Dodgson, M. (1993), 'Learning, Trust and Technological Collaboration', *Human Relations*, 46: 77–95.

Gabarro, J. J. (1978), 'The Development of Trust, Influence and Expectations', in A. G. Athos (ed.), *Interpersonal Behavior*. Englewood Cliffs, NJ: Prentice-Hall.

Gambetta, D. (1988), 'Can We Trust Trust?', in D. Gambetta (ed.), *Trust*.

Gellner, E. (1988), 'Trust, Cohesion and the Social Order', in D. Gambetta (ed.), *Trust*.

Gewirth, A. (1982), 'Human Rights and the Prevention of Cancer', in A. Gewirth (ed.), *Human Rights*. Chicago: University of Chicago Press.

Held, V. (1968), 'On the Meaning of Trust', *Ethics*, 78: 156–9.

——(1984), *Rights and Goods*. New York: Free Press.

Hofstede, G. (1979), 'Value Systems in Forty Countries: Interpretation, Validation and Consequences for Theory', in L. H. Eckensberger, W. J. Lonner, and Y. H. Poortinga (eds.), *Cross-Cultural Contributions to Psychology*. Lisse: Swets & Zeitlinger, 389–407.

Horsburgh, H. J. N. (1960), 'The Ethics of Trust', *Philosophical Quarterly*, 10: 343–54.

——(1962), 'Trust and Social Objectives', *Ethics*, 72: 28–40.

Hosmer, L. T. (1995), 'Trust: The Connecting Link Between Organizational Theory and Philosophical Ethics', *Academy of Management Review*, 20: 379–403.

Jones, T. M. (1995), 'Instrumental Stakeholder Theory: A Synthesis of Ethics and Economics', *Academy of Management Review*, 20: 404–37.

King, J. B. (1988), 'Prisoner's Paradoxes', *Journal of Business Ethics*, 7: 475–87.

Liebrand, W. B. G., Messick, D. M., and Wolters, F. J. M. (1986), 'Why We Are Fairer Than Others: A Cross-Cultural Replication and Extension', *Journal of Experimental Social Psychology*, 22: 590–604.

Luhmann, N. (1979), *Trust and Power*. Chichester: Wiley.

Mayer, R. C., Davis, J. H., and Schoorman, F. D. (1995), 'An Integrative Model of Organizational Trust', *Academy of Management Review*, 20: 709–34.

Messick, D. M., Bloom, S., Boldizar, J. P., and Samuelson, C. D. (1985), 'Why We Are Fairer than Others', *Journal of Experimental Social Psychology*, 21: 480–500.

Michalos, A. C. (1990), 'The Impact of Trust on Business, International Security and the Quality of Life', *Journal of Business Ethics*, 9: 619–38.

Noreen, E. (1988), 'The Economics of Ethics: A New Perspective on Agency Theory', *Accounting, Organizations and Society*, 13: 359–69.

Puffer, S. M. and McCarthy, D. J. (1995), 'Finding the Common Ground in Russian and American Business Ethics', *California Management Review*, 37: 29–46.

Rawls, J. (1971), *A Theory of Justice*. Cambridge, Mass.: Harvard University Press.

Sabel, C. F. (1993), 'Studied Trust: Building New Forms of Cooperation in a Volatile Economy', *Human Relations*, 9: 1133–70.

Sako, M. (1991), 'The Role of "Trust" in Japanese Buyer–Supplier Relationships', *Ricerche Economiche*, 45: 449–74.

——(1992), *Prices, Quality and Trust*. Cambridge: Cambridge University Press.

Scanlon, T. (1990), 'Promises and Practices', *Philosophy & Public Affairs*, 19: 199–226.

Sellerberg, A.-M. (1982), 'On Modern Confidence', *Acta Sociologica*, 25: 39–48.

Shell, G. R. (1991), 'Opportunism and Trust in the Negotiation of Commercial Contracts: Toward a New Cause of Action', *Vanderbilt Law Review*, 44: 221–82.

Solomon, R. C. (1992), *Ethics and Excellence*. New York: Oxford University Press.

Thomas, D. O. (1978), 'The Duty to Trust', *Proceedings of the Aristotelian Society*, 79: 89–101.

Thomas, L. (1989), *Living Morally*. Philadelphia: Temple University Press.

Tullock, G. (1967), 'The Prisoner's Dilemma and Mutual Trust', *Ethics*, 77: 229–35.

Zucker, L. (1986), 'Production of Trust: Institutional Sources of Economic Structure, 1840–1920', *Research in Organizational Behavior*, 8: 53–111.

Conclusion: Trust—Conceptual Aspects of a Complex Phenomenon

REINHARD BACHMANN

1. TOWARDS AN ADEQUATE RESEARCH PERSPECTIVE ON TRUST

The foremost problems relating to the analysis of trust seem to be connected to the understanding of the role of the institutional environment in which business relations are embedded. In particular, this issue is highly relevant from the perspective of business relationships, as has been suggested by Granovetter (1985), Streeck (1992), Grabher (1993), Deakin, Lane, and Wilkinson (1994), Lane and Bachmann (1996, 1997), and others who emphasize the social quality of economic behaviour. This perspective argues in favour of a multidisciplinary approach to the study of relationships between economic actors instead of an approach which solely relies on the premises of mainstream economic theory. Admittedly, what is on offer within the latter tradition of thought and analysis is often highly developed in formal terms but obviously has considerable problems in coming to grips with the complexity of real-world phenomena. Thus, it appears to be empirically more fruitful to adopt a multidisciplinary perspective which takes the social context of business relations into account, and focuses on the multilayered process of their social shaping.

The neo-classical approach, game theory, and transaction cost economics would be misjudged if one assumed them to completely neglect the relevance of institutions. But looking a bit closer at mainstream economic theory reveals that within this tradition, these are considered as *parameters* of individual actors' decisions rather than as elements of an integral framework which shapes the economic interactions between individuals and organizations. In other words, conventional economic theory tends to conceptualize institutions as external variables which take the form of certain values determining—together with other factors—the behaviour of 'hyperrational' individual actors (cf. Lane, as well as Deakin and Wilkinson, both in this volume). This view, however, is blind to the procedural and reflexive aspects of the social formation of business relationships, and thus needs to be substantially complemented by inputs from other social sciences such as sociology, legal studies, organization theory, and philosophy. The multidisciplinary approach is based on the premise that the socio-institutional context of economic relationships deserves special attention if individual relationships are to be understood and—as many of the latest contributions to the debate on trust show—this perspective is increasingly assumed to be most appropriate for explaining the quality of co-operation within and across the boundaries of business organizations.

Also, comparative research appears to be very useful in bringing light on the problems of governance structures of intra- and interorganizational relations. This approach can be seen as highly illuminating in its own right, but—furthermore—it also confirms that a socio-institutional framework which is specific to certain regions, nation states, and sometimes even larger geographical areas plays a major role in determining the quality of relationships and economic performance (Hofstede 1991). Of course, there are also other factors such as the structure of the industry or global market conditions, which belong to the wider 'contractual environment' (Deakin, Lane, and Wilkinson 1994), and which decide upon whether business relationships are either more based on trust or more adversarial. But comparative research can single out such factors and show how strongly the *institutional* framework shapes the forms and quality of economic relationships (Burchell and Wilkinson 1997; Deakin and Wilkinson in this volume). The latter is understood to consist of the legal system, the status and functions of trade associations, economic state policy, the financial system, and the systems of industrial relations and training (Lane and Bachmann 1996).

Comparative research can thus make very clear that the institutional order, in which the cultural specificities—among other factors—manifest themselves, provides the basic patterns of economic actors' social interaction. The contributions to this book which explicitly adopt a cross-national comparative perspective (Mari Sako, Simon Deakin and Frank Wilkinson) leave no doubt on this matter. But also those chapters which focus on the problem of how to reconstruct the link between trust at the interpersonal level and the institutional framework (Jörg Sydow), as well as those which try to answer the question of how to create trust within a given business system (John Child, and John Humphrey) widely agree on this insight: trust-based relationships and the generation of trust in economic relationships are highly dependent on the nature of the institutional environment in which they are embedded.

2. THE LIMITS OF ONE-DIMENSIONAL APPROACHES TO UNDERSTANDING TRUST

The questions which arise in the context of analyses which focus on the institutional framework are complex and much more difficult to answer than formalistic models, which view institutions merely as exogenous factors, allow for. Within social theory, the most crucial issues of the interdependence between social actors' behaviour and the role of the institutional framework have generally been referred to by discussions on the so-called 'micro-macro-link'. This, of course, is a long-standing debate throughout the history of the social sciences, and many contemporary contributions to 'grand theory', such as Giddens' 'structuration theory' (1984), place greatest emphasis precisely on this question (1984). In the discussion on trust this issue is of central importance with regard to understanding why individual social actors are more inclined to trust each other under the conditions of a certain institutional environment, and why they tend to distrust one another in other circumstances.

In this volume, Jörg Sydow draws heavily on Giddens' conceptual framework, and applies it to the problem of how trust is created and reproduced through the institutional order of a business system which—according to this view—is both the conditional basis and the result of the patterns of economic actors' social relationships. Through a recursive process which links together social interaction and institutional structures, Jörg Sydow argues, borrowing from Giddens, trust production is facilitated through 'knowledge', 'norms', and 'resources of social action'. Within this process, which includes all three of these dimensions of social reality, trust is permanently either reproduced or challenged. Both the 'virtuous circle of cooperation' and the 'vicious circle of distrust' (Womack, Jones, and Roos 1990) can be perpetuated in this way as Jörg Sydow shows in his chapter.

Christel Lane (in the introductory chapter, and—borrowing from her—John Child in this volume) also differentiates between three general approaches to the same problem: 'calculative trust', 'norm-based trust', and 'cognition-based trust'. Under closer examination, this classification is in its essence quite similar to Giddens' view and Sydow's suggestion that trust should be analysed in terms of 'resources', 'norms', and 'knowledge'. Both Christel Lane and Jörg Sydow seek conceptual links between interpersonal relations and the institutional framework, and come to answers which are highly compatible with each other despite the fact that they differ slightly in terminology. While 'norms' are explicitly identified in both approaches, 'knowledge' and 'cognition' can easily be recognized as being very closely connected concepts, and it is also not difficult to see that 'calculating' social actors tend to consider their 'resources' before they make their decisions. Christel Lane's classification, however, is in some aspects easier to handle. In particular, it shows that three broad, but distinct traditions of social thought are referred to here; traditions which Giddens and Sydow seem to have completely amalgamated in their conceptual view. At least for analytical purposes it seems to be quite useful to keep these traditions separate as this allows for an easier reconstruction of the anatomy of the social phenomenon of trust.

It is not surprising that all of these three forms—or better: dimensions—of trust are in one way or another present in all of the contributions to this volume. Julia Porter Liebeskind and Amalya Lumerman Oliver, for example, seem to deem trust a quite rational matter. In their analysis of changing patterns of relationships between molecular biologists they see trust as being closely connected to individual scientists' interests and calculations. George Brenkert explicitly examines the normative implications of trust, and John Humphrey places strong emphasis on the observation that the institutional framework produces specific forms of tacit knowledge providing the relevant contexts of meaning and signification. The rest of the contributions to this volume might be more difficult to categorize but also frequently refer to one or more of these dimensions of trust.

Wherever one's theoretical preferences may lie, it can be concluded that trust is such a complex phenomenon that it does not fit completely into any of the three conceptual approaches. An adequate understanding of this phenomenon, thus, needs to draw on all of these traditions of theoretical thought. That is to say, trust can neither be seen as an entirely cognitive phenomenon, nor solely as a norm-based behaviour, nor can it be adequately reconceptualized as being completely based on calculation. Instead, all these dimensions are obviously important in some sense when trust is under consideration. In some ways it looks as if trust can only be adequately described in a terminology of 'neither/nor'. In the literature on network relations in which trust plays a particularly important role (Lorenz 1988; Powell 1990) this terminology is frequently employed and proves how difficult it is to find suitable terms for a social mechanism which is as multidimensional as the concept of trust.

3. THE CALCULATIVE DIMENSION OF TRUST

Trusting someone means having *some* information about the future behaviour of the potential trustee but certainly not as much as one would want to have. This seems to be an intrinsic featue of trust (Simmel 1950). Only in a situation in which social actors have *partial* information about what is likely to influence the potential trustees' future behaviour, trust is both needed to allow for co-operation and possible to be established in a social relationship. If one has complete information about all factors influencing another social actor's decisions, trust is redundant and co-operation can be achieved by matching each other's resources which can be utilized to underpin their interests. In the case of a complete absence of information, trust would seem to be too risky and thus unlikely to emerge.

There cannot be much doubt that trust can—with some restrictions—be reconceptualized in terms of incomplete information and risk. For this reason it could be assumed that a trustor will sometimes be in a position where he/she *explicitly* considers whether he/she finds the risk of being betrayed acceptable and whether there are means to reduce this risk within the given situation. However, it is debatable whether one should go as far as to claim that placing trust in someone can be analysed in the same terms as used to describe betting on horses, for example, which Coleman (1990) suggests in his Rational Choice-based theory of trust. It might well be true that the very idea of betting is that those who place a bet have incomplete information about the outcome of the race. But at the same time the gamblers have (or ideally should have) all information they could possibly get about the conditions and circumstances in which the race takes place. This is the reason why the horses are presented to the gamblers before the race starts so that they can judge upon their condition, and why information about other gamblers' behaviour is supplied as long as bets are taken. The only factor one cannot assess in the case of betting is fate, but the rest is calculable and many successful gamblers are indeed completely calculative in their behaviour. That this is somewhat different when trust is concerned should not be overlooked.

It has been argued against Coleman, that the expression which he suggests as underlying the potential trustor's behaviour[1] pretends formalistic accuracy where there cannot be any, as the difficulty lies in the translation of circumstances specific to a given situation into the values for insertion into his formula (Preisendörfer 1995). However, the more important difference between trusting and betting is located elsewhere, namely in the fact that the concept of betting implies calculative behaviour on the one hand and pure fate on the other, whereas the nature of trust, by contrast, requires that the trustors' decisions are in a certain sense *loosely* connected to calculative considerations, and that fate is not an important factor at all in influencing the trustee's behaviour.

Obviously, there is a fine distinction between basing a decision on a calculation and including calculative elements in a process of decision-making. While a trustor can never (and would not intend to) base his/her decision completely on a calculation which would, as we have seen, leave neither room nor need for trust, a trustor will normally also not engage in 'blind trust'. Thus he/she would not completely ignore calculative considerations where these are possible and where they can be referred to in order to reduce the risk of being betrayed. But the difference between pure calculation and trust is that the latter is constitutively based on a social form of rationality presupposing that the trustee is not merely to be taken as the passive object which is to be assessed as accurately as possible but also as a social *actor* who is free to either comply with the trustor's expectations or to disappoint his/her assumptions. Both the trustor and the trustee can be conceptualized as social actors with mutual expectations about each other's future behaviour who can (and it is indeed likely that they will) change their behaviour with reference to what the other side expects him/her to do. In other words, when a trustor expects a potential trustee to behave trustworthily and the trustee him-/herself can expect the trustor to make this expectation, this might well contribute to the trustee's decision to actually behave trustworthily. By contrast, it is hard to assume that a racehorse will be impressed by the odds on him winning a race. For this reason trusting is in its very logic much more complex than a calculation over a given set of variables whether they include a factor of fate or not.

Those contributions to this volume which emphasize the link between trust and goodwill instead of predictability (implicitly) confirm this insight into the social logic of trusting (e.g. Mari Sako). But there remains much analytical work to be done to spell out what 'goodwill' precisely means within a business relationship and what its social function is in regard to establishing a basis for trust. That both predictability and goodwill are necessary ingredients of trust while none of them alone is sufficient to explain how it can be created and differentiated from other mechanisms to enable or enforce co-operation between social actors—such as, for example, power—, is shown by Cynthia Hardy, Nelson Phillips, and Tom Lawrence (in this volume). Their argument can be taken as another indication that trust tends to be a 'hybrid' phenomenon between calculation and predictability on the one hand, and goodwill and voluntary exposure to the risk that the trustee might cheat, on the other hand.

4. TRUST AND NORMS

The same logic of 'neither/nor' appears to apply with reference to social norms. In most cases these seem to play a certain role when someone decides to trust or not to trust another social actor. But hardly anyone would trust a potential business partner only because a social norm required such behaviour. Nor would anyone refrain from trusting someone if a norm was in place which required social actors to always remain suspicious in business relationships. Social norms are often not strong enough to entirely control social actors' behaviour. In particular, this can be observed when other factors such as, for instance, profit interests conflict with a social norm of behaviour. But more important: often there exists not even a norm to which social actors could take recourse when they are to decide whether to trust or not to trust someone. The general social norm connected to trust could not be vaguer. It seems to require social actors to find their own decision without falling into the extremes of 'blind trust' and complete distrust.

Comparative studies on business systems, however, reveal that there are some interesting differences between business systems in this regard. In Asian business systems, for example, it is obviously very important to avoid behaviour which might be interpreted as a sign of distrust (Sako 1992; Child in this volume). Here the social norm to trust business partners seems to be considerably stronger than in Europe or America. But, as John Child in his chapter shows with reference to China, the norms which requires social actors to trust each other are often closely connected to rules of social inclusion and exclusion. Only within families or clans, which are based on a common history and mutual exchanges of favours, the norm of trust applies whereas almost the opposite is true for the external relationships across the boundaries of these communities. In European and American business systems, by contrast, the social norm to trust each other seems to be weaker, but at the same time, more universalistic. Thus the difference between 'friend' and 'stranger' is less clear-cut in these systems and does not mean too much, at least within business relations. Here, referring to formal standards, for instance, would not necessarily be seen as a sign of distrust, whereas that would most likely be the case in Asian systems. In certain circumstances such references could even be seen as a facilitator of stability and co-operation in European business environments (Arrighetti, Bachmann, and Deakin 1997).

In this volume, George Brenkert explicitly looks at the normative implications of trust. Drawing on Rawls' philosophy, he makes fine distinctions between ethics, morality, and the social preconditions of both. In his chapter he explores the possibility of international business ethics and the question of whether trust can play a role in their establishment. In particular, when the boundaries of cultural settings and of institutional frameworks are transcended, as it is the case, for example, in Sino-foreign joint ventures, which John Child analyses in this volume, the question of whether values and norms could serve as a reliable basis of trust is most obvious. However, it is open to debate whether John Child presents a generalizable insight in suggesting that norm- and value-based trust which arises in interpersonal exchanges should only be taken as the highest stage of the evolution of trust (after calculative trust and cognitive trust in the earlier phases of a growing economic relationship). George Brenkert's argument, in contrast, seems to imply a different assumption, namely that trust is a basic precondition of morality in that it provides a minimum of commonality of values and norms. In his view the possibility of an international business ethics is based on the assumption that even 'basic trust' (Brenkert) always has some normative quality which enables contractors from different cultural and institutional backgrounds to find a level of co-operation between them. This does not mean that norms come only into play when a relationship is already quite far developed in terms of stability and trust. Rather, the opposite seems to be the underlying notion in George Brenkert's argument.

Generally, the relationship between morality and social interaction deserves some special attention if we are to avoid misleading conclusions. On the one hand there is indeed some common ground between moral values and social norms, but on the other hand, it is also important to see the difference between them. Social norms, at least with reference to Parsons, can be understood as a mode of co-ordination of social interaction, whereas a moral postulate which may, for instance, require altruistic behaviour has implications which surely cannot be captured by a purely sociological understanding of norms and values. As Christel Lane in the introductory chapter of this volume points out, analysing the function of social norms in a Parsonian manner means to adopt a view which lays emphasis on the social embeddedness and the mechanisms of social control instead of taking a utilitarian approach which assumes that social actors are driven by instrumental rationality and self-interest. In that sense values and norms are reconstructed as the 'cement' of society which guarantees its order and stability. Trust, in this perspective, appears as a mechanism which fulfils a certain role in regard to the self-preservation and the functionability of a given social system. Due to the fact that Luhmann (particularly in his early writings) draws heavily on Parsons' theory, his analysis of trust takes a similar standpoint. Both theorists carefully avoid any moralistic undertones in their argument, even when they analyse the *social function* of 'moral obligations'. Against the background of their analysis of social norms it can be concluded that these are not *per se* a moral issue. Moral philosophy which takes an interest in trust can be based on the analysis of social reality, but it would be very problematic to draw on moral claims and postulates for the purpose of analysing social reality. Thus, the analysis of the normative dimension of trust may indeed be utilized for establishing a universalistic business ethic (cf. Brenkert, in this volume), and the role of ethics within business systems is an interesting subject for the analysis of the quality of business relations. But certainly, one should carefully refrain from interpreting social reality in terms of moralistic postulates for altruistism, trust, trustworthiness, or any other behaviour.

5. COGNITION-BASED TRUST

Tacit knowledge is highly important with regard to how trust works and how it is created. Focusing on this dimension of trust reveals that the basic categories and cognitive frames which underlie social actors' perceptions and decisions play a major role in the 'stucturation' (Giddens) of their interactions. They allow as much for expectations about other social actors' future behaviour as calculation and norms do. At least this is the case when the actors involved are sharing the same set of meanings and interpretations within what ethnomethodology has called a 'world-in-common' (Garfinkel). While calculation is an explicit process, and norms are usually internalized and *partly* withdrawn from social actors' consciousness, cognitive frames and scripts do their job in a tacit manner. However, the latter are not less efficient as a result of this characteristic. Rather the opposite seems to hold true. It can even be argued that a central precondition of the efficiency of cognitive scripts and frames is that they usually are not apparent to social actors on the level of consciousness, and are thus very difficult to challenge (Powell and DiMaggio 1991). Giddens, Luhmann, and the New Institutionalist approach within organization theory strongly agree on this insight, albeit with slightly different arguments when it comes to detail.[2]

At the same time it should be seen that this perspective on explaining the generation of trust is also limited and has to be conceptually complemented by both norm-based aspects of trust and the calculative elements within a trust-based relationship. One of the reasons for the limitations of the cognitive approach is that in some cases there simply is not too much 'world in common' between social actors. This situation, for instance, underlies John Child's and John Humphrey's analyses of the Indian and the Sino-Western cases of business relations (both in this volume). Nevertheless social actors obviously can find ways of trusting each other even in these situations. In the Chinese case John Child describes a common strategy of Western firms which is mainly based on mutual calculativeness and the deliberate acceptance of the dominance of the Western firm by the Chinese partner. Looking at the Indian business system where very few institutional guarantors of goodwill and shared business values and beliefs exist, John Humphrey suggests, that the trustworthiness of a business partner must be monitored in order to establish a basic form of trust.

From this perspective one could argue that those forms of trust which are predominantly based on individual calculation and social norms are systematically linked to an environment which lacks a strong institutional basis, while the existence of reliable institutions provides large stocks of shared background beliefs allowing for a form of trust which is largely generated beyond individuals' consciousness, i.e. through common habits and practices. High-trust systems such as the German business environment seem to depend upon the specific features of a strong institutional framework which operates on the grounds of common understandings within shared frames of interpretation. Business systems with a lower level of trust, such as for example India or China, appear not solely, but predominantly, to be based on normative and calculative mechanisms of trust production.

One could of course also argue that institutional arrangements can provide an incentive structure for calculative social actors and one could indeed admit this possibility without slipping into the formalistic trap of conventional economics. But it would be hard to reconcile this view with empirical evidence if one went so far as to assume that this was the *only* way in which institutions mould the form and content of what individual social actors expect in regard to each other's future behaviour. Surely, this possibility can be taken as a confirmation of the assumption that the role of the institutional environment in which business relationships are embedded is particularly relevant when the creation of a high level of trust is (to be) achieved. Neither Rational Choice nor New Institutionalism would reject the insight into the general importance of institutions, and into the centrality of the problem of how to reconstruct the relationship between social interaction and the institutional framework of a given social system.

All three approaches of explaining the creation of trust, namely the cognitive, the normative and the calculative perspectives, seem to be *partially* right as all these aspects (shared knowledge, internalized social norms and calculation over interests and resources) may—depending on the specific circumstances—to some degree be conducive to the constitution of trust. This is precisely the insight which is presented in Jörg Sydow's argument (in this volume) and in Giddens' 'theory of structuration', respectively. What is shown in these approaches, however, is that the full complexity of the problem only becomes visible when the relationship between interpersonal action and social institutions is considered in the light of the named aspects of trust.

6. INTERPERSONAL TRUST AND INSTITUTIONAL SOURCES OF TRUST

Particularly when trust is concerned, it seems to be unrealistic if one assumes that the interpersonal level of social action and the institutional framework could be conceptualized as being linked together in a deterministic way. Rather, these levels should be seen as being *loosely coupled*. On the one hand, a given type of institutional arrangement cannot be seen as entirely determining a certain quality of interaction, which would mean to *either* trust *or* distrust another social actor. But on the other hand, it would also be false to believe that the institutional framework is *not* highly influential on the decisions of the potential trustor, and that it could not be conducive to enhancing trust in social relationships (Lane and Bachmann 1996; Simon Deakin and Frank Wilkinson in this volume). Norms, frames, and calculative considerations are mechanisms which contribute to establishing the link between the interpersonal relationship and the institutional environment, and it seems that these mechanisms complement one another when the specific form of co-ordination of interaction can be described as being based on trust (Bachmann and Lane 1997). Trust as opposed to power, for example, can be viewed as a constitutively semi-conscious process in which institutional arrangements can be understood as playing a particularly significant role.

While most of the authors of this volume agree on the importance of institutionally generated forms of trust in complex modern societies none of them would, of course, claim that this is the *only* way of producing trust

among economic actors. However difficult and time-consuming the creation
of trust merely on the basis of individual experiences in face-to-face situations may be, this mode of trust production should indeed not be completely ignored. Julia Porter Liebeskind and Amalya Lumerman Oliver (in
this volume) present a detailed analysis of interpersonal trust relationships
in the biotechnology sector and describe how credibility is established
among small groups of scientists. This chapter provides particular insight
into the role of trust at the micro-level of social interaction. However, it is
important to note that even their analysis explains the dynamics within
interpersonal reationships with recourse to changes in the contractual environment. The commercialization of research and the legal status of intellectual property are shown as being highly influential on the intensity and
quality of relationships. Drawing on Zucker (1986) one could discern here
'process-based trust' and 'characteristic-based trust', and contrast it with
'institutional-based trust'. Only the reliable production of the latter form of
trust, Zucker argues, is sufficient to ensure the efficient functioning of
advanced economies. A highly generalized (institution-based) mode of
trust production is thus taken as a vital precondition for the development of
complex socio-economic systems. Luhmann (1979) largely confirms this
insight into the importance of a strong and coherent institutional framework for the constitution of institutionally based trust, or 'system trust'—to
use his expression.

   The identification of different modes of trust production has given rise to
an important discussion, but has also caused confusion about how to use the
terms 'institutional-based trust' and 'system trust'. To avoid such problems
it is of central importance not to mix up the *source* of trust with the question
of who or what should be assumed to be the *object* of trust. Jörg Sydow (in
this volume) makes a considerable effort to clarify these categories in that
he suggests using the term 'institutional-based trust' only where the source
of trust is concerned, and the term 'system trust' when the object of trust is
not an individual but a social system such as a firm or any other organization. However, in this matter he skips some of the most crucial questions
which are involved here.

   More than 'institutional-based trust', the term 'system trust' has been
used in both ways, i.e. referring to social systems either as the source or as
the object of trust. The necessity of differentiating both meanings is obvious
for logical reasons. At the same time, however, in many cases it can be very
difficult to decide who or what the object of trust really is. When social
actors decide to trust their business partners, e.g. with reference to the
quality of a delivered product, they themselves might not be able to say
whether they have more faith in the competence and goodwill of their
business partners *or* in the institutional system within which this transaction
takes place and which produces the social standards controlling their business partners' expectations and behaviour.

Luhmann's work on trust (1979), which is most frequently referred to within the theoretically oriented part of the literature on inter-organizational relationships, is a good example of starting off with a very clear distinction between the source and the object of trust. But in the course of developing his argument he becomes uncertain about it. His complete approach seems to centre upon the question of how the inherent risk of trust can be reduced to such a degree that social actors can find it acceptable and thus are more inclined to trust one another than this would seem possible without this reduction in risk. In answering this question Luhmann suggests that institutions such as legal regulation play an important role here in that they make it less likely that a trustee will behave untrustworthily. No doubt, this argument implies the assumption that institutions are a *source* of trust between social actors. At the same time, however, Luhmann sometimes uses the term 'system trust' in a way which seems to be connected to the argument that modern societies need impersonal forms of trust in the sense that social actors place their trust in the functioning of abstract systems such as the monetary system, the educational system, or the legal system of a given society, and not so much in the individual social actors' integrity. Individuals are then only seen as trustworthy in so far as they can be assumed to comply with the rules guaranteed by the institutional order, irrespective of whether it is sanctions that prevent calculating social actors from cheating or whether it is the tacit 'structuration' of their expectations and actions that achieves this. In any case, at this point of the argument one can see how the concepts of source and object of trust are closely inter-linked, although they seem to be quite different in logical terms.

Giddens (1990) draws heavily on Luhmann's ideas here (as Christel Lane discusses in the introductory chapter of this volume), but he seems to develop his argument in the opposite direction. He starts with a notion of 'system trust' which implies that social actors are confident that 'expert systems' such as air traffic systems or—one might also assume—legal systems can generally be trusted because they are large-scale abstract social systems which can be expected to function according to highly universalistic rules, irrespective of whether an *individual* actor—for whatever reason—might in particular circumstances consider cheating or not. But, of course, Giddens would never believe that individual actors are completely irrelevant when the object of trust is under consideration. Rather, he shows quite convincingly that individual actors are important at the 'access points' of social 'expert systems' (Giddens 1990). These are seen as representing and constantly confirming the trustworthiness of the system (cf. also Jörg Sydow in this volume). In other words, the functioning of the legal system, for example, would in this perspective be seen as being constitutively dependent on the social interactions in which individual lawyers and judges engage in specific situations. Like any other 'expert system', the legal system is only assumed to exist and to be permanently reproduced through the concrete individual behaviour of the relevant social actors. Thus one could conclude that in the end it is individual social actors rather than abstract institutional arrangements who are attributed trustworthiness or untrustworthiness.

However, there might still be a slight difference between Giddens' conceptualization of the problem and what is implied in the initial thrust of Luhmann's argument. While Luhmann's theoretical conceptualization of the problem of trust starts with the questions of how two social actors can find reasons to trust each other, and in what sense the nature and quality of the institutional order might help them to make their decisions, Giddens' approach hinges on the question of why social actors can under normal circumstances be fairly confident about what other actors within their shared social reality expect them to do or intend to do. This latter perspective seems to focus more on how social actors look at the structures of the social systems in which their action takes place, rather than at the other social actors who are conceptualized as only representing the functionability of an abstract system. But, of course, Luhmann's social actors can be equally understood as representing a social system which in his view is taken as the central reason why they can be trusted.[3]

Given the current state of the discussion, it is very difficult to decide whether there is a fundamental difference in how both theorists reinterpret the concept of trust. Obviously, there are different perspectives to be reconstructed and—in theory—it should be possible to adopt one of these specific theoretical views consistently, and either see systems as the source *or* the object of trust. Both ways are viable conceptual strategies but at some point one has to accept the logic of the empirical world, which often seems to be vague here. This can be taken as another indication that trust is difficult to force into conventional categories of theorizing.

7. TRUST AND POWER

As several contributions to this book point out, trust is not the only way to co-ordinate social actors' expectations. In many ways a high level of trust may be advantageous for a business system (Barney and Hansen 1994; Fukuyama 1995). But at the same time trust is fragile and thus one could at least seriously think about whether there exist other mechanisms which are equally apt to ensure that social actors can efficiently co-ordinate their interactions; and indeed one can certainly find such devices. Power, for instance, can be seen as a social mechanism which in many respects— although by no means in all respects—works in a way similar to trust (Bachmann and Lane 1997).

Cynthia Hardy, Nelson Phillips, and Tom Lawrence as well as Jörg Sydow (both in this volume) include the problem of how to reconstruct the relationship between trust and power, and also show that there are quite different ways of approaching this relationship. One of the very basic decisions here seems to be whether one joins the politically oriented argument which suggests a critique of power as an unacceptable means of establishing—or enforcing, if this was to be preferred—co-operation between social actors, or whether one supports those theoretical views which suggest that power is to be seen as a universal feature of any social relationship. The first position is represented by 'critical theorists' such as Habermas (1984/7) and strongly supported by Cynthia Hardy, Nelson Phillips, and Tom Lawrence (in this volume) while the second perspective is preferred by Luhmann as well as by Giddens (and Jörg Sydow in this volume).

The politically critical approach is important in so far as it enables one to insist that there might be differences in what is openly declared by social actors and what their hidden intentions are. Cynthia Hardy, Nelson Phillips, and Tom Lawrence (in this volume) discuss the strategy of the management of a firm who wished to close down a production site without being honest with their workforce. While the management made the workers believe that they could be trusted they in fact used this strategy to enforce their intentions. In this case power was veiled behind a façade of trust which was established purely for instrumental reasons. It seems to be important to recognize such discrepancies and to be able to criticize such behaviour. Cynthia Hardy, Nelson Phillips, and Tom Lawrence suggest with good reason that this presupposes that trust and power should be conceptually clearly differentiated. However, in more analytical terms, the commonalities between trust and power should equally be noted.

With reference to Luhmann (1979) and systems theory more generally, it could be argued that power is a mechanism which—in its basic function—is apt to do the same job as trust: it can be utilized to co-ordinate expectations of social actors and thus to enable them to co-operate with each other. Here, the underlying notion is that trust and power could—under certain conditions—be seen as 'functional equivalents' (Luhmann 1984), which leads to the question of whether it would be possible to replace trust by power or to combine both mechanisms with one another, if one of them should prove to be not sufficient to produce the required level of co-operation (Bachmann 1997).

Of course, this question is highly relevant with regard to the problem of how to ensure co-operation in circumstances where the reliable production of a sufficient amount of trust cannot be assumed because of an unstable institutional environment as discussed for the cases of India and China by John Humphrey and John Child (in this volume). It may be right to suggest that the institutional framework of a socio-economic system is not invariable as it can be changed by social action if a great number of individual actors persistently confirm the need for a tighter net of social regulation. Thus, there is no reason why one should assume that the institutional framework of a national or regional business system could not be strengthened, but without doubt, it usually takes much time and effort to achieve such changes. If at the same time, however, it is true that trust which is generated on the interpersonal level cannot really compensate for a lack of institutionally produced trust in complex societies, power—understood as a mechanism alternative or complementary to trust—might be necessary to create the amount of social cohesion which is needed to ensure effective co-operation between social actors

One might indeed argue that in some cases it is simply unavoidable to build on individual resources of power which might manifest themselves in rigid contract clauses and/or refined procedures of quality assurance of inputs, if trust cannot be taken as pre-existent. In some situations this might well be a viable strategy to compensate for a lack of trust, or even to establish more stability which could *then* be taken as a basis of trust creation (John Humphrey in this volume). This assumption links into what has been shown by Arrighetti, Bachmann, and Deakin (1997) and what also Mari Sako (in this volume) admits, namely that detailed contracts, for instance, need by no means generally be seen as detrimental to the constitution of trust. At least with reference to the highly regulated German system one could observe that rather the opposite holds true. However, for other systems such as the British or the American ones, one gets the impression that there is a clearer division between trust and power as different means of establishing co-operation between business partners. Thus, power needs to be seen as a double-faced mechanism. In some cases it may be incompatible with trust (Sako 1992) and in some sense it can be taken as being supportive to the production of trust.

The relationship between trust and power seems to be another intricate facet of the concept of trust. In one sense both mechanisms can be viewed as alternative modes of co-ordinating social interaction. This understanding seems to be particularly adequate when one focuses on the interest of an individual social actor or on the question of what his/her considerations might be before he/she decides to establish a specific relationship with a business partner predominantly on the basis of trust or on the basis of power (Bachmann and Lane 1997). Although one might argue with good reason that virtually all relationships carry some features of both trust and power, rather than simply being built on 'blind trust' or 'total power', it clearly makes a difference whether one or the other mechanism becomes dominant in a specific relationship. Thus, in many cases trust and power can be understood as being able to increase each other's potential or compensate for each others' deficits regarding their function as co-ordinators of social interaction. A social actor may, for instance, trust his/her business partner up to a certain limited amount of money being at stake but might perhaps consider his/her power resources before he/she risks more than this sum. Equally, an actor may be inclined to use his/her power resources as far as possible but at a certain point in a relationship perceive the limits of power and turn to trust in order to enhance the mutual profitability of the relationship. In other words, sometimes—but by no means in every case—it might be sensible to accept some extra risk in order to make some extra benefits achievable.

This approach to conceptualizing trust and power can be taken as a first step to understand the interrelationship between both mechanisms. However, when the scope of the analysis is widened and the institutional framework in which the relationship is embedded comes into the picture, the conceptual link between trust and power becomes much more complicated. Against the background of a coherent and strong institutional framework, power indeed seems to be an important facilitator—if not a precondition—of the creation of trust, rather than an alternative mechanism to co-ordinate social interaction. The form of power which is referred to in this view, however, greatly differs from power based on individual resources, which someone who is about to decide upon whether to build a relationship predominantly on trust or on power might consider using. Rather, it is an impersonal form of power which is embodied in the structures of a legal system, a state policy or in the rigid and hierarchical structures of a powerful trade association. This form of power, which is fundamentally different from individually usable resources of power such as capital or a dominant position in the market, has significant consequences where its relationship to trust is concerned.

A closer look at the institutional sources of trust production reveals that power in the form of hierarchy and structural domination can in fact enable social actors to trust each other at the interpersonal level rather than being an alternative mode of co-ordinating interfirm relations. From this perspective trust presupposes power. Only where 'process-based trust' is concerned and where power is based on individual resources, can trust and power be conceived as 'functional equivalents' which might serve as alternatives complementing each other, or even come into conflict, if social actors misinterpret each other's intentions. In the case of 'institutional-based trust', powerful institutions fuel the creation of trust (Bachmann and Lane 1997).

It is difficult to say whether the institutional form of power itself could be seen as sufficient to ensure co-operation if it was not assumed, at the same time, to provide a basis for the constitution of trust. This question might arise in a somewhat exceptional situation in which trust-based relationships between economic actors are massively questioned through political campaigns which embrace conflict and adversarialism while the institutional order of the business system largely keeps its hierarchical structures. Horst Kern (in this volume) suggests that the current crisis of the German model is due to such a situation. Accordingly, the underlying assumption of the argument implies that the core of the German problem is linked to inconsistencies between the institutional and the ideological level of the business system.

Along the lines of Horst Kern's analysis, it can be argued that in a situation of rapid change, a strong and coherent institutional framework might not necessarily produce a high level of trust. In normal circumstances, however, one can expect more coherence between the structural and the ideological characteristics of business systems, and empirical research can show how hierarchy and domination embodied in the institutional structures of the system—'system power' in other words—reduces uncertainty and absorbs risks, and thus makes it easier for individual social actors to trust each other. This can generally be seen as a mode of trust production which is much more reliable and efficient than what Zucker (1986) calls 'process-based trust', i.e. trust developed out of a specific relationship between individual social actors without significant reference to the institutional framework. However, there are also specific disadvantages associated with over-regulated business systems which should not be completely overlooked.

8. TRUST AND LEGAL REGULATION

As Simon Deakin and Frank Wilkinson (in this volume) point out, classical mainstream socio-legal studies (Macaulay 1963; Beale and Dugdale 1975) as well as some newer contributions to the debate (e.g. Sitkin and Roth 1993) suggest that the true quality of business relationships is to be found in the forms of informal understanding and practices which are not part of the contract itself, but lie 'beyond contract' (Fox 1974, with reference to employment contracts). Within this literature one can even find the conclusion that written and legally binding contracts should be seen as indicating a low level of trust, and that detailed contractual arrangements are inimical to the development of trust. But in this argument two assumptions are made which rather seem to be a hindrance than a help to understanding the nature of the contract, at least where an interorganizational contract is concerned. *First*, this view builds on the problematic conceptualization of the contract which separates it from the social context in which it is agreed and interpreted, and, *secondly*, the central function of the contract is misjudged if emphasis is almost exclusively laid on the idea that agreements can be enforced with reference to contracts if one side does not comply with what he/she had promised to do.

No doubt, there always exists the possibility of legal sanctions when a contract is agreed. This is certainly *one* strong reason why legally binding contracts are frequently used. However, other functions of the contract should not be ignored. For instance, contracts are also planning devices which means that they can be understood as documents containing information about agreed delivery dates and prices, which enables both business partners to co-ordinate their supply, production, and sales processes. From this perspective, contracts fulfil a co-ordination function in a purely technical sense and ensure what Frank Wilkinson calls 'technical cooperation' (Wilkinson, forthcoming).

But even when a contract is viewed in its function as deterring from opportunistic behaviour and cheating it is worth noting that it is usually not designed to actually mobilize the sanctions which the contractors refer to in their agreement. According to Luhmann (1979), legal arrangements only provide for the *possibility* of sanctions and this alone is in most cases sufficient to reduce uncertainty and risk in that it enables the contractors to establish expectations about each other's future behaviour. If legal sanctions need to be activated and contractors take their disputes to the courts, the legal arrangement has failed in what its main function was.

Seen from this point of view detailed and written contracts, on the one hand, and a high level of trust, on the other, are not necessarily inimical to each other. Instead, trust can even be enhanced by making use of legal provision as Simon Deakin and Frank Wilkinson point out (in this volume). From this perspective, the threat of legal sanctions needs not be omitted. It rather should be noted that these play an important role in the creation of trust when they remain in the background. While Mari Sako (in this volume) finds such a view only fruitful when trust is understood as 'contract trust' as opposed to 'goodwill trust', Simon Deakin and Frank Wilkinson more generally agree with what Luhmann suggests, namely that 'legal arrangements which lend special assurance to particular expectations and make them sanctionable . . . lessen the risk of conferring trust' (Luhmann 1979: 34). However 'the structure of the trust relationship requires that such calculation should remain latent . . . purely a reassuring consideration' (ibid. 36).

The second of these quotes contains an expression which is difficult to understand and points back to what we discussed earlier (in this concluding chapter) with reference to the dimensions of trust. The difficulty here lies in the problem of whether calculative behaviour should be assumed at all when the contractors refer to the sanctions implied in legally enforceable arrangements. On the one hand one might feel inclined to agree with this view, but on the other hand, it is hard to imagine how to behave calculatively in an implicit manner, or 'latently', as Luhmann puts it. The first interpretation would indeed miss the point in Luhmann's argument. From his perspective social norms as well as legal norms do their job not so much through threats and deterrence but rather by more subtle mechanisms which we have described earlier with reference to the cognitive dimension of trust. However, all three dimensions of trust which we have differentiated seem to come together here, which confirms what we said about the limits of one-dimensional approaches to the theory of trust.

Turning to empirical observations now shows that there are some further issues involved in the relationship between legal regulation and trust. According to Mari Sako's comparative research (in this volume) there are significant country-specific differences as to what the influence of certain aspects of contracts is on the quality of interfirm relationships. This is an interesting finding which indicates that contracts in themselves are not to be seen as isolated from the social context in which they are produced and applied. Simon Deakin and Frank Wilkinson (in this volume) as well as David Marsden (in this volume) strongly confirm this insight in that they show with reference to different forms of contracts (interfirm contracts and employment contracts) that legal norms are highly intertwined with social norms and practices, and that only their combination determines what can be deemed the quality of a relationship. This, however, is quite different from asserting that contracts themselves are negligible and that the quality of relationships is only determined by factors which lie beyond the contract.

Only against the background of this insight, can the role which contract law and—more generally—economic legislation play in the process of shaping relationships within and between organizations, be assessed adequately. Legal regulation, for instance, may require contractors to comply with certain standards of behaviour, e.g. to pay for goods within a certain period of time after delivery. Thus, such requirements can become a compulsory and legally binding term within contractual relationships. But if this should not remain merely abstract theory it needs to be interlinked with other elements of the institutional framework which equally support the notion of having general standards in business behaviour, such as that which, for instance, prevails in the case of the German system (Lane and Bachmann 1996; Simon Deakin and Frank Wilkinson in this volume).

Strong interlinks between the individual contracts, contract law and other elements of the institutional framework of the business system can be assumed to be conducive to establishing stable relationships based on trust and 'good faith' rather than adversarialism and the threat that individual resources of power will be used extensively. By contrast, the absence of a strong and coherent socio-legal framework can lead to a high degree of uncertainty. This might then result in a serious lack of co-ordination of economic exchanges, as seems to be the case in many developing countries, or in a 'battle of contracts', which has been reported with regard to the British context (Sako 1992). In the latter case contracts are used as a tool for maximizing one's interests individually, and not as a confirmation of general standards of business behaviour.

9. TRUST, PERFORMANCE, AND ECONOMIC POLICY

Much of the research on intra- and interorganizational co-operation shares the assumption that trust-based relationships will inevitably entail competitive advantages. With reference to this premise, the literature on 'industrial districts' (Sengenberger, Loveman, and Piore 1990; Pyke and Sengenberger 1992, etc.), for instance, argues that certain geographical regions such as Baden-Württemberg or the Emilia Romagna show superior economic performance because of the very close co-operation which characterizes the horizontal and vertical relationships between their typically small- and medium-sized firms. In a similar vein, the debate on the Japanese influence on Western industries (Oliver and Wilkinson 1988; Morris and Imrie 1992, etc.) suggests that the Japanese production model owes its success to very highly developed forms of co-operation and trust both between employers and employees, and between buyer and supplier firms. More generally, the 'industrial networks' literature (Jarillo 1988; Sydow *et al.* 1995, etc.) looks at what makes partnership relations between organizations attractive, and largely agrees that there must be a close link between trust and performance (also in this context cf. Barney and Hansen 1994; Fukuyama 1995).

These strands of research have not only found an empirical correlation between both phenomena but also present good theoretical reasons why trust can foster economic success, in that they show that close co-operation allows for the pooling of know-how and risk, and that it keeps a balance 'between market and hierarchy', to use Transaction Cost Economics terms (Williamson 1985). Within this mixture, it is claimed, lies the secret of success. Although this argument without doubt points in the right direction, the need to specify the implied assumptions with regard to certain conditions which must be fulfilled before they hold true becomes ever clearer today.

In this volume, Mari Sako generally confirms that a high level of trust can significantly fuel the competitiveness of a business system, but she treats it as a question to be answered with reference to empirical evidence rather than as a conceptual premise of her argument. This approach, which is increasingly recognized as more suitable than orthodox theoretical assertions, seems to be linked to the observation that the current performance of the Japanese and the German economies casts considerable doubt on the assumption that trust *necessarily* results in competitiveness. Horst Kern (in this volume), who has intimate knowledge of the German system, is even more critical about the over-generalization of the argument that trust and competitive success are intrinsically linked together. In his chapter he rather points out that 'blind trust' is very unlikely to produce a high level of flexibility and innovativeness.

Against the background of the innovation crisis which became apparent in Germany in the past five years or so (Audretsch 1995) Horst Kern's argument must indeed be taken seriously, even if it is at first sight difficult to reconcile with the arguments which emphasize the advantages of very stable and close relationships. On reflection, trust needs to be balanced with incentives to occasionally transcend the boundaries of the familiar. But this is not necessarily ensured merely by long-termism and stability. The latter may, on the one hand, fuel a certain form of flexibility which is based on good-faith practices and which may indeed be seen as conducive to incremental innovation of products and production processes. On the other hand, however, too close relationships also seem to disencourage social actors to take the risks which are connected to fundamental innovation. The claim that trust has a high potential to stimulate performance is not false, but needs to be specified with reference to such differentiation. The future discussion will have to put strong emphasis on this issue, and also will have to clarify the conditions under which trust creates both stability *and* a high level of innovation. Cross-national comparative studies seem to be very appropriate for learning more about these conditions and, thus, rate high on the research agenda.

With regard to economic policy, these questions are urgent. The modernization of advanced economies seems to be heavily dependent on solutions to the problem of how to make use of elements of both co-operation and competition in a fruitful combination (Bachmann forthcoming). But also with reference to developing business systems these problems, and the question of what could be seen as an appropriate means of fostering the production of *trust towards creativity*, should not be overlooked. Currently, we simply need to have more knowledge on how to achieve this goal. What we already can see against the background of empirical evidence and theoretical argument, however, is that neither creativity and innovation, nor co-operation and trust are likely to evolve spontaneously at the level of individual interaction.

One of the tools for controlling the quality of economic relationships between social actors on which emphasis has been laid (in this concluding chapter as well as by some of the authors of the other chapters), is legal regulation. Simon Deakin and Frank Wilkinson (in this volume) leave no doubt that the creation of trust in buyer–supplier relationships can be strongly influenced by contract law. But this also applies to employment contracts (Marsden in this volume) and contracting in the field of commercially exploitable co-operation in science and research (Porter Liebeskind and Lumerman Oliver in this volume). That these forms of relations and contracting are not separate issues but highly interlinked with the mechanisms which decide upon the quality of interfirm contracting can only be inferred at the current state of research. Much more work needs to be done to fully understand the relations between these different forms of contracting and how they link into each other.

However, legal regulation should not be seen as the only important tool of economic policy. There are, as we have argued earlier, also other elements of the institutional environment of relationships which should be taken into consideration. As yet, we equally know little about how different elements of the institutional framework such as legal regulation, the status and the role of trade associations, the financial system, etc. interact with each other. These issues need to be studied very thoroughly through comparative research which has to draw on the specific know-how of all disciplines which are represented in this book. Only then is there a hope that economic policy in the future can be based on a better understanding of how social actors engage into economic exchange relations and how the economic systems of modern societies work. At present, it has to be admitted that we are not yet in a position to have more than rudimentary answers to the problems which economic policy has to encounter, but the debate on the role of trust in business relations has made significant advances in recent years. These are broadly reflected in the chapters of this volume which presents a quite good picture of where we stand and which are the central questions to be answered in order to achieve a comprehensive understanding of the complex interrelations between the conditions and the consequences of trust within and between organizations.

NOTES

1. Coleman's theory of how a social actor decides whether to trust or not to trust someone else is based on the simple expression pG <or> $(1 - p)V$, where p is the probability that the trustee will behave in a trustworthy fashion, G is the potential gain to be made if this should turn out to be true, $(1 - p)V$ the risk that the trustee cheats, and V is the potential loss which might occur if the latter holds true. In all cases in which 'greater than' $(>)$ is to be inserted into the expression Coleman suggests that trust is invested by the potential trustor, whereas he/she refrains from trusting the potential trustee if 'less than' $(<)$ connects the two sides of the expression (Coleman 1990: 99).

2. While Giddens focuses his interest predominantly on the social process which interlinks social actors' decisions to institutional arrangements, Luhmann's systems theoretical approach as well as New Institutionalism, place more emphasis on the explanation of why problems of co-ordination of social interaction can be solved. The latter approaches look at their object from an *ex post* point of view, which assumes that the problems being studied have already been solved. Giddens, by contrast, seems to be more interested in the actual

process of how these problems are tackled (or left unsolved) by the social actors involved.

3. Also, it may be worth noting that in the light of their more general major works (Giddens 1984; Luhmann 1984) one would even be inclined to interpret Luhmann's approach as being more oriented towards the question of how social systems operate whereas Giddens' interest seems much more to include the social problems which occur on the inter-personal level.

REFERENCES

Arrighetti, A., Bachmann, R., and Deakin, S. (1997), 'Contract Law, Social Norms and Inter-firm Cooperation', *Cambridge Journal of Economics*, 21/2: 329–49.

Audretsch, D. B. (1995), 'The Innovation, Unemployment and Competitiveness Challenge in Germany', WZB discussion paper. Berlin: WZB.

Bachmann, R. (1997), 'Kooperation und Vertrauen in zwischenbetrieblichen Beziehungen', in S. Hradil (ed.), *Differenz und Integration: Verhandlungen des 28. Deutschen Soziologiekongresses, Dresden, 7–11 Oct.* Frankfurt: Campus, 255–70.

——(forthcoming *b*), 'Reducing Risk in Knowledge Partnerships', in F. Blackler, D. Courpasson, B. Elkjaer, and K. Legge (eds.), *Knowledge Workers and European Competitiveness*. London: Sage.

——and Lane, C. (1997), 'Vertrauen und Macht in zwischenbetrieblichen Kooperationen—zur Rolle von Wirtschaftsrecht und Wirtschaftsverbänden in Deutschland und Großbritannien', *Managementforschung*, 7: 79–110.

Barney, J. B. and Hansen, M. H. (1994), 'Trustworthiness as a Source of Competitive Advantage', *Strategic Management Journal*, 15: 175–90.

Beale, N. and Dugdale, T. (1975), 'Contracts Between Businessmen: Planning and the Use of Contractual Remedies', *British Journal of Law and Society*, 2: 45–60.

Burchell, B. and Wilkinson, F. (1997), 'Trust, Business Relations and the Contractual Environment', *Cambridge Journal of Economics*, 21/2: 217–37.

Coleman, J. (1990), *Foundations of Social Theory*. Cambridge, Mass.: Harvard University Press.

Deakin, S., Lane, C., and Wilkinson, F. (1994), 'Trust or Law? Towards an Integrated Theory of Contractual Relations Between Firms', *Journal of Law and Society*, 21/3: 171–95.

Fox, A. (1974), *Beyond Contract: Work, Power and Trust Relations*. London: Faber and Faber.

Fukuyama, F. (1995), *Trust. The Social Virtues and the Creation of Prosperity*. New York: Free Press.

Giddens, A. (1976), *New Rules of Sociological Method*. London: Hutchinson.

——(1984), *The Constitution of Society*. Cambridge: Polity.

——(1990), *The Consequences of Modernity*. Cambridge: Polity.

Grabher, G. (1993) (ed.), *The Embedded Firm: On the Socio-Economics of Industrial Networks*. London: Routledge.

Granovetter, M. (1985), 'Economic Action and Social Structure: The Problem of Embeddedness', *American Journal of Sociology*, 91: 481–510.

Habermas, J. (1984/7), *The Theory of Communicative Action*, 2 vols. Cambridge: Polity.

Hofstede, G. (1991), *Cultures and Organizations: Software of the Mind*. London: McGraw-Hill.

Jarillo, J. C. (1988), 'On Strategic Networks', *Strategic Management Journal*, 9: 31–41.

Lane, C. and Bachmann, R. (1996), 'The Social Constitution of Trust: Supplier Relations in Britain and Germany', *Organization Studies*, 17: 365–95.

——— (1997), 'Cooperation in Inter-firm Relations in Britain and Germany: The Role of Social Institutions', *British Journal of Sociology*.

Lorenz, E. H. (1988), 'Neither Friends nor Strangers: Informal Networks of Subcontracting in French Industry', in D. Gambetta (ed.), *Trust: Making and Breaking Cooperative Relations*. Oxford: Blackwell, 194–210.

Luhmann, N. (1979), *Trust and Power*. Chichester: Wiley.

—— (1984), *Soziale Systeme*. Frankfurt: Suhrkamp.

Macaulay, S. (1963), 'Non-contractual Relations in Business', *American Sociological Review*, 45: 55–69.

Morris, J. and Imrie, R. (1992), *Transforming Buyer–Supplier Relations: Japanese Style Industrial Relations in a Western Context*. London: Macmillan.

Oliver, N. and Wilkinson, B. (1988), *The Japanization of British Industry*. Oxford: Blackwell.

Powell, W. W. (1990), 'Neither Market nor Hierarchy: Network Forms of Organization', in B. M. Staw and L. L. Cummings (eds.), *Research in Organizational Behavior*, 12: 295–336.

—— and DiMaggio, P. J. (1991) (eds.), *New Institutionalism in Organizational Analysis*. Chicago: Chicago University Press.

Preisendörfer, P. (1995), 'Vertrauen als soziologische Kategorie', *Zeitschrift für Soziologie*, 46: 263–72.

Pyke, F. and Sengenberger, W. (1992) (eds.), *Industrial Districts and Local Economic Regeneration*. Geneva: International Institute for Labour Studies.

Sako, M. (1992), *Prices, Quality and Trust: Inter-firm Relationships in Britain and Japan*. Cambridge: Cambridge University Press.

Sengenberger, W., Loveman, G., and Piore, M. (1990), *The Re-emergence of Small Enterprises: Industrial Restructuring in Industrialised Countries*. Geneva: International Institute of Labour Studies.

Simmel, G. (1950), *The Sociology of Georg Simmel*, ed. K. H. Wolff. New York: Free Press.

Sitkin, S. B. and Roth, N. L. (1993), 'Explaining the Limited Effectiveness of Legalistic "Remedies" for Trust/Distrust', *Organization Science*, 4/3: 356–92.

Streeck, W. (1992), *Social Institutions and Economic Performance*. London: Sage.

Sydow, J., Windeler, A., Krebs, M., Loose, A., and van Well, B. (1995), *Organisation von Netzwerken*. Opladen: Westdeutscher Verlag.

Whitley, R. (1992) (ed.), *European Business Systems*. London: Sage.

Wilkinson, F. (forthcoming), 'Co-operation, the Organisation of Work and

Competitiveness', Working Paper Series, University of Cambridge/ESRC Centre for Business Research.

Williamson, O. E. (1985), *The Economic Institutions of Capitalism*. New York: Free Press.

Womack, J. P., Jones, D. T., and Roos, D. (1990), *The Machine that Changed the World*. New York: Rawson.

Zucker, L. (1986), 'Production of Trust: Institutional Sources of Economic Structure, 1840–1920', *Research in Organizational Behavior*, 6: 53–111.

INDEX